THE PAGEANT
OF AMERICA

R.K.

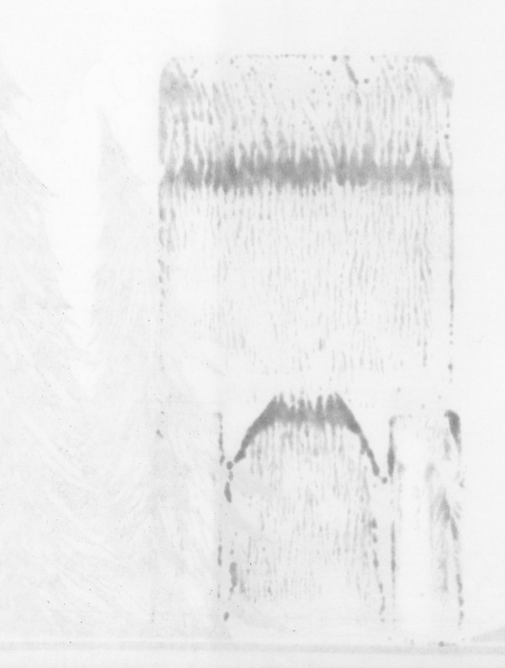

Independence Edition

VOLUME IV

THE PAGEANT OF AMERICA

A PICTORIAL HISTORY OF THE UNITED STATES

RALPH HENRY GABRIEL

EDITOR

PETER GUILDAY   HARRY MORGAN AYRES

ASSOCIATE EDITORS

OLIVER McKEE   EDWIN MIMS, JR.

ASSISTANT EDITORS

CHARLES M. ANDREWS   ALLEN JOHNSON
HERBERT E. BOLTON   WILLIAM BENNETT MUNRO
IRVING N. COUNTRYMAN   VICTOR H. PALTSITS
WILLIAM E. DODD   ARTHUR M. SCHLESINGER
DIXON RYAN FOX   NATHANIEL WRIGHT STEPHENSON

ADVISORY EDITORS

DAVID M. MATTESON

INDEXER

From the painting by Charles R. Patterson (1878–), owned by B. L. Allen, New York

THE CLIPPER SHIP "GLORY OF THE SEAS"

THE MARCH OF COMMERCE

BY

MALCOLM KEIR

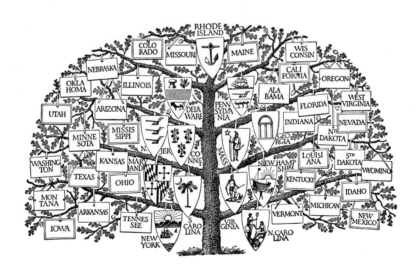

NEW YORK
UNITED STATES PUBLISHERS ASSOCIATION
TORONTO · GLASGOW, BROOK & CO.

TABLE OF CONTENTS

THE EVOLUTION OF AMERICAN COMMERCE

A RCHÆOLOGISTS, digging in the great mounds left by the Indians of the upper Mississippi valley, have found shells from the shores of the Pacific, obsidian from the Rockies, copper from the Lake Superior region, stones for making pipes from Minnesota and Canada, and wampum from the Atlantic. Trade was a common activity in Indian life. Within the acknowledged domains of divers tribes were different desirable commodities; salt deposits, flint quarries, pigments for paint, or shells for beads. Sometimes the owners allowed neighbors to come and exploit for themselves the natural resources after paying a tribute; at other times the possessors used the particular articles which they controlled for trade. Though at first the white man could not speak the Indian's language, when he held out a handful of ornaments and pointed to a pile of beaver skins, the Indian knew what he meant. In such a manner John Smith secured much needed corn from his dusky neighbors for the settlement on the banks of the sluggish James. Scarcely had the existence of the New World been heralded in Europe before white men were penetrating its unknown and dangerous fastnesses, seeking to discover what desirable commodities they might contain. The sixteenth century saw the Spanish resort to predatory warfare, that primitive practice out of which peaceful trade evolved, to bring down the rich empires of the Aztecs in Mexico and the Incas in Peru.

In the same century the English were stirred with the excitement of new and distant ventures. Merchants, meeting on London streets, paused to gossip of the latest news from the Levant, that land of Arabian nights, whither English traders, backed by an English company, had gone. Or they talked of Russia to be reached by way of the Baltic from the shores of which broad rivers led into the little known interior. Here the Muscovy Company exchanged English goods for the commodities to be found at the fairs of the inland trading marts. Other Englishmen were in India looking with dazzled eyes upon the accumulated wealth of an ancient civilization. English traders were faring forth to the ends of the world — the precursors of empire. England was slow to exploit the undeveloped continent of America beyond the Atlantic where Spain, in the sixteenth century, stumbled upon fabulous wealth. But, in the seventeenth, English villages sprang up along the coast from Maine to the Carolinas. About the habitations grew fields of wheat and maize, tobacco and rice. From the northern hamlets fishermen put off in boats for cod and mackerel. Moving westward from the settlements could be seen, from time to time, traders leading pack horses along the forest trails that led to the Indian villages.

When the English frontier in North America was but a fringe of cabins beside the ocean, trade was scarcely more developed than among the Indian tribes who lived in the forest. Most of the people labored to wrest a living from the soil and were forced to be content to consume little more than their acres produced. There were no shopkeepers in early Plymouth or primitive Boston. As the settlements became more firmly established, ships coming from England offered their miscellaneous cargoes to the people of the port at public auction. The transactions were by barter, for money was practically non-existent. The ships sailed home with a load of supplies obtained from the people of the colony. Time saw these coast hamlets grow into vigorous and populous communities. The self-sufficiency of the early household was modified as itinerant craftsmen, shoe-makers, weavers, and tinkers, went from house to house. But their labors did not lead to commercial activities, for the work was done upon the consumer's premises and with the consumer's materials. As the eighteenth century came on, crude roads took the place of the forest trails, and ferries were established at the river crossings. Shipyards appeared in the northern ports and a colonial merchant marine began to take form. Life grew steadily more complex in the American communities as the century progressed. Division of labor increased and the specialist became more common. One of the most important of these was the merchant who appeared in New England and the middle colonies.

Commonly the merchant owned one or more ships, built in the yards of New England or Long Island, and manned by sailors from the northern ports. The captain was both a seasoned mariner and a trader. The merchant, living perhaps in Providence or New Haven, would buy directly from the household producers a cargo of rum. The ship cap-tain, then, turning his prow eastward, would make the coast of Africa and exchange the rum for a batch of wild negroes rounded up in the jungles of the Sudan or the Congo. With these safely on board he would hurry before the warm trade winds along the "Middle Passage" to the West Indies. He might stop at Barbados where he would notify the sugar planters of his arrival. His negroes would be exchanged for a little sugar and much molasses together with some other tropical products to take back to New Haven where the molasses would be sold to the household distillers of rum. This was the famous "triangle of trade." But it was only a part of the merchant's activities. He might send a boat direct to the West Indies, laden with lumber or with food stuffs. Many a ship captain, leisurely following the coast to the southern colonies, put in at port after port and, if he were a skillful bargainer, made a profit on every transaction, exchanging his goods for new cargoes as he went. Sometimes two years might elapse before his weather-beaten ship put back into the home port and he reported in person to his employer. In addition to the voyages mentioned, ships constantly plied between the colonial ports and the mother country. Such was the trading organization within the eighteenth-century English colonies. Land transportation was so difficult and costly that most of the popu-lation lived within easy reach of the sea or of navigable rivers. As the century drew to a close, retailers became common in the more important towns and the merchant, either himself, or through his ship captain, bought and sold through these. The shops, however, tended to enhance the importance of the merchant class. The successful among them built up fortunes. They were the American capitalists of the eighteenth century and a sort of commercial aristocracy in the seaport towns.

In the seventeenth and the first half of the eighteenth centuries Englishmen thought of their overseas colonies almost wholly in terms of trade. The British Empire was a busy one. Englishmen had no time for vast imperial dreams which had enticed French-men like La Salle into the wild interior of North America. Instead, the men of Britain thought of profits, both individual and national. The business men of **London and Bristol**, conservative yet enterprising, accepted without question the current theory that colonies existed solely for the benefit of the mother country. They were, no doubt, frequently annoyed at the vigor with which Spain applied this principle of mercantilism. That Government centered all trade with New Spain in one Spanish port and two or three towns in the New World. The English trader who defied this monopoly might lose his life. The Dutch in their dealings with their East India islands were no better than the Spaniards. These were days when men thought that they could confine the natural flow of commerce within highly artificial channels. England's commercial regulations for her colonies, expressed in the Navigation Acts (Vol. VIII), were, perhaps, the mildest of any. They granted benefits as well as imposing burdens and the burdens were lessened by widespread evasion.

The Revolutionary War was a cataclysm sending, for the time being, the whole structure of commercial interchange within the British Empire crashing down. When it was over, disillusioned American merchants discovered that independence meant, for many of them, "dependence upon nothing." They who, with the British, had enjoyed a monopoly of the commerce with the English sugar islands in the West Indies were now foreigners, excluded from their old-time trade. The death from starvation between 1780 and 1787 of some fifteen thousand negro slaves in the West Indies was evidence of what a dislocation the war and the new conditions had brought. The list of American commodities that could lawfully be imported into Great Britain was restricted largely to naval supplies. Nor were the French or Spaniards any more obliging in offering opportunities to the Americans to do business with their own West India islands. Necessity drove the American merchants to strange lands and distant peoples in search of trade. Their ships rounded Cape Horn and coasted as far north as the Columbia River. In 1784 the *Empress of China* weighed anchor in New York harbor outward bound for Canton. Fortune smiled on this venture. The American challenge to Britain in the Far East had begun.

Among the first measures undertaken by the strong government established by the Constitution were some to aid American shipping. The merchant marine grew apace. Ten years after the Treaty of 1783, the United States had a tonnage exceeding that of any other nation in the world save Great Britain. Its foreign trade ranked next to that of England. In this year began the series of wars between England and France which was not to end until Waterloo had been fought. During these wars American merchants and shipowners won fat profits from the neutral trade. The coffee houses of New England hummed with excitement as the shipping news of the early years of the nineteenth century was discussed. The profits of the Americans excited the jealousy of their British competitors. England, mistress of the sea and fighting desperately to overthrow the colossus of the Continent, issued Orders-in-Council intended to restrict the activities of the Americans and to injure France. Napoleon fought back with decrees which made it dangerous for Americans to obey the British orders. President Jefferson retaliated with his Embargo of 1807. After a period of unprecedented prosperity, the American merchant marine fell upon hard times. The depths were reached when the United States was drawn into the war against England. Then most American ships were either tied up to the wharves or were armed as privateers. These went out to lie in wait along the important sea lanes and to prey upon British commerce. The events, however, which caused disaster to American merchant shipping aided materially in bringing to the United States the Industrial Revolution which had been developing in England since the middle of the eighteenth century.

One of Alexander Hamilton's most famous public papers is his *Report on Manufactures*, submitted to Congress (1791) while he was Washington's Secretary of the Treasury. But the "manufactures" which he listed were, for the greater part, articles fabricated by men and women in their homes or the little shops attached thereto. The thrifty Puritans of Connecticut, in particular, turned often from their disheartening struggle with a stony soil to the making of small articles. About 1740, according to President Dwight of Yale, one William Pattison, a native of Ireland, settled at Berlin, Connecticut, and began the manufacture of tinware. The sequel to that event was the Yankee tin peddler who merged later into the peddler of "Yankee notions." Dwight, stanch Congregationalist that he was, looked with some disfavor upon this breed, whose activities were ubiquitous. "Every part of the United States is visited by these men. I have seen them on the peninsula of Cape Cod, and in the neighborhood of Lake Erie. . . . They make their way to . . . Canada; to Kentucky; and, if I mistake not, to New-Orleans and St. Louis. . . . Many of the young men, employed in this business, part, at an early period with both modesty, and principle. Their sobriety is exchanged for cunning, their honesty for imposition; and their decent behaviour for coarse impudence. Mere wanderers, accustomed to no order, control, or worship; and directed solely to the acquisition of petty gains; they soon fasten upon this object; and forget every other, of a superior nature. . . . [The peddler] has an assortment of merchandize to offer his customers. He carries pins, needles, scissors, combs, coat and vest buttons, with many other trifling articles of hardware; and children's books, and cotton stuffs made in New England." It might be added that from his alleged distressing habit of palming off wooden nutmegs upon unsuspecting housewives, Connecticut received the name of the "Nutmeg State."

The Yankee peddler, a distinctive early nineteenth-century type, was the humble distributor of manufactured goods. The outlet to a market which he offered called into being a great variety of manufacturing enterprises in Connecticut. With the coming of the industrial revolution, factory products rapidly replaced those of household fabrication. The merchant of former times frequently financed the new enterprise and, in some cases, gave up his commercial work for that of manufacturing. At other times he became the agent of a factory and concentrated his energies upon the distribution and sale of its products. Finally many a merchant, feeling the limitations of an agent dealing in a single line, developed into a wholesaler or jobber. By the end of the first quarter of the nineteenth century the old-time merchant, as he was known in those fateful years just before the Revolutionary War, had largely disappeared from American life. The foundation for the distributive system of modern times had been laid. Simplicity was the outstanding characteristic of this commercial structure. The factory, the wholesaler or jobber, and the retailer were the chief elements. No complex organization was needed, for, relative to later times, the manufactured commodities were few. Moreover, American factories could never supply the demands of a rapidly developing and expanding nation. It was a "seller's market"; the buyer took what he could get and was thankful. During the same years economic sectionalism found its sharpest manifestation.

Trade had made possible the development of the lower South into a region with a single staple — cotton. By flatboat and steamboat foodstuffs from the upper Mississippi valley were brought down the Father of Waters to New Orleans whence they were carried along the coast to be distributed throughout the cotton kingdom by means of the rivers which flowed into the Gulf and Atlantic. Droves of mules, those indispensable plantation animals, raised in Kentucky and Tennessee, were driven across the mountains and through the Saluda Gap to the Carolinas and Georgia. The planter procured the manufactured articles that he needed from the factories of the Northeast or from England. The Erie canal and later the Pennsylvania system carried quantities of manufactured goods from the Northeast to the Northwest and brought back the products of the central plains. The United States, in the development of its vast domains, had advanced to sectional specialization of function. It had passed the period of economic dependence upon Europe.

Nowhere was the freedom and initiative of the new age more clearly manifested than in the merchant marine. The news of the Treaty of Ghent in 1815 brought endless activity to the wharves of the shipping ports. As fast as the privateers came in, their guns were dismounted and they were hurried into commission for the activities of peace. New vessels began to slip from the ways to take up the old challenge to the merchant shipping of the late enemy. The boat which made its leisurely way from port to port still remained and increased in numbers. The "tramp," as it began to be called, still carries no inconsiderable part of the world's commerce. Soon after the War of 1812, however, lines of packet ships, making regular runs between ports, appeared on the Atlantic. Between Liverpool and New York they foamed, under a heavy spread of sail, each ship trying to outdo the others. In the words of H. U. Faulkener: "Generations of New England shipbuilding had produced the most skilled artisans in the world, and northern Europe had sent many of her shipwrights, drawn here by high wages. To man these ships there were the aggressive and intelligent American sailors who appeared equally at home on the cod banks, in the whaling ships, or on the rigging of a transatlantic packet. Notwithstanding higher wages, it cost less to run an American vessel, for a smaller crew was required."

The acme of the old American merchant marine was the clipper ship, built for speed and long voyages. Their shapely hulls surmounted by bellying canvas expressed the genius of the American people as did no other nineteenth-century construction.

> "I touch my country's mind, I come to grips
> With half her purpose thinking of these ships,
> That art untouched by softness, all that line
> Drawn ringing hard to stand the test of brine,
> That splendour of fine bows which yet could stand
> The shock of rollers never checked by land.
> That art of masts, sail crowded, fit to break,
> Yet stayed to strength and backstayed into rake,
> The life demanded by that art, the keen
> Eye-puckered, hard-case seamen, silent, lean, —
> Earth will not see such ships as those again."

London shippers followed with amazement the course of clippers like the *Flying Cloud*, which sped before the wind from New York to China in almost unbelievable time. In such vessels Americans dominated the Pacific trade. But their day was brief. Already steam had been adapted to ocean transport and already the iron hull was pointing to the great steel ship of the future. In the new types Americans were destined not to excel. The Civil War marked the end of a glorious epoch.

It also marked the beginning of what proved to be a revolutionary change in the life of the American people. Four years after Grant and Lee sat down together in the farm-house at Appomattox, was hammered home, at Promontory Point in the western mountains, the golden spike which completed the construction of the first railroad to span the continent. Twenty years later the nation was covered with a railroad network which bound its distant parts together and which penetrated the isolation of all but the most inaccessible mountain and desert regions. In less than the span of a generation the United States had become an economic unit. The semi-isolation of the sections before the war disappeared. Sectional specialization, however, was not abandoned, for that is based on the immutable facts of physiography and climate. The cotton belt, the corn belt, and the wheat region remain fixed. The New England factory could now draw its raw products from distant Oregon, while oranges from the groves of California could be sold in the Atlantic seaports. The United States became a huge market for the buying of raw materials and the selling of finished products, a market with a common language, a common standard of living, with no dislocating tariff barriers, and increasing rapidly in buying power as the wealth of the nation mounted. Such a market, when existing side by side with matchless natural resources, transformed America, in the last quarter of the nineteenth century, into a highly developed industrial nation. (See Vol. V.) Mass production made its appearance. The retail shops which served the American people, from the general store of the country crossroads to the great department store of the urban centers, were filled with an amazing amount and variety of articles.

The simple marketing machinery of the first half of the nineteenth century proved inadequate to meet the needs of the tumultuous years which marked its end or that first quarter of the twentieth century when the United States swept into the position of the first industrial nation of the world. Changing conditions brought the inevitable experiments with the marketing organization. Some manufacturers tested the possibilities of direct sale to the consumer; others sought to be wholesalers as well as producers. Wholesale houses, in their turn, tried their fortunes at manufacturing and at retailing. The experiments resulted in some modification of the former organization of distribution, but also in the demonstration of its essential soundness. Through the channels of trade marked out before the Civil War still flow the great bulk of the commodities which pass from the producer to the consuming public. But industrialism brought a fundamental change to commerce. The shipping rooms of countless factories were piled high with a wealth of products which must be sold. Competing manufacturers vied with one another in making articles that would please the public. The day of the seller's market passed and that of the buyer's had dawned. No longer must the man or woman who went to the store take the meager offerings of the counter; they had now many things from which to choose. The manufacturer must cater to their desires, and solicit their patronage. The result was the rise of advertising. By every known method for the communication of ideas the producer trumpets abroad the excellence of his wares. He hires an advertising specialist who studies the product, the channels of trade, and the needs or peculiarities of the consuming public. Advertising is a corner stone of modern industry. It is the most striking addition to the simple marketing machinery of the early decades of the nineteenth century.

Another is the mail-order house. That institution sends to the remotest corners of the land its bulky catalogue filled with pictures and alluring text. The family in the lonely mountain cabin turns its pages and beholds the things that may be theirs. A letter is sent and, in course of time, the article desired is at the nearest express or post office. The amazing catalogue of the mail-order house is the lineal successor to the Yankee peddler. The contrast in the variety and cheapness of the articles it offers in comparison with the commodities piled in the wagon of the itinerant vendor is the contrast between two industrial eras. Moreover, the persuasive guile of the peddler who passed but once, perhaps, along the same road has given place to the guarantee that the article, which for any reason is unsatisfactory, may be returned. The mail-order house, like the peddler, wins small profits from small transactions; the difference between the two lies primarily in the volume of business.

The World War marked a significant turning point in American commercial evolution. Up to 1913 the great bulk of commodities shipped from the ports of the United States were raw products drawn from the forests, the mines, and the farmlands of the new country. After that conflict had ended, American manufacturers, with a vastly greater productive capacity because of the demands of the war, sought beyond the national borders for raw materials and for markets. American merchants began to build up an organization especially for the export trade. American companies sent agents to foreign countries to investigate commercial opportunities and to sell their goods. They established branch houses, branch factories, and even banks in distant lands. The development is still young. More and more the business interests of the United States look to the national Department of Commerce as the chief agency for the gathering of commercial information the world over. The aggressive entry of the United States into the world market in competition with other industrial powers marks a new epoch in the commercial history of the country. What the end may be no man can foresee.

Commerce, the exchange of desirable commodities, is almost as old as human society. Few are the tribes of undeveloped peoples that have been found which did not understand its meaning. It has remained, however, for the United States in the twentieth century to demonstrate more fully than any other people the power of commerce to ameliorate the lot of the masses of mankind. A shrewd observer has summed up the achievements and ideals of twentieth-century American trade: "I have long felt that the chief contribution of the United States to progress has been in the wide distribution of what might be called the 'good things of life.' In learning, in culture, and in the fine art of living, we have probably not reached the peaks of many earlier and even some modern nations. As we learn more of ancient civilizations we come to realize that the Egyptians, Babylonians,

Greeks, and Romans lived richly, thought deeply and cultivated the best that life offers. That is, the select few did. The mass of the people existed in hopeless slavery, their lot being no better than that of the common beasts of burden. In the United States we teach the idea that the door of opportunity is open to all. Probably we have not yet reared a man with an intellect equal to that of Aristotle, but we have, with free universal education, almost eliminated illiteracy. . . . We have few roads equal in construction to those built two thousand years ago by the Romans, but we have more roads and superior facilities of transportation. Through our postal, telegraph, and railroad systems, communication and travel are cheap and easy, and open to all. The tables of the Egyptian kings were heaped with delicacies, gathered from all parts of the known world, but their subjects lived on scant rations of coarse, rough food. Poetry was written, sculpture carved, temples were constructed, fabrics woven, and plays presented — for the rulers and their sycophants. But for the masses there was no hope. They were not considered in the scheme of things. When we visit art museums today and inspect the craftsmanship exhibited in articles more than a thousand years old, we are shamed by the comparison with our modern factory-made products.

"It is only on second thought, when we realize that a few centuries ago only kings enjoyed the luxuries which are today common necessities, that we get the proper thrill from twentieth-century achievements. This, then, I believe to be the great contribution of America; a universal education through public schools, universal access to all literature through the public libraries, universal opportunity for communication through cheap postal rates, and finally, universal enjoyment of comforts and conveniences through a factory system which supplies goods at a price so low that many millions today live in comparative luxury. . . . The vision of the majority of American manufacturers is to produce products which will be universally used — to make goods so well and so cheap that they may find a place in every home. This is a democratic vision. Our advertising and salesmanship are tuned to the democratic idea. . . . In no other country have merchants and manufacturers caught this idea because their 'markets' are circumscribed by centuries of thinking in terms of 'royalty' and 'upper classes.' In the United States the market consists of 'the population.'" (The *William Feather Magazine*, November, 1924.) For a nation to ameliorate the lot of the masses of its people is no mean achievement. This is, unquestionably, one of America's greatest contributions to the civilization of the world.

RALPH H. GABRIEL

CHAPTER I

THE COMMERCE OF THE COLONIES

THE expanding commercial interests of fifteenth-century Europe brought about the two great discoveries of a water route to India around the southern end of Africa, and of new continents beyond the Atlantic. (See Vol. I.) In less than half a century after Columbus' epoch-making voyage Spain had developed an extensive and highly profitable colonial empire in the New World. Portugal, meanwhile, pursued the India trade. France, England and Holland were not quite ready to take advantage of Columbus' discovery when news of it was brought to their capitals. A century and a quarter elapsed before they had established significant plantations on the west shore of the Atlantic. The seventeenth century, however, found nationals of all three in America busy with the pioneer work of laying firm foundations for their communities. The French were in the north, in the peninsula of Nova Scotia and along the banks of the St. Lawrence. From the latter region enterprising *coureurs de bois* made their way into the country of the Great Lakes in the continental interior in pursuit of the lucrative fur trade; and explorers, of whom La Salle was the greatest, charted the waterways from the Gulf of St. Lawrence to the Gulf of Mexico. France claimed the great interior lowland of North America.

The English never dreamed the vast dreams of the French. They merely established a row of settlements along the coast from Maine to Georgia, the latter colony being neighbor to the Spaniards in Florida. For diverse reasons a large population flowed from the British Isles to the overseas plantations, augmented in the eighteenth century by immigrants from Sweden and Germany. The English colonies became relatively populous and powerful communities occupying, when compared with French imperial claims, a restricted territory. From the point of view of the mother country the continental colonies comprised the temperate zone part of an empire that extended into the tropics of the West Indies.

The Dutch in the heyday of their seventeenth-century commercial greatness established a foothold at the mouth of the Hudson and in the very midst of the English possessions. But before the century closed they had been expelled. In the following century the French were also driven from the continent. In 1763 Great Britain reigned supreme from Florida northward. When the last of the French and Indian wars had come to an end, British statesmen began to survey with increased attention the characteristics and peculiarities of the empire which had grown up in the Western world and with which the people of their nation enjoyed much lucrative trade.

1 Detail from a map, *Nova Scotia, Drawn from Surveys by T. Kitchin*, engraved for the *London Magazine*, 1749

2   From the painting *The Ships of Columbus*, by J. L. G. Ferris (1863–), in Independence Hall, Philadelphia

COLUMBUS SEEKING THE INDIES

WHEN the three small ships of the Genoese sailor stood out to sea from the harbor of Palos, Spain had embarked upon the greatest commercial venture of her history. Columbus had a vision of new lands and of a possible route to the Orient. The old familiar trade routes leading eastward from the Mediterranean were difficult, and at times the Turks in Asia Minor were obstructing them. The trading centers of southern Europe were shifting westward as sailors began to risk more and more the broad Atlantic and explore its shores. The Portuguese had assumed the leadership in this and were pushing their prows steadily farther down the African coast. Under such circumstances Spain granted the petition of Columbus and introduced a new continent to an astounded world. The desire for glory loomed large in the mind of the admiral, but the possibilities of trade and the extension of Christianity stirred the Spanish court to action.

LATER SEARCHES FOR THE ROUTE TO THE EAST

FOLLOWING Columbus, many explorers, Spanish, French, English, crossed the Atlantic to the newly discovered lands, pushing ahead to the frozen regions of the Antarctic and to the frigid waters where Esquimaux fished. The Spaniards found two civilizations, one on the Mexican plateau and the other perched high in the mountain valley in Peru. From these centers they sent many shiploads of silver and other valuable commodities across the ocean to the motherland (see Vol. I). Magellan, following the coast of South America, entered the strait which bears his name, sailed through it, the first European to cross the vast Pacific, and, dying, sent his remaining ship home.

3   English explorer's view of the Arctic barrier, from Sir Martin Frobisher. *De Martini Frobisseri Angli Navigatione in Regiones Occidentis et Septentrionis Narratio Historica,* Norimb: 1580

CENTURIES OF DISCOURAGEMENT

BUT the Straits of Magellan were far to the south of the equator. Generations of seamen skirted the northern coast, penetrating the rivers in the hope of finding a cleft in the annoying dike that prevented further progress to the eastern *El Dorado*. The thought of explorers and even of early colonists turned toward the search for the headwaters of that river which emptied into the western ocean. Frobisher, Hudson and later Cook all tried in vain to parallel Magellan's feat. Trade was the magnet that drew them into the dangerous ice-filled waters of the north.

4   From the painting *The Northwest Passage*, by Sir John E. Millais (1829–1896) in the Tate Gallery, London

5   Share of stock in The Virginia Company, dated May 23, 1610, from the original in the Egerton Mss., British Museum, London

TRADE AND THE FOUNDING OF COLONIES

LONG before explorers had demonstrated that the northwest passage was blocked by ice, Englishmen and Frenchmen had turned their attention to the exploitation of the continent which John Cabot had been the first to visit. Raleigh had tried a private venture at the end of the sixteenth century and had failed. A few years later two English commercial companies obtained from King James a charter of incorporation, modelled on those of trading organizations which had built up English trade in European ports, and undertook to found settlements in the New World.

THE LONDON AND PLYMOUTH COMPANIES

THE first of the two new companies was made up of "certain knights, gentlemen, and merchants" in and about London, the second of "sundry knights, gentlemen, and merchants" in and about Plymouth. The venture of the London Company became the first permanent English outpost of commerce in America. The year after the beginning of Jamestown, in 1607, the Frenchman, Champlain, started the settlement at Quebec, at which point French merchants hoped a lucrative fur trade with the Indians would develop.

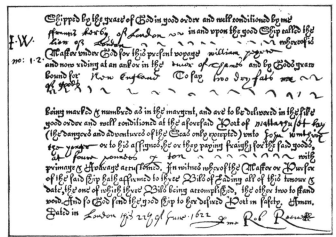

6   Bill of lading for goods from London to Plymouth, 1622, from the original in the Massachusetts Historical Society

OCTROY,

By de Hooghe Mogende

Heeren Staten Generael/verleent aende West-
Indische Compagnie/in date den derden
Junij 1621.

JN 'S GRAUEN-HAGHE,
By Hillebrant Iacobsz, Ordinaris ende Ghesworen
Drucker vande Ed: Mo: Heeren Staten van Hol-
landt en Weft-Vrieslandt, Anno 1621.

7 Title-page of the Charter of the Dutch
West India Company, 1621, from the
original issue at The Hague, 1621

THE NEW ENGLAND FISHING INDUSTRY

WITH the earliest settlements established
as commercial enterprises designed to
benefit adventurers in the home countries, and with no definite common tie
attaching the settlements to one another,
it was natural that the first commerce of
any account was of the type now called
"foreign trade." The first trade to attain
any degree of prestige was that in fish.

DUTCH TRADE AND COLONIZATION

NOT to be outdone, the commercial men of Amsterdam organized a company and put a trading post at the southern tip of Manhattan Island and
another up the Hudson River. The Atlantic, so long unknown, within
a century and a half after Columbus had found its western margin,
was dotted with the sails of many ships carrying commodities back
and forth between the Old World and the New.

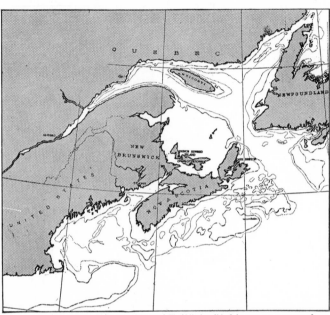

8   Chart of a section of the "Continental Shelf," simplified from a map prepared
by the Department of the Interior, Ottawa

The waters of the Atlantic bordering America are comparatively shallow owing to the presence of an extensive submerged "shelf" that in former geological eras was a part of the American mainland. All parts of this
"shelf" offshore abound in marine life because the shallowness makes feeding and propagating easy. But
that portion of the shelf northward from Cape Cod has the advantage not only of water of no great depth,
but of coolness derived from the inflow of cold currents from the Arctic. This cool shallow ocean is the
favorite haunt of cod, halibut, herring, mackerel and many other varieties of fish. Moreover, the North
Atlantic coast of America is intricately indented with inlets and bays which afforded excellent harbors for
fishing craft. The mainland of the region, being glaciated, was not ideally fitted for agriculture. These
factors taken together made the North Atlantic the scene of the greatest fishing industry. The South Atlantic
had a narrower shelf, warmer water, fewer harbors, and a land well adapted to profitable agriculture. (For a
fuller account of American fisheries, see Vol. III.)

FRENCH FISHERMEN ON THE GRAND BANKS

ALTHOUGH it is likely that John Cabot reported the discovery of
the North Atlantic fishing grounds, found on his voyage of 1497,
the French were the first to exploit extensively the rich food
supplies found in these northern waters. Vessels from Brittany
touched at Newfoundland as early as 1504, and within the same
generation as many as fifty houses were put up by them in
Newfoundland. The French became so interested in these
fishing grounds that they sent Cartier upon expeditions in two
successive years (1534–35) to seek out the best places for the
fishing industry.

9 Fishers of "Nova Francia" with their catch, vignette
from a map in Johann Blaeu, *Grooten Atlas oft Werelt-
Beschryving, Vol. VIII*, Amsterdam, 1664

THE STRUGGLE FOR THE FISHING BANKS

NEARLY fifty years later (1583) the British began to take active part in developing the fish resources of the area. Then Sir Humphrey Gilbert voyaged to Newfoundland and claimed it for the British crown. For almost one hundred and fifty years French and British vied with each other in the development of the fishing resources and at times fought for exclusive possession of the valuable fishing rights and the territory adjacent to the fishing grounds. In this struggle the New England colonists inevitably became involved. Although England in the end wrested Canada from her ancient rival, France retains to this day two small islands off the south shore of Newfoundland where cod may be dried and where French fishermen may make their headquarters during the fishing season.

10   English Fishing Fleets, from Guillaume de l'Isle, *Atlas Nouveau*, Amsterdam, 1733, after Henry Popple, London, 1733

THE FOREIGN TRADE IN FISH

IN the foreign trade there were three markets for the fish. The highest grades of the best fish went to Spain and Portugal where the dominant religion of these countries made the eating of fish compulsory at more frequent intervals than is now the case. The second grades of fish were sold to the islands in the Atlantic near Europe. They were also carried to the West Indies where they were sold to the plantations for use as food for slaves. From Spain and Portugal the American shipmasters brought back wine and fruits. Wine came also from the Canary and Madeira Islands. From the British West Indies the return cargo was sugar, molasses, rum, wine and slaves. A flourishing trade developed with the French West Indies, whose rum, excluded from the wine and brandy producing mother country, was absurdly cheap. Although the fish trade centered at Marblehead, Gloucester, Salem and Boston, the small draft of commercial vessels permitted many a little port to share in the commerce based on fish. The whole encircling arm of Massachusetts Bay eventually was dotted with villages whose prosperity depended on the sea. From the Kennebec to the Delaware the odor of fish permeated trade.

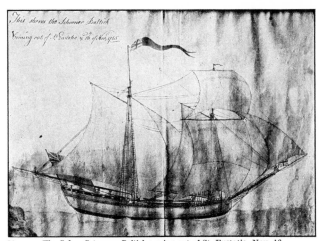

11   The Salem Schooner *Baltick* coming out of St. Eustatia, Nov. 16, 1765, from the water color in the Essex Institute, Salem

12   Whales in New York Harbor, from the original sketch by Jasper Danckaerts, 1679, in the
                        Long Island Historical Society, Brooklyn

THE COLONIAL WHALING INDUSTRY

A PARTICULARLY interesting branch of the colonial fishing business was the whaling industry.   The earliest explorers in New England waters mentioned the number and size of the whales they saw there.   After settle-

ments were made in New England dead whales cast up on the shore by the sea were utilized.   These were cut up, the bone extracted and the remainder tried out for oil.   As this limited resource soon proved insufficient, small boats sailed off shore in pursuit of living whales which, when successfully harpooned, were towed to the beach for cutting, boning and oil-trying.   Eventually, voyages to the deep sea extending over months were taken by whalers, and the whale products were prepared for market while the boats were far out upon the ocean.   (For whaling, see Vol. III.)   Sailors "off soundings" despised slovenly, lubberly whalers and few self-respecting seamen would sign for a whaling voyage.   Whaling crews were largely "green hands."

13   Harpooning whales off Canadian coast, detail from "Mappemonde peinte sur par-
chemin par ordre de Henri II, Roi de France," in Jomard, *Les Monuments de la Géographie*,
Paris, 1862

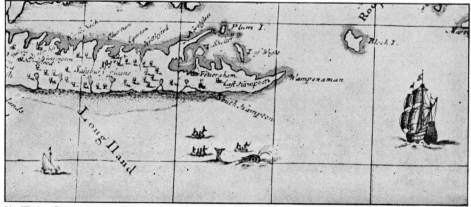

14   Whales off Long Island, detail from R. Morden, *Map of ye English Empire in ye continent of America,* London, 1700(?)

15   Colonial Shipwrights at work, from Willis J. Abbot, *The Story of our Merchant Marine*, New York, 1919.
Illustration by Ray Brown, courtesy of Dodd, Mead & Co.

THE SHIPBUILDING INDUSTRY

A BY-PRODUCT of the extensive colonial fishing industry was shipbuilding, the fisheries creating a large and constant demand for boats. Upon the land was a seemingly unlimited extent of forest containing, among other valuable woods, the prized white pine whose tall straight trunks were unequalled for masts and yards. Skilled shipwrights were attracted to the region, and young men from the colonies entered the trade eagerly, for it became a sure means of steady employment at good wages. The boats constructed being small, as compared with present ships, shipyards could be set up on any of the innumerable little inlets and bays as well as on the larger harbors. In fact, some boats were built at a considerable distance inland and brought to the shore on wheels or rollers.

16   From an engraving *A South East View of ye grea' Town of Boston in New England in America*, 1743, published by William Price, after a drawing by William Burgis in 1723, in the Massachusetts Historical Society, Boston

BOSTON THE SHIPPING CENTER FOR NEW ENGLAND

THE first New England built boat was the *Blessing of the Bay*, launched in 1631, and the first boat of American construction to sail up the Thames was seen on that river in 1638. With this start, colonial shipyards eventually turned out boats literally by the hundreds. To be sure, most of the vessels were small, but a large number were big enough to rank with the best of the ocean ships of that age. At the time of the Revolution, more than two thousand ships, or almost a third of all the British bottoms engaged in commerce, were American built, and naturally a considerably larger percentage of the commerce-carriers engaged in colonial traffic came from American yards. Although the New England shipwrights, and especially those of Massachusetts, constructed most of the colonial boats, many were built also in New York and Pennsylvania.

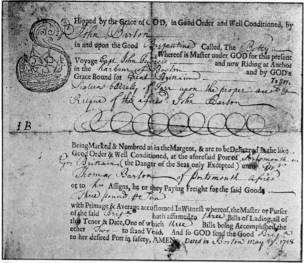

17　A New England shipping bill, Boston, 1718, from the original in the
Essex Institute, Salem

EARLY EXPORT TRADE

ALTHOUGH fish was the mainstay of New England's commerce, the colonists were not limited to this one kind of product. The extensive forests supplied almost as much cargo as the fisheries. Aside from ships built in America and sold abroad, the forests furnished shiploads of masts and spars and planks. Staves, clapboards, pearl ash, tar, potash and miscellaneous lumber were also sent out in large quantities. Rum, made in New England, was an important export; so also were many varieties of provisions other than fish. Horses, sent to the West Indies from Rhode Island and the Connecticut valley, were an interesting cargo.

THREE–CORNERED COMMERCE

To support commerce several factors are necessary, a difference of resources, a difference of economic development, or a difference in national tastes and aptitudes. Some of these differences were present to encourage interchange between England and her overseas colonies. Maritime Britain needed the ships and the spars and masts which came from the northern forests and also the tar and turpentine from the southern woodlands. The people of the British Isles eagerly sought the furs which the traders collected from the American wilderness. The use of tobacco had become widespread in the land of Raleigh and the plantations of Maryland, Virginia and North Carolina furnished many shiploads of the fragrant leaf. The lowlands and river bottoms of South Carolina produced rice for the tables of Europe. The wharves of the tropical islands of the West Indies were piled high with barrels of sugar and molasses. A supply of raw materials was the chief advantage that England derived from her distant possessions. But the mother country was naturally more advanced in economic development than the colonies. The English people were manufacturers as well as traders and the colonists needed manufactured goods.

The conditions of the British Empire gave rise to a triangular trade in the Atlantic. A ship in Boston might load with whale oil and spars for London where the cargo was exchanged for manufactured goods consigned to customers in Barbados. In the latter colony the hold would be filled with molasses to be taken to Boston to be distributed to the rum distilleries. The same ship might then reload in Boston with lumber, low grade fish, and wheat and put off for the French colony at Hayti to exchange for a cargo of molasses. The tropical West Indies needed the food and timber of the temperate north. The exports from the northern colonies to England were relatively small; the New Englanders paid for their heavy imports of manufactured goods by the profits flowing from their trade with other parts of the empire and from the carrying of commodities.

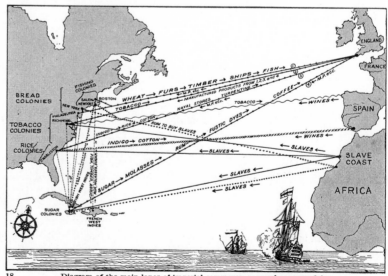

18　　Diagram of the main lanes of imperial commerce, expressly prepared for
The Pageant of America by Edwin Mims, Jr.

COMMERCE OF NEW YORK STATE

IN New York's early commerce, furs took the place occupied by fish in New England's trade. New Amsterdam first, and New York city later, led all the colonial ports in the export of furs. The natural waterways of the Hudson and Mohawk, tapping the Adirondack and Catskill regions, to say nothing of the Finger Lake area occupied by

19

English Colonists trading with Iroquois, vignette from William Faden, *North American Atlas*, London, 1777

the Iroquois Indians, afforded easy access for trappers and traders to the fur territories as well as a natural approach to the Indian population of New York. The fur trade waned as settlement increased; but up to the time of the Revolution, New York was the leading exporter of pelts bought from the Indians.

20   New York in 1732, from an engraving of the view on the "Great Map" in Henry Popple, *British Empire in America*, 1733

THE LIMITATIONS OF EARLY NEW YORK

IN spite of its fur trade, New York, during the colonial era, did not have the relative importance in commerce that the city has since possessed. This was due to the fact that the Hudson valley was relatively narrow and bounded by hills and mountains. Penetration of the valuable Mohawk valley was blocked by the Iroquois Indians who claimed this territory. New York city therefore lacked the contributory and trading region enjoyed by its rival Atlantic ports. Beside the fur trade, in which it was preëminent, New York sold considerable quantities of provisions, horses, hogs and hog products, lumber and lumber products to the West Indies. Much of New York's commerce was carried on by New England merchants.

21   New York Harbor in 1740, from *Manual of the Corporation of the City of New York*, New York, 1858

22   The New Market, Philadelphia, from a sketch by Thackara, in the
                    Columbian Magazine, February 1788

THE COMMERCE OF THE MIDDLE COLONIES

PENNSYLVANIA, West Jersey and Delaware centered their colonial trade at Philadelphia, although Burlington, Gloucester, Salem and Wilmington each had a substantial commerce of its own. Much of the trade of these smaller ports, however, was local in nature; Philadelphia was always the great mart. As in New York, the fur trade was one of the first to develop in importance in Pennsylvania and Philadelphia. It was soon supplemented by the commerce in tobacco, a product which the Lancaster Valley region of Pennsylvania still produces in large quantities. The extensive growing of tobacco, such as took place further south, did not last long in Pennsylvania but soon gave way to cereals, which with flour and other provisions early appeared in Philadelphia's exports. The fur and tobacco of Philadelphia were sold by direct commerce in Europe, but the other products entered the West Indian trade. Philadelphia was one of the leading colonial ports and became the largest of the seaboard cities. Part of its preëminence was due to the rich hinterland with easy access to its excellent harbor.

23   View of Philadelphia Market, 1799, from an engraving by William Birch
          in the Emmet Collection, New York Public Library

An AGGREGATE and VALUATION of the Exports from the Port of Philadelphia, with the number of Vessels and Tonnage employed therein Annually, distinguished from the year 1771 to 1774

N. B. Calculated from Jan. 5. 1771, to Jan. 5. 1774 exclusive; each year distinguished, viz.

Year	No. square rigged vessels	No. sloops and schooners	Amount of Tonnage	Barrels of flour	Barrels of bread	Bushels of wheat	Bushels of Indian corn	Barrels of beef and pork	Barrels of hams	Tons of iron	Barrels of Tar	Barrels of pitch	Barrels of turpentine	1000 Feet plank & boards	1000 Staves and heading	1000 Hoops	1000 Shingles	No. walnut logs	Feet of mahogony	Tons of mahogony	Tons of lignumvitæ	Tons of logwood	Chests of dear-skins	Pounds of furs	Tons of pot-ashes
1771	361	391	46654	252744	38520	51609	259441	5059	778	3358	2693	214	3143	1724	6188	195	1937	63	108441	24	169	93¾	902	161½	
1772	370	390	46841	284872	50504	92012	159625	5849	782	2205	4877	543	1569	4075	5867	978	1765	204	142962	42½	425½	164	1200	66	
1773	426	370	46972	265967	48183	182391	179217	8587	1062	15646	5672	264	1722	3309	51141	1245	5254	79	63255	30	195½	37	40	13¾	

Tons of pearl-ashes	Cwt. of brown sugar	Pounds of loaf sugar	Gallons of molasses	Gallons of rum	Tons of wine	Tons of oil	Barrels of fish	Bushels of flax-seed	Pounds of bees wax	Boxes spermaceti candles	Boxes of tallow candles	Boxes of soap	Kegs of Lard	Boxes of chocolate	Cwt. of coffee	Bushels of fish	Pounds of cotton wool	Barrels of beer	Pounds of feather	Pounds of rice	Kegs of starch	Value in Sterling.
136¼	1185	79116	52621	204456	24	22	5128	110412	29261	683	873	2936	399	479	501	64468	2200	1336	25970	258376	349	£651,534 : 14 : 10¼
25	5198	51408	19681	247635	118	42	5776	85794	50140	1004	1078	3231	734	385	296	42803	5840	1798	40725	534974	1053	784,254 : 4 : 2
57¼	4578	84240	39403	277693	17286	4588	6430	68681	64546	514	1165	3743	732	306	1639	39192	25070	1394	31696	998400	700	720,135 : 13 : 7¼

24   Chart of Shipments from Philadelphia, 1771–74, from *The Pennsylvania Magazine*, 1775

THE PECULIARITIES OF SOUTHERN TRADE

THE commerce of colonial Maryland and Virginia was quite different from that of the other continental colonies. The two possessed one staple, tobacco, greatly desired abroad but obtainable then only in America. Upon the cultivation and sale of this one product, Maryland and Virginia founded their economic life; they grew it almost to the exclusion of everything else. They could sell it easily in England, and its money value there was at times enormous. Consequently, the southern colonists were able to buy freely what they needed in Europe; their purchases including a wide variety of luxuries.

In contrast with the other colonies, therefore, the foreign commerce of Maryland and Virginia was directly with Europe. But the shipping in which this trade was conducted was for the most part British-owned. The plantation owners were country gentlemen, not merchants, traders or ship captains. Since most of the plantations were on the tidewater, there was no great port for the direct trade, but instead many plantations had their own ship-wharves where commerce was carried on. Sole reliance upon tobacco had its unfavorable side; when the European market was glutted American planters suffered financial reverses.

25   A Virginia Tobacco Wharf, detail from *A New and Correct Map of North America*, engraved and published by Matthew Albert and G. F. Lotter, London, 1784

COASTWISE TRADE

NEXT to the foreign trade of the colonies, the coastwise commerce between the colonies themselves, bulked large in value and quantity. Citizens of the settlements from the Kennebec to the Delaware engaged in this commerce, and all the colonies bought and sold from one another. In addition, much of the trade was collec-

tive and distributive in character. That is, small boats gathered the products of many little places and took the articles to some large port for overseas shipment. Likewise, at the greater ports, European merchandise was loaded aboard the small craft and distributed to the villages along the coast or on the navigable rivers. Although all the settlements had many common resources, there were several distinctive differences that gave rise to intercolonial coastwise trade. Thus New England had its fish, livestock and rum; the middle colonies had provisions, animals, meat and beer; the southern plantations had tobacco

26   Sailing Notice, from the *Newport Mercury*, June 24, 1765, in the John Carter Brown Library, Providence, R. I.

and rice; and the West Indies tropical products. All of these commodities were traded back and forth between the various colonies, and the total of such trade created a commerce of no small volume and value. Most of this commerce was water-borne because overland transport of freight was practically impossible.

27   Sailing Notice, from *The Pennsylvania Gazette*, April 12, 1750, in the New York Public Library

28   Sailing Notice, from *The Pennsylvania Gazette*, March 20, 1750, in the New York Public Library

29   From a mezzotint, 1791, by S. R. Smith, after the painting
                    The Slave Trade by G. Morland

THE SLAVE TRAFFIC

ONE important item of colonial commerce was the purchase, shipment, and sale of African slaves. The negroes were brought from the interior of their native continent to the coast on the Gulf of Guinea. Here they were loaded aboard English or into New England ships to be carried to the West Indies. Some slaves were taken directly to the continental colonies but in general the people in these regions preferred to purchase partly civilized and trained negroes from the West Indies rather than attempting to break in wild negroes. Among the colonial ports which sent out their vessels to engage in the human traffic on the Atlantic, Newport, Rhode Island, was preëminent.

THE BRITISH MERCANTILE THEORY

NECESSARY to an appreciation of the character of American colonial commerce is an understanding of the theory and practice of the British in respect to national wealth and colonial administration. The British, in common with all other advanced nations, believed completely in the theory of mercantilism. It was supposed that trade could not be mutually advantageous; one party to an exchange must be a gainer and one a loser. Every country, therefore, tried to be as nearly self-sufficing as possible, but at the same time endeavored to force every other country to buy as much as possible from itself. Everyone believed that money and gold should be kept at home. In respect to colonies, Britain, in common with all Europe, was of the opinion that oversea possessions should be administered like plantations. The colony should be encouraged to produce raw materials needed by the mother country, and compelled to purchase from the home nation the manufactured articles which it produced. The colony was to be prohibited from exploiting raw materials or manufacturing commodities that competed seriously with those furnished by the mother country.

With these theories in mind, Parliament passed legislation, the king issued mandates, and trade bodies enacted ordinances to bring the American colonies in practice into accord with the precepts. The result in laws were the bounties, preferential duties and drawbacks, offered to Americans for producing certain desired articles. At different times and for short or long periods such favors were extended to naval stores, lumber, indigo, silk, tobacco, pig and bar-iron, molasses, whale-fins and flax. Except in the case of indigo, none of these favors produced results commensurate with the expectations. Artificial stimulation seldom has had a permanent beneficial effect upon commodity production.

30   Commerce on the Thames, 1616, from the reprint, published by the Topographical Society of
           London, 1883–84, of the original "Visscher View of London, 1616" in the British Museum

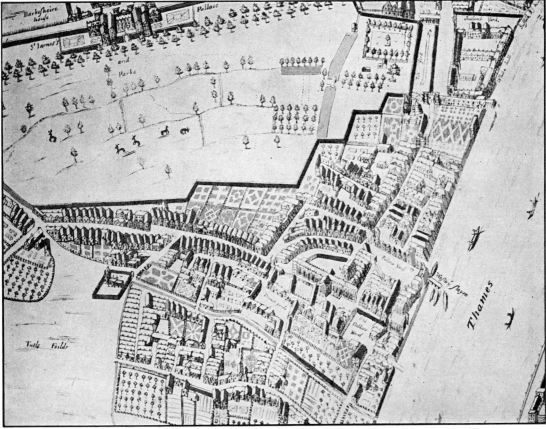

31   Center of Imperial Control, London, from the reprint, published by the Topographical Society of London, 1658

PARLIAMENT IMPOSES RESTRAINTS ON COLONIAL COMMERCE

In accordance with the prevailing doctrine of mercantilism and colonial administration, a number of Parliamentary acts were passed that affected American colonial commerce and industries. There were three acts passed, beginning in 1651, relating to navigation and trade, two administrative acts, and one concerning molasses. The purpose of these various measures was to exclude foreigners, primarily the rival Dutch, from colonial commerce and the carrying trade, and to limit the field of activity of colonial shipmasters and merchants. They also sought to insure that England should be the focus of the commercial activities of the colonies and that British workmen should not lack raw materials nor the manufacturers a colonial market for their wares. During the decade preceding the Revolution, Parliament endeavored to secure revenue by taxing commerce in addition to regulating it. Since Parliament was distant and often ill-informed and the legislation intended primarily for the benefit of England rather than the colonies, the various laws tended to hamper the commerce of the colonies. To be sure, the colonists evaded, ignored and violated some of this legislation where it served American purposes so to do. These facts, together with lax administration of the laws by the British, mitigated the severity of the acts.

(403)

Anno quarto

Georgii III. Regis.

C A P. XXVI.

An Act for granting a Bounty upon the Importation of Hemp, and rough and undressed Flax, from His Majesty's Colonies in *America.*

WHEREAS the Encouragement of the Importation of Hemp, and rough and undressed Flax, from His Majesty's Colonies and Plantations in America, will be a Means of furnishing this Kingdom with Sail Cloth and Cordage (so essentially necessary for the Supply of His Majesty's Royal Navy, as well as for Ships employed in the Merchants Service) at more reasonable Rates than at present, and will also tend to make the Supply of the said Materials cheaper and less precarious, and be a Means of employing and enriching His Majesty's Subjects within the said Colonies and Plantations: May it therefore please Your most Excellent Majesty, that it may be enacted; and be it enacted by the King's most Excellent Majesty, by and with the Advice and Consent of the Lords Spiritual and Temporal, and Commons, in this present Parliament assembled, and by the Authority of the same, That from and after the Twenty fourth Day of June, One thousand seven hundred and sixty four, every Person or Persons who shall, within the Time appointed by this Act, import or cause to be imported into this Kingdom, directly from any of His Majesty's English Colonies or Plantations in America, in any Ship or Ships that may lawfully trade to His Majesty's Plantations, manned as by Law is required, any hemp,

S 3 2

32   First page of printed copy of the Act Granting Bounty to Colonial Merchants, in the New York Public Library

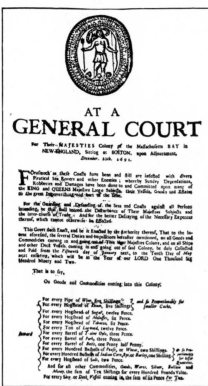

33 An Act of the Massachusetts Bay Colony, Dec. 22, 1691, imposing import and export duties on all goods entering or leaving her harbors, from the original broadside in the Massachusetts Archives, Boston

COLONIAL LAWS REGARDING COMMERCE

The colonies themselves were imbued with the theory of mercantilism and passed measures intended to conserve, protect or enhance production, trade and commerce. Although different in detail, these colonial enactments were similar in general to the English legislation. They comprised import and export duties, embargoes, bounties and charges for harbor and wharf-services. Even taxation of commerce for the purpose of revenue rather than for regulation was included in the colonial laws. These colonial measures, too, had considerable influence in shaping commerce, particularly the intercolonial coastwise trade. Politically they were a factor of disunity tending to separate the colonies rather than bring them together. Economic disharmony and political discord were intimately related.

In this same act of 1691 another important characteristic of mercantilism is clearly demonstrated: "It is Ordered, That from and after the last day of January next Ensuing, none of the French Nation be permitted to take up their Residence, or be in any of the Sea-Port, or Frontier Towns within this Government, but such as shall be Licensed by the Governour and Council.

"Nor shall any of said Nation open Shop, or Exercise any Manual Trade in any of said Towns, without the Approbation of the Select Men of such Town first orderly obtained. On pain of imprisonment. . . ." These provisions were more important in a military than in an economic sense and should be set against the background of the first of the French and Indian Wars which had broken out two years before.

THE TRADE OF THE CAROLINAS

Toward the close of the colonial period, the Carolinas developed a trade similar to that of Virginia and Maryland. The most valuable crops involved were rice and indigo. Under the stimulus to trade offered by these products, ardently desired in Europe, Charleston grew almost to rival Philadelphia and Boston as a commercial center. In nearly every other respect, the Carolina commerce was akin to that of Virginia and Maryland except that it was not established so early in colonial history. In the northern section of the proprietary province tar, resin, turpentine, and ship supplies were produced from the great pine forests and exported abroad. For, like northern neighbors, they depended upon British and Yankee ship captains and merchants to carry and dispose of their products.

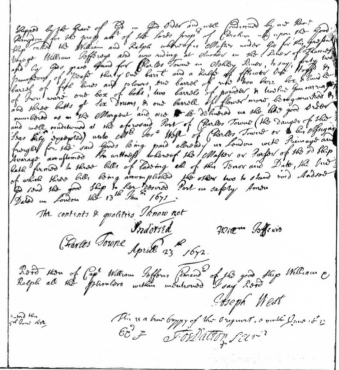

34   Bill of lading for goods shipped from Charleston, 1672, in Historical Commission of South Carolina

CHAPTER II

THE OLD MERCHANT MARINE

IN 1764 George Grenville, Chancellor of the Exchequer, had begun to strengthen and to render more effective the Navigation Acts which had been on the statute books of England since the previous century. In his opinion England, just emerging from a desperate war with France, needed to examine the commercial phases of her empire. The mercantilist theory that the colonies should be developed in the interest of the mother country was in his mind as he put through the Sugar Act of 1764 against the illegal trade between New England and the French colonies in the West Indies (see Vol. VIII). Neither Grenville nor the majority of his contemporaries realized that on the continent of North America communities had come into existence which were bound to chafe under any attempt to restrict their economic development. One of the fundamental causes of the Revolution was this failure of the British Government to realize that the time was at hand when the American colonies should be allowed to grow as they would without the hampering restrictions of the mercantilist policy.

In 1783, when thirteen former English colonies found themselves recognized as an independent nation, they faced a commercial situation a little disconcerting. They were still dependent upon the former mother country for the great part of their manufactured goods. They hoped to make a commercial treaty with England which would restore at least some of the privileges which they had once enjoyed as members of the British Empire. But when John Adams went to London with this in view, he failed completely. To the British the Americans were now foreigners. The old Navigation Acts to which the latter had objected were now enforced against them in exactly the same way as they were enforced against the Dutch or the French. So the Americans were compelled to seek new opportunities for trade.

For this adventure they had a serviceable merchant marine which was, in part at least, the result of benefits they had derived from the Navigation Acts. In the seventeenth century England had decreed that imperial trade should be in English ships manned by English crews. This included New England vessels and New England seamen. Freed from competition with the vigorous Dutch, therefore, New England had developed ships and sailors. In half a century after the close of the Revolution this nucleus was to develop into one of the great merchant marines of the world.

35 The ship *Recovery* of Salem, from a copy of the original painting by William Ward, 1799, in the Peabody Museum, Salem

36 Commerce in the harbor of New York during the Revolution, from a lithograph by George Hayward
in D. T. Valentine, *Manual of the Corporation of New York*, New York, 1858

COMMERCE DURING THE REVOLUTION

THE Revolutionary War had an evil effect upon American commerce. The cod and whale fisheries were brought practically to a standstill, for both British men-of-war and privateers ravaged them. The crippling of the fisheries was a staggering blow to New England. Since a large share of American commerce had been with England herself and with the West Indies, the British navy effectually blocked these two avenues of traffic. With the falling off of commerce and the closing of the British market for American ships, the industry of ship-building declined. Nevertheless, through-out the war some American commerce was

37 A Revolutionary privateer, *The Rising States*, from the model in the Peabody Museum, Salem

carried on despite the risks involved. Trade with Holland and France, for example, was carried on through the Dutch island of St. Eustatius in the West Indies. "This rock," commented Admiral Rodney, "only six miles in length and three in breadth, has done England more harm than all the arms of her most potent enemies, and alone supported the infamous American Rebellion." Rodney's devastation of the island was practically complete. Furthermore, many former merchant vessels and fishing boats — one estimate is that there were two thousand — became privateers. The continental market of Europe was open to Americans, even if England was closed to them. The southern colonies particularly continued to export their products throughout the conflict, although naturally in reduced quantities. The war, therefore, seriously impaired commerce, without, however, causing it to stagnate.

38 A post-war sailing vessel, *The Friendship*, built at Salem, 1797, from the model in the Peabody Museum, Salem

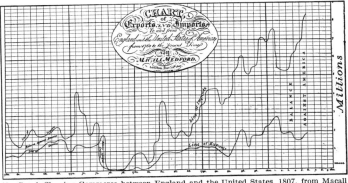

AT the Court at St. *James's*, the 24th of *March*, 1786,

P R E S E N T,

The KING's Moſt Excellent Majeſty in Council.

WHEREAS by an Act paſſed in this preſent Seſſion of Parliament, intituled, " An Act " for further continuing, for a limited Time, an Act " made in the Twenty-third Year of the Reign of " His preſent Majeſty, intituled, An Act for pre- " venting certain Inſtruments from being required " from Ships belonging to the United States of Ame- " rica; and to give to His Majeſty, for a limited Colonies belonging to the Crown of Great Britain in America; and that, until further Order, there ſhall be allowed and paid the ſame Drawbacks on the Exportation of any Sort of Foreign Hemp, or Foreign Iron, exported from Great Britain into any Britiſh Colony or Plantation in America, or into the Terri- tories of the United States of America, or any of them, as are or may be allowed by Law upon the Ex-

39   British General Order for regulating trade with America, Great Britain and the British West Indies, 1786, from a copy in the Library of Congress

EFFECT OF THE AMERICAN REVOLUTION ON COMMERCE

TRADE customs, practices and personal relationships are hard to change; even war does not always disrupt them permanently. Thus it is no cause for surprise that after the Revolution most American commerce continued to be associated with the British Isles. Even the trade between America and the continent of Europe continued to flow by way of England. Political bonds were broken by the war, but commercial ties were only temporarily loosened; when hostilities ceased, the commercial attachments were strengthened and soon were more tightly joined than ever.

But the Revolution greatly weakened the American commerce with the West Indies. After the war, the United States was a foreign nation to the British islands in the Caribbean,

40   Graph Showing Commerce between England and the United States, 1807, from Macall Medford, *Oil without Vinegar, and Dignity without Pride; or British American and West India Interests Considered*, London, 1807

and American ships or merchants were as rigidly excluded from traffic there as if they were Dutch or French; the British continued their mercantilist policy of keeping British trade in the hands of the British. Their rigid rule was evaded quite successfully, although illegally, by Americans, but the West Indian commerce from this time on became relatively less important.

AMERICAN TRADE IN THE MEDITERRANEAN

IN these circumstances, American commercial interests sought new outlets. They were found in the Baltic, the Mediterranean, the Yellow Sea, and the Indian Ocean. New or enlarged markets for American goods were found in Russia, Holland, Denmark and Prussia. The Mediterranean countries proved to be good markets, but commerce in that region was highly adventurous for American shipmasters by reason of the depredations of the Barbary pirates (see Vol. VI). The infant United States was unable until 1815 to beat the pirates into a proper regard for the American flag. Meanwhile, many American captains traded profitably in the Mediterranean by using forged or otherwise fraudulent British ship-papers.

41   The ship *Hercules* of Salem at Naples, 1809, from the painting in the Peabody Museum, Salem

Laſt Sunday ſailed for China, the ſhip Empreſs of China, Captain Green. A correſpondent remarks, that notwithſtanding the many difficulties he may have to encounter with, as being the firſt ſhip from this new nation, to that rich and diſtant part of the world, from his character as an able and ſpirited navigator, we may from a pleaſing preſage of that ſucceſs which every friend to his country wiſhes him, And to the gentlemen, whoſe ambition to diſcover new reſources of wealth, by forming new channels for the extenſions of our commerce, a contemplation on the ſervices they are rendering their country, muſt ſufficiently compenſate for the riſque of their property.

42   Notice of the sailing of *The Empress of China*, from *The Independent Gazette; or the New York Journal Revived*, New York, Feb. 26, 1784

NEW YORK, May 12.

We have the ſatisfaction of announcing the arrival of the Ship Empreſs of China, Capt. Greene, commander, from the EAST-INDIES, at this port, yeſterday, after a voyage of fourteen months and twenty-four days. She ſailed from this port about the 15th of February, 1784, and arrived at Canton in Auguſt, having touched at the Cape de Verdes—ſhe took her departure from China the firſt of laſt January, and in return touched at the Cape of Good Hope, from whence ſhe made her paſſage here in about two months.—The crew during this long voyage have been remarkable healthy. The carpenter, who went out in a bad ſtate of health, died on the homeward paſſage.

We learn that Captain Greene met with polite uſage during his ſtay in Canton—the Britiſh Commodore was the firſt who ſaluted his flag on his arrival there.

43   Notice of the return of the *Empress of China*, from *Louden's New York Packet*, May 12, 1785

THE *EMPRESS OF CHINA* SAILS FOR CANTON

THE most interesting new development in American commerce, however, was marked by the sailing in 1784 of a New York ship, the *Empress of China*, for Canton. For fifteen months Chinese merchants and dignitaries traded their silks and teas for the strange products of these unfamiliar visitors. When Samuel Shaw returned again to New York, his account aroused such interest that it was read aloud in the halls of Congress. The profits realized from this voyage opened the eyes of American men of commerce to a new field of endeavor, and they began an amazing chapter in American maritime annals. A Philadelphia-built ship, the *Canton*, made the voyage to China and return in 1785–87.

44   The *Canton*, from the model in the Philadelphia Commercial Museum

THE *GRAND TURK* SAILS FROM SALEM

THE *Empress of China* was sent to Canton by New York capitalists, but her supercargo was a Bostonian, Major Samuel Shaw. Boston and all maritime New England could not fail to be interested in the voyage and the profits of the *Empress* venture, and soon after Shaw's return many New England vessels were experimenting with the new commercial outlet in China. The *Grand Turk* of Salem, Massachusetts, was the first New England boat to turn her prow into the waters of the Far East. Her voyage was so profitable to her sponsors that New England merchants and shipmasters rushed into the trade by the score.

45   Samuel Shaw, from an engraving by J. Andrews, in Freeman Hunt, *Lives of American Merchants*, New York, 1858, after the portrait by John Johnston (1752–1818)

46 The *Grand Turk*, from the painting, 1786, by a Chinese artist on a punch bowl, in the Peabody Museum, Salem

THE "CHINA TRADE"

In time, two ports, Boston and Salem, took precedence over all others in this "China trade." Each port established a commercial system peculiar to itself, Boston ships sailing to China by way of the Pacific Northwest, and Salem

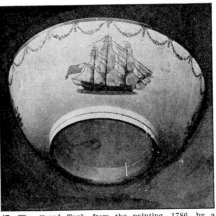

47 The *Grand Turk*, from the painting, 1786, by a Chinese artist on a punch bowl, in the Peabody Museum, Salem

ships by a route that took her vessels to the Cape of Good Hope and the East Indies on the way to Canton.

48   Cape of Good Hope, from an engraving in the *European Magazine*, 1800, by S. Rawle, after a drawing by C. Thomas

A GOLDEN HIGHWAY

Boston ships to the Far East, sailing westwardly around the Horn, and Salem ships sailing eastwardly around the Cape of Good Hope retrieved the loss of the commerce with the West Indies which had been crippled by the Revolution and its aftermath. So it came to pass that the commerce with the Far East which in the fifteenth century had led to the discovery and exploration of America, helped to save the United States in the infancy of its independence. Perhaps the China trade was not as great as the illicit trade that continued with the West Indies but it was of vital importance at a critical time.

49   From the painting *Canton Factories, 1840*, in the Peabody Museum, Salem

50   Ship *Columbia* in Oregon, 1790, from the contemporary sketch by George Davidson
in the Bostonian Society, Boston

THE FAR EASTERN TRADE

THERE was a good market in America for the wares of China and the Far East, for teas, spices, silks and china were in demand; and what could not be sold in our own domestic market was easily disposed of in Europe. The trouble at the beginning of the Far East commerce was that America had little to offer to the Far East in exchange for Oriental goods. The two voyages of Captain Robert Gray in the ship *Columbia* solved the problem for the Bostonians. On September 30, 1787, Gray sailed from Boston, rounded Cape Horn and spent the next year and a half along the coast of what is now Oregon, Washington and British Columbia. The object of this long visitation was to secure a cargo of skins of the sea otter. The waters of the Northwest coast abounded in these sea animals; in China the fur was in great demand among the rich mandarins. So the *Columbia* filled her hold with skins and then sailed for Canton. There the furs were exchanged for tea and the *Columbia* sailed back around the world to Boston where she arrived in August, 1790, the first vessel to carry the American flag around the globe. This voyage blazed the way for the Boston-China trade. A second voyage took Gray to the Northwest coast in 1792. On this occasion, he discovered the river that he named after his vessel, the beginning of a train of events that eventually united the Pacific coast to the great American republic. Prior to the opening of the Boston-China trade the Celestial Empire had procured prized furs overland at great expense from Russia. American furs undersold the Muscovite.

51   Ship *Columbia* Attacked by Indians in Juan de Fuca Straits, from a contemporary sketch by
George Davidson in the Massachusetts Historical Society

52   View of Honolulu, from James Hunnewell, *Journal of the Voyage of the Missionary Packet, Boston to Honolulu,*
1826, Charlestown, 1880, engraving by Kalama after the drawing, 1837, by E. Bailey

TRADE IN THE SOUTH SEA

WHEN Gray returned to Boston after his first voyage in the *Columbia,* he brought with him a native of "Oyhyhee" as the name was then currently spelled. Later traders out of Boston to Canton by way of the Northwest coast found it profitable to break their Pacific voyage by a stop at the Hawaiian Islands. The crew were relieved by the chance to get fresh food instead of the steady sea-diet of "salt horse," as pork was called, and the men also found much to delight them, animate and inanimate, during the stay — often prolonged — among the islands.

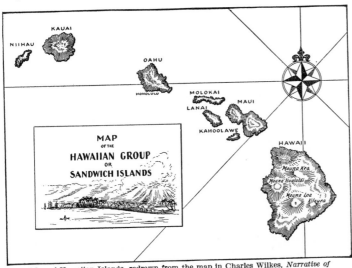

53   Map of Hawaiian Islands, redrawn from the map in Charles Wilkes, *Narrative of the United States Exploring Expedition,* Philadelphia, 1845

THE AMERICANIZATION OF HAWAII

THE economic justification for making Hawaii a stopping place on a commercial voyage was the opportunity afforded to fill out the cargo with sandalwood. This pleasant-smelling commodity grew wild in the islands but was rare and highly valued in China. Adding it to a cargo collected on the Northwest coast insured merchant captains of easy sales in Canton. Missionaries as early as 1820 traced the wake of commercial ships to Hawaii. These messengers of the gospel were unusually successful and in course of time made Christianity the practically universal religion among the natives. The descendants of these missionaries and early commercial people made up that American population who in the eighteen nineties played such a large part in bringing about the annexation of Hawaii to the United States. The acquisition of the Hawaiian Islands was destined to be of great importance in furthering American trade in the Pacific.

54   The Barge *Cleopatra,* Salem ship purchased by rulers of Hawaii, from the painting in the Peabody Museum, Salem

55   Ship *America*, from the water-color by Corné, in possession of Peabody Museum, Salem

A LEISURELY TRAFFIC

SINCE large ships could not be maneuvered easily on the Northwest coast because of sand bars, shallow inlets and islands, the China trade at the beginning was confined almost entirely to boats from sixty-five to ninety

56   Ship *Belisarius* (built 1794), from a painting by Corné, in the Peabody Museum, Salem

feet long, little more than fishing boats according to modern standards. These small vessels were heavily armed and well-manned because nearly all the first trading was interspersed with warfare between the natives and the crews. To prevent fouling on the long cruises, the small trading vessels were sheathed with copper. Despite this precaution, the China traders, before the day of the clipper, were more noteworthy for the leisurely fashion of their voyages than they were for speed. Inasmuch as the cargo for the Canton market had to be collected gradually, with many calls at innumerable stopping places along the Pacific, speed was hardly an essential for the trade. The time was to come, however, when, with the determination of the United States to challenge Britain's supremacy in the tea-carrying trade, speed became so important a factor in this commercial interchange with the Orient that the swiftest sailing ships were employed.

57   Captain James W. Chever, Privateer *America*, from a crayon portrait in the Peabody Museum, Salem

58   Ship *Boston*, from John R. Jewitt, *A Narrative of the Adventures of the Ship Boston*, 1815

59   The Pagoda Anchorage, Whampoa, 1840, from a painting in the Peabody Museum, Salem

FEATURES OF THE CHINA TRADE

THE vessels trading with China could not go to Canton itself but were halted at an international anchorage called Whampoa. There the cargoes were transferred to small Chinese river craft and carried up the river to Canton to great warehouses called hongs. A few Chinese merchants had a monopoly of commerce at the hongs and acted as intermediaries between foreign traders and the Chinese people. Certain of these Chinese merchants became fast friends of some of the American traders, aided them in countless ways and reposed unusual confidence in them. Several American fortunes grew out of such international friendships. Year by year the invasion of China by western goods and western traders increased, but China always sold more than she bought. Opium was foisted upon China in an effort to balance British-Chinese trade.

60   Shamien Consulates, Canton, about 1860, from a painting in the Peabody Museum, Salem

THE BURNING OF THE CANTON FACTORIES

IN 1856, the Canton factories were destroyed by fire during the war between the Chinese and British forces. Since then the little island of Shamien has been taken for foreign residences, although China alleviated strict segregation.

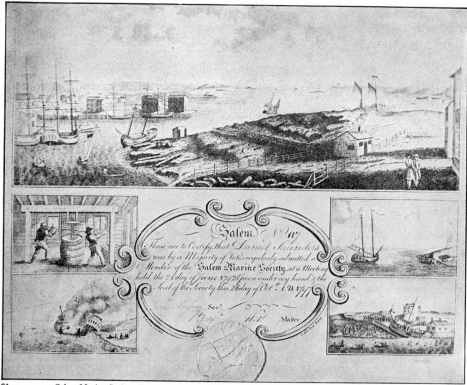

61   Salem Marine Society Certificate of Membership, from the original in the Essex Institute, Salem

SALEM BOATS SAIL EASTWARD

ALTHOUGH the China trade was inaugurated by the *Empress of China*, a ship sent out from New York, that city was never as prominent in the commerce as Boston. Neither Philadelphia nor Baltimore shared the honors with Boston to any extent. It was Boston's next-door neighbor, Salem, that was her greatest rival in Oriental commerce. Salem, faced with the same problem of securing a cargo salable in the East, found a different solution from Boston's Northwest-Hawaii practice. Salem ships sailed east, not west. Spain, Portugal, the Dutch East Indies, the Philippines and both coasts of Africa, to say nothing of the tiny islands that dot the southern Pacific ocean, soon became familiar with the house flags on the vessels that belonged to the Derbys, Princes and Crowninshields of Salem. A vessel out of Salem would be loaded and emptied of half a dozen cargoes before she returned from her final destination in the Orient.

62   From the painting *Launch of the Fame* at Salem, 1802, in the Essex Institute, Salem

63   Salem ships loading coffee at Mocha, Arabia, from a water-color, about 1820-25,
in the Peabody Museum, Salem

SALEM IMPORTS FROM THE ORIENT

SALEM vessels roved all Asiatic waters in search of articles salable in America and capable of trans-shipment across the Atlantic to Europe. Thus alongside the bales of Indian cottons on Salem's wharves there might be found bags of coffee from Mocha and Java, tin from the Gaspar Straits, spices from the Malay Archipelago and especially pepper from the northwest coast of Sumatra. Indeed, Salem for a time was not merely the principal place of sale for pepper in America: the whole Western world looked to this small port for the supplies of this necessary condiment.

64   Brig *Herald* (built 1832), off Dixcove, Gold Coast, Africa, from a water-color in the Peabody Museum, Salem

SALEM'S TRADE WITH INDIA

JUST as Boston specialized in trade with China, so Salem put most of her energies into commerce with India; what Canton stood for among Bostonians, Calcutta meant to Derby and his neighbors. But Calcutta was not the only Indian terminus for Salem ships; they were well known in Bombay, Rangoon and Bengal. Boston boats returned home laden with silks and tableware, while Salem wharfs were piled with Indian cotton goods, spices and wine.

65 Elias Hasket Derby, 1803–80, from the portrait by
James Frothingham in the Peabody Museum, Salem

66 Joseph Peabody, 1757–1844, from the portrait by
Charles Osgood in the Peabody Museum, Salem

TWO SALEM MERCHANTS

SALEM shipowners as well as Salem ships were known throughout the mercantile world. Chief among the men who contributed to the glory of this famous port were Elias Hasket Derby and Joseph Peabody. The son of Richard Derby, famous merchant and privateer of the Colonial period, the brother of John Derby who arrived in England with the first news of Lexington, himself interested in at least eighty of the privateers that during the Revolution had sailed from Salem, Derby was the greatest of those who, in the period after the Revolution, opened the Eastern trade. It was he who sent the *Grand Turk* to China. He was also the first

67 Thomas Handasyd Perkins, 1764–1854, from the portrait by Thomas Sully (1783–1872) in the Boston
Athenæum

to raise the American flag at Calcutta and Bombay, the first at Mauritius and the Isle of France. His son Elias, Jr., he sent as special agent to reside in the East and build up the Derby trade. Following the War of 1812, the wealthiest Salem merchant was Joseph Peabody, who continued the Salem trade with China and India until his death in 1844. "Seven thousand sailors signed articles in the counting-room of Joseph Peabody and went to sea in his eighty ships which flew the house flag in Calcutta, Canton, Sumatra, and the ports of Europe until 1844. These were mostly New England boys who followed in the footsteps of their fathers because deep-water voyages were still 'adventures.' . . ." — RALPH D. PAINE, *The Old Merchant Marine*, The Chronicles of America Series, New Haven, 1920.

A GREAT BOSTON MERCHANT

THE China merchants of Boston were an aristocracy of wealth and culture which dominated the social life of New England during the Federalist period. Not least among the great merchants was Thomas Handasyd Perkins, one of the earliest traders on the Northwest and China coasts and founder of the great mercantile house of J. & T. H. Perkins. This house erected the famous Perkins & Co. branch at Canton in 1803 and put in charge John Perkins Cushing, who remained at Canton for over thirty years and became the most wealthy and respected foreign merchant in China.

68   Southeastern View of Nantucket, Mass., from J. W. Barber, *Historical Collections of Massachusetts*, Worcester, 1839

THE REVIVAL OF THE WHALING INDUSTRY

MEANWHILE, the whaling industry annihilated by the Revolution began to show signs of new life. Whalers from Nantucket and New Bedford followed the Boston merchantmen around Cape Horn and chased their mammalian prey all along the coasts of South and North America from the southern tip of Chile to the Russian holdings in the Bering Sea. The whalers, too, ventured to the islands far out in the Pacific, from Tahiti to Honolulu. The whale oil was sold in England, France and Spain. But the domestic market in America, forced by the Revolution to become accustomed to tallow candles, did not readily return to spermaceti from Nantucket. Thus whaling did not revive as completely as the merchant commerce of Boston and Salem.

69   New Bedford, Mass., in 1808, from the painting by William A. Wall, courtesy of the State Trust Co., Boston

THE FISHING FLEETS DESTROYED BY WAR

THE fishermen were not so fortunate as the merchantmen after the Revolutionary War. The fleets had been destroyed by war or neglect, the ranks depleted and the survivors impoverished. It took years for the fishing fleets to regain numbers and vigor, and hardly had they done so when the Embargo and Non-Intercourse Acts and the War of 1812 prostrated them a second time.

70   Marblehead "heel tapper" fishing schooners, from a fireboard painting about 1800, in the Marblehead Historical Society, Marblehead, Mass.

71   From the painting *Crowninshield's Wharf, Salem*, during the embargo, 1807, by M. Macpherson after George Ropes,
in the Essex Institute, Salem

AMERICAN SHIPPING HAMPERED BY ENGLAND AND FRANCE

WHILE Yankee enterprise was carrying the Stars and Stripes to the far corners of the world, events in Europe were creating a situation fraught with uncertainty for the American skipper. In 1793 France and England clashed. With but little respite, war continued until the final overthrow of Napoleon at Waterloo in 1815. As the nineteenth century opened, neutral American shipping began to enjoy unparalleled trading opportunities. British sea power drove to cover the merchant marines of France and other enemy nations. At the same time French warships and privateers harassed the English merchant shipper. At the very moment when trade with Asia had become firmly established, trade with war-ridden Europe began bringing in rich profits. Maritime America prospered as never before. But the harvest was short-lived. In 1806 began a battle between England and Napoleon each seeking to prevent the neutral Americans from aiding the other. Merchants from Boston and Salem were buffeted by British orders-in-council and Napoleonic decrees. President Jefferson sought to compel the European belligerents to respect his nation's neutral rights by an economic boycott. The story of the Embargo of 1807 is told elsewhere (see Vol. VIII); suffice it to say here that, when orders came from the national government to tie up at the home wharf all shipping save that engaged in the coast trade, New England was bitter. The act was avoided as much as possible. When, finally, the United States declared war against Britain (see Vol. VI), New Englanders openly opposed the conflict. Despite the obnoxious British actions against Americans the followers of the ocean highways felt greater friendliness for the British than for the French and considered the former their greatest bulwark against the tremendous power of Napoleon.

THE WAR OF 1812

THE Embargo and Non-Intercourse Acts crippled American commerce most seriously, but the War of 1812 virtually wiped it out. The British blockade was thorough (see Vol. VI) and before the end of the war embraced the whole Atlantic coast line, so that few daring ship captains were able to evade its vigilance. New England merchants and mariners sulked sullenly at home, but numerous privateers were fitted out. For eight long years after 1807, except for a brief interval just prior to the War of 1812, American commerce carriers and fishing boats for the most part rotted at their anchors in their home ports.

72   The Letter of Marque Brig *Grand Turk*, saluting Marseilles, 1815, from the painting by
Anton Roux (1765–1835) in the Peabody Museum, Salem

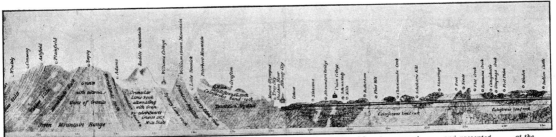

73   Section of a map of the geologic profile of the Erie Canal, from Cadwallader D. Colden, *Memoir prepared . . . and presented . . . at the Celebration of the Completion of the New York Canals*, 1825

AN ERA OF INTERNAL IMPROVEMENTS

THE United States that emerged from the Peace of Ghent was not the same nation that had been prostrated by Jefferson's Embargo Act. The eight years that bore so heavily upon our foreign and coastwise commerce saw the sowing of seeds which, in ripening, changed all of our commercial relations. The privation of the period taught the lesson that our nation, if it hoped to survive, must be economically less dependent. Since we were weakest in manufacturing, national self-sufficiency required us to develop this aspect of our economic life. The War of 1812 did more than anything heretofore to develop and strengthen this phase of industry. To shield manufacturing in its infancy protective tariffs were inaugurated. The war had shown the vital need for inland waterways; so the conflict was followed by an era of internal improvements.

74   View of the entrance of the Erie Canal at Albany, from Cadwallader D. Colden, *Memoir prepared . . . and presented . . . at the Celebration of the Completion of the New York Canals*, 1825

These, when completed, tended to focus attention upon domestic commerce rather than upon foreign trade. Moreover, with the close of the war, the population ceased to be concentrated along the Atlantic seaboard: there were successive waves of westward migration and settlement, a flood that never ceased until the continent was covered with people and a market at home was created larger in extent, fully as diverse and more easily served than any previously known in foreign trade.

Although our overseas commerce continued to follow the traditional routes after the War of 1812, certain details of the trade began to change. The textile mills of New England and New Jersey furnished the merchants with an outbound cargo to China and somewhat relieved the captains of ships from picking up commodities from port to port on their outward journeys. Soon the protective tariff compelled homeward coming ships to abandon Oriental textiles (except silk) in favor of textile raw materials, fruits, wines, tea, coffee and spices.

75   Early view on the Erie Canal, from an engraving by Peter Maverick after a drawing by Henry Inman in possession of the publishers

76   Loading ice at Boston for shipment to India, from a photograph taken about 1870, in possession of Joseph G. Minot, Boston

THE TRADE IN ICE

ONE of the most interesting of the new articles of trade was ice. As early as 1805, Frederic Tudor sent a cargo of ice gathered from a pond near Lynn to Martinique in the West Indies. Ridicule at home and the fears of sailormen that the ice would melt and swamp the boat did not hold Tudor back from his experiment. The first shipment of ice to the West Indies was a failure, but Tudor did not despair; he continued to experiment with the packing, stowing and sale of this strange commodity until by 1812 he had established a small but regular and profitable trade with the Carib Islands. The business was gradually extended after the war until in 1833 Tudor astonished the shipping world by sending a cargo of ice to Calcutta. This started a long-distance ice business that by 1850 served every large port in the southern part of the United States, the West Indies, South America and the Far East. It kept a large number of men employed in New England winters gathering the crop in ice houses and forwarding it to the storage houses on and near Gray's Wharf, a landing place the name of which was soon changed to Tudor Ice Wharf. The ice traffic expanded and prospered until, within the memory of living men, artificial ice manufacture killed it. Unusual commodities carried to strange markets color the whole history of commerce.

77   Negroes unloading ice in the West Indies, from S. G. Goodrich, *A System of School Geography*, Hartford, Conn., 1836

THE GOLDEN AGE OF WHALING

FOLLOWING the War of 1812, the whaling industry was rapidly revived and soon entered its Golden Age. Nantucket, the ancient leader in whaling, soon came to the fore, but by 1843 was surpassed by the rival port of New Bedford. The latter city had a more capacious deep-water harbor; it was located on the mainland, and became possessed of railroad connections with the large city markets. From 1843 onward, New Bedford was the chief whaling center of the world, but besides Nantucket it had competitors in Stonington and New London, Connecticut, Provincetown and Edgartown, and in fact many another place from Cape Cod south through Long Island Sound. Whaling and its allied industries such as cooperages prospered until Colonel Drake in 1859 went to Oil Creek, Pennsylvania, and drilled the first petroleum well. Thereafter the fishery declined rapidly, but it has never been completely extinguished. In form whaling was coöperative, the whole crew sharing the risks and profits.

78   New Bedford at the height of the whaling industry, from an engraving by Wellstood & Peters for *The Ladies Repository*, about 1845, after drawing by J. W. Hill

EUROPEAN COMMERCE

So much has been said about the West Indian and Far Eastern commerce that the importance of European commerce may have been obscured. Measured by volume or value, the trade with Europe has always been the largest single item in American overseas traffic. This fact was emphasized in 1816 when the Black Ball packet line was established between New York and Liverpool. This was the first packet line across the Atlantic to sail under the Stars and Stripes. The Red Star line followed in 1821, and then came the Swallowtail

79   The Packet Ship *Isaac Webb*, of New York, from *Gleason's Pictorial*, May 17, 1851

line. The same year Thomas Cope of Philadelphia started his packet line with the *Lancaster* and *Tuscarora*.

A packet line or liner is a vessel that sails regularly between two or more specific ports on a schedule, and carries whatever traffic (passenger and freight) happens to offer. Obviously, liners cannot be established profitably until the commerce between two ports is so large that each voyage of the liner is assured a full cargo. It is important, therefore, to note that the first American packet line was between New York and Liverpool, and the date was the year following the Peace of Ghent. The *Isaac Webb* was of the Black Ball line, and built by William H. Webb. She sailed from New York to Liverpool in seventeen days.

THE AMERICAN PACKET SHIP

THE American packet line ships were so comfortably fitted and so fast as compared with other contemporary sailing vessels that the packet eventually got the cream of the transatlantic traffic — passenger, express and mail. The packet ship was among liners what the clipper became among chartered freight carriers until clippers themselves were added to line vessels.

"The Atlantic packets brought a different order of things, which was to be continued through the clipper era. Yankee sailors showed no love for the cold and storms of the Western Ocean in these foaming packets which were remorselessly driven for speed. The masters therefore took what they could get. All the work of rigging, sail-making, scraping, painting, and keeping a ship in perfect repair was done in port instead of at sea, as was the habit in the China and California clippers, and the lore and training of the real deep-water sailor became superfluous. The crew of a packet made sail or took it in with the two-fisted mates to show them how.

"From these conditions was evolved the 'Liverpool packet rat,' hairy and wild and drunken, the prey of crimps and dive-keepers ashore, brave and toughened to every hardship afloat. . . ." — RALPH D. PAINE, *The Old Merchant Marine*.

The glamor of the seaman's life often upon close inspection fades to misery.

80   The Clipper Ship *Dreadnought*, Capt. Samuel Samuels, on her record voyage of 13 days, 8 hours, New York to Liverpool, from the painting by D. McFarlane, courtesy of the Massachusetts Institute of Technology, Clark Collection

81   Packet Ship *Emerald* of Boston, after the painting owned by
William O. Taylor, Boston

THE *EMERALD* CROSSES IN SEVENTEEN DAYS

SIX years after the New York Black Ball line was started the Boston and Liverpool line was inaugurated (1822) at Boston. Owing to lack of cargoes out of Boston, this line soon failed. A second venture failed in 1827 from the same cause. One of the famous ships of the Boston and Liverpool line during its short existence was the *Emerald*. In 1824 she made a record passage from Liverpool to Boston under Captain Philip Fox of Cohasset, arriving just seventeen days out of port. This record for a westward passage was seldom, perhaps only once, surpassed by a sailing vessel, and then by a clipper five times her size.

82   Arrival of a Train line packet at the Boston pier, from *Ballou's Pictorial*, March 10, 1855

83   From the painting *Packet Daniel Webster*, in the Massachusetts Institute
of Technology, Clark Collection

TRAIN LINE PACKETS

THE Train line was the first successful Boston-owned packet line. It was founded in 1844 by Enoch Train, a Boston merchant in the South American and Baltic trade. He persuaded Donald McKay to abandon the enterprises at Newburyport and transfer the shipyards to the outskirts of Boston to build the first Train packet, the *Joshua Bates*. He was so impressed by McKay's work that he commissioned him to build a number of other ships for the Train line. The *Ocean Monarch*, the *Daniel Webster*, the *Washington Irving*, the *Anglo-American*, and other famous packets for the Train line were built in quick succession.

NEW FEATURES OF COASTWISE TRADE

FOLLOWING the Revolutionary War and before 1830, the coastwise commerce of the United States in general continued to be a collective and distributive adjunct to foreign trade; but several new important features were noticeable. In the first place, coastwise trade was limited to American ships by law (1817), the motive in part being to provide a "nursery for seamen." But more important from the commercial point of view was the beginning of a new kind of interstate coastal trade. This was occasioned by the building, at Pawtucket, Rhode Island, in 1790, of the first cotton mill in America and the rapid spread in New England of cotton manufacture (see Vol. V). At the same time, cotton-growing in the South received an enormous impetus from the invention of the cotton gin in 1792. The North wanted raw cotton, the South needed cloth, so the two products were traded and transported back and forth by coastwise commercial carriers. This traffic eventually grew to great proportions.

In time other northern manufactured articles were shipped coastwise to southern markets, and tobacco as well as cotton was brought back on the return voyage. Traffic originating in the new West, the Mississippi valley, and deposited at New Orleans, was also gathered by coastwise trading boats and distributed all along the Atlantic coast. Coal, too, became an important item in coastwise trade.

Before the Revolutionary War, coastwise commerce was strictly subordinate to foreign trade, but the geographic specialization of industries that arose after that conflict gave rise to an ever-expanding coastwise intersectional traffic legally monopolized by American ships and traders.

COASTWISE PACKET LINES

THE inauguration of packet lines across the Atlantic was an immediate and direct incentive to the coastwise trade. The certainty of getting goods taken from New York, Philadelphia or Boston to Liverpool encouraged men with saleable products to ship them coastwise to one of these packet ports. At first the increase of coastwise trade was cared for by ordinary chartered freight vessels, but it was not long before the volume of local coastwise freight was enough to encourage the inception of coastwise packet lines running regularly between specific Atlantic ports. Each of the principal ports had its local coastwise packet lines radiating from it, and there were even some coastwise packet lines that traversed the entire coast. New York was the focal point for the greatest number of lines, but Boston, Philadelphia and Baltimore had almost as many.

For Boston.
The Sloop
RICHARD ALFRED.
Edwd. Clawson Master,
Burthen about five hundred barrels, part of her Cargo being engaged. For the remainder of Freight or Passage [having good accommodations] apply to the master on board at Smith's Wharf, or to,
HAYS and POWER.
Howard Street.
June 13.   d

For New-York,
The Sloop ROVER,
Abm. Bird, master, jh
A regular trader, and a good substantial vessel. She will be dispatched with all possible expedition. For freight or passage apply on board, at Smith's wharf, or to   ISAIAH MANKIN,
Who offers for sale at very reduced prices, to close sales,
320 quintals Codfish, in good order, and 2000 Sugar Moulds.
may 24   d

84   From *America and Commercial Daily Advertiser,* Baltimore, Md., July 7, 1808

Richmond, February 12, 1810.
JUST ARRIVED,
THE SLOOP MARY,
Daniel Brown, Master,
From Rhode Island, and now lying at William Wilson's old lower Wharf, has got on board
400 bushels Potatoes,
30 bbls. Cyder,
15 do Apples,
1000 lbs. Cheese,
500 lbs. Butter,
8 quintals Cod Fish,
4 bbls. Manhaden Fish,
10 bushels Onions,
All of an excellent quality.
February 16.   2t¶

85   Coastwise Shipping Notices, from the *Enquirer,* Richmond, Va., February 16, 1810

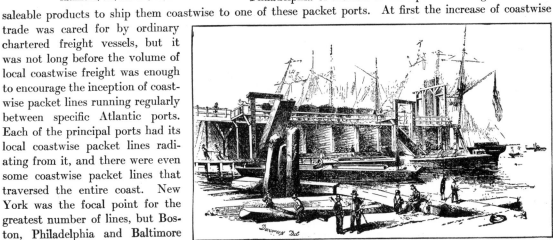

86   Loading Vessels at Port Richmond, Philadelphia, Terminal of Reading Railroad, from *Gleason's Pictorial,* Jan. 15, 1853, engraving by Gulick after the drawing by Devereux

87 Ship *George*, from the water-color, 1820, by Edward Stone in possession of George H. Allen, Manchester-by-the-Sea, Mass.

NEW SHIPS FOR NEW CONDITIONS

THE War of 1812 marked the passing of the old, leisurely sea trade. Competition had grown keener. In the former time American merchant ships had been small, with full rounded bows. Their light draught enabled them to pass over the sand bars obstructing many a harbor — even such a harbor as Salem's. In far-away seas, moreover, where strange coasts were uncharted, unbuoyed and unlighted, small craft could feel their way with safety where great vessels might easily be lost. But these sturdy little ships, so well adapted to the conditions they met, were unsuitable for the carrying trade that developed after the war. The smaller ports were crowded aside by the larger ones; trade became more direct and unbroken. The ship which wandered from port to port picking up and disposing of a number of cargoes was replaced by the packet ship in the Atlantic and, in the Orient, by the vessel that steered straight from the home port to its destination. So American ships were made larger. The cod and mackerel were studied by the shipwrights for lines that make for speed. One of the most famous of the newer boats was the Salem frigate, *George*. Twenty-one voyages she made to India and none of them exceeded one hundred days. Her best time was a voyage from Calcutta home in eighty-nine days. The triumph of this record lay in the fact that the shortest time of British boats was one hundred and fifty days from Calcutta to the nearer port of London. Not all the American superiority was due to design; as much is attributable to seamanship.

GRIFFITHS' CLIPPER SHIP *RAINBOW*

WHEN international commercial rivalry narrowed to questions of speed, ships like the *George* were insufficient; it was men, more than ship design, that enabled the *George* and similar American vessels to astonish the world. In 1841, a young New York draftsman named John Willis Griffiths (1809–82) proposed to make a ship with a knife-like concave prow, greatest width amidship instead of forward, and a hull with a dead rise from amidship to the narrow stern. Old salts jeered the new idea. When Griffiths persuaded a New York-China merchant to risk an order for a ship to be built according to his design, a storm of controversy raged around both of these revolutionaries. William H. Aspinwall, the merchant, winced under the adverse criticism leveled against him for encouraging such a lunatic as Griffiths and almost drew back. After two years of construction, the new vessel was ready for launching in January, 1845. A hostile crowd turned out expecting to see her sink when she left the ways. That ship was the *Rainbow*, the first renowned clipper.

The *Rainbow's* maiden voyage to China started in February, and she was back in New York in September, having paid her cost (forty-five thousand dollars) and her owners an equal sum in profit. On her second voyage she was so fast that she herself brought back to New York the news of her arrival in Canton: she had made the round-trip faster than any other boat could sail one way from Canton to New York — out in ninety-two days and back in eighty-eight days. Griffiths became the maritime hero of the day. The *Rainbow* started a brief but glorious era in American annals of the sea. In the opinion of foreign competitors American captains took seemingly foolhardy chances. They carried too much sail in brewing gales and refused to seek refuge when disaster loomed over a tumultuous sea. They weighed anchor in the teeth of storms or romped into port in the height of a gale. Such recklessness sometimes resulted in shipwreck, but more often fortune smiled on captains who nicely calculated between daring and bravado.

88 From the painting by Worden Wood, in possession of the Submarine Signal Corporation, Boston

THE SAILING OF THE
SEA WITCH

WHEN Griffiths' second clipper, the *Sea Witch*, was launched, she was accorded a reception befitting a national event. She sailed from Hong Kong to New York on returning from her first voyage in eighty-one days; the next year she reduced this by three days, and once she brought the record down to seventy-three days. No sailing vessel has ever come from China to New York in a shorter time. There was in those days no Panama Canal to shorten the route to the Orient. The clippers with canvas spread to the wind sped down the coast of South

89   From the painting by W. E. Nerton, in the Massachusetts Institute of Technology, Clark Collection

America, passed the Straits of Magellan, and turned west across the vast Pacific. The sailing ships which, following this route, could make Canton from New York in seventy-three days, are to be reckoned among the greatest triumphs of human ingenuity.

GOLD IN CALIFORNIA

HARDLY had the clipper ship been developed when gold was discovered in California. The rush of men and supplies that followed placed a hitherto unequaled premium on sailing-ship speed. The voyages were from American ports to American ports, and, as a consequence, the ships in the trade were limited to those carrying the American flag. Here was a great incentive to American ship designers, builders and captains. Speed became the mania of the sea, and every voyage to San Francisco a race — usually only against time, but many times an actual contest between ships. No ship but the clipper could qualify over a course fourteen thousand miles long. The first clipper, the *Memnon*, reduced by sixty days the former record of one hundred and eighty days between New York and San Francisco. The *Sea Witch*, when sent to San Francisco soon after the *Memnon*, raced through the Golden Gate ninety-seven days after leaving New York. But even the *Sea Witch* did not hold the honors long. Within seven months Donald McKay, an East Boston shipbuilder, sent out over the course one of his clippers, the *Flying Cloud* (No. 94). Her record, far surpassing that of every rival, proved her one of the greatest sailing ships ever laid down.

90   Shipping card advertising clipper service to California, in the New York Historical Society

91   Shipping card advertising clipper service to California, in the New York Historical Society

IV—4

92   From a lithograph by Chandler after a daguerreotype by Southworth and Hawes, courtesy of Charles H. Taylor, Boston

DONALD McKAY, SHIPBUILDER

DONALD McKAY was born of Scotch stock in Nova Scotia and his boyhood was spent amid the maritime surroundings of Shelburne, his birthplace. While still a young man, he emigrated to New York and found employment in a shipyard. When he learned the trade of shipbuilder he went to Newburyport, Massachusetts, where he first worked for a local shipbuilder and then became a partner in the business. His first great opportunity came when he attracted the favorable attention of Enoch Train, the founder of the Train line of packet-ships. Backed by Train, a shipyard under Donald McKay's direction was established in East Boston. There he built several boats for the Train lines, acquiring the equipment, experience and reputation that stood him in such good stead immediately afterward, when the California fever demanded the best of ships. Judged by the records won by his ships in the stiffest competition, McKay justly may be called the greatest shipbuilder of his day. Others too deserved honor but McKay merited the supreme distinction.

THE CLIPPER
STAG–HOUND

McKAY turned his attention to the difficulties of spars and rigging strong enough to support two hundred feet of canvas rising to the sky-sail pole and spreading two hundred and sixty feet. He launched in 1850 his first clipper, the *Stag-Hound*, a vessel that holds the sailing record of thirteen days from Boston Light to the Equator, three days faster than any other sailing ship has ever covered the distance. She also has the second-best record for sailing time between San Francisco and Honolulu.

93   From the lithograph in the Marine Museum, Boston, courtesy of Charles H. Taylor

94   The *Flying Cloud*, from a lithograph, 1852, in the Bostonian Society, Old State House, Boston

THE *FLYING CLOUD*

BUT the greatest clipper that McKay — or anyone else — ever built was the *Flying Cloud*. Seven months after the *Sea Witch* had hung up the record of ninety-seven days, New York to San Francisco, the *Flying Cloud*, on her maiden voyage, stormed over the course in eighty-nine days.

95   Launching of the *Flying Cloud*, from *Gleason's Pictorial*, May 10, 1851

"A NATIONAL EVENT"

THIS record, never beaten, has been equalled only twice, once by the *Flying Cloud* herself in 1854, and once by the clipper, *Andrew Jackson*, in 1860. During twenty-six consecutive days the *Flying Cloud* had covered a distance of five thousand nine hundred and twelve miles, an average of two hundred and twenty-seven miles a day. On one day, after rounding the Horn, she made three hundred and seventy-four miles, the fastest day's run for any sailing ship up to that time. An editorial in the *New York Commercial* applauded the event: "It is a truly national event and points clearly and unmistakably to the preëminence upon the ocean which awaits the United States of America." The following description appeared in *Gleason's Pictorial*, May 10, 1851: "She is two hundred and thirty feet long, has forty-one feet extreme breadth of beam, twenty-one feet depth of hold, thirty inches dead rise at half-floor, eight inches swell or rounding of sides and three feet sheer. Not only is she the longest & largest clipper ship but she has the sharpest ends. . . ." Few sights could have been more thrilling than the *Flying Cloud* smothered with canvas scudding to port before a stinging breeze.

96   Loading the *Flying Cloud*, from *Gleason's Pictorial*, May 31, 1851

97   The Clipper Ship *Great Republic*, from a lithograph in the M. H. de Young Memorial Museum, San Francisco

BUILDERS OF FAMOUS CLIPPERS

BUT Donald McKay's reputation does not rest with the *Flying Cloud*. Of all the clippers that raced from Atlantic ports to San Francisco only twenty-two passages were made round Cape Horn in less than 100 days. Of these seven were made by five ships built by McKay: the *Flying Cloud*, the *Flying Fish*, the *Great Republic*, the *Romance of the Seas*, and the *Glory of the Seas* (see frontispiece in color), the first two having each two such runs to their credit. But Griffiths and McKay were by no means the only builders of famous clippers. There were half a dozen others whose ships were record-breakers. America was challenging the age-old supremacy of Britain. The time was to come when the maritime glory of the United States was to fade, but in the middle years of the nineteenth century the Stars and Stripes flew above the greatest ships that the world had seen. The builders, the captains, and the vessels themselves were significant of the genius of the American people.

CLIPPERS SAIL TO CHINA

SIMULTANEOUSLY with the discovery of gold in California, another incident resulted in an increased enthusiasm for clipper ships. In 1849 and 1854 Great Britain abandoned the last vestiges of the Navigation Acts, those laws that had sought to confine British imperial trade to British ships. Immediately American clippers made a bid for this traffic, especially that in the Far East and Australia. Clippers hailing from our Atlantic seaboard and voyaging to San Francisco found it advantageous to jaunt across the Pacific for a cargo in China or India which could then be carried to London. There a loading for America could be secured for the homeward trip across the Atlantic.

The first genuine clipper to sail up the Thames was the *Oriental*, belonging to A. A. Low & Brother, of New York. Upon this voyage, in 1850, she had brought a cargo of tea from China to London in ninety-one days, a passage so swift that it was hardly believed at first. English people watching from the banks of the Thames feared for the supremacy of their merchant marine, a fear that events for a time justified.

98   The Clipper Ship *Flying Fish*, from Basil Lubbock, *The China Clippers*, Glasgow, 1914

99 The Clipper Ship *Surprise*, from the painting in the Massachusetts Institute of Technology, Clark Collection

AMERICAN CLIPPERS TO LONDON

CLOSE upon the *Oriental* came the *Surprise*. London and Britain went clipper mad. The lines of the American boats were copied in dry dock and British shipyards began to construct clippers themselves. But the American clippers continued to run away with the express trade — such as tea — between Britain and her dependencies. The discovery of gold in Australia led to the use of clippers between London and Melbourne. The two British packet-companies, *White Star* and *Black Ball*, bought or chartered American clippers to compete against each other. These clippers, too, made records that were previously considered impossible.

CLIPPER CARGOES

SHIPS called "clippers," but not of the later accepted clipper design, appeared in the smuggling of opium from India to China late in the 'thirties and continued until after the mid-century. These vessels were all small because they carried a compressed cargo and sought shallow remote uncharted harbors. They possessed speed as their great essential because they had to beat against the treacherous currents off China and contend with monsoons and typhoons. Moreover, their inbound cargo, opium, and their outbound lading of silver were a sure temptation for Chinese pirates, escape from whom demanded fast sailing. Most of the opium clippers were British, but Americans too owned and operated them. The last of the American opium clippers were the sister ships *Minna* and *Brenda*, 300 tons, built in 1851 at Portsmouth, New Hampshire, for John M. Forbes of Boston. The repeal of the British Navigation Laws in 1849 caused Americans to build their first high-speed clippers to capture the tea cargoes from China to Liverpool or New York. The California trade and the tea trade were often combined in a continuous voyage round the world. The returns from a single voyage sometimes equaled the original cost of the ship. The *Surprise*, the second clipper to arrive at the Golden Gate in 1851, after a voyage of ninety-six days, had a cargo list that filled a manifest twenty-five feet long. Her freight in San Francisco was worth seventy-eight thousand dollars. Another McKay ship, *The Sovereign of the Seas*, arriving in San Francisco in 1852 sold her cargo for eighty-four thousand dollars. Toward the end of the era frequently wheat was a return cargo.

100 View of San Francisco, 1849, from a colored lithograph by Le Breton published in Paris, in possession of the publishers

101   Traveling conditions aboard ship during the Gold Rush, from *L'Illustration*, Paris, 1849

GOLD IN AUSTRALIA

MORE often the clippers crossed the Pacific either to Honolulu for a cargo of whale oil, or to China for a load of tea destined for London, Liverpool or New York. In the tea trade the clippers so diminished the sailing time of the leisurely stately British "Indiamen" that the Yankees got the bulk of the cargoes even though they charged double the rates asked by the British. Under these circumstances yards at Aberdeen and Glasgow began to turn out British clippers. But due to one cause or another, the British clippers never made the sustained records of the Yankees. In 1851 gold was discovered in Australia where Melbourne repeated the hectic history of San Francisco. Clippers, American and British, carried passengers, mail and supplies to Australia and brought back gold dust and wool. The gold in small amounts was concealed in the staterooms of passengers who with the officers stood constant armed guard against piratical mutinies of the crews. Soon the British Black Ball and the White Star lines, both equipped with American and British clippers, contested the Australian business. Their rivalry put a premium upon speed and again the American-built ships ran away with the prizes.

THE ZENITH OF OUR MERCHANT MARINE

THE clipper was an exceptional ship built for unusual services where speed was the first requisite. During the decade when the clipper was mistress of the seas, the bulk of commerce requiring no premium upon haste was carried in vessels designed for their carrying capacities. What race horses are to draft animals, clippers were to the unostentatious but sturdy, chunky, reliable burden-carriers of the ocean. Between the two types, the United States, immediately preceding the Civil War, carried almost three-fourths of her own commerce and a considerable proportion of the commerce of the rest of the world. This was the zenith

of the American merchant marine. During the Civil War, iron ships, steam-driven, came into prominence, and Americans had then no especially favorable circumstances to give them preëminence in this new type of merchant-men. Furthermore, the land offered safer, more lucrative opportunities than the sea, both for capital and labor; so the clipper ship was the last defiant challenge of American shipbuilders and mariners to the merchantmen of the world.

102   The Merchant Ship *City of Mobile*, from *Frank Leslie's Illustrated Newspaper*, May 10, 1856

CHAPTER III

LANDWAYS AND WATERWAYS

WHEN in the middle of the nineteenth century the clipper ship brought the old American merchant marine to the acme of its development, the westward moving frontier of the United States had established continuous settlements halfway across the continent with outlying communities in the Far West in Oregon and California. Important as was communication between America and foreign countries, connection between the various parts of the rapidly expanding nation itself was more vital. Improved methods of transportation from one inland community to another became a prime need of the early nineteenth century. American enterprise set itself to the solution of the problem.

In the decade of the seventeen nineties "internal improvements," to use a phrase that remained current for nearly half a century, began in the United States. The long war of the Revolution had so engrossed the attention of Americans and had so absorbed their capital that the bettering of communications was impossible. The post-war period was marked by the impotence of the central government and also by a severe financial depression which reached its culmination about 1785. These years immediately following the Revolution, so aptly called by Fiske the "Critical Period," saw many different elements among the newly independent American people suffering grave discomfort. The maritime merchants were seeking new trading opportunities outside the British Empire. The substantial men who lived in the principal cities were taking losses as the government bonds which they had purchased during the war declined in value. The farmers who lived fifty miles or more from the coast or navigable water were stagnating in poverty because of their inability to get any important part of the produce of their acres to the eastern markets.

The decade of the seventeen nineties brought changes which made easier a start toward the solution of some of these problems. A stable government had been established under the new Constitution and conservative statesmen were in control. The depression of the previous decade gave way to a growing prosperity. The credit of the nation was established by Hamilton's brilliant and daring financial measures with the result that the European investor looked with a more friendly eye upon American enterprises that were brought to his attention.

Under these more favorable circumstances began what has been called the "Turnpike Era." Improved highways increased the areas from which produce could be brought into the coast cities and even penetrated far into the stagnant rural "back country," bringing to the farmer there the invigorating touch of the market. Turnpike and bridge companies became almost a craze as the eighteenth century merged into the nineteenth, and the shares of these companies offered the first important opportunities for stock trading in America. Later the Turnpike Era gave way to the "Canal Era" as the great opportunities of water communication became clear. The years from the completion of the Erie canal in 1825 to the disastrous national panic of 1837 saw Americans digging canals on an unprecedented scale, frequently providing means of communication far in advance of their needs. The panic brought the Canal Era to an end; when the nation had recovered from its losses, the railroad had superseded the artificial waterway.

NEWS! NEWS!!

AARON OLIVER, *Poft-Rider,*

WISHES to inform the Public, that
he has extended his Route; and that he now
rides thro' the towns of *Troy, Piltftown, Hoofick, Ma-*
pletown, part of *Bennington* and *Shaftfbury, Peters-*
burgh, Stephentown, Greenbuſh and *Schodack.*

All commands in his line will be received with thanks, and executed with punctuality.

He returns his fincere thanks to his
former cuftomers; and intends, by unabated diligence,
to merit a continuance of their favours.

O'er ruggid hills, aud vallies wide,
He never yet has fail'd to trudge it;
As fteady as the flowing tide,
He hands about ths NORTHERN BUDGET.

June 18, 1799.

103 From *The Northern Budget,* Troy, N. Y., June 18,
1799, in the American Antiquarian Society, Worcester

TRAVEL IN THE MIDDLE COLONIES

THE King's Path was an early road
joining New York and Philadelphia,
and by the time of the Revolution
it was possible to journey by land
from New York to Savannah by
way of Philadelphia and Baltimore.
But travel over the colonial roads
was largely limited to journeys of
necessity. Post-riders toiled over
them on horseback, and occasional horse-pack trains carried goods
from one place to another. Wagons and coaches were seldom to
be seen, but in the winter pungs and sleighs occasionally made an
appearance. The only long distance road over which commercial
traffic was regularly driven prior to the Revolution was that between New York and Philadelphia, after 1732.

A CORDUROY ROAD ACROSS A SWAMP

WITH the break-up of winter, eighteenth-century roads in America
turned into seas of mud. In dry weather the dust was almost as
bad as the rainy season's sloughs. In swampy places an improvement was made by placing logs close together across the roadway
and covering them lightly with earth. This corduroy road did indeed serve as a bridge over the mud, but was so exceedingly rough
and uneven that it not only lamed horses but speedily jolted a
wheeled vehicle to pieces. The townships and counties were too
poor, however, to construct better highways. In remote corners
of the United States corduroy roads persist, twentieth-century re-
minders of eighteenth-century conditions. Even a rough and dangerous roadway is preferable to letting mud interfere with traffic.

THE POST RIDER

LONG before the clipper ship became Queen of the Seas, the
attention of Americans had been drawn to the necessity for
developing communication by land as a means of securing
economic independence. The wars of 1776 and 1812 had
brought home the dangers of having to depend on foreign
markets. Waterways had sufficed for the early colonies,
settled for the most part on the shores of rivers or by the sea,
but as settlements were pushed toward the interior the demand
for roads became acute. Local roads between villages, following
Indian trails, had been begun early in the seventeenth century;
but these had been largely horse-paths incredibly difficult to
traverse. A beginning toward trunk-line roads was made in
1654, when the Common Road between Boston and Providence
was opened, and later continued as the Shore Road to New
York. Eventually another road, the Boston Post Road, connected Massachusetts Bay and the Hudson River.

104   Express Rider (Ginery Twichell), from Worcester to Hartford, from a print, courtesy
of the Worcester Bank and Trust Co., Worcester

105   From a photograph by Clifton Johnson

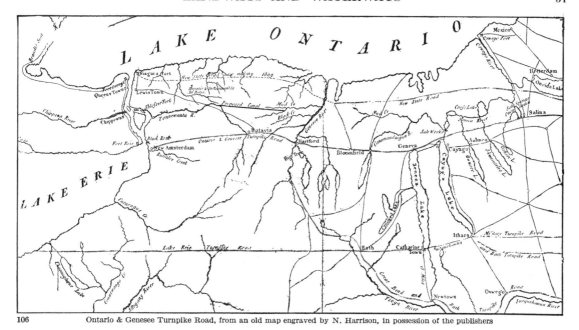

106   Ontario & Genesee Turnpike Road, from an old map engraved by N. Harrison, in possession of the publishers

NEW YORK AND PENNSYLVANIA ROADS

AFTER Yorktown the demand for land transportation became insistent, and what could not be done by publicly authorized funds was accomplished by private capital. The State of Pennsylvania took the lead, granting in 1792 a charter to a private company to build a road between Philadelphia and Lancaster, which two years later was opened for use. At intervals long poles armed with sharp spikes were thrown across the road to stop traffic. At these poles the wayfarer had to stop to pay a fee for the use of the road: and the piked poles were then turned out of the way so that his conveyance could pass. The road was therefore nicknamed the Lancaster Turnpike, and all such roads thereafter took the name "turnpike" from it.

The Lancaster Pike was such a financial success that it was soon imitated in all parts of the country. These turnpikes were the first improved roads in America and greatly stimulated travel. Most of them were absorbed into the state highway system and made free, but a few still survive. Toll barriers are more rare than toll roads; a sign is sufficient.

107 Toll-bridge on The Old Newburgh Turnpike, after a drawing by Harry Fenn in *Picturesque America*, New York, 1872

SOUTHERN ROADS

BALTIMORE, always commercially aggressive and ambitious, countered Philadelphia's turnpike construction by building at very heavy expense thoroughfares to the west, the Baltimore-Reisterstown, and the Baltimore-Frederick turnpikes.

View from Bushongo Tavern 5 miles from York Town on the Baltimore road

108   View on the Baltimore Road, from *Columbian Magazine*, 1786–90 (?)

109   Sketch Map of the Wilderness Road, from Thomas Speed,
                    The Wilderness Road, Louisville, 1886

THE WILDERNESS ROAD

A FULL generation before the first turnpike was built in Pennsylvania, a trail into the wilderness beyond the Appalachians had been blazed by Daniel Boone. In order to open the "promised land" west of the mountains, Boone organized a small band of intrepid explorers and frontiersmen to hew a path from the last Western settlements in North Carolina to the heart of the recently revealed Kentucky country. At the very beginning of the Revolutionary War, Boone and his friends began the work that led eventually to a continental empire. The small band set out from Fort Watauga on a branch of the Holston River in North Carolina, Boone with a tomahawk blazing a path through the forest, while his companions followed, felling the smaller trees and cutting away the underbrush. This continued until the party had passed through Cumberland Gap. There they turned north along a well-defined Indian trail, the Warriors' Path, running almost straight north from Cumberland Gap to a point on Lake Erie now in the vicinity of Sandusky, Ohio. Boone incorporated about fifty miles of this Path into his own roadway, turning westward at a point near the present town of Manchester. Here herds of buffalo had trampled a veritable street through the forest to central Kentucky, and at the end of this "street" Boone established Boonesborough on the Kentucky River. Throughout the Revolution, hundreds of people, with their cattle and goods, passed over the road first called Boone's Trace and then the "Wilderness Road." After the war, the Wilderness Road became for a time the principal land artery for Western civilization; over it journeyed the grandparents of Abraham Lincoln. Ungraded, cluttered with stumps, and full of holes, the Wilderness Road was far from being a "highway"; but it served the purposes of its time.

110   Cumberland Gap, from an engraving after the drawing by Harry Fenn in
                    Picturesque America, New York, 1872

111   Fur traders on the Missouri attacked by Indians, from *Harper's Weekly*, May 23, 1868, after a sketch by W. M. Cary

THE CUMBERLAND ROAD IN THE EAST

THE Wilderness Road was only the first of many by which the Middle West was reached. The strategic points were the Cumberland Gap, Louisville, Cincinnati, Nashville and Vincennes. The roads connected these points and diverged from them into surrounding territory. At first settlers found the roadways on the whole safer than the waterways, because immigrants could travel in bands for mutual aid and defense along the roads. River journeys were subject to the hazards of current, snags and falls; and, since the travelers on the water could not gather together in groups, each boat, raft or canoe ran the gauntlet of Indians on the shore. When the riverways became the more popular routes to the West, the *termini* of the older land roadways were still the focal points for travelers, for all of them, except the Cumberland Gap, were at junctions of roads and waterways. Immigrants poured over these roads and the waterways in such numbers that as early as 1792 Kentucky was admitted as a state, followed in 1796 by Tennessee. Ohio was ready for statehood by 1803, but when she had been admitted to the sisterhood of commonwealths a new problem arose. The existing transportation routes provided for the northern and the southern sectors of the West of that time, but the central section was without means of communication. So the same bill that proposed statehood for Ohio also carried provision for a road from the East through the center of the new West. This highway was called at first the Cumberland Road. Afterward, when it was extended, it became known as the National Road.

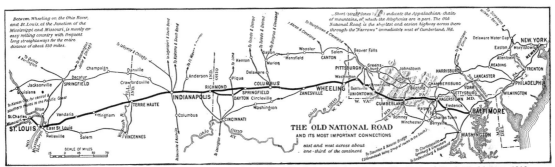

112   Map of the old National Road, originally known as the Cumberland Road, from Robert Bruce, *The National Road*, Washington, 1916

THE NATIONAL, OR CUMBERLAND, ROAD

A CONGRESSIONAL committee in 1802 recommended a road from Cumberland, Maryland, to Wheeling, Virginia. Work was started in 1808, but the road was not opened as far as Wheeling until 1817. It took three Presidents, ten Congresses, and fourteen governmental acts to get the road to that point within the nine years.

Indiana came into the Union in 1816 and Illinois two years later; within another two years Missouri was made a state. The proposal was then made to carry the National Road as a government enterprise across Ohio, Indiana and Illinois to the Mississippi. Although Congress appropriated money for surveys of the extension and also for actual construction, many people, among them President Monroe, began to question the right of Congress to pass such acts. The National Road therefore became an issue in national politics, and as a governmental enterprise it never got beyond Vandalia, Illinois, which it reached in 1852.

The United States Government spent from seven to ten million dollars in constructing this highway. The eastern part of the road was built eighty feet wide with a thirty-foot section in the center made of crushed stone a foot deep, covered with gravel. For the early nineteenth century this construction was excellent; by the time the road had been built as far as Terre Haute, Indiana, the railroad had proved a success and interest in the National Road lagged. From Terre Haute to its terminus at Vandalia, Illinois, the National Road was merely a dirt highway. Interest in highways for the purpose of interstate traffic lapsed until the arrival of the age of the automobile.

113 The old Cumberland Road to-day, from a photograph, courtesy of the Department of Roads, Washington

114 Mile post on the Cumberland Road, in the Kentucky State Historical Society, Frankfort

115 Old toll house, Cumberland Road, from a photograph, courtesy of the Department of Roads, Washington

LIFE ON THE HIGHWAY

BETWEEN 1808 and 1852 the National Road played an important part in the economic life of the regions it served. From 1827 to 1850 it was the principal route between the Atlantic and Ohio. Farmers drove cattle and hogs over it all the way from Indiana to Baltimore. Trains of pack horses or pack mules loaded with freight were constantly passing over the highway in both directions. Added to the throng were packmen on foot and immigrants both afoot and asaddle, in stage coaches, or in Conestoga wagons. It was always busy, teeming with life, color and motion. The chief hindrances to land travel were streams, large and small. Along the bridle paths a rider forded the stream if it was shallow enough, otherwise he swam his animal. Even after roadways had replaced bridle paths, the necessity for fording nearly all streams persisted. Vehicles were built high above the ground, the sides and ends as nearly water-tight as possible, becoming a kind of boat, either propelled by swimming horses, pulled by ropes, or pushed by poles.

Union Hall,

VINCENNES, IA.

TEE subscriber respectfully informs the *travelling public*, and the citizens generally, that he has purchased, and now occupies, that eligible & long established tavern stand, on Main street, where ladies & gentlemen who favor him with a call, shall be accommodated in comfortable village style.

There is a *FERRY* attached to the premises, which shall be attended to in such a manner as to deserve public patronage.

WM. PRICE.

September, 1825.

116 A Tavern-keeper's poster, from Seymour Dunbar, *History of Travel in America.* © 1915, courtesy of the publishers, the Bobbs-Merrill Company, Indianapolis

117 Land Travelers in Virginia, from a sketch by F. O. C. Darley, in B. J. Lossing, *Our Country*, New York, 1876–78

118   From the mural painting *Old Coaching Days*, by C. Y. Turner (1850–1918) in the Wisconsin State Capitol

THE MICHIGAN ROAD

THERE were at least two other roads of importance: the Michigan Road and the Natchez Road. The first was secured by treaty with the Potawatomi Indians in 1826, providing for the cession of a strip of territory 100 feet wide extending from Lake Michigan to the Wabash River, together with a section of good land next the road for each mile of the road. For this grant the Indians received the equivalent of $114,000 in goods and privileges. The road passed through Indianapolis to Madison on the Ohio River and was built by Indiana largely from the proceeds of the sale of the sections of land ceded by the Indians alongside the one-hundred-foot thoroughfare. The roadbed was relatively well built, averaging a width of twenty-four feet, and consisting in some places of seasoned oak timbers twenty feet long and a foot square, covered with one and a half feet of soil. It rapidly became the principal route between the Ohio River valley and Lake Michigan. Before railroads were built it was secondary only to the Cumberland Road as an aid to the settlement of the Middle West. It was also a large factor in the undoing of the Indians who sold the land through which it ran.

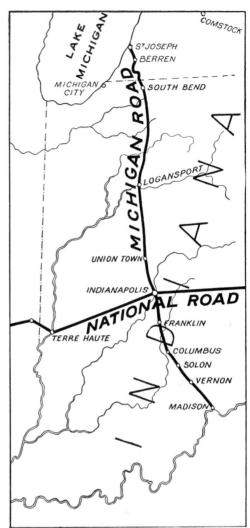

119 Redrawn from S. A. Mitchell, *Travellers' Guide through the United States*, engraved on steel by J. H. Young & D. Haines, Philadelphia, 1838.

THE NATCHEZ ROAD

A QUARTER of a century earlier, the Natchez Road had been obtained by the treaties of 1801 and 1803 with the Chickasaw and Choctaw Indians, who had given "permission to the President of the United States to make a convenient wagon road through their land. . . ." The "Old Natchez Road" connecting the settlements of Nashville and New Orleans provided a means of communication, travel and traffic between Kentucky or Tennessee and the lower Mississippi valley. When the Michigan Road was built, there was a highway from New Orleans to Lake Michigan running north and south to match the east-west artery provided by the National Road. The main current of migration being westward the National Road was of greater economic worth than the Michigan and Natchez Roads.

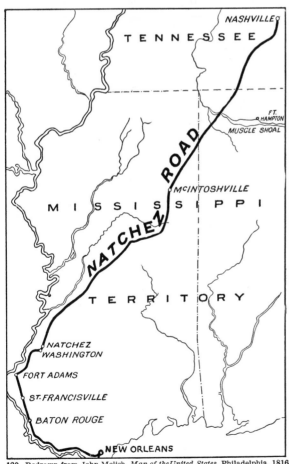

120 Redrawn from John Melish, *Map of the United States*, Philadelphia, 1816.

121   Ferry on the Susquehanna, about 1830, from an aquatint by Strickland after a drawing by
J. L. Morton, in possession of the publishers

FERRY TRANSPORTATION

EVENTUALLY where broad or deep watercourses interrupted a traveled roadway, some household near by would maintain a ferry. The crossing was usually known by the name of the family that operated the ferry. Many of the ferries were rafts without sides, or large raft-like boats with side boards, propelled by large-bladed oars called sweeps. The ferries were a picturesque aspect of early America. Travelers were wont to note their experiences with them. Ferrying some of the larger streams when the spring floods were on was frequently a matter of no little hazard. State inspection of these public carriers was practically unknown and the traveler had his choice of using the facilities offered at the particular locality or of changing his itinerary.

122   Ferry-boat to Brashear City, on Berwick Bay, La., from *Harper's
Weekly*, Oct. 20, 1866, after a drawing by Alfred R. Waud

123   Ferry across Oil Creek, Pa., from an engraving in possession
of the publishers

CABLE FERRIES

ON streams with a strong current a cable was stretched across to which the ferry was attached by a loop or pulley. The ferry itself had a movable side board. This was let down when the ferry had been pushed or pulled from the shore, and the current striking against the board caused the ferry, held to its course by the cable, to move just as wind blowing against sails produces a forward motion in a sailboat. Ferries of this sort are used to-day. Sail ferries were employed on the largest streams or bays.

124   From Edward King, *The Great South*, 1875

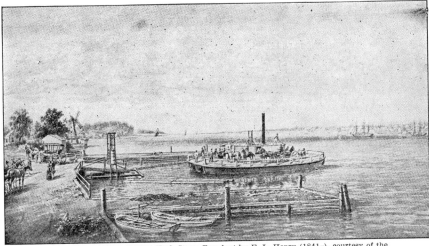

125　From the painting *Paulus Hook Steam Ferryboat* by E. L. Henry (1841–), courtesy of the
Title Guarantee & Trust Co., New York

THE STEAM FERRYBOAT

ONE of the first uses of the newly invented steamboats was in ferry service. Fulton himself built a boat on the catamaran principle to carry six to ten carriages and three hundred passengers. This ferry, operating at Paulus Hook, reduced the crossing from three hours to nineteen minutes.

CORDUROY BRIDGES

OVER smaller streams bridges early made their appearance; first a mere tree felled across a brook, then with the coming of wheeled vehicles parallel logs were thrown across a stream with smaller poles laid across to form a corduroy bridge. Somewhat smoother floors were obtained by using larger logs flattened with a broadax on the upper side. Europeans were quick to contrast the temporary wooden bridges of the early United States with the stone structures of the old world. America was new; at first there was neither capital nor labor for stone bridges. The wooden bridge was not only symbolic of the makeshifts of a young country but also of the cheapness and prevalence of wood. Crude wooden bridges may still be seen in remote lumbering districts.

126　Corduroy Bridge, Mount
Mansfield Road, after a drawing by Harry Fenn in *Picturesque America*, New York, 1847

127　From an engraving *Indiana Knobs*, by A. W. Graham, after the drawing by G. N. Frankenstein,
in possession of the publishers

128   Log Bridge, Lake Memphremagog, from a steel engraving after the drawing by W. H. Bartlett

THE LOG BRIDGE

THE simple log bridge could be carried across wider streams by means of piers made of log pilings. Some of these, though serviceable, were extremely crude, while others were more elaborate. The traffic determined the structure.

PILE BRIDGE ACROSS LAKE CAYUGA

VERY long bridges across relatively shallow waters were made possible by means of continuous piling, on which was laid a board floor. Side rails were sometimes added and sometimes omitted. This bridge, built while western New York was still a frontier region, is significant of the energy and ability of the men who led the westward advance of the American population.

129   From a steel engraving *Bridge at Norwich, Connecticut*, after the drawing by W. H. Bartlett, in N. P. Willis, *American Scenery*, London, 1860

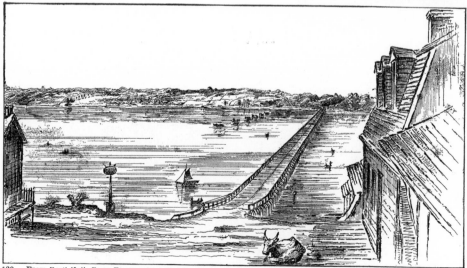

130   From Basil Hall, *Forty Etchings from Sketches Made with the Camera Lucida in North America*, Edinburgh, 1829

STONE–PIER BRIDGE AT ZANESVILLE, OHIO

YET these pioneer wooden bridges, however great an advance they marked over former attempts, could not be permanent. For log pilings were subject to rapid decay and to destruction by floods and ice floes. Whenever road travel warranted, stone piers replaced the earlier

131   From a lithograph in A. Welby, *A Visit to North America and the English Settlements in Illinois.*
London, 1821

structures built on wooden piles. The Zanesville bridge shows the transition from the frontier makeshift to the structure that was built for permanency.

132   Covered Bridge Across the Congaree, S. C., from Basil Hall, *Forty Etchings from Sketches Made with the Camera Lucida in North America*, Edinburgh, 1829

133   From a steel engraving *Bridge at Glens Falls on the Hudson*, after the drawing by W. H. Bartlett, in N. P. Willis, *American Scenery*, London, 1860

THE COVERED BRIDGE

STONE piers proved more durable but did not prevent the bridge floor from disintegrating rapidly under the attacks of weather. To meet this difficulty a shed was built above the floor. Some of the earliest covered bridges had sides and roofs made of log slabs, but most of them were closed in with boards on the side and shingles on the roof. This type of covered bridge became general throughout the country. The covered bridge with stone piers was the first and most picturesque solution of the problem of building a bridge that would last from generation to generation. Many of them have stood for more than a hundred years and are still in use. However, the automobile and concrete are causing their rapid disappearance.

IV—5

134   From Herrmann J. Meyer, *Universorum*, New York, 1851

LONG COVERED BRIDGE ACROSS THE SUSQUEHANNA

COVERED wooden bridges, some of which spanned streams of a mile in width, began to be supplanted by iron structures at the time of the Civil War. The iron bridge, however, in its brief day, before its place was taken by concrete, never completely drove out the old-fashioned covered wooden bridges. Indeed many of them are still in use in New England and elsewhere.

STONE BRIDGE ON THE OLD CUMBERLAND ROAD

THE first eastern sections of the National Road (Cumberland Road), those between Cumberland and Wheeling, were, as a general rule, more substantially built than the western sections beyond the Ohio. The former were furnished with bridges of stone masonry. "Its numerous and stately stone bridges, with handsome turned arches, its iron mile posts, and its old iron gates, attest the skill of the workmen engaged on its construction, and to this day remain enduring monuments of its grandeur and solidity." — THOMAS B. SEARIGHT, *The Old Pike*, Uniontown, Pa., 1894. Some of these bridges even to-day, after a hundred years of service, are almost as good as when they were first built, although occasionally a little narrow for automobile traffic. These old stone bridges built by the government of the United States show clearly the ability of the Americans of the early nineteenth century when sufficient capital was available.

135   From a photograph, courtesy of the United States Bureau of Roads, Washington, D. C.

WINTER TRAVEL

BEFORE roads were improved and turnpikes constructed, many a family that owned no wheeled vehicle nevertheless possessed a sled or sleigh. The winter season not only granted fuller leisure for travel but the cold and snow provided a way. The frost froze the streams and made them passable on a bridge of ice, while the snow afforded a smooth highway through the forest and across the cleared spaces. Winter therefore was the season of travel. Extensive journeys of several days or weeks were often undertaken in December and January.

136   Old Sleigh, in the collections of the Mattatuck Historical Society, Waterbury, Conn.

137 Early stagecoach, from a wood engraving by Alexander Anderson, in the Mattatuck Historical Society, Waterbury, Conn.

138 An American stagecoach, in Basil Hall, *Forty Etchings Made with the Camera Lucida in North America*, Edinburgh, 1829

DISCOMFORTS OF EARLY STAGECOACHES

"THE American stagecoaches are such as experience has found out to be most suitable to the American roads, and you have not ridden in them five miles before you long for the delightful springing of four horses upon the level roads of England. They are something between an English stage and a French diligence, built with all the panels open, on account of the excessive heat of the summer months. In wet weather these panels are covered with leather aprons, which are fixed on with buttons, a very insufficient protection in the winter, as the wind blows through the intermediate spaces, whistling into your ears, and rendering it more piercing than if all was open. Moreover, they are no protection against the rain or snow, both of which find their way in to you. The coach has three seats, to receive nine passengers. But the most disagreeable feeling arises from the body of the coach not being upon springs." — MARRYAT, *A Diary in America, with Remarks on its Institutions*, 1840

139 A Concord coach, from a wood engraving on an early stagecoach poster, in possession of the publishers

THE CONCORD COACH

THESE first cumbersome coaches were replaced gradually throughout the entire country by the "Concord coach," first constructed at Concord, New Hampshire. It was lighter than the European vehicle and progressively changed its shape from the oval to the rectangular. These changes in shape at first permitted the roof to be used for baggage, and in time for outside seats. The most prized outside seat, however, was on the driver's box. For inside passengers the rectangular shape gave more headroom and more light and air and vision except in inclement weather when side curtains sealed the inside passengers in a jolting box. The stagecoach was picturesque; it has never ceased to stir the imagination of later generations. But, as it sped over the partly improved roads of the early nineteenth century, now perhaps crossing a swift stream on a primitive ferry, now sinking a wheel in a bottomless mud hole and requiring to be lifted out by great exertion, it was not notable for comfort. The twentieth-century traveler has little conception of the lot of his forefathers.

140 From the painting *The Evening Mail*, by Stanley M. Arthurs, in possession of the artist

141   Philadelphia cart, 1845, from a contemporary sketch by
A. Kollner, in possession of the publishers

142   New Jersey cart, 1846, from a contemporary sketch by
A. Kollner, in possession of the publishers

PRIMITIVE CARTS, 1845–46

OCCASIONALLY in the eighteenth and early nineteenth centuries the two-wheeled peasant's cart of Europe could be seen on American highways. But this vehicle so common in France or Ireland was ill adapted to American conditions. Distances were greater in the New World and a conveyance was needed that could carry a larger load. The ox rather than the more specialized horse was the common draft animal and oxen were better adapted to hauling a four-wheeled wagon.

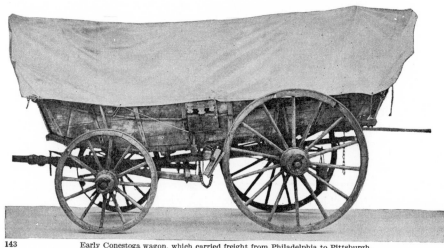

143   Early Conestoga wagon, which carried freight from Philadelphia to Pittsburgh,
from the original in the Carnegie Institute, Pittsburgh

THE CONESTOGA WAGON

THE long-distance freight carrier was the Conestoga wagon, named from Conestoga, Pennsylvania, where the type originated. The body of this wagon was high from the ground and had a peculiar curved shape, to hold the goods in place on hills and help to float the vehicle in crossing deep streams. The Conestoga wagon was a crude boat on wheels.

To protect the freight from weather, hooped-shaped slats were cleated at intervals along the sides and arched over the center of the wagon. On these arched hoops canvas was drawn so as to make a tent over the entire wagon body.

144   Conestoga wagon, which traveled in 1811 from Baltimore to
Ohio, from the original in the Chicago Historical Society

145   From the painting *Travel in 1830*, by Stanley M. Arthurs (1877–), in possession of the artist

THE FREIGHT CAR OF THE TURNPIKE

ALL the turnpikes were filled with these wagons, some operated singly, some in long trains and carrying everything known at the time. The Conestoga wagon was the freight car of the turnpike.

Likewise the same vehicle was used by emigrants transporting their families and goods to a new home. When the West — both Middle and Far — was opened, the Conestoga was practically the only wheeled vehicle extensively employed by migrants. Beyond the Mississippi it was given the new name "prairie schooner." The "covered wagon" has a place in American history alongside the "Mayflower."

146   From the painting *Conestoga Wagons on the National Road*, by C. W. Jefferys (1869–),
in possession of the publishers

147 Advertisement of stage coach service between Philadelphia and New York, from the *New York Gazette or Weekly Post Boy*, May 28, 1767

149 From the painting *Country Tavern on the Boston Post Road*, by Stanley M. Arthurs (1877–), in possession of the artist

ORGANIZATION OF THE COACH INDUSTRY

BOTH the stages and the conestoga wagons were operated for commercial profit. Both fell into two classes: those that ran upon schedule between specified places and those that were for hire to undertake any kind of journey. To use nautical terms, there were "liners" and "tramps."

The business organization was generally that of entrepreneurship or partnership. A man drove a coach or wagon which he owned between two or more towns; or a group of men hired drivers and controlled the movement of several coaches or wagons.

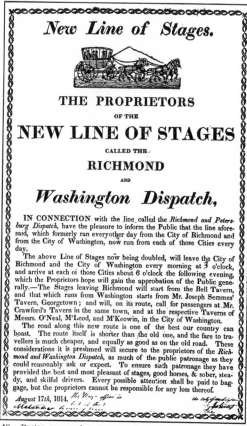

148 Poster announcing stage coach service between Richmond and Washington, 1814, from the original in the New York Historical Society

LONG–DISTANCE STAGE TRAFFIC

To accommodate long-distance traffic there were operators' associations which arranged connecting schedules. There were similar agreements or associations between stage or wagon lines on the one hand, and boat or ferry lines on the other. Thus separate links of a long journey were joined so as to form a continuous chain. There was competition within the "links" and between different "chains." A person could, if he so desired, furnish and pilot his own conveyance both for short and long journeys.

THE COACHING TAVERN ON THE POST ROAD

THE flood of travel and commerce over roads and turnpikes created scores of highway inns and taverns. These were roughly divisible into two classes: those that catered to the stagecoach travelers and those that sought the patronage of wagoners, drivers of the freight carriers and poorer imigrants driving their own conveyances.

The coaching inns were the *de luxe* establishments, and their customs were in the unbroken tradition transplanted from England. In lieu of newspapers and letters the tavern was the source of all news. The landlord was known far beyond the confines of his vicinity, and his tavern was rated according to the fame

150 A Relay on the Old Boston Post Road, from a drawing by T. de Thulstrup
in *Harper's Weekly*, Mar. 6, 1886

of the host. Good food and drink and a reputation for good cheer and story-telling brought patronage to an inn. Often, of course, particular taverns were stations on a coach route where horses were changed and travelers slept or ate. In such cases the traveler had no choice of a stopping place, but the coach proprietors selected the particular inn because of its repute.

BOSTON, Plymouth & Sandwich MAIL STAGE,

CONTINUES TO RUN AS FOLLOWS:

LEAVES Boston every Tuesday, Thursday, and Saturday mornings at 5 o'clock, breakfast at Leonard's, Scituate; dine at Bradford's, Plymouth; and arrive in Sandwich the same evening. Leaves Sandwich every Monday, Wednesday and Friday mornings; breakfast at Bradford's, Plymouth; dine at Leonard's, Scituate, and arrive in Boston the same evening.

Passing through Dorchester, Quincy, Weymouth, Hingham, Scituate, Hanover, Pembroke, Duxbury, Kingston, Plymouth to Sandwich. Fare, from Boston to Scituate, 1 doll. 25 cts. From Boston to Plymouth, 2 dolls. 50 cts. From Boston to Sandwich, 3 dolls. 63 cts.

N. B. Extra Coaches, &c. to be had of the proprietors, at Boston and Plymouth, at their houses. STAGE BOOKS kept at Boston's blacksmith's, Boston, and at Bradford's, Plymouth.

LEONARD & WOODWARD.

BOSTON, November 12, 1810.

51 Poster of Boston Mail Stage Service, 1810, from the original in the Bostonian Society, Old State House, Boston

THE WAGON TAVERN

THE wagon taverns were poorer, meaner establishments, often notable for their roistering. The wagoners, unable to afford even the meager luxuries of private bedrooms, spread their own bedding, which they had brought with them, on the floor of

152 Old-Time Tavern, Wolf Creek, Tenn., from a photograph by Clifton Johnson

the one large common room — the dining room or taproom by day — where they slept side by side. They were a rough lot, but mixed with them were folk of gentler strain whom poverty forced to seek the cheapest lodging on a journey to a new home.

153   Running the Rapids of New River, Virginia, from an engraving by M. T. Boyd after the drawing by W. L. Sheppard, in *Harper's Weekly*, February 21, 1874

THE FIRST CANALS

ROADS, important as they were, in the early nineteenth century were eventually second in importance to waterways in the development of early American domestic commerce. The river furnished a highway free of toll, but was interrupted by rapids and falls, causing a break in the continuous carriage of freight. Boats had to be discharged of their cargo below a rapid and the packages one by one carried around the obstruction. The boat, if it were small enough, was hauled too, or carried to a point where the stream was again free; otherwise the journey of the goods was continued in another boat. This process, often repeated on a single waterway, was slow, laborious, and so expensive that most heavy or cheap commodities were barred from long-distance transportation. Consequently, the first waterway improvements were short canals around rapids or falls, providing unbroken transportation of commodities, and, by the reduction of costs, extending the range of goods that could be transported.

The first canal of importance in America was one of this sort authorized by the Virginia Legislature in 1785. It was seven miles long and extended from Richmond to Westham, sufficient to carry laden boats around the falls in the James River at this point. Similarly, a small canal was built in 1797 to avoid the Patopwick Falls in Massachusetts. The Bow Canal in New Hampshire was finished in 1812. The Connecticut River was early improved by means of canals. Flatboatmen were able to pole their craft over the rapids of the lower Connecticut, but an abrupt fall of fifty feet in the neighborhood of the present city of Holyoke, Massachusetts, interrupted further progress upstream. In 1792, a canal company was chartered, backed with capital supplied by Amsterdam bankers, and a canal around the fall was opened for traffic in 1794. The tolls charged indicated how expensive the previous portage must have been, two dollars and fifty cents per ton of freight or one thousand feet of lumber, together with an excess charge of twenty-five cents a ton for the tonnage capacity of the boat; that is, the cargo paid one fare and the boat itself another.

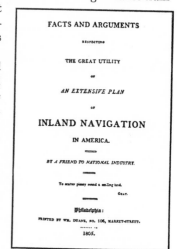

FACTS AND ARGUMENTS

RESPECTING

THE GREAT UTILITY

OF

AN EXTENSIVE PLAN

OF

INLAND NAVIGATION

IN AMERICA.

BY A FRIEND TO NATIONAL INDUSTRY.

To scatter plenty round a smiling land.
GRAY.

Philadelphia:
PRINTED BY WM. DUANE, NO. 106, MARKET-STREET.
1805.

154   Pamphlet urging internal navigation, 1805, title-page of the original in the New York Public Library

155   The Market or Passage boat and the Dispatch boat, used on canals, from an engraving in Robert Fulton, *A Treatise on the Improvement of Canal Navigation*, London, 1796

Following this canal, others were constructed. There was a three-mile canal at Turner's Falls that cut off a six-mile bend and falls in the river; at Bellows Falls a canal a mile long got around a fifty-foot fall, and there were canals at two points near the present town of Hanover, New Hampshire. Likewise, below the original canal near present-day Holyoke, canals were constructed in the lower river at what is now Windsor Locks. At a later time, in the late 'twenties and early 'thirties, a canal was dug in the old geological Connecticut River valley which in effect turned the river trade back into the ancient channel at Northampton, Massachusetts, and continued it to the outlet at New Haven, Connecticut. If all these canals had been in operation at once, the Connecticut River would have been navigable from Saybrook, Connecticut, nearly to its source close to the Canadian boundary, with a branch between Northampton and New Haven.

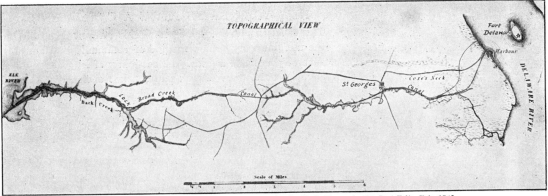

156   Chesapeake & Delaware Canal, from an engraving by H. S. Tanner in the *Port Folio*, Feb. 1825

THE "CANAL ERA"

NOT all the early canals were constructed to avoid river obstructions; many of them were dug to connect existing waterways and so extend the usefulness of both. The Middlesex Canal of Massachusetts was of this character, connecting Boston Harbor with the Merrimac River. It was incorporated in 1779, begun

157   James Sullivan, President of the Middlesex Canal Co., from the portrait by Gilbert Stuart (1755–1828) in the Massachusetts Historical Society

in 1795 and finished in 1808 at a cost of over half a million dollars. It diverted from Portsmouth, New Hampshire, to Boston considerable commerce in lumber, cord wood, potash, stone and grain. In like manner it was proposed in 1764 to join Chesapeake Bay with the Delaware River. Work on this canal was begun in 1804, but was soon halted not to be revived until 1822. Similarly, the Susquehanna (at Middleton) and the Schuylkill (at Reading) were to be united by canal. This enterprise was started in 1791, but for various reasons it was not finished until 1827. In 1792, the Western Company was chartered by New York state to provide a navigable waterway from Hudson River to Lake Seneca and Lake Ontario. A second company was chartered at the same time (the Northern Inland Lock and Navigation Company) to construct a canal from the Hudson River to Lake Champlain. Virginia and North Carolina jointly authorized in 1787 a canal to join Chesapeake Bay and Albermarle Sound. This work was known as the Dismal Swamp Canal and was finished in 1794. The Santee Canal, twenty-two miles long, brought the Santee River in South Carolina to the doors of Charleston.

All of these canals were of local usefulness. The "Canal Era," from 1817 to 1837, was ushered in by the Erie Canal.

158   From a drawing *Middlesex Canal at North Billerica, Mass.*, 1825, by William Barton, in possession of A. W. Stearns, Boston

159 Elkanah Watson, 1758–1842, from the portrait by Ezra Ames (1768–1836), after the original portrait by J. S. Copley, in the Albany Institute and Historical and Art Society

NEW YORK STATE PLANS A CANAL SYSTEM

THE canals about the falls in navigable streams demonstrated the usefulness of the new method of communication and men naturally began to consider the possibility of lengthening these artificial waterways. Here again a prime obstacle was lack of capital. By this time much of the money of small investors was being put into turnpike companies and bridge companies. The National Road to cross the mountains and join East and West suggested the possibility of a canal to perform the same function. Christopher Colles was one of the first enthusiasts. Elkanah Watson envisaged the utilization of the Mohawk pass between the Catskills and the Adirondacks for a canal that would tie Lake Erie to the Hudson River. In 1791, Watson began an active campaign of propaganda for internal improvements in general, and particularly

160 C. Christopher Colles, 1738–1821, from the original portrait by J. W. Jarvis (1780–1840) in the New York Historical Society

for canal building. The next year he was appointed a state commissioner to explore and make recommendations for a canal through the western part of New York. As a result of his report in 1791, the Western Inland Lock Navigation Company was formed, and by 1796 had made the Mohawk River navigable from its mouth to Fort Stanwix (Rome). In 1810 the route of the Erie Canal was surveyed. This began a work that raised New York to economic leadership.

161 From an engraving by Henry Inman (1801–46), after the portrait by Asher B. Durand (1796–1886), in the Print Room, New York Public Library

DE WITT CLINTON, 1769–1828

DE WITT CLINTON became a commissioner and a stanch advocate of the project which seemed to many a conservative, a quite impracticable, dream. The supporters of the Erie Canal, recognizing its national importance, hoped that the waterway would be built by the United States Government. In its time the Erie Canal was an undertaking quite as stupendous as the later Panama Canal. There was a strong nationalist group in Congress during and immediately after the War of 1812. John C. Calhoun in 1817 proposed his famous "Bonus Bill" which provided that the bonus paid by the second Bank of the United States for its charter should be expended by the national government for internal improvements. When President Madison vetoed this measure, the hopes of the supporters of the Erie Canal for government aid were dashed. In the same year, in spite of bitter opposition, the New York legislature passed a law providing for a system of canals and improvements from the Lakes to the sea. Having failed not only to interest the national government but also Ohio and Indiana, the state of New York undertook the gigantic project alone. On July 4, 1817. digging began.

162 From the mural painting *Entering the Mohawk Valley*, by C. Y. Turner (1850–1918) in the De Witt Clinton High School, New York

163 From the mural painting *The Marriage of the Waters*, by C. Y. Turner in the De Witt Clinton High School, New York

INAUGURATION OF THE ERIE CANAL

SECTIONS of the Erie Canal were opened as finished. The fifteen-mile strip from Utica to Rome was ready for traffic in 1819. Four years later the waterway was opened from Utica to Rochester. In the same year Utica was connected with the Hudson and Albany. In 1825 the entire work was finished so that boats might proceed from Buffalo to New York city.

As each of these sections was opened for business, celebrations of increasing duration and enthusiasm were held. The final celebration began at Buffalo October 26, 1825, when the *Seneca Chief*, a canal boat, started from Buffalo with Governor Clinton and other notables aboard. This boat and its passengers had a continuous ovation as it passed along the canal until it arrived in New York Bay near Sandy Hook on November 4. There Clinton poured a cask of lake water into the sea to symbolize the "marriage of the waters." For ten days the *Seneca Chief* had been greeted with cheers, tin horns, bells, whistles and cannon. Its passengers had paused to view parades and to partake of banquets. The enthusiasm was comparable to that produced by some great national victory. As a matter of fact this outburst was not a mistake, for the Erie Canal became a vital factor in American progress.

164 Fireworks celebration of opening of canal, from a contemporary engraving by Richard Willcox in possession of the publishers

Celebration

Of the Passage of the first Boat from the Grand Canal into the Hudson, at the City of Albany, on Wednesday, October 8, 1823.

Order of Arrangements.

1. A National Salute to be fired at sunrise, and the bells to ring. At which time the joint committee will proceed to the junction of the Erie and Champlain Canals, and there join the Canal Commissioners and Engineers on board a Canal Boat; from thence down the canal. On their arrival at the Basin at Gibbonsville, they will be received by another Boat, with the Military Association and a Band of Music on board. The two boats, with such others as may join them, will then move on to the city of Albany, where they will arrive at 11 o'clock.

2. The different vessels in the harbor to be dressed with flags, and moored in a line in front of the Basin.

3. A Band of Music to be stationed opposite the Lock.

4. The Artillery, with field pieces, to be stationed on the Pier in front of the Lock.

5. A detachment of Artillery, with heavy field pieces, to be stationed on the high ground west of the Lock.

6. The State and Municipal Authorities, Military Societies and Citizens will assemble at the Mansion-Houses at 9 o'clock, A. M. and will be escorted to the lower Lock by the Military.

7. At 11 o'clock the Top Stone of the Lock at the termination of the Erie and Champlain Canals, will be laid by the Grand Chapter of the State of New-York, according to masonic rule.

8. When the first boat passes into the Hudson, salutes to be fired by the Artillery on the pier and high ground, during which National Airs to be played by the Band, &c. and the boat will then be taken in tow by 12 Yawls, each manned by a Captain and six oarsmen, and proceed down the Basin into the river, and thence round to the head of the Pier.

9. After the landing of the Canal Commissioners and other gentlemen from the Boats, a procession will be formed in the following order:—

MILITARY, under the command of Major-General Solomon Van Rensselaer, Marshal, assisted by Major R. I. Knowlson and Capt. John Koon, in such order as the Marshal shall designate in General Orders.

Sheriff and City Marshal.
Common Council and Committee of Arrangements.

CANAL COMMISSIONERS.

Engineers and Assistant Engineers.
Commissioners of the Albany Basin.
Canal and Basin Contractors.
Rev. Clergy.
The Governor and Suit, Lieutenant-Governor, Chancellor and Judges of the Supreme, Circuit and United States Courts.
Senate and Officers.
The Heads of Departments.
Members of Congress and Civil Authorities of the United States.
Officers of the United States Army and Navy.
BAND.
Military Association.
Fire Department, including Engine, Hook and Ladder, and Axe Companies.

SOCIETIES.

Cincinnati.
Grand Chapter of Royal Arch Masons.
Society for the promotion of Useful Arts.
Albany Lyceum.
St. Andrew's Society.
St. Patrick's Society.
Mechanics' Society.
Cordwainers' Society.

CITIZENS and STRANGERS.

10. A signal gun will be fired by the Artillery on the Pier, when the procession will move under discharges of Artillery, through North Ferry, Market and State-streets, to the Capitol Square. The bells will ring during the moving of the procession.

Ceremonies to be performed in a Pavilion at the Capitol Square.

11. An address to the Throne of Grace by the Rev. Dr. Chester.

12. His Honor the Mayor, in behalf of the Common Council and the Citizens of Albany, will deliver an Address to the Canal Commissioners, on the successful completion of Canal Navigation to the city of Albany.

13. National Air by the Band.

14. Benediction by the Rev. Mr. Leonard.

15. A Feu-de-joie by the Military.

16. Fire Works to be exhibited in front of the Capitol in the evening, to commence at 7 o'clock.

| CHARLES E. DUDLEY, ESTES HOWE, JAMES GIBBONS, EBENEZER BALDWIN, FRIEND HUMPHREY, JOHN CASSIDY, CONRAD A. TEN EYCK, HAWTHORN McCULLOCH, HENRY W. SNYDER. | COMMITTEE OF COMMON COUNCIL | WILLIAM JAMES, JOHN STILWELL, JAMES B. DOUGLASS, SAMUEL A. FOOT, JOHN N. QUACKENBUSH, PETER GANSEVOORT, ISRAEL SMITH, JOSEPH RUSSELL, SOL. VAN RENSSELAER. | COMMITTEE OF CITIZENS |

165 Broadside celebrating the opening of the Erie Canal, from the original in the New York Historical Society

166   Western end of the Erie Canal at Buffalo, from Basil Hall, *Forty Etchings from Sketches Made with the Camera Lucida in North America*, Edinburgh, 1829

RAPID DEVELOPMENT ALONG THE CANAL

BEFORE the Erie Canal was opened, it had cost one hundred dollars to move a ton of freight from Buffalo to New York, and the journey required at least twenty days. The canal carried the same amount of freight for ten dollars and did it in eight days.

From the first it was jammed with traffic. Upper New York state and the Middle Western states poured surplus farm products into the canal boats at Buffalo; at New York the boats were filled with manufactured articles and supplies for the interior. With a market thus opened, farm products increased in price on the farms and land values went up. In New York farm products were lowered in price because so many more were offered. This situation induced immigration to the Middle West, and hordes of men, women and children went to new homes by way of the canal. The intermediate canal towns, such as Rochester and Syracuse, felt the new flood of life at their doors and could tap the traffic in either direction; the canal itself furnished employment to many, and business sprang up everywhere along its course. The commodities piled at New York city created a demand for ocean shipping, a need for banking facilities, a desire for all kinds of middlemen to handle the business, and a voracious market for all kinds of labor. From this time the metropolis at the mouth of the Hudson sprang into the foremost place among American cities, the leading importing, exporting, commercial banking, manufacturing and population center. To this day the bulk of the business, population, commerce, manufacture and wealth of the entire state of New York is in the zone of the Erie Canal. Of the larger communities only Binghamton, Elmira, and Jamestown lie outside the canal area.

167   From the painting *Before the Days of Rapid Transit*, by E. L. Henry (1841–1919). © J. C. Klackner & Co., New York

TRAFFIC ON THE ERIE CANAL

THE Erie Canal was three hundred and sixty-two miles long, twenty-eight feet wide at the bottom and forty feet at the surface. Its waters were four feet in depth. Although the whole work cost New York state some eight million dollars, the traffic over the canal was so great that by 1837 the tolls had paid the cost and provided for operating expenses. There was so much business that by 1835 the canal had to be enlarged.

The traffic was both passenger and freight. For the former there was the packet boat and the line boat. The packet was luxuriously fitted and pulled by superior horses, with a view to speed; it charged a cent or two more per mile than other boats. The line boat was less comfortably fitted and moved at a rate of two miles an hour, but it afforded cheap transportation for the many emigrants to western lands.

168   From the model of a sectional canal boat used on the Old Portage Road, in the Carnegie Institute, Pittsburgh

CANALS THAT FOLLOWED THE ERIE

THE completion of the Erie Canal and the consequent enhancement of the importance of New York city was a blow to all the other principal Atlantic coast cities. Each of them endeavored to find a way to connect its own port with the continental interior. Boston proposed to build a canal across Massachusetts, including

169   From a lithograph *Canal Barge at the Summit of the Allegheny Portage,* in the Philadelphia Commercial Museum

the Berkshire Hills, to join Massachusetts Bay with the Hudson River and Erie Canal, but before this plan was fully matured the railroad appeared and changed the direction of Boston's efforts. Pennsylvania proposed and built an elaborate system of public works to join Philadelphia and Pittsburgh. But the Keystone state had no pass like that of the Mohawk River across the mountains and the eastern escarpment of the Cumberland plateau barred the way from Philadelphia to Pittsburgh. No canal could go over it. As a consequence the canal boats in sections were carried over the ridge on an inclined railway. So great were the difficulties that the Pennsylvania canal

system never became a serious rival of the Erie route. Baltimore also sought by means of the Chesapeake and Ohio Canal to penetrate the Middle West. This canal, built at vast expense, and very slowly because of the natural difficulties in the way, never reached its goal. Indeed, it did not reach Cumberland (one hundred and

fifty miles) until 1850. New York state had the only natural nearly water-level route between the Atlantic and the Middle West, and other cities turned to the railroad for the solution of their problems. The Atlantic coast cities did not cease their rivalry with the construction of canals but carried their competition onward in the railroad era when each struggled for advantages in railroad rates. The strife over canals was but the beginning of a long campaign whose end is not yet in sight.

170   From the painting *Old State Portage Railway Crossing the Alleghenies,* in the Philadelphia Commercial Museum

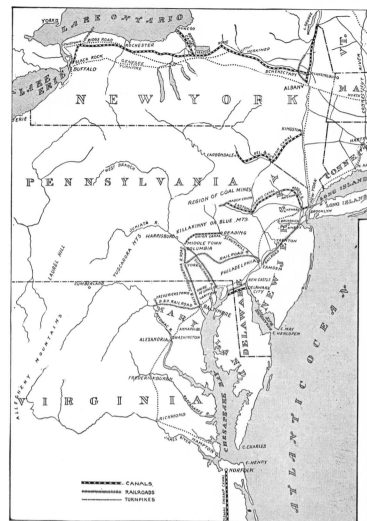

171 Early Eastern Canals, and the railroads built up around them, simplified from the *Map of the Routes through the Middle and Northern States*, etc., published by G. M. Davidson, Saratoga Springs, N. Y., 1833, in the New York Public Library

THE ANTHRACITE CANALS

To join the Atlantic with the Middle West was only one of the objectives of the canal builders. Waterways were built as outlets for the anthracite coal region in the mountains of eastern Pennsylvania to Philadelphia, New York and Baltimore. The first system was a canalization of the Schuylkill River from Mount Carbon to the Quaker City. This way was opened in 1826. Soon afterward the Lehigh River was similarly improved. From the point at Easton where the Lehigh empties into the Delaware the state of Pennsylvania built another canal connecting Easton with Bristol, thus avoiding the treacherous upper reaches of the Delaware and the long elbow by way of Trenton. It also deprived Trenton and thus New Jersey of the larger share of the coal traffic. Three canals brought coal to New York city: the Morris and Essex Canal, built from Phillipsburg (across the Delaware from Easton) to Jersey City; the Delaware and Raritan, connecting Bordentown and New Brunswick; and a third running between Honesdale, Pennsylvania, and Rondout, New York, on the Hudson. Baltimore got its anthracite by means of a canal that improved the Susquehanna, called the Susquehanna and Tidewater Canal. Most of these waterways were built by private capital but with state aid. Their significance lay in the fact that anthracite was a comparatively new fuel but enormously popular because no other coal was then known in America except the small soft coal deposit near Richmond, and some unavailable soft coal near Pittsburgh. From the three ports anthracite was distributed by vessels along the Atlantic coast, where it competed with soft coal brought from Great Britain.

172 From an engraving, about 1839, after the drawing *View on the Susquehanna at Liverpool*, by W. H. Bartlett, in possession of the publishers

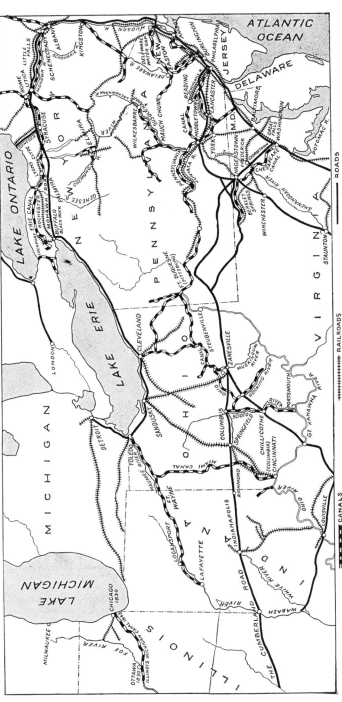

173   Map of Mid-Western Canals and Railroads, 1850, and the westward spread of Eastern Canals and Railroads, based on a map in A. B. Hulbert, *Paths of Inland Commerce*

MIDDLE WESTERN CANALS

A THIRD object of the canal builders of the Canal Era (1817–37) was to join the Great Lakes with the Ohio and Mississippi rivers and their branches. The first of these canals, authorized by Ohio in 1825, started at Portsmouth on the Ohio River, followed the Scioto River northward to about the center of the state and at Akron swung northeastward to Cleveland. In 1830, the whole route was ready for business. A second canal was projected from Cincinnati northward along the great Miami River, across country to the Maumee River and along that stream to Toledo on Lake Erie. This waterway was started in the same year as the Portsmouth-Cleveland enterprise and was completed a year later. By 1833 Ohio had some four hundred miles of internal waterways, with connections to New York city. At about the same time Indiana began the construction of a trunk-line canal, the Wabash and Erie. Starting at Fort Wayne, this work was carried southwestward to Lafayette where it joined the Wabash River and thus gave an outlet to the Ohio at Evansville. From Fort Wayne northward to the Lakes the most practicable extension of the canal seemed to be eastward to form a junction with the Cincinnati-Toledo canal of Ohio. Financial and political and natural difficulties arose constantly in the progress of this venture, so it was not until 1851 that the entire project was finished. That state dug a short canal from Chicago to La Salle where it met the Illinois River. Illinois found her task easier. Since this stream is an affluent of the Mississippi and since Illinois was a raw pioneer region in 1848 when the canal was constructed, no other waterway was then required to satisfy her needs.

174 Raft at Dubuque, Iowa, from Henry Lewis, *Das Illustrirte Mississippi-Thal*, Düsseldorf, 1844–45

THE MISSISSIPPI RAFT

BEFORE the local canals in Ohio and Indiana were built, the ordinary route from the Middle West was furnished by the rivers of the Mississippi system, of which New Orleans was the great southern metropolis and Pittsburgh, Cincinnati, Louisville and St. Louis the northern outposts. The southern tiers of counties in Ohio, Indiana and Illinois, bordering on the rivers, were the first to be settled; the first capital of Indiana was at Corydon, about midway between Louisville and Evansville.

The simplest instrument of river commerce was a great log raft, loaded with pork, grain, or whatever the settler had to sell, and floated down stream on the long journey to New Orleans. At that city the farm stuffs were sold and the raft, too, was broken up and disposed of in the market. The raftsmen then either walked back to their homes through the forests, a tedious and dangerous journey of from three to nine months, or took ship at New Orleans for an Atlantic port whence they made their way overland to their distant cabins on the frontier.

175   Sketch of a Flatboat, from an engraving in Collot, *Voyage dans l'Amérique Septentrionale*, Paris, 1826, after a drawing, 1796

THE MISSISSIPPI FLATBOAT

THE crudity of the log rafts was soon improved by building sides and a cabin upon a flat bottom. This type of boat was the principal commerce-carrier on the western rivers before the day of steamboats and on eastern rivers before the construction of canals. Coal, grain, flour, all kinds of agricultural produce passed downstream in these unwieldy boats, driven by the current and guided by one or more long sweeps. Flatboats ranged in size from forty feet to ninety feet in length and from ten to twenty feet in width. Their crews consisted of five or six men who managed the sweeps and conducted business negotiations. Usually the flatboats that arrived at New Orleans were broken and the lumber they contained sold.

176   From a lithograph *Bound Down the River*, by Currier & Ives, 1870

177   Early Bull Boat on the Missouri, from a drawing in the Missouri Historical Society.   © Pierre Chouteau

THE MISSOURI BULL BOAT

THE bull boat was ordinarily about twenty-five feet long and twelve or fifteen feet wide. The frame consisted of long pliable poles, intersected at right angles by shorter ones, and made water tight with a covering of dressed buffalo hides. The result was a craft of lightness, and little draft.

178   Mackinaw or Cordell Boat, 1785, from a drawing in the Missouri Historical Society.   © Pierre Chouteau

THE KEEL BOAT

A MODIFICATION of the flatboat was the keel boat, with a heavy timber along its bottom to take the shock of river obstructions. Keel boats, unlike the flatboat, were occasionally forced upstream by setting-poles or by towlines, with occasional help from a sail. But operation against the current was slow, arduous and expensive and seldom employed for commercial purposes.

Some keel boats and flatboats were fitted out as a sort of general store and, floating downstream, carried commodities to dwellers along the river; a peddler afloat instead of with pack or wagon.

179   Keel Boat, 1810, from *Kansas State Historical Society Collections*, Vol. IX, Topeka, 1906

IV—6

180   Harbor of New Orleans, from Basil Hall, *Forty Etchings from Sketches Made with the Camera Lucida in North America*, Edinburgh, 1829

THE MISSISSIPPI FLATBOAT TRADE

THE first immigrants into the territory of the western rivers found that the only products they could sell with profit, after paying for long and expensive transportation, were furs and skins, lead ore, ginseng and whisky. These were durable, easily carried, and had a high value for their bulk and weight. The proceeds of the sale were invested in salt, gunpowder, indispensable small iron products and calico, all articles that could stand long, costly journeys.

When the right of deposit was granted by the Spanish at New Orleans, and later in 1803 when Jefferson made the fortunate bargain that resulted in opening the Mississippi waterways, flatboats and keel boats by the hundreds carried from the upper rivers to New Orleans such articles as tobacco, pork, flour, grain, whisky and brandy. But since it took thirty men three months to push a flatboat upstream from New Orleans to Cairo, very few such passages were made. Until 1817, only twenty barges made the northward journey per year, and of course each barge was limited to one trip. It was cheaper and more convenient to haul stuff from Philadelphia to Pittsburgh by horses, at one hundred and twenty-five dollars a ton, than to force it upstream from New Orleans. Pittsburgh therefore became the distributing center for imports into the river country, while New Orleans was the gathering point for stuff exported from the river farms.

The constant increase of immigrant travel by way of Philadelphia and Pittsburgh was in part responsible for improvements in the roadway and the development of facilities for travel and freight. Conestoga wagons made the journey in twenty days, and as many as three thousand passed over the route in a year. Later, with the building of the National Road, an alternate route from Baltimore via Wheeling was available. With these improvements in the East, the riverways became jammed with flatboats, keel boats and rafts, to carry products and people downstream. The picture shows the flatboats moored at New Orleans side by side with ocean shipping; where the river journey ended the deep sea traffic began.

181   The Interior of a Mississippi Flat Boat, from *Les Voyages du Naturaliste Ch. Alex Le Sueur dans l'Amérique du Nord (1815–1837)*, reprinted by E. T. Hamy in the *Journal de la Société des Américanistes de Paris*, Vol. 5, Paris, 1904

182   Warsaw, Illinois, from Henry Lewis, *Das Illustrirte Mississippi-Thal*, Düsseldorf, 1844–45

THE PASSING OF THE FLATBOAT

THE crude flatboat and keel boat remained until the middle of the nineteenth century an important factor in carrying downstream commodities, like hay and coal, of great bulk and relatively low value. In 1846 more than two thousand flatboats arrived at New Orleans, many the property of farmers carrying their own produce. Nine years later the number had shrunk to seven hundred and eighteen. By 1860 the flatboat as an important factor in the carriage of river freight had disappeared. The combination of railroads and steamboats had practically driven it from the inland rivers. With the passing of these crude boats (which had their origin in frontier times) passed also one of the most picturesque phases of river life. Almost from the beginning the flatboatmen were a class apart, and as rough and crude as any group in American life. Floating day after day down the Father of Waters, they fought, danced, and gambled with what little money they possessed. They knew the dives of every river port from Cincinnati to New Orleans; no one could mistake them as they wandered the streets of the latter city. Their disappearance marked the passing of frontier conditions along the Mississippi and Ohio and the advent of advanced commercial methods and more polished business agents.

183   From the painting *The Jolly Flatboat Men*, by George Caleb Bingham (1811–1879)
in the Mercantile Library, St. Louis

CHAPTER IV

THE SPREAD OF THE STEAMBOAT

THE Mississippi flatboat emphasized the natural waterways which lay within the boundaries of the United States. By the terms of the treaty of peace which brought the Revolution to an end, the Father of Waters was the western boundary of the new United States with Spain in control of all territory on its right bank. In the east the Merrimac, Connecticut, Delaware, Susquehanna, Potomac, James, Savannah, and, most of all, the Hudson offered natural water routes to the region which lay back of the Atlantic coast. They served well the needs of the people who lived east of the Appalachian mountains. During the Revolution, however, a trickle of immigrants had begun crossing to Kentucky and Tennessee and, after the war, the movement became a flood. In their early days these trans-montane settlements were separated from the coast region by both great distance and by difficult country. Naturally they turned to the rivers at their very doors to float what goods they had for export down the Mississippi to New Orleans. So long as Spain held one bank of this potential artery of trade and completely controlled its mouth the freedom of American development west of the mountains was seriously threatened. Men feared that these communities would separate themselves from the states east of the Appalachians and make what terms they could with the foreigner across the Mississippi. The purchase of Louisiana in 1803 changed entirely the western situation. The Mississippi from source to mouth was American, destined within less than half a century to be one of the greatest of American commercial highways.

Neither the western nor the eastern rivers, however, could be used to advantage as commerce carriers in the days of sailing ships. It was no accident that the first practical steamboat made her test voyage on an American river under American management. No country in western Europe had such distances as the United States to conquer in the development of its commercial life and few had rivers to compare with the streams of the New World. Rivers offered, west of the Appalachians, practically the only solution of the problem of long distance transportation and the steamboat was necessary to make upstream navigation practicable. When the technique of building and handling this new craft had been mastered, and when the rivers had been cleared of some of the worst of the dangerous snags that had accumulated from time immemorial, these waterways played for a space a vital part in the development of the life of the American people. The Mississippi River trade was more significant for American history than the brilliant exploits of the clipper ships. The latter marked the brilliant ending of a cycle, but the former was the beginning of a development not yet completed. Without the Mississippi valley this country would be shorn of much economic power, and without the river the vast fertile interior would have waited many years for settlers and for means of marketing the settlers' products. Accessibility is a key to nature's storehouse; the Mississippi system provided this key.

THE RISE OF THE STEAMBOAT

ALTHOUGH Robert Fulton deserves credit for inventing and operating the first practicable steamboat, and though his famous journey in the *Clermont* from New York to Albany in 1807 is properly regarded as the starting point of steam navigation, at least eight Americans had invented boats pro-

184   Jonathan Hull's Pioneer Steam Tug, 1737, from Jonathan Hull, *A Description and Draught of a New-Invented Machine*, London, 1737

pelled by steam and had actually constructed sixteen steamboats that operated under their own power before the *Clermont* was even planned. The first of these prior inventors was John Fitch, a native of East Windsor, Connecticut. Fitch's boat, operated on the Delaware River in 1786, was forced through the water by mechanical paddles. There were six of these on each side, alternately raised and lowered by means of power derived from a steam engine. The boat was built by Brooks and Wilson of Philadelphia and was forty-five feet long with a twelve-foot beam. Its speed was scarcely three miles an hour. It is apparent that Fitch tried to reproduce by mechanical means the motion a man used in paddling a canoe.

185   Plan of John Fitch's 1786 Steamboat, from *The Columbian Magazine*, Philadelphia, January, 1787

186   The Second Experimental Boat of Fitch, 1787, from an engraving by J. W. Orr in *One Hundred Years' Progress*, Hartford, 1871

FITCH'S PERSISTENT EXPERIMENTS

THE following year Fitch launched a second, somewhat larger, boat in which the paddles were not banked, but individualized, each one on a separate crank and suspended by their middle just as a man would grasp it. This vessel, called the *Perseverance*, made a trip of twenty miles in 1788 from Philadelphia to Burlington in three hours and twenty minutes. Fitch's third boat, the *Thornton*, had more power and in 1789 and 1790 was run on the Delaware at a speed of eight miles per hour. After 1790 it was run regularly on the Delaware as a

packet boat and covered some thousand miles before it was retired. In 1797 Fitch experimented with another boat, a small yawl, which he ran on Collect Pond in New York city. Canal Street now covers one of the outlets of this pond. On this boat Fitch tried both paddle wheels and a screw propeller. Derided or ignored, sunken in poverty, a disappointed, embittered man, Fitch committed suicide at Bardstown, Kentucky, in 1798.

187   Model of Fitch's 1797 Steamboat, in the collection of the New York Historical Society

188   Oliver Evans' *Oruktor Amphibolos* (reconstruction), from a
photograph. © Rau Studios, Philadelphia

THE "STEAM MANIA"

SAMUEL MOREY of New Hampshire, who began experimenting with a steamboat in 1790, built a paddle-wheel steamer which in 1794 ran from Hartford to New York at a speed of about five miles an hour. This boat had the paddle wheel at the stern. A later boat of Morey's, built at Bordentown on the Delaware, was operated with two side paddle wheels. Others who were seized with the "steam mania," as it was derisively called at the time, were William Longstreet, of New Jersey, whose boat made five miles an hour against the current of the Savannah River in 1790, and Elijah Ormsbee of Connecticut, who made paddles to imitate ducks' feet and operated them by steam in a boat that he navigated from Cranston to Providence and Pawtucket and return. Oliver Evans, who invented the high-pressure steam engine and tubular boiler, applied it to moving boats as well as highway wagons and mills. Steam dredges built by him, such as the *Oruktor Amphibolos*, operated in 1804 through the water under their own power. Robert R. Livingston, afterward associated with Fulton, built a steamboat and ran it on the Hudson. John Stevens of Hoboken, New Jersey, experimented with a half-dozen different steamboats after 1791 and eventually hit upon the idea of the screw propeller in place of the more usual setting poles, paddles, oars or paddle wheels. Stevens himself, however, soon discarded the screw propeller in favor of paddle wheels, and it was not until years later — in 1839 — that the screw propeller received further attention.

RUMSEY'S STEAMBOAT

BENJAMIN FRANKLIN, who had a finger in nearly every pie that was cooking during his lifetime, was a member of an association headed by James Rumsey, a native of Maryland, that proposed to try Franklin's idea of propelling a boat by sucking in water at the bow and ejecting it at the stern. A boat was built and run on this principle by Rumsey in 1787, a steam pump being the means of ejecting the water. Rumsey had in 1784 exhibited a steamboat before General Washington at Bath, Virginia. In this earlier boat the power had been steam applied by cranks to a series of setting poles. Fitch, who had applied for state monopolies

189   The engine of John Stevens' screw-propelled steamboat,
1804, in the Stevens Institute, Hoboken, N. J.

over steamboats, contested Rumsey's inventions, so Rumsey took his ideas to London but died there in 1792, before they came to practical fruition. An Englishman, Dr. John Allen, in 1730 had propelled a canal boat by ejection, using a hand pump. In 1738 David Ramsey, also an Englishman, added a steam pump. So the American Rumsey was not unique.

190   James Rumsey's steamboat, from the model in the United States
National Museum, Washington

ROBERT FULTON, 1765–1815

ROBERT FULTON, the father of the steamboat, was an artist by profession. While in London in 1786, living with the famous American painter, Benjamin West, but giving most of his time to the study of engineering, he met Rumsey frequently and must have talked steamboats with the Maryland inventor. During his residence abroad, he also met Robert R. Livingston, American Minister to France, who was interested in steamboat invention. Livingston secured for Fulton the plans of Fitch's steamboats, and the two carefully studied all the attempts so far made in America and Europe in steamboat construction.

192   Model of the engine of Fulton's steamboat *Clermont*, 1807, in the United States National Museum, Washington, D. C.

FULTON'S PRELIMINARY EXPERIMENTS

BEFORE he returned to America, Fulton, through Livingston's influence, induced the British Government to permit him to take with him a steam engine and boiler from the best British builders of the day, Boulton & Watt. Robert Fulton returned home in 1806 and engaged Charles Brown of New York, a contractor, to build the hull of a vessel according to Fulton's plans. Into this boat, which was one hundred and forty feet long, of sixteen-foot beam, and of twenty-eight inches draft, the Boulton & Watt's engine was set. The craft was launched in the spring of 1807 and christened "The North River Steamboat of Clermont," the latter term being the name of Livingston's Hudson River country estate. August, however, arrived before the vessel was fully prepared for her maiden trip. The *Clermont* contained nothing that was original with Fulton, all of its parts having been tried by earlier experimenters. Yet Fulton deserves the honor and credit he won, since he was the first man to assemble working parts that operated together with practical success for commercial purposes.

"FULTON'S FOLLY"

WHILE fitting for her first voyage, the *Clermont* was dubbed "Fulton's Folly"; and on the day of the maiden trip a great crowd gathered at the wharf to jeer. When the *Clermont* chugged out into the stream and moved northward on her course the crowd was at first struck dumb with amazement, and then stimulated to tumultuous cheers. To rivermen unprepared for her advent the *Clermont* was a

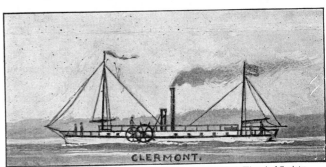

CLERMONT.

193   From the drawing by Richard V. De Witt in the New York Historical Society

terrifying sight, for her dry pine fuel sent clouds of smoke from the tall thirty-foot stack, accompanied by flashing sparks and an occasional sustained fire at the top of the funnel and for many feet above it, the whole effect heightened by the clanking and groaning of her machinery. This apparition, advancing steadily over the water against wind and tide, caused superstitious rivermen aboard the regular craft — so it was said — to jump overboard or run their boats aground. "Some besought Providence to protect them from the approaches of the horrible monster which was marching on the tides and lighting its path by the fires it vomited."

194   From the mural painting *First Passage of the Steamer Clermont to Albany, August 17, 1807*, by C. Y. Turner
(1850–1918), in the Hudson County Court House, Jersey City, N. J.

FULTON'S COMMENT ON THE FIRST TRIP OF THE *CLERMONT*

ROBERT FULTON himself wrote to a friend named Barlow a description of his passage to Albany and return on the first voyage of the *Clermont:* "My steamboat voyage to Albany and back has turned out rather more

195   From the painting *A Strange Craft on the Hudson,* by
Stanley M. Arthurs (1877–), in possession of the artist

favorably than I had calculated. The distance from New York to Albany is one hundred and fifty miles: I ran it up in thirty-two hours and down in thirty. I had a light breeze against me the whole way both going and coming, and the voyage has been performed wholly by the power of the steam engine. I overtook many sloops and schooners beating to windward and parted with them as if they had been at anchor. The power of propelling boats by steam is now fully proved. The morning I left New York there were not perhaps thirty persons in the city who believed that the boat would ever move one mile per hour or be of the least utility; and while we were putting off from the wharf, which was crowded with spectators, I heard a number of sarcastic remarks. This is the way ignorant men compliment what they call philosophers and projectors. Having employed much time, money and zeal in accomplishing this work, it gives me, as it will give you, great pleasure to see it fully answer my expectations; it will give quick and cheap conveyance to the merchandise on the Mississippi, Missouri and other great rivers, which are now laying open their treasures . . . and, although the prospect of personal emolument has been some inducement to me, yet I feel infinitely more pleasure in reflecting on the immense advantage my country will derive from the invention."

196   The enlarged *Clermont,* from the drawing by Richard V. DeWitt,
in the New York Historical Society

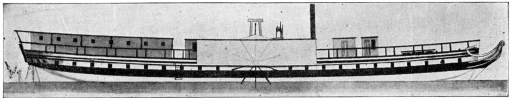

197   Plan of the *Chancellor Livingston*, from a diagram by Klinckowstrom after an original plan by
Robert Fulton, in the New York Historical Society

FULTON'S OTHER STEAMBOATS

Two weeks after her trial trip, the *Clermont* began to make regular scheduled commercial voyages between New York and Albany. The advertised charge was seven dollars for the entire trip one way, or one dollar for every twenty miles for less than the full voyage. The running time was set down as thirty-six hours. The boat made stops along the way to pick up and discharge passengers and even took on passengers in the middle of the river from rowboats or sailboats that put off from the shore where there was no scheduled stop. Boatmen or innkeepers were allowed a shilling a person for bringing out passengers in this manner. During the winter of 1807–08, the *Clermont* was enlarged. She continued to do service until July, 1814, when she was withdrawn in favor of a later Fulton-Livingston boat, the *Richmond*. Meanwhile, Fulton and his associates had put the *Car of Neptune* into service in 1808, the *Paragon* in 1808, and the *Fire Fly* in 1812, all of which, like the *Clermont* and afterward the *Richmond*, plied between New York and Albany. No part of the original *Clermont* was invented by Robert Fulton. His success lay in adapting properly the work of other men to practicable ends. After the *Clermont*, Fulton made original improvements and adjustments which he patented.

198   Chart showing progress in Hudson River steamboat construction, courtesy of *The Nautical Gazette*, New York, 1906

THE FULTON–LIVINGSTON MONOPOLY

ROBERT LIVINGSTON obtained from the New York Legislature a state monopoly of steamboat operation. This annulled a similar grant made to John Fitch. Fulton, having been made a joint beneficiary, shared with Livingston exclusive control of steam navigation in New York. They had a right to seize the boat of any competitor and exact a money penalty in addition for every trip he had made. Not satisfied with control of the Hudson, they applied in 1809 for a Federal patent on steamboats, which they secured, and with their associate Nicholas Roosevelt, they induced Louisiana in 1811 to grant them an exclusive monopoly of the lower Mississippi. A small one-hundred-ton steamboat called the *New Orleans* was built at Pittsburgh by them and started in October on the first voyage made by steamboat on inland waters. The *New Orleans* reached the city of her baptism in January, 1812. Efforts on the part of rivals to break the steamboat monopoly, though retarded by fear of litigation, had begun as early as 1810. The great test of the Fulton-Livingston monopoly came when one Thomas Gibbons opened a ferry line between Elizabethtown, New Jersey, and New York city as a rival to a line operated by Aaron Ogden under a license from the monopolists. Cornelius Vanderbilt was captain of one of the two boats of Gibbons' line. Ogden applied to New York courts for an injunction against Gibbons, which was granted; but the case was appealed and carried finally to the United States Supreme Court, which, in February, 1824, handed down a decree in favor of Gibbons. This broke the monopoly and permitted anyone to operate steamboats without paying tribute to the Fulton or Livingston estates.

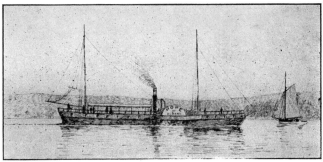

199   Steamer *Hope*, 1811, rival of Fulton's steamboats, from a contemporary wood engraving in S. W. Stanton, *American Steam Vessels*, New York, 1895

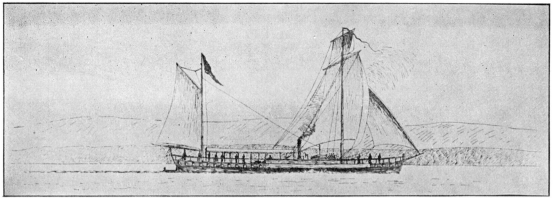

200   Fulton steamer *Paragon*, from an engraving after a drawing by Robert Fulton, in S. W. Stanton, *American Steam Vessels*, New York, 1895

THE SPREAD OF THE STEAMBOAT

WHEN the decree of the Supreme Court in 1824 destroyed the Fulton-Livingston monopoly, steamboats began to appear in considerable numbers in response to impatient demand. Several new companies began operating boats on the Hudson, between New York, Albany and intermediate points. Other lines ran from New York to New Jersey towns, Elizabethtown, Amboy, New Brunswick, Keyport, and Red Bank. On the Delaware, steamboats were put in service between Philadelphia, Bordentown, and Trenton. Likewise, the lower Delaware saw several steamboats making regular passages out of Philadelphia, Chester, or Wilmington. Baltimore established connections to points on Chesapeake Bay. In addition, there were steamboats serving towns on Long Island Sound, the Connecticut River, the Thames River, Narragansett Bay and Massachusetts Bay. Some of these lines were links in through passenger services. A traveler from Philadelphia to New York, for example, journeyed by boat to Bordentown (or Trenton), thence by stage to New Brunswick (or Amboy), and again by boat to New York city.

201   Captain Henry M. Shreve, from an engraving after the portrait by D'Almaine, in the *Democratic Review*, 1848

RIVER STEAMBOATS IN WEST AND SOUTH

THE *New Orleans*, which in 1811 steamed from Pittsburgh to New Orleans, was put in passenger and freight service between the metropolis and Natchez, but was sunk two years later in collision with a partially submerged tree stump. Several other steamboats, built at Pittsburgh and run through to New Orleans, were in local service along the Mississippi River, and did duty in the War of 1812 in the transportation of food, ordnance, ammunition and troops. In 1816, the *Washington*, under Captain Henry M. Shreve, made two round trips between New Orleans and Louisville and in the upstream journeys took less than a fourth of the time required by bargemen and pole-boatmen. These trips removed the doubt of the practicability of upstream steamboat service, and soon steamboats were plying regularly between local points on the rivers, such as Cincinnati and Louisville, and for through trips between Pittsburgh and New Orleans.

In contrast with the East, where the early boats were designed principally for passenger service, western river boats were important as freight carriers. After 1815, some also towed vessels upstream from the river's mouth to New Orleans. The earnings of these first steamboats is suggested by the record of one boat which in 1817, from one round trip between New Orleans and Louisville, returned eight hundred dollars a day, making a total profit which more than equaled the original cost of the vessel.

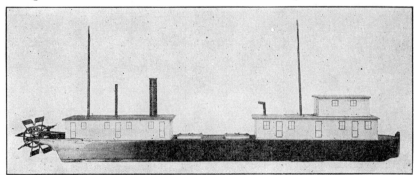

202   Model of the *New Orleans* in Carnegie Institute, Pittsburgh

DIFFICULTIES OF WESTERN RIVER STEAMBOATS

VOYAGES upon early western river steamboats were exciting, hazardous adventures, for few boats lasted intact for more than three years. The rivers were full of trees and rocks, the current, channel, and river depths were constantly changing and steamboat accidents or wrecks occurred frequently. The boats, too, used wood fuel, except in the upper Ohio where coal was obtainable, so that the sparks from the boats' own stacks sometimes set them afire. Furthermore, all the boats were fitted with high-pressure engines because of their compactness,

203   Steamboat disaster on the Ohio, 1868, from *Harper's Weekly*, December 26, 1868

cheapness, and ease of operation. But engines designed to withstand a pressure of one hundred pounds were often subjected to two hundred pounds in order to get up power enough to pull the boat off from banks,

204   Snags in the upper Missouri, 1833, from a lithograph after the painting by Carl Bodmer, in Prince Maximilian de Nieu-Wied, *Travels in North America, 1832–34*

over snags, or to get steerage way in a raging downstream current. In addition, races between boats were everyday occurrences; and, when a race was on, precautions were forgotten. So explosions, and fires with explosions, sent many a boat, together with its human freight, to disaster. Collisions were frequent, owing either to carelessness, or the difficulties of navigation on rivers full of curves and fierce currents or eddies. The resultant destruction of property and human life was appalling. Yet everyone disregarded the risks, and boats, literally by the hundreds, plied the rivers of the Mississippi system.

THE RIVER PILOT

MARK TWAIN has left a vivid account of the education of the river pilot. Said an old hand to an apprentice: "You see this has got to be learned. . . . A clear starlight night throws such heavy shadows that if you didn't know the shape of the shore perfectly you would claw away from every bunch of timber because you would take the black shadow of it for a solid cape; and you see you would be getting scared to death every fifteen minutes by the watch. You would be fifty yards from shore all the time when you ought to be within fifty feet of it. You can't see a snag in one of these shadows, but you know exactly where it is, and the shape of the river tells you when you are coming to it. Then there's your pitch-dark night; the river is a very different shape on a pitch-dark night from what it is on a starlight night. All shores seem to be straight lines, then, and mighty dim ones, too; and you'd *run* them for straight lines only you know better. You boldly drive your boat right into what seems to be a solid, straight wall (you knowing very well that in reality there is a curve there) and that wall falls back and makes way for you. Then there's your gray mist. You take a night when there's one of those grisly, drizzly, gray mists, and then there isn't *any* particular shape to a shore. A gray mist would tangle the head of the oldest man that ever lived. . . . You only learn the shape of the river; and you learn it with such absolute certainty that you can always steer by the shape that's *in your head* and never mind the one that's before your eyes." — *Life on the Mississippi*, pp. 103–04.

205   From an engraving after the sketch *That's A Reef*, by Harley, in Mark Twain, *Life on the Mississippi*, Boston, 1883

MORE PERFECT ADAPTATION

As time passed the boats operating on the Mississippi River system were adjusted more and more perfectly to their work. They also increased in size and the luxuriance of their fittings.

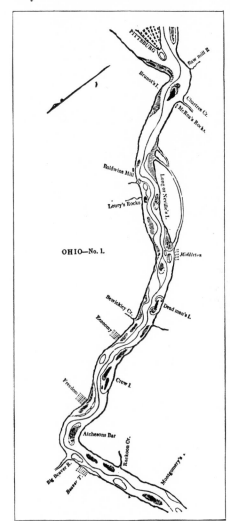

207   Chart of the Ohio below Pittsburgh, from Samuel Cumings, *The Western Pilot*, Cincinnati, 1839

Competition placed great premium on speed, when, before the days of the railroad, the steamboat offered the only good means of passenger transportation. The boat which broke a record was sure to be the subject of lively comment in all the river towns at which she stopped. In 1817 the *Enterprise* made the upstream journey from New Orleans to Louisville in twenty-five days, two hours, and four minutes. Seventeen years later the *Tecumseh* cut the time to eight days and four hours. In 1853 the *A. L. Shotwell* covered the distance in four days, nine hours, and nineteen minutes. Boats on the run from New Orleans to Natchez showed a like increase of speed. In 1814 the *Comet* made Natchez in five days and ten hours, a record which was cut by the *Tuscarora* to one day and twenty-one hours in 1834. In 1853 the *Natchez* made the trip in seventeen hours and a half. In each case the last record showed a six-fold increase in speed over the first. At the wheel stood pilots, past-masters of their difficult art, driving the great vessels at top speed through the dark hours of night. The passengers were a mixed lot, immigrants seeking western homes, backwoodsmen journeying to the bright lights of cities, gentlemen enjoying travel in novel surroundings, and deft-fingered gentry preying upon the others. Cargoes were local country products and imports from the East.

THE WESTERN PILOT.

Directions for Map No. 1.—Ohio River.

From the landing at Pittsburgh, on the Monongahela side, keep near the right shore, and, at high water, pull directly out into the Alleghany current, which sets strong over to the left shore. At low water, when nearly up with the point, keep over to the left, towards O'Hara's glass-works, which will carry you clear of the bar at the point, and of the Monongahela bar on the left.

Brunot's Island. _____ 2¼

Channel to the right, and near the right shore, round the head bar of the island, and then incline towards the island, and pass near its foot, to avoid a bar on the right below.

Neville's, or Long Island. _____ 5   7¼

Channel to the right. About three-fourths of a mile above Neville's island, keep to the right, to avoid the bar at its head, and pass pretty close to Baldwin's mill dam ; and, when past it, close in to the right shore below, then turn short across for the island, and keep near the island shore until you approach a small sandy island, when you must keep to the right, and pass betwixt the latter and Lowry's rock, which lies on the right, opposite. A quarter of a mile below the small sandy island, keep to the left round the head of Duff's bar, and near to Neville's island shore, until you are within a mile and a quarter of its foot, then turn quick to the right, and approach within fifty yards of the right shore, and when nearly up with Hog island, incline to the left, and keep one third of the river on your right, which will carry you clear of the bar at the foot of the island, and the shore bar on the right. After passing Middletown bar, incline to the left.*

Dead Man's Island. _____ 9¼   17

Channel to the right. As you approach the island, keep well towards the right shore, round the large bar at the head of the island, then keep to the left, well over to the island, round a bar on

* I am informed that an artificial channel has been cut to the right of Woollery's trap. In that case, it will be necessary to incline to the right, after passing Middletown bar, and keep three-fourths of the river on the left, until you are past Woollery's trap.

B   9

206   Directions for the Use of the Chart, from Samuel Cumings, *The Western Pilot*, Cincinnati, 1839

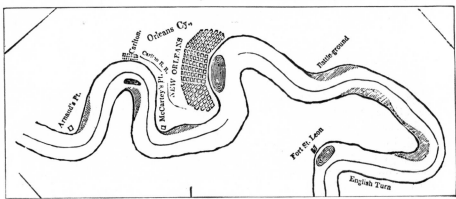

208   Chart of the Mississippi River around New Orleans, from Samuel Cumings, *The Western Pilot*, Cincinnati, 1839

209   Mississippi steamboat taking on wood, from *Ballou's Pictorial Drawing-Room Companion*, June 7, 1856

THE PROBLEM OF FUELING

WOOD-BURNING vessels on voyages of a thousand miles had to make frequent stops to take on fuel. Fueling stations were set up along the river courses, clearings to which settlers could bring wood for storage and sale. As most of them had no dock or wharf, the steamer was run ashore at the desired point. Deck hands were supposed to bring the wood aboard, but, as haste was essential, passengers could help in the job: if they did this, they received a discount on their fare. Many accidents occurred at fueling stations because occasionally the extra weight of fuel grounded the boat so that she could not back off, or broke her wheels in trying to creep out to deep water. It was customary to keep steam up during fueling so as to have extra power to get away; but, unfortunately, in the prevailing excitement, the engineer sometimes neglected to keep his boilers full of water and they would blow up.

210   Fueling station on the Mississippi, from a lithograph in Henry Lewis,
Das Illustrirte Mississippi-Thal, Düsseldorf, 1844–45

211   Cotton plantation on the Mississippi, from a lithograph in Henry Lewis,
Das Illustrirte Mississippi-Thal, Düsseldorf, 1844–45

THE TRADE OF THE SOUTHERN PLANTATIONS

COINCIDING with the appearance of the steamboat on the Western rivers came the rush to settle the rich cotton lands of Mississippi and Louisiana for the growing of cotton and sugar. The great plantations proved an excellent market for the farmers of the upper waterways, for cotton growers wasted no time, land, or effort on other products. As the planters became more prosperous, they bought more goods in New Orleans through their permanent agents, and less from occasional flatboatmen. This practice tended to discourage flatboat traffic and to encourage through traffic by means of steamboats. Although upstream steamboat navigation began as early as 1814, the volume of traffic in that direction never approximated that which rode with the current. Sugar and coffee were carried northward by water and also heavy machinery. There was in addition a large local movement of freight north from New Orleans to the cotton and sugar plantations. By far the most of the manufactured articles used in the river territory, however, came from the East; and, so far as they entered river traffic, they swelled the downstream volume. But the passenger traffic upstream was large; for along with the round-trip steamboat passengers who patronized the upstream service, a great many people who came down the current in their own boats went back by way of steamer.

212   Natchez, Miss., from a lithograph in Henry Lewis, *Das Illustrirte Mississippi-Thal*, Düsseldorf, 1844–45

THE GROWTH OF TRADE IN THE MIDDLE WEST

As the river country filled with settlers, changes appeared in the steamboat commerce. There was less emphasis upon the through journeys, such as those from Pittsburgh or Louisville to New Orleans, and more attention to shorter local traffic such as that from Louisville to Cincinnati, or Memphis to St. Louis. The more important upper-river towns began to develop their own manufactur-

213   From a lithograph *Louisville, 1836*, by Doolittle and Munson after the drawing by T. A. Evans, courtesy of R. C. Ballard Thruston, Louisville, Ky.

ing and so became less dependent upon the East. Rolled and cast-iron products, for example, were manufactured in Cincinnati and Pittsburgh. Likewise the Ohio hogs that once were driven overland to Baltimore for slaughter — as many as five thousand in a drove — were dressed and packed at Cincinnati. Indeed, Cincinnati was the first great meat-packing center in America and attained the nickname, "Porkopolis." The best market for these hog products was in the Southern plantations. Pittsburgh, Cincinnati and Louisville also manufactured steam engines, barrels, rope, cotton and wool cloth, liquors and beverages, all of which found their way into the steamboat commerce. Another important change was the growth of population

214   Memphis levee before the Civil War, from an engraving after the sketch by Porte Crayon, in *Harper's Weekly*, March 15, 1862

in the neighborhood of the Missouri River with a consequent swelling of commerce upon that stream centering at St. Louis. This traffic was not confined to farmstuff but included furs, skins and minerals, the latter chiefly lead. This commerce fortunately took the place of the freight lost on the Ohio River to the canals that connected with the Great Lakes and the Erie Canal. A large water-borne business was built up between the Ohio River towns and St. Louis; but this traffic was decidedly one-sided, being mostly westbound manufactured articles. St. Louis sent her own products collected from the Missouri River country down the Mississippi River to New Orleans and with the proceeds purchased Eastern or Ohio Valley manufactures.

215   From the painting *St. Louis in 1832*, by George Catlin (1796–1872), in the Mercantile Library Association, St. Louis

216   The levee at Pittsburgh, from an engraving by J. P. Davis after a drawing by "H. F."
                        in *Every Saturday*, March 25, 1871

THE ACME OF STEAMBOAT DEVELOPMENT

"AFTER a period of gaudy ornamentation, 1830–40, steamboat architecture settled down, as has that of Pullman cars today, to sane and practical lines, and the boats gained in length and strength, though they contained less weight of timber. The value of one of the greater boats of this era would be about fifty thousand dollars. When Captain Bixby made his celebrated night crossing of Hat Island a quarter of a million dollars in ship and cargo would have been the price of an error in judgment, according to Mark Twain, a good authority. The *Yorktown*, built in 1844 for the Ohio-Mississippi trade, was typical of that epoch of inland commerce. Her length was one hundred and eighty-two feet, breadth of beam thirty-one feet, and the diameter of wheels twenty-eight feet. Though her hold was eight feet in depth, yet she drew but four feet of water light and barely over eight feet when loaded with five hundred tons of freight. . . . The *Yorktown* had forty private cabins. It is interesting to compare the *Yorktown* with *The Queen of the West*, the giant British

steamer built for the Falmouth-Calcutta trade in 1839. *The Queen of the West* had a length of three hundred and ten feet, a beam of thirty-one feet, a draft of fifteen feet, and sixteen private cabins. The building of this vessel led a writer in the New York *American* to say: 'It would really seem that we as a nation had no interest in this new application of steam power, or no energy to appropriate it to our own use.' The statement — written in a day when the Mississippi steamboat tonnage exceeded that of the entire British Empire — is one of the best examples of provincial ignorance concerning the West." — ARCHER HULBERT, *The Paths of Inland Commerce*, pp. 181–82.

217   Ohio River steamboat pushing flotilla of coal barges, from a painting
                        in the Carnegie Institute, Pittsburgh

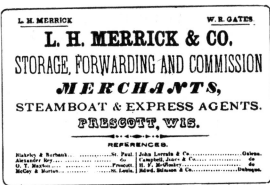

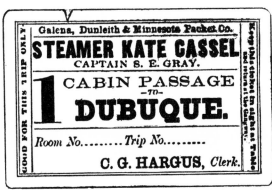

218 Business Card of Mississippi Freight Agents, from a facsimile of the original, in George B. Merrick, *Old Times on the Upper Mississippi,* Cleveland, 1909, courtesy of A. H. Clark Co.

219 Mississippi Steamboat Ticket, from a facsimile of the original, in Geo. B. Merrick, *Old Times on the Upper Mississippi,* Cleveland, 1909, courtesy of A. H. Clark Co.

WESTERN STEAMBOAT FINANCING

BARON DE GERSTER, traveling through the United States about 1840, made careful computations concerning Western river steamboat financing, which are quoted in J. H. Morrison's *History of American Steam Navigation,* as follows:

ORIGINAL COST OF *FRANKLIN*

For the hull at $25.00 per ton	$ 5,000.
For two steam engines	12,000.
For joiner work in cabins	4,000.
Furniture, draperies, equipment	9,000.
TOTAL	$30,000.

MONTHLY OPERATING EXPENSES

1 captain and 2 clerks	$ 200.
2 pilots	200.
2 engineers and 2 assistants	250.
2 mates	80.
1 carpenter	30.
2 cooks	80.
1 steward and 6 waiters	140.
1 chambermaid	20.
10 firemen	200.
6 common laborers	120.
38 persons with wages totaling	$ 1,320.
785 cords of wood and a few tons of coal	1,775.
Provisions for 100 persons per mo.	1,440.
Total expense per trip of 150 miles at $1 per mile	150.
Average profit	$ 240.
Average trips per season	270.
Average profit per trip	$ 240.
Average profit per year	64,800.
First cost of boat	$30,000.

YEARLY EXPENSES FOR *FRANKLIN*

Current expenses for 9 months season	$40,500.
Salary, captain and clerks who remain with the boat the 3 months idle time	1,000.
Repairs and general depreciation	10,500.
Insurance, 7 to 9 percent. on three quarters of value	1,350.
Miscellaneous	1,150.
	54,500.
Less board for passengers and crews	14,000.
Expense for boat alone	$40,500.

Boat operates 150 miles per day equaling 40,500 miles for 9 months season or $1.00 expense per mile.

AVERAGE REVENUE PER TRIP OF 150 MILES

62 cabin passengers at $4.00	$ 248.
63 deck passengers at 1.00	63.
25 tons goods at 3.00	75.
Transporting U. S. Mail	4.
Total average revenue per trip	390.
Total monthly expenses, without repairs	$ 4,495.

Hence boat earns more than double its first cost in its first year of service.

Average length of service before wrecked, sunk, burned or sold for junk — three years.

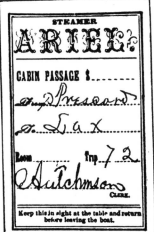

220 Mississippi Steamboat Ticket, from Merrick, *Old Times on the Upper Mississippi,* courtesy of A. H. Clark Co.

MISSISSIPPI STEAMBOAT RATES

THE steamboat rates on the Mississippi between 1812 and 1819 were:

NEW ORLEANS TO LOUISVILLE

THROUGH TRAFFIC

Freight rate:

Heavy goods, per pound	$	.04½
Light goods, per pound		.06
per ton		112.00

Passenger fare:

Upstream; time, 20 days	$125.00
Downstream; time, 10 days	70.00

NEW ORLEANS TO NATCHEZ

LOCAL TRAFFIC

Freight rate:

Per pound	$	.00¾
Per barrel		1.50
Per ton		15.00

Passenger fare:

Upstream	$ 30.00
Downstream	15.00

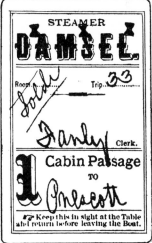

221 Mississippi Steamboat Ticket, from Merrick, *Old Times on the Upper Mississippi,* courtesy of A. H. Clark Co.

IV—7

222   From the painting, 1853, *Bateaux à Vapeur Geants*, by H. Sebron, in
Tulane University, New Orleans

THE GOLDEN AGE OF MISSISSIPPI COMMERCE

THE three decades from 1830 to 1860 are generally called the "Golden Age" of Mississippi commerce, for each year saw an increase in the volume and value of the business done on that stream which reached its highest point in 1860. This record was due in part to the ever greater amount of cotton, sugar and molasses shipped into New Orleans from the lower Mississippi River region, and in part to the constant addition to the volume of business originating in the Missouri River territory and focusing at St. Louis. Yet the signs of decay were not lacking. Trade on the Mississippi River system was doomed to decline, as earlier it had on the Ohio. For the numerous local canals joining Ohio, Indiana, and Illinois with the Great Lakes and the Erie Canal diverted more and more commerce from the traditional North-South route to the East-West one. This influence was vastly intensified by the building of railroads. What saved the Mississippi until 1860 was the fact that through railroad connections did not until after the Civil War penetrate the Missouri country, nor parallel the Mississippi, nor form a network in the territory drained by the Mississippi. As a consequence, the steamboat ruled the commerce of the Mississippi valley until after the war between North and South.

A FAMOUS RIVER RACE

THE most famous river steamboat race occurred in June, 1870. The *Natchez*, commanded by Captain Thomas P. Leathers, had steamed to St. Louis from New Orleans in three days twenty-one hours and fifty-eight minutes, a record that provoked a challenge from Captain John W. Cannon of the *Robert E. Lee*. In providing for the race, Captain Cannon removed all the rigging outfit and superstructure of the *Lee* that would catch the wind; he also sent a boat ahead to provide that coal should be ready on floats in the river, so that coaling could take place without stopping the *Lee*. For the trip, Captain Cannon refused all business, both passenger and freight. The *Natchez*, on the other hand, made no special preparations and took on board both passengers and freight. The two boats left New Orleans within five minutes of each other in the middle of the afternoon of June 30, 1870. The world was notified of the race by telegraph and cable and its whole progress was as eagerly watched as an international yacht race. All along the actual route people lined the banks, and at the cities or larger towns thousands of people cheered their choice of the two contenders as it hove in sight. For three days the race lasted, with the boats in sight of each other the whole time below Cairo, except where river-bends hid the view. Being better prepared, the *Lee* jumped into the lead from the start and gained consistently on her more heavily laden rival. At Cairo, the *Lee* lost the *Natchez*, for the latter was hampered by a fog and ran aground; but the *Lee* kept up her pace until she reached St. Louis, three days, eighteen hours and thirty minutes after she had left her wharf in New Orleans. The *Lee* had made a great record, one that many an old riverman had deemed impossible.

Thousands of people greeted the victorious *Lee* at St. Louis and her captain was given a banquet by the city. In a sense the race was a final exhibition of the spirit of the great days of the Mississippi River steamboat. A few years later the railroad had relegated these giants of the middle of the century to a place of secondary importance. The river boats of the present have little splendor.

223   From a Currier & Ives lithograph, *The Great Mississippi Steamboat Race*,
1870, courtesy of the Kentucky State Historical Society, Frankfort

BACKWARDNESS OF THE GREAT LAKES TRADE

In 1836, when there were hundreds of steamboats plying the Ohio, the Missouri and the Mississippi Rivers, together with their tributaries, there were only forty-five passenger steamboats on the Great Lakes. The reasons for this disparity are not hard to find. The great Western rivers were natural highways of com-

224   View of Buffalo Harbor, from a lithograph by Imbert in Cadwalader D. Colden, *Memoir in Celebration of Completion of the New York Canals*, New York, 1825

merce. The steamboat made it possible to use them. The Lakes, on the contrary, were solitary inland seas lacking border settlements and with scarcely a half dozen good harbors. The rapids of the St. Lawrence cut off communication with the sea, the Niagara River interrupted communication between Ontario and Erie, and the Soo rapids separated the upper and lower lakes. On the lakes themselves, therefore, there was no possibility of through traffic. Furthermore, the whole lake region was outside the range of western navigation and settlement, for it could not be reached easily from the Ohio-Missouri-Mississippi system either by water or overland, and the route by way of the Hudson and Mohawk was impracticable until the Erie Canal was completed in 1825. As a consequence, the first lake steamer *Walk-in-the-Water*, whose initial voyage was in 1818, ran for three years without earning its cost, although the fare from Buffalo to Detroit was only eighteen dollars for cabin passengers.

WALK–IN–THE–WATER

The *Walk-in-the-Water* was built at Black Rock, New York. Her engine was made in New York city, carried in sloops to Albany and thence to Buffalo overland in wagons hauled by three, and sometimes four, teams of horses. It took nearly a month to transport the machinery and parts from Albany to Buffalo. The vessel itself was one hundred and thirty-five feet long, with a thirty-two foot beam. In addition to her engine, she carried sails, being rigged as a brig.

The captain, one John Fish, piloted her out of Buffalo on her maiden voyage on August 20, 1818, arriving in Detroit toward the end of the second day. The vessel ran regularly between the two places with stops at intermediate points during the next three years. On November 1, 1821, she was wrecked in Buffalo Bay during a heavy gale. During the three years, despite the fact that she had no steam competitor, she paid only one dividend to her owners. Her successor was the *Superior*, built in 1822 at Buffalo. The machinery was that of the wrecked vessel. Although the *Superior* was soon converted into a sloop-rigged sailing boat for carrying lumber, other steamboats slowly appeared on the lakes. By 1836 there were forty-five in service, all designed to carry passengers, but occasionally taking small amounts of freight. Lake steamships began to overthrow sail vessels when canals connecting the lakes were built; for sail boats navigated these waterways with more difficulty than steam.

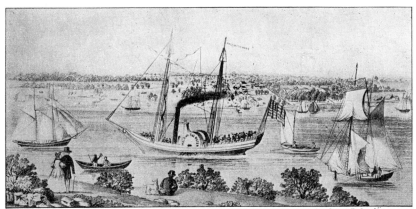

225   Detroit in 1820, showing the *Walk-in-the-Water*, the first steamboat on the Great Lakes, from a lithograph in *Wisconsin Historical Collections*, Madison

226   Ships passing through locks of the Welland Canal.   © Detroit Publishing Co.

THE WELLAND AND SOO CANALS

THE completion of the Erie Canal in 1825 brought a rush of settlers to the Lake region, who used the Lakes and the canal as a means of sending their surplus products to the Eastern seaboard markets. Soon afterward the Welland Canal removed the menace of the Niagara River and canals were started in Ohio and Indiana to connect the Lakes and the Ohio-Mississippi River systems. In 1865, when the first Soo Canal was built, the Lakes became a continuous waterway, connected on the east by the Erie Canal with the Atlantic and on the south by means of the Ohio canals with the Ohio River. In 1856, two hundred and forty-five steam vessels and one thousand and six large sailing boats operated on the Great Lakes as freight and passenger carriers.

OPENING THE LAKES REGION TO SETTLERS

UNTIL the building of the Erie Canal, the shores of the Great Lakes were almost unknown to white settlers. Detroit was a frontier fortress, Milwaukee a hunting ground, Chicago a fortified trading post, Cleveland a small band of Connecticut Yankees, and Buffalo a tiny village. But the opening of the Erie Canal brought immigrants to the lands bordering the Lakes. Northern Ohio began to fill with people and the tide of population pressed onward first into Indiana, then upward into Michigan, then beyond into Illinois, and finally into Wisconsin. With settlement, trade began. The outlet for the Lake region was New York city, reached by the Erie Canal, but the Great Lakes themselves were gigantic natural extensions of the New York public utility. For a short fifteen years New York State itself furnished most of the eastbound canal traffic. During those years, however, the lake region filled with settlers; so that, beginning in 1839, the shipments eastward over the Erie Canal coming from west of New York were greater in volume than those from western New York State. The canals built in Ohio, Indiana and Illinois contributed to the Erie Canal, being constructed to furnish outlets for the prairie farmers by waterways to the large eastern markets.

227   From the painting *Detroit Harbor, 1794*, by C. T. Chapman (1860–) in the steamer *Greater Detroit*. © Detroit and Cleveland Navigation Co., Detroit

228   From a lithograph *Chicago in 1820* by J. Gemmell, in the Chicago Historical Society

THE GROWTH OF COMMERCE

OHIO with its three canals was at first the leading grain-shipping state, but Indiana, Illinois and Wisconsin crept up on their rival after the railroads were built. Eventually Chicago became the center of the grain trade. Besides grain, a great quantity of lumber was carried eastward over the Lakes; copper appeared on the lists after 1845, and iron after 1855. The grain and the copper were destined for the Atlantic coast; but much of the lumber was used in new construction in the states near the Lakes, while the iron went into furnaces in Pennsylvania, New York and Ohio. As compared with the eastbound traffic, the westward lake commerce was lighter but more valuable, being mostly manufactured textiles, leather goods, small metal wares and articles needed on the farm or in the shipment of farm products.

THE CHARACTER OF LAKE COMMERCE

IN 1830, the total tonnage of vessels engaged in Great Lakes commerce was scarcely seven thousand, but the growth of Lake commerce, keeping pace with the enormous increase elsewhere, employed in 1860 a tonnage capacity on these inland waters of four hundred and fifty thousand. Steamboats, however, made but slow headway against sail: in 1860, only one hundred and four thousand were accredited to steam-driven vessels, or less than a third of the total. The reason for this was that as Lake commerce dealt with heavy, bulky, raw materials, grain, lumber, copper and iron ore, cheapness rather than speed was essential in this traffic. West-

bound trips were always light or in ballast, and steamers were obliged to cut their rates in that direction to secure their share of the manufactured goods moving westward. The steamboats got practically all of the passenger business until the railroads captured most of this traffic after 1857. The railroads never ousted passenger steamers. Between Buffalo, Cleveland, and Detroit, for example, passenger steamers retained popularity.

229   From a colored aquatint, 1837, *City of Detroit, Michigan*, engraved and painted by W. J. Bennett, after a sketch by Frederick Grain. © I. N. Phelps Stokes, New York

230 *The Phoenix*, from a painting, artist unknown, in possession of the Stevens Institute of Technology, Hoboken, N. J., courtesy of F. De R. Furman

THE STEAMSHIP IN COASTWISE COMMERCE

UNTIL the Civil War, the steamboat in America proved its greatest usefulness upon rivers and inland or protected waters such as Chesapeake Bay, Long Island Sound or Massachusetts Bay. The steamers conquered river currents, and operated in sheltered bays with a speed and regularity impossible for other boats hampered by calm, fogs and tides. But for ocean service the American steamboat was for a long time less advantageous than the highly developed sailing vessel. The sea-going steamers were small, mere copies of river or sound craft, and had no more speed than the well-designed sail-packet-boats. Marine engine design, moreover, was still faulty, and accidents on the seas were more hazardous than on a river or bay. Perhaps credit should be given to the *Phoenix* as the first American steamboat in coastwise service, although she made but one trip, in 1809, to get from New York around to the upper Delaware River. Several other early steamers took at least one coastwise voyage to get them from one river service to another, or from a river to a bay. Thus the *Sea Horse* made a remarkable sea run in 1819 from New York to New Orleans. Hermaphrodites — part steamer, part sail — were tried out in coastwise service in the 'twenties, such as the steam brig *New York*, running between New York and Norfolk in 1822–23; but these boats were withdrawn because they were more expensive to operate than the regular sailing packets and made no better time. A good many sound and bay steamers were transferred to coastwise service in the 'twenties and 'thirties, running between New York, Baltimore, Wilmington, Charleston, Havana and New Orleans. But these boats failed of financial success and the frequency with which they met sea disaster made them unpopular. In coastwise trade, therefore, the sail packet had no real rival until the 'forties.

Travelling.

INTERCOURSE BETWEEN PHILADELPHIA & BALTIMORE.
The following, shewing the extent of the intercourse between Philadelphia and Baltimore, was furnished to the editor of the REGISTER by an intelligent and enquiring traveller, and is, probably, pretty accurate.

The means of the "Union Line," for the conveyance of passengers and goods from city to city, via Frenchtown and Elkton, on the waters of the Chesapeake, and New Castle on those of the Delaware, are—

  5 steam boats in the Chesapeake,
  2 ditto in the Delaware,
  3 sloops in the Chesapeake,
  2 ditto in the Delaware,
  18 four horse stages,
  12 heavy waggons—

Employing about 159 men and 160 horses.

By this line, passengers may leave Philadelphia or Baltimore early in the morning, and make the journey between them at an early hour in the evening, via Elkton and New Castle. The chief intercourse however, is maintained by the line of boats which leaves Philadelphia at 12, noon, and Baltimore at 5 P. M. and respectively end the journey at from 9 to 11 A. M. at Philadelphia, and as from 3 to 5, A. M. at Baltimore. Goods (generally carried by the packets and the heavy waggons) commonly reach either city from the other in from 3 to 4 days.

In the year 1818, it is believed there were about 30,000 full passengers between these cities, to and from, besides-way passengers, and the freight carried by the sloops and waggons might amount to $40,000.

The following calculation of capital, costs, and profit is interesting, though not pretended to be given as accurate:

5 steam boats, at $40,000 (on average)		$200,000
5 sloops,	4,000	20,000
18 stages,	200	3,600
12 waggons, with gears	150	1,800
150 horses.	100	15,000
Miscellaneous, say		10,000
		$250,400
Cr. 30,000 passengers—at $6		$180,000
Way-passengers		20,000
Freight of goods, in the packets		40,000
		240,000
Dr. Fuel for steam boats	$30,000	
Wages of 150 men, 300 days, at $1 per day	47,700	
"Wear and tear," 25 per cent. on capital	62,600	
Horse feed	30,000	
To cover all losses, superintendence, wharf-rents, &c. &c. and for profits	69,700	
		$240,000

231 Analysis of coastwise trade, Baltimore and Philadelphia, showing early use of steamboats, from *Niles' Register*, June 26, 1819

COASTWISE STEAMER OF THE 'FORTIES

By 1840 the railroad had become an assured fact. In the West steam river boats hastened commerce and travel; but communication between the Gulf or the South Atlantic coast on the one hand and the North Atlantic on the other was confined to the vagaries of sail-ships by sea and stagecoaches by land. One went from New Orleans to Mobile by steamer via Lake Pontchartrain, from Mobile to Augusta by stagecoach, from Augusta to Charleston (or Savannah) by steamer, from Charleston (or Savannah) to Norfolk by stagecoach, from Norfolk to Baltimore by sail packet or steamer, from Baltimore to Wilmington, Delaware (or Philadelphia), by stagecoach, from Wilmington (or Philadelphia) to Trenton by river steamers, from Trenton to New Brunswick (or Perth Amboy) by stagecoach, and from New Brunswick (or Perth Amboy) to New York by steam ferry. Parts of these journeys could be taken by railroad (see No. 232).

The alternative was a river steamer to Pittsburgh, thence by stage to Philadelphia, where the two routes joined. Both routes were slow and expensive. Freight went between New Orleans and New York by sail-vessel for the entire distance. The rates were relatively cheap, but no one ever knew when a consignment of goods would arrive at port, for storms, calms and fogs interrupted the service. So men began to question anew the feasibility of steam coastwise service.

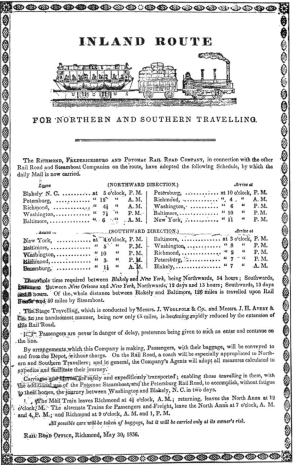

INLAND ROUTE

FOR NORTHERN AND SOUTHERN TRAVELLING.

The Richmond, Fredericksburg and Potomac Rail Road Company, in connection with the other Rail Road and Steamboat Companies on the route, have adopted the following Schedule, by which the daily Mail is now carried.

Leave				Arrive at			
(NORTHWARD DIRECTION.)							
Blakely, N. C.	at 5 o'clock, P. M.			Petersburg,	at 10 o'clock, P. M.		
Petersburg,	" 12 " A. M.			Richmond,	" 4 " A. M.		
Richmond,	" 4½ " A. M.			Washington,	" 6 " P. M.		
Washington,	" 7½ " P. M.			Baltimore,	" 10 " P. M.		
Baltimore,	" 6 " A. M.			New York,	" 11 " P. M.		
(SOUTHWARD DIRECTION.)						Arrive at	
New York,	at 4 o'clock, P. M.			Baltimore,	at 3 o'clock, P. M.		
Baltimore,	" 5 " P. M.			Washington,	" 8 " P. M.		
Washington,	" 10 " P. M.			Richmond,	" 2 " P. M.		
Richmond,	" 3 " P. M.			Petersburg,	" 7 " P. M.		
Petersburg,	" 11 " A. M.			Blakely,	" 7 " A. M.		

The whole time required between Blakely and New York, being Northwards, 54 hours; Southwards, — hours. Between New Orleans and New York, Northwards, 12 days and 13 hours; Southwards, 13 days and 8 hours. Of the whole distance between Blakely and Baltimore, 126 miles is travelled upon Rail Road, and 50 miles by Steamboat.

The Stage Travelling, which is conducted by Messrs. J. Woolfolk & Co. and Messrs. J. H. Avery & Co. in the handsomest manner, being now only 6¾ miles, is becoming rapidly reduced by the extension of this Rail Road.

☞ Passengers are never in danger of delay, preference being given to such as enter and continue on the line.

By arrangements which this Company is making, Passengers, with their baggage, will be conveyed to and from the Depot, without charge. On the Rail Road, a coach will be especially appropriated to Northern and Southern Travellers; and in general, the Company's Agents will adopt all measures calculated to expedite and facilitate their journey.

Carriages and Horses are safely and expeditiously transported; enabling those travelling in them, with the additional use of the Potomac Steamboat, and the Petersburg Rail Road, to accomplish, without fatigue to their horses, the journey between Washington and Blakely, N. C. in two days.

The Mail Train leaves Richmond at 4½ o'clock, A. M.; returning, leaves the North Anna at 12 o'clock, M. The alternate Trains for Passengers and Freight, leave the North Anna at 7 o'clock, A. M. and 4, P. M., and Richmond at 9 o'clock, A. M. and 1, P. M.

All possible care will be taken of baggage, but it will be carried only at its owner's risk.

Rail Road Office, Richmond, May 30, 1836.

232 Broadside advertising inland railroad and steamer connections, 1836, in the South, from the original in the Library of Congress

MAIL–CARRYING STEAMERS

As early as 1840 there had been manifested on the part of various of the growing ports along the Atlantic seaboard a desire for improvement in coastwise service. When this became acute it was met by lucrative mail-carrying contracts, authorized by Congress in 1845 and 1847. This resulted in the inauguration of a steam coastwise line between New York and Charleston in 1846, with the steamship *Southerner*, followed by the steamship *Northerner*. By this time ship designers and builders had learned how to construct a steam-propelled vessel that was stanch and seaworthy; marine-engine design had also improved during the last two decades. With the success of the steam-line to Charleston, other lines were started between New York and Savannah, New Orleans, Norfolk, and Havana.

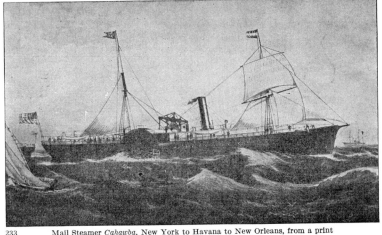

233 Mail Steamer *Cahawba*, New York to Havana to New Orleans, from a print in the New York Historical Society

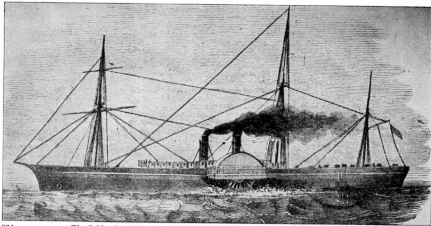

234 *The Golden Gate,* from the *Illustrated American News,* New York, July 26, 1851

FIRST PACIFIC MAIL STEAMERS

THE most spectacular coastwise project was a triple service, the United States Mail Steamship Co., running between New York and Panama by way of Atlantic ports, a water-and-land journey across the Isthmus of Panama, and steamer service from Panama to San Francisco by the Pacific Mail Steamship Co. If it had not been for the mail subsidy and the gold rush of 1849 the Pacific Mail Steamship Co. could hardly have survived its high costs. Despite these various steam coastwise ventures, the coastwise trade for the most part remained with the sail vessel until after the Civil War. Packets and clippers were a match for any steamer then built, and their service was familiar and not easily supplanted.

235 Steamship *Savannah,* from a print in the Bostonian Society, Boston

THE *SAVANNAH* CROSSES THE ATLANTIC

IN 1819 was launched a small vessel, the *Savannah,* which had been laid down as a sailing vessel but in the course of the work had been fitted with steam boiler and engine. Her total cost was fifty thousand dollars. After several trial voyages the *Savannah,* on May 24, 1819, started across the Atlantic, the first vessel in the world to brave the open ocean with steam. She used her sails however for five hundred and sixty-eight hours out of a total of six hundred and forty-eight hours. This nevertheless does not dim the *Savannah's* prestige, for she was the first vessel to use steam power at all in deep waters. She was pursued for a whole day off the coast of Ireland by the British revenue cruiser *Kite,* whose captain thought her afire.

THE *SAVANNAH* BECOMES A SAILING PACKET

FROM Liverpool, the *Savannah* went to St. Petersburg (Leningrad), using her engine for ten out of thirty-three days. After cruising about the Baltic for cargo, she returned to the port whose name she bore after a rough and dangerous passage. She then made a coastwise journey to New York, stopping at Washington. At New York the *Savannah's* machinery was removed and she was converted into a sailing

236   Log of the *Savannah*, from the original in the United States National Museum, Washington

packet as originally designed. The *Savannah's* failure as a steamship was not mechanical but commercial. She was a small boat and her machinery, together with the space required to store her wood fuel, cut her cargo capacity below the point required to pay expenses. The *Savannah's* life under sail was equally brief; on November 15, 1821, while on a coastwise run, she was driven ashore by a violent storm and wrecked beyond reclamation. America had thrilled the world with the first transatlantic steamship, the *Savannah*. But it was not until the late 'forties that another ship under the American flag used steam to cross the Atlantic. Up to the Civil War, our sailing packets and then our clippers recognized no superiors in the world's commercial fleets. Marine engines and other machinery were still crude and costly. Americans saw no reason why they should run risks in disturbing a situation already entirely satisfactory.

BRITISH COMPETITION ON THE ATLANTIC

WITH the British circumstances were different. From the first their experiments with steam, supported by the Government, had been on salt water, not on rivers as in America. They were anxious to recover superiority on the high seas. On April 23, 1838, there arrived in New York not one but two British steamships, the *Sirius* out of Portsmouth, and the *Great Western* cleared from Bristol. The performance of these two vessels was so convincing that it was at once recognized that a new epoch in Atlantic navigation had begun. The

237   Steamship *Britannia*, from a water color in possession of the Cunard Steamship Company, Ltd., New York

Sirius and *Great Western* showed the British the way to recapture the Atlantic traffic lost to American sail. The British Government, which had itself operated Channel steamers, offered a lucrative mail contract, in effect a subsidy, to a line of steamers that should run between Britain and America by way of Halifax. In 1840, the Cunard Company secured this contract and, on July 4, sent the *Britannia* from Liverpool to Boston by way of Halifax. With the backing of the British Government the service has remained unbroken to the present.

238   Steamship *Washington*, from a lithograph by N. Currier in the New York Historical Society

THE OCEAN STEAM NAVIGATION CO.

FOR seven years Americans, confident in their supremacy in sail, watched the Cunard steam vessels with apathetic eyes. But when the Cunarders began regularly to beat the sail packets across the ocean, and so took the cream of the passenger and express freight traffic, the Americans awoke to their danger. Congress took a hint from Parliament and awarded subsidies in the form of mail contracts. In 1847, a mail contract of two hundred thousand dollars a year was awarded to the Ocean Steam Navigation Co., an American steamship line proposing to operate between New York and Bremen. With the contract secured, this company, on June 1, 1847, put the *Washington* into service; the *Herman* was added on March 2, 1848. But the hopes of the Americans were dashed, for the Cunarders regularly beat these two boats by from two to four days time in crossing the Atlantic.

239   United States Mail Steamer *Adriatic*, from *The Illustrated London News*, December 19, 1857

THE COLLINS LINE

IN 1847 a mail contract was awarded to the New York and Liverpool United States Mail Steamship Co., popularly called the "Collins Line," after the name of its principal promoter. The Collins put into service first the *Atlantic*, then the *Pacific*, *Arctic* and *Baltic*. These vessels, the last word in luxurious passenger accommodations, were fitted with the best mechanical equipment, and cost nearly three million dollars each. The Collins Line accomplished its purpose: its boats were more attractive to passengers than the Cunarders, and they beat the time of the Cunarders across the Atlantic regularly by from seven to eighteen hours. During the first years of operation, the ships averaged only eighty-six passengers per voyage; but as their fame spread their passenger list rapidly increased. The Collins records, however, were obtained only by excessive costs of operation. The strain in making every voyage a race against time regardless of wind or wave told upon the boats, and occasioned terrific expense for repairs. Although Congress in 1852 raised the mail contract from three hundred and eighty-five thousand dollars to eight hundred and fifty-eight thousand dollars a year, the Collins Line never made money for its backers. It beat the British, it attracted the best passenger and freight trade, and it was the most famous steamship line of its day, but it was a financial failure.

240   The Collins Fleet, from *Gleason's Pictorial*, March 4, 1854

241   Edward K. Collins, from the portrait by Thomas W. Wood in the Chamber of Commerce, New York

THE FAILURE OF THE COLLINS LINE

THE misfortunes of the Collins Line began in 1851 when the *Atlantic* broke her shaft nine days out from Liverpool and had to proceed to port under sail. This accident was costly in money and reputation, but was not irreparable. In 1854, the *Arctic*, speeding through a fog and bound for New York, collided with another boat near Cape Race and was a total loss, carrying down Collins' wife and two children. To take her place the Collins Line began building another vessel called at first the *Antarctic* but afterward the *Adriatic*. In 1856, the *Pacific* sailed from Liverpool and was never heard from. There were two hundred and eighty-eight persons aboard. In addition to these disasters, the Collins Line mail subsidy aroused sectional animosity, and in 1857 Congress reduced the Collins subsidy from eight hundred and fifty-eight thousand dollars a year to three hundred and forty-six thousand dollars. Complete failure was now inevitable. In January, 1858, the *Baltic* made her last voyage as a Collins ship. In the Civil War she was chartered by the United States and, in 1870, sold to Bostonians who converted her into a sail ship which was wrecked in 1880. The *Adriatic* made one voyage in 1858 for the Collins Line and was then sold to the British Lever Line, operating between New York and Galway. Thus passed the Collins Line. The British Government continued to back the Cunard Company which, with the demise of the Collins Line, resumed its rule of the waves.

VANDERBILT ENTERS THE TRANSATLANTIC FIELD

THE Ocean Steam Navigation Company and the Collins Line were not the sole American essays in the Atlantic steamship business. In 1848, the Black Ball Line, famous for its sail packets and clippers, put on one steamship, the *United States*, running between New York and Liverpool. After one year this vessel was sold to Prussia. In 1849, the Livingston Line — New York and Havre Steam Navigation Company — received a government mail contract for one hundred and fifty thousand dollars a year. In 1850, it put the *Franklin* on the ocean route. This boat was lost in 1854 and replaced by the *Arago*. In 1851, the *Franklin* was given a companion in the *Humboldt*. This ship foundered in 1853 and was replaced in 1855 by the *Fulton*. The Livingston Line never made the record runs of the Collins Line and got very little public recognition. The *Arago* and the *Fulton* were chartered by the government for war service in 1861.

Commodore Vanderbilt tried to break into the transatlantic field both with and without government mail subsidies. At various times he entered the steamships *Vanderbilt*, *Illinois*, *North Star*, *Ariel*, and *Ocean Queen* in the Atlantic service, but none of them made many trips. Not even Vanderbilt could make this kind of ship business a commercial success. At the time of the Civil War, therefore, Americans were not serious contenders for honors and business in overseas steam shipping. What salt-water steam-borne commerce we possessed was limited to the coastwise trade and the Pacific coast business.

242   Cornelius Vanderbilt, 1794–1877, from an engraved portrait in J. C. Buttre, *American Portrait Gallery*, New York, 1877

CHAPTER V

THE RAILROAD AGE

THE United States in the days of Presidents Washington, John Adams and Jefferson was in the stagecoach and turnpike phase of the evolution of transportation. The craze for canal building which manifested itself after the completion of the Erie Canal was contemporaneous with Andrew Jackson's overshadowing influence in national life. The era of the dependable transatlantic packet ships, of the great clippers, of the fleets of steamboats tied up to the wharves of the river ports of the Ohio and the Mississippi, and of the experimental American steamship lines, was a time of swift national expansion in the 'forties and of the equally swift development of sectional antagonisms in the 'fifties.

Experiments with railroads went on side by side with the building of canals. But the former were still at the beginning of their development when the "canal era" was in full swing. In the times of Jackson the relative merits of railroads and canals was a familiar question for debate with the victory usually going to the advocates of the waterways. The canal epoch came thus early because its mechanical and engineering problems were relatively simple. The use of boats had long been familiar to Americans and the canal required merely the development of a craft of light draft that would always be used on water that was perfectly calm. The digging of the "big ditch" itself was largely a matter of workmen and the engineering problems of carrying the canal across streams or of lifting it up a grade by locks were not difficult. At a time when the industrial development of the American people was just beginning men naturally preferred the canal, which they could understand, to the railroad, the possibilities of which they were quite unable to foresee.

The railroad presented an almost infinite number of technical problems that must be solved before it could become in any large sense a commercial success. Fundamental was the development of the locomotive, an extremely complicated piece of machinery. Nearly a century elapsed before the engine was brought to perfection. But the locomotive was only a part of a complex whole. The problem of roadbed and rails was almost equally vital; there are few who ever pause to consider the vast amount of study and experimentation that lies behind the steel rail that carries the modern train on its endless journeys. In addition there have been questions of the form of cars, of brakes and couplings, and in some respects most complicated of all, of problems of organization and control. The modern railroad is one of the greatest triumphs of the human mind and will. It was not the work of a decade or even of a generation. The canals and the Mississippi River steamboat traffic were products of the first half of the century; the railroad required nearly the whole of the nineteenth and part of the twentieth centuries to bring it to the peak of its development.

EARLY GRANITE TRAMWAYS

THE application of the railway does not begin with the introduction of the locomotive: both in Europe and America there were railways before there were movable steam engines. Benjamin Outram built the first horse-railway in the suburbs of London in 1801. The first tramway in America, built in 1826, extended from the granite quarries of Quincy, Massachusetts, to the Neponset River, a distance of three miles: it was used to get out the stone for the Bunker Hill monument. At its steepest portion this tramway was operated by a stationary steam engine; over the rest of the line horses pulled the cars. In 1827, a similar tramway was operated by the Delaware & Hudson Canal Company between Honesdale and the Company's coal mines at Carbondale, a distance of some sixteen miles

243   First car used on the Quincy Railway, from a replica, based on contemporary description, courtesy of the Granite Railway Co., Quincy, Mass.

earlier than the Quincy tramway. About 1795, there was a short one on Beacon Hill, Boston, used to lower bricks from a kiln to the highway; and another was constructed at the Thomas Leiper stone quarry in Delaware County, Pennsylvania, in 1809. In 1811, at Falling Creek, Virginia, a railed inclined plane about a mile long was employed to lower powder-mill products to a magazine. Gravity supplied the power for the loaded cars which were hauled back by a rope around a huge drum attached to a water wheel.

244   Bronze tablet, 1921, commemorating the original horse-drawn railway in America, courtesy of the Granite Railway Co., Quincy, Mass.

OTHER RAILWAYS PRIOR TO THE LOCOMOTIVE

AT first the tramways were considered an improved variety of turnpike providing a smooth path over which one horse could haul some fifteen times the ordinary load.

245   Baltimore & Ohio Passenger Car, 1830, reconstruction by Heinmiller, courtesy of the Baltimore & Ohio Railroad Co.

The tramway company, like the turnpike company, was to furnish the highway, upon which any one who desired could drive his own wheeled vehicles with his own animals, paying toll for the use of the track. That this scheme would lead to the utmost confusion was perceived even before the locomotive rendered it imperative that one company should control both track and rolling stock. But the idea that the railway was a public highway died hard. As late as the 'nineties, the Long Island Railroad furnished special trains on particular days to bring loaded farm wagons, horses and farmers into the Brooklyn city markets, the loaded wagons going on specialized flat cars, the horses in box cars and the farmers in a coach. In other words, the railroad transported the farmer's vehicle and its motive-power instead of freighting the farmer's produce. Such confusion as to the function of a railroad after sixty years of use is significant of the perplexity of the first Americans who were confronted with the problem of the proper organization of tramway service.

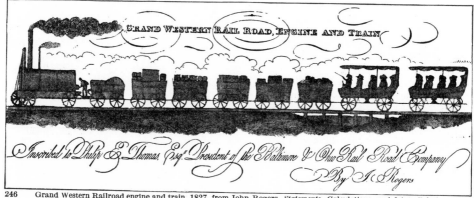

246   Grand Western Railroad engine and train, 1827, from John Rogers, *Statements, Calculations, and Hints Relative to Railroad Building*, Baltimore, 1827, dedicated to the president of the Baltimore & Ohio Railroad

PIONEER BRITISH EXPERIMENTS

WITH the tramway in successful operation, it needed only the invention of a locomotive to usher in the era of railroads. For fifty years after Watt gave the world his steam engine in 1773, other inventors toyed with the idea of making a steam engine move itself. Among Americans who experimented with steam road wagons or steam locomotives were Oliver Evans, Benjamin Dearborn, and John Stevens. Many British inventors, including Richard Trevithick, also experimented with the problem. The weakness in all their machines was that they could not produce steam as rapidly as they used it, nor did their engines have enough power to move quickly or to pull more than their own weight.

247   Road trial of Richard Trevithick's steam locomotive, 1801, from Edith K. Harper, *A Cornish Giant*, London, 1913

THE SUCCESS OF THE *ROCKET*

IN 1829, the progress of British invention justified a competitive trial held by the Liverpool and Manchester Railway. At this test the *Rocket*, an engine invented by George and Robert Stephenson, father and son, was the victor. The *Rocket* combined two features which enabled it to eliminate the faults of its predecessors and competitors; it had a tubular boiler and a forced draft. Stephenson's boiler exposed the maximum of heating surface to the burning fuel, and the forced draft, occasioned by turning the exhaust steam from the cylinders into the stack fanned a fire fierce enough to produce steam faster than it was used. Thus, although Stephenson alone is not to be credited with the invention of the locomotive, he was responsible for setting forth a practicable combination of known principles by which for the first time the machine desired by other inventors was obtained. Consequently his fame is deserved. George Stephenson did not suffer in a material way after his invention proved its worth. He became a manufacturer of locomotives and a consultant in building railroads.

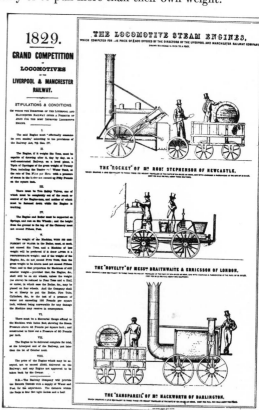

248   Three British engines, 1829; from a contemporary lithograph, courtesy of the South Kensington Museum, London

GEORGE STEPHENSON, 1781–1848

GEORGE STEPHENSON, born near Newcastle, England, on June 9, 1781, was the son of a fireman of a stationary engine in a coal mine. At the age when most boys are just beginning to go to school, young Stephenson went to work, first on a farm and then with his father. By the time he was fourteen, he had become his father's assistant. Unable, through lack of education, to satisfy his curiosity concerning his fascinating engine, he learned to read and attended night school to acquire the rudiments of mechanics; he also learned the trade of watchmaker. Stephenson's opportunity came in 1813 when he was commissioned by the Kellingworth Colliery to build an engine to move a loaded coal-tram from the colliery to a shipping port nine miles distant. As a result of his success with this, he was able to get the promoters of the Stockton and Darlington Railway, who had planned to use horses for motive power, to make trial of a Stephenson locomotive. Thus came into being the first steam railroad in the world. With the winning of the Liverpool and Manchester Railway prize of £500, Stephenson became, and for the rest of his life remained, the most successful locomotive builder in Great Britain and all Europe.

249 From *Historical Portraits*, 1919, after the original portrait by Henry W. Pickersgill in the National Portrait Gallery London, courtesy of Oxford University Press, New York

THE *STOURBRIDGE LION* IN AMERICA, 1829

ENGLISH engines came to America through the action of the proprietors of the Carbondale Railroad, the coal tramway of the Delaware & Hudson Canal Company. Through their civil engineer, Horatio Allen, whom they sent to England, they ordered three locomotives, one with riveted flues of large size from Foster, Rastrick & Company of Stourbridge, and two with tubular boilers from Stephenson & Company of Newcastle-on-Tyne. The *Stourbridge Lion* was operated at Honesdale by Horatio Allen on August 9, 1829. The locomotive proved so heavy (eight tons) that it was pronounced unsafe on the frail bridges and trestles of the Carbondale Railroad and was discarded. This trial, however, was the first time a practicable locomotive ran upon a permanent railroad track in America, and Allen, though it was the only time he ever ran an engine, has the distinction of being the first American locomotive engineer. The Stourbridge engine received its name

250   From a replica of the original *Stourbridge Lion*, in the United States National Museum, Washington

from a painting of a lion's head on the front of the engine's boiler. The *Lion*, stored in a shed by the Carbondale Railroad, was picked to pieces by souvenir hunters, and what was too heavy to carry away was eventually sold by the railroad for old iron. Later the historical value of this engine caused a search for its parts, some being recovered. The two engines built by Stephenson & Company arrived somewhat later. They were stored in an iron warehouse in New York city, exhibited occasionally but never used. These engines were similar to the Stephenson *Rocket*, and if they had been given a trial at once they would have had the historical place now assigned to the *Rocket* itself, for the latter did not make its famous trip until October 14, 1829.

251   Horse treadmill car on the Baltimore & Ohio, from William H. Brown, *The History of the First Locomotives in America*, New York, 1874

252   Sailcar on the Baltimore & Ohio, from William H. Brown, *The History of the First Locomotives in America*, New York, 1874

THE BALTIMORE & OHIO RAILROAD

THE first railroad constructed in America with the definite aim of carrying passengers and freight was the Baltimore & Ohio. It was chartered in 1827, and the laying of the rails began on July 4, 1828, Charles Carroll, the only living signer of the Declaration of Independence, lifting the first shovelful of earth. The first section of thirteen miles, from Baltimore to Ellicott's Mills, was opened in May, 1830. The promoters experimented with various sorts of power. One was a flat car fitted with a treadmill operated by a horse. Upon its trial trip this contrivance was upset by a stray cow on the tracks and the device was condemned. Another experiment, also unsuccessful, was made with a sailcar, the *Meteor*, a sailboat on wheels.

253   Peter Cooper, 1791–1883, from an engraved portrait by George E. Perine, New York, in possession of the publishers

254   Peter Cooper's *Tom Thumb*, a reconstruction, courtesy of the Baltimore & Ohio Railroad

PETER COOPER'S *TOM THUMB*

PETER COOPER was the next inventor to offer ideas to the Baltimore & Ohio Railroad; he was influenced in part by the fact that he owned some land whose value would be enhanced if this railroad proved a success. Cooper built a tiny steam locomotive with a boiler about the size of those that now stand by the kitchen stove and with flues constructed of gun barrels. Other parts were proportionately small and crude. This engine was called the *Tom Thumb*. With it Cooper made a few trial runs upon the partially finished railroad in 1830.

255   Trial of speed between *Tom Thumb* and a horse car, from William H. Brown, *The History of the First Locomotives in America,*
New York, 1874

THE *TOM THUMB* RACES A HORSE

WITH the data secured from his small model, Cooper reconstructed the *Tom Thumb* and operated it again on August 28, 1830, over the full thirteen miles of the road, attaining a speed of four miles an hour, pushing a car with twenty-four passengers. A few days later there was a challenge race between the *Tom Thumb* and a horse-drawn car over the double track from Ellicott's Mills to Baltimore. The gray horse led at the start but the locomotive caught up with it and passed it; then a belt slipped and the horse reached Baltimore first. During the following year, horses served as the motive power on the Baltimore & Ohio.

256   The locomotive *York*, 1831, reconstruction, courtesy
of the Baltimore & Ohio Railroad

257   Baltimore & Ohio locomotive, 1837, reconstruction,
courtesy of the Baltimore & Ohio Railroad

THE *YORK*

DESPITE the victory of the gray horse over the *Tom Thumb*, the Baltimore & Ohio officials retained a bias in favor of steam locomotives. Accordingly, on January 4, 1831, they offered in an advertisement a prize of $4,000 for the most approved engine which should be delivered to the road for trial on or before the first of June, 1831. For the second-best engine there was a prize of $3,500. The requirements were that the engine should not weigh more than three and a half tons, that it should be capable of a speed of fifteen miles an hour, and able to draw upon the level a load of fifteen tons. In response to this offer three locomotives were submitted in competition, but only one fulfilled the requirements. The prize winner was designed by a watchmaker named Phineas Davis, a member of the firm of Davis and Gartner of York, Pennsylvania. The Davis locomotive was named by its maker the *York*, but the Baltimore & Ohio Railroad men named the type "the grasshopper." Davis built several more locomotives for the Baltimore & Ohio after the plan of a modified *York*, and as late as 1889 three of these early "grasshoppers" were still in service. Among the engines built by Phineas Davis for the Baltimore & Ohio was the *Traveler*. This locomotive, similar to the *York*, had the distinction of being the first designed for freight service. It remained in service until 1893.

258   The locomotive *Atlantic*, 1832, reconstruction, courtesy
of the Baltimore & Ohio Railroad

259   The *Best Friend*, from William H. Brown, *The History of the First Locomotives in America*, New York, 1874

THE CHARLESTON & HAMBURG RAILROAD

FOLLOWING closely upon the construction of the Baltimore & Ohio Railroad came the Charleston & Hamburg, chartered by South Carolina in 1829. This road was planned from its inception for the use of steampower, and horse-drawn cars were never used in its regular traffic. However, the horse treadmill and sailing locomotive were given trials on this road just as they were on the Baltimore & Ohio. Horatio Allen, civil engineer in charge of construction, advised from the first the adoption of steam locomotives, for, said he,

260 The *Flying Dutchman*, from William H. Brown, *The History of the First Locomotives in America*, New York, 1874

"There is no reason to expect any material improvement in the breed of horses, while, in my judgment, the man is not living who knows what the breed of locomotives will place at command." The Charleston & Hamburg, rather than the Baltimore & Ohio, therefore, has the honor of being the first railroad in America constructed for steam. In March, 1830, the Charleston & Hamburg contracted with the West Point Foundry of New York city for a steam locomotive capable of a speed of ten miles an hour. This locomotive was called at first *The Best Friend of Charleston* and was generally spoken of as *The Best Friend*. It was shipped to Charleston by ocean-sailing packet and arrived late in the fall of 1830. At the trial in November it ran off the track, but after re-railing and changing certain parts the engine developed a speed of thirty miles an hour without load, and twenty-one miles an hour pulling four loaded passenger cars. *The Best Friend* was put into service in January, 1831. Its fireman in June, 1831, was a negro who did not like the sound of steam escaping from the safety valve; so he sat on the valve, with the result that the boiler blew up and the fireman's thigh was broken. This was the first locomotive accident in America.

261   From a contemporary lithograph in the United States National Museum, Washington, D. C.

THE LOCOMOTIVE *WEST POINT*

SOUTH CAROLINA RAILROAD had ordered another locomotive in 1830, which was delivered in February, 1831, but was not satisfactory at first and did not go into regular service until July 15, 1831. It was called the *West Point*, the second American locomotive built for practical work. To calm the passengers' fears of another explosion the executives placed between the locomotive and the passenger cars a car piled with cotton bales.

262   From the painting *The First Railroad Train in New York*, by E. L. Henry, original, 1894, in the Albany (N. Y.) Institute and Historical and Art Society. © G. C. Klackner

THE LOCOMOTIVE *DE WITT CLINTON*

UNDER a charter granted by the New York Legislature in 1826, the Mohawk & Hudson Railroad Company built in 1831 its original line from Albany to Schenectady, a distance of about seventeen miles, the primary

263   The original *De Witt Clinton* engine and coaches, reproduction from a pageant, courtesy of the New York Central Railroad. © Janet M. Cumings

link in the present New York Central system. The road was at first operated with horse-drawn cars, but the success of the southern railroads with locomotives led to the ordering, from the West Point Foundry in April, 1831, of a locomotive to which was given the name *De Witt Clinton*. The first public trial of the engine pulling a train of cars was on August 9, 1831. The engine employed wood fuel and the passengers were showered with sparks from the stack, so that some had their clothing burned in spots while others put up umbrellas to ward off the fiery rain. The cars were coupled with heavy chains about three feet long, and, when they started and stopped, the venturers were jerked off their seats as the chain-slack was taken up or the cars crashed together. The passengers themselves cut fence rails and wedged them between the cars to reduce the hazards of the journey.

THE MEETING OF THE WAYS, OR THE FIRST RAILROAD TRAIN

SPECTATORS thronged the right of way to catch a glimpse of the mechanical marvel that was to surpass the horse and that animal began a long and painful contact with human inventions that traveled at an astonishing rate and emitted terrifying noises. The spirited horse did not become adjusted to the age of machines until the high-powered motor car had practically driven him from the highway. Stanley M. Arthurs has caught the feeling of one of the most significant moments in American history. The era of the stagecoach ends as the little locomotive rattles along the rails. The leisurely and easy-going times of the eighteenth and early nineteenth centuries are forever past now that the little locomotives have in turn given place to the constantly accelerating speed and comfort of the modern express, of the automobile, and of the airplane.

264   From the painting *The Meeting of the Ways*, by Stanley M. Arthurs (1872–), in the possession of George C. Hetzel, Ridley Park, Pa.

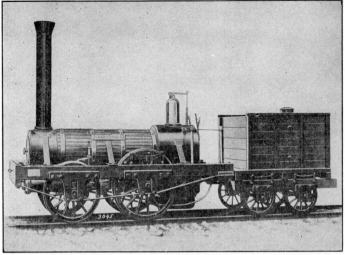

265   The locomotive *Old Ironsides*, courtesy of The Baldwin Locomotive Works, Philadelphia

THE LOCOMOTIVE
JOHN BULL, 1831

THE *John Bull*, the first locomotive used on the Camden & Amboy Railroad, was built in England and shipped "knocked down" to America. The parts were finally assembled by a youngster named Isaac Dripps. Before the *John Bull* was assembled, Matthias Baldwin saw it and was influenced by it in constructing *Old Ironsides*, the first locomotive on the Philadelphia, Germantown & Norristown Railroad, and also the first product of the Baldwin Locomotive Works of Philadelphia.

JOHN BULL ENGINE AND TRAIN, WITH COWCATCHER, 1831

THE invention of the cowcatcher is credited to Isaac Dripps of the Camden & Amboy Railroad. British railroads operated in thickly settled regions with rigid trespass laws, but American lines frequently ran through open country over an unfenced right of way where existing trespass laws were enforced loosely. Some device to sweep wandering animals out of the way of locomotive wheels therefore became imperative. Dripps built a low truck attached to the front of the locomotive. The cowcatcher was at first provided with long pointed wrought-iron bars projecting a few inches above the tracks, but these actually impaled recalcitrant beasts who disputed the right of way with the locomotive. A heavy bar like an automobile bumper was then attached to the prongs at right angles to the track. Modified and developed from these primitive beginnings the cowcatcher became an integral part of the American locomotive, persisting through the years, and giving it a distinctive appearance.

PHILADELPHIA. GERMANTOWN, AND NORRISTOWN RAIL-ROAD. LOCOMOTIVE ENGINE.

NOTICE.—The Locomotive Engine, (built by M. W. Baldwin, of this city,) will depart DAILY, when the weather is fair, with a TRAIN OF PASSENGER CARS, commencing on Monday the 26th inst., at the following hours, viz:—

FROM PHILADELPHIA.	FROM GERMANTOWN.
At 11 o'clock, A. M.	At 12 o'clock. M.
" 1 o'clock, H. M.	" 2 o'clock, P. M.
" 3 o'clock, P. M.	" 4 o'clock, P. M.

The Cars drawn by horses, will also depart as usual, from Philadelphia at 9 o'clock, A. M., and from Germantown at 10 o'clock, A. M., and at the above mentioned hours when the weather is not fair. The points of starting, are from the Depot, at the corner of Green and Ninth street, Philadelphia; and from the Main street, near the centre of Germantown. Whole Cars can be taken. Tickets, 25 cents.   nov 24-3t

266   An early announcement of the Philadelphia, Germantown & Norristown Railroad, from the original in possession of The Baldwin Locomotive Works, Philadelphia

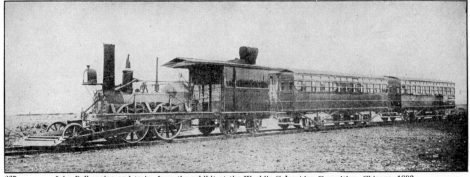

267   *John Bull* engine and train, from the exhibit at the World's Columbian Exposition, Chicago, 1893.
© Rau Bros., Inc.

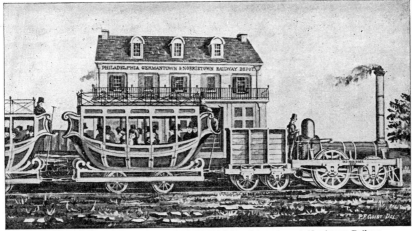

268   First Railway Train in Pennsylvania, 1832, Philadelphia, Germantown & Norristown Railway,
by P. F. Goist, courtesy of the Historical Society of Pennsylvania

NEW RAILROAD PROJECTS

THE Baltimore & Ohio, the Charleston & Hamburg, and the Mohawk & Hudson were the leaders in experimental railroad construction. The practicability of the new form of transportation needed no further proof to encourage a number of other railroad projects, and as soon as the smallest link was ready for traffic it was opened to the public. Thus by 1835 people and goods were moving by rail over the completed portions of the New York & Harlem Railroad in New York, the Camden & Amboy Railroad in New Jersey, the Philadelphia, Germantown & Norristown Railway, the Columbia Railroad, the Philadelphia, Wilmington & Baltimore Railroad and the Reading Railroad in Pennsylvania. In New England by that time three railroads radiated from Boston, one north to Lowell, one west to Worcester and one south to Providence. In the same year the original railroad, the Baltimore & Ohio with about seventy miles of track, carried nearly one hundred thousand passengers. By 1835 the steam railroad was an accepted fact in the United States.

EARLY OPPOSITION TO RAILROADS

IN its infancy the railroad, being a new transportation enterprise, had to combat the opposition of investors in competitive businesses as well as the prejudices of the people inimical to novelties. Owners of turnpikes and canals, both private and public, vigorously belittled and actively thwarted the ambitions of railroad promoters. Tavernkeepers and their retainers, bound to the interests of turnpikes, canals, and highways, dreaded the popularity of railroads and used all their influence to prevent the spread of the new system of travel. Draymen in towns and freighters over land, two-fisted fighting breeds, hampered and limited in every way in their power the development of railroad endeavors. Farmers — of all people in the United States now perhaps the most vitally interested in railroads — gloomily visioned the doom of highways or canals and consequently the elimination of important markets for farm stuff, ruminated upon this obvious immediate effect of the railroads upon existing farm business, and unresponsive to or unaware of the enlarged opportunities offered by them, blocked railroad charters and protested railroad building. Other people less personally involved in the new ventures yet were prejudiced against them. A few said it was sinful to travel at the frightful speed of fifteen miles an hour since the Lord's intentions were manifest when he provided men and animals with legs but made them incapable of sustained speed. Some were afraid to ride on the cars and some were made ill by the unaccustomed motion. Others claimed that railroads were dangerous to users — of which they had plenty of evidence — and equally dangerous to innocent bystanders because the trains frightened animals. All this opposition was soon smothered in the public acclaim for the new transportation.

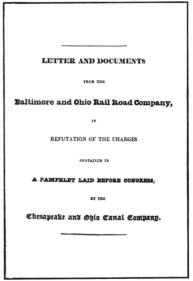

LETTER AND DOCUMENTS

FROM THE

Baltimore and Ohio Rail Road Company,

IN

REFUTATION OF THE CHARGES

CONTAINED IN

A PAMPHLET LAID BEFORE CONGRESS,

BY THE

Chesapeake and Ohio Canal Company.

269   Title-page of a pamphlet, illustrating the hostility of canal and railroad, in the New York Public Library

270 The locomotive *Experiment*, the first to employ the swivel truck, courtesy of the Baltimore & Ohio Railroad

THE BUILDING OF AN "AMERICAN TYPE" LOCOMOTIVE

STEPHENSON's success with the *Rocket* made his rigid, massive machine the standard in England, and his influence is apparent in British locomotives to this day. In America, there was no authoritative locomotive builder; and even the British engines, imported in 1830 and 1831, were soon cast aside. Our railway construction, our rails, curves, and hills, presented a different set of problems. The first problem in producing the "American type" locomotive was to build a machine that could swing around sharp curves. This was met by placing a separate truck under the forward part of the boiler, and attaching it to the frame by a king bolt in the center. This was first suggested by Horatio Allen, in a report dated May 16, 1831, to the Charleston & Hamburg Railroad, but the first practical use of it was made in the fall of 1831 by John B. Jervis, chief

271 John B. Jervis, 1795–1885, from an engraved portrait in Lillian C. Buttre, *American Portrait Gallery*, New York, 1877

engineer of the Mohawk & Hudson Railroad. Ross Winans of Baltimore adapted the idea to cars in 1834 and claimed prior invention of it for locomotives, thereby involving himself in lawsuits lasting for twenty years in which he was eventually defeated. The swivel truck was the first great American improvement in locomotives that enabled them to meet peculiar American railway conditions.

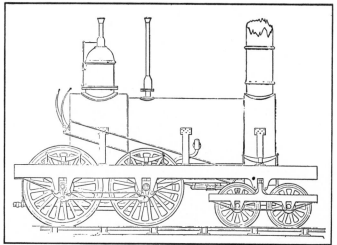

272 Henry R. Campbell's first design for an eight-wheeled locomotive, 1836, from a copy of the original drawing in Joseph Harrison Jr., *The Locomotive Engine*, Philadelphia, 1872

273 Ross Winans, from an engraved portrait in *Harper's Weekly*, 1861

"CAMPBELL" ENGINE

THE locomotive's grip on the rails must be greater than the resistance of the cars in the train; otherwise the admission of steam to the cylinders would simply spin the driving wheels of the locomotive and fail to start the cars. The British secured this grip of adhesion in the Stephenson engine by making the engine of considerable weight and so pressing the driving wheels hard against the track. Such British engines, however, proved too heavy for American tracks. The problem of getting the necessary grip on the rails without unduly increasing engine weight was solved in 1836 by Henry R. Campbell of Philadelphia, who used two pairs of driving wheels on each side of the locomotive, each pair connected by a rod. This arrangement of driving wheels was so speedily and widely adopted that together with the swivel truck it established the American type of locomotive.

THE AMERICAN TYPE

SINCE our original locomotives were either imported from Great Britain or influenced in their design by British experience they did not fit well into American environment. We could not afford heavy expenditures for rights of way or track; so our inventors were called upon to produce locomotives that would run safely on hastily constructed tracks full of sharp curves and relatively steep grades. The first step toward an "American type" locomotive was the general adoption of the service truck to carry the weight of the forward part of the boiler instead of

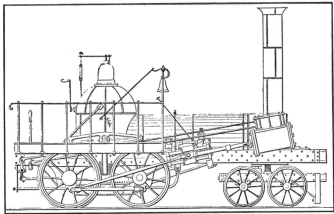

274   The *Hercules*, 1837, as arranged with Harrison equalizing levers, from Joseph Harrison, Jr., *The Locomotive Engine*, Philadelphia, 1872

two wheels whose axles were held rigidly by the frames. Horatio Allen in 1831 designed for the South Carolina Railway Company an engine called the *South Carolina* which had a four-wheeled truck attached to the forward part of the boiler by a king bolt or center pin around which the truck could swing to accommodate the wheels to curves. He recommended trucks for cars. In the same year John B. Jervis invented a swivel truck for use on a locomotive for the Mohawk & Hudson Railroad. Three years later Ross Winans of Baltimore patented the application of the principle Allen and Jervis had adopted for locomotives, to passenger and other cars.

The Allen and Jervis locomotives of 1831 used one pair of drive wheels which were rigidly attached to the frame. Henry R. Campbell of Philadelphia in 1836 patented the use of two pairs of driving wheels but these were also rigid. It remained for Joseph Harrison, Jr., of Philadelphia to bring forth his "equalizing beam" before the difficulties with drivers were solved. His engine, the *Hercules*, satisfied the operating condition that each drive wheel have a controlled vertical motion without varying greatly the pressure of the wheel upon the track. The effect of the equalizing beam or lever (now called equalizer) was to distribute the engine weight equally on all of the driving wheels with a tripod arrangement enabling the engine to adjust itself to any surface. The engine with four connected driving wheels and a four wheel truck became the American type.

THE HEADLIGHT

THE first American railroads ran only in the day time. But with the rapid growth of passenger traffic it became necessary to haul freight at night. On rare occasions in the early days, when passenger trains were run after dark, a pilot engine was sent ahead to feel out the way for the passenger locomotive engine. This soon became impracticable, and an effort was made to equip the engine with some sort of headlight. Horatio Allen on the Charleston & Hamburg Railroad piled a small flat car with sand and then built a bonfire of pine knots upon it. The engine pushed this bonfire ahead of itself, the flame being hidden from the engineer's eyes by the front of the boiler while the glare lighted the track ahead. Soon afterward a huge candle lantern was put on the front of the locomotives for night service. Later, about 1840, a reflector in the lantern intensified the feeble candle rays. After 1859, when petroleum was discovered, kerosene lamps replaced the candles. Gaslights supplied from storage tanks came next and finally electric headlights. The latter have been steadily improved until they resemble battleship searchlights in their intensity.

275   Early headlight, from an engraving after the painting *The Danger Signal*, by Jervis McEntee, in *Art and Artists*, 1876

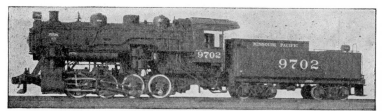

276   Modern switching locomotive, courtesy of the Baldwin Locomotive Works, Philadelphia

TYPES OF LOCOMOTIVES

SINCE the improvement of the flexible beam-truck by Matthias Baldwin in 1842, American locomotive design has been differentiated according to the work the engine had to do. A switch engine, moving great weights and consequently requiring a high degree of cohesion between its drive-wheels and the track, is so arranged that all or most of the weight rests upon the drives. Suburban passenger engines likewise require considerable weight on the drivers in order to get a quick start, and larger drivers (and hence larger boilers, etc.) to maintain high speed. Freight engines to pull heavy loads and surmount steep grades require power, obtainable only by great engine size, the weight of which must be distributed over several sets of drivers.

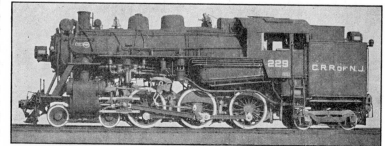

277   Modern suburban locomotive, courtesy of the Baldwin Locomotive Works, Philadelphia

278   Modern mountain freight locomotive, courtesy of the Baldwin Locomotive Works, Philadelphia

A THREE–IN–ONE LOCOMOTIVE

THE locomotive has shared in the improvements applicable to all steam engines. It was found in stationary engines that the expansive power of steam is not always exhausted by the work it does in one cylinder and may be run into two or more cylinders, pushing a piston in each, with a corresponding gain in power for a given amount of fuel. The "compound" principle is widely used in locomotives, in spite of the fact that it is complicated and costly to maintain. The steam superheater likewise first appeared in stationary engines but was eventually brought into service upon locomotives. This device receives the steam from the boiler and heats it to a higher temperature before admitting it to the cylinders. This process does not add to the expansive power of steam but it gives greater duration to the maximum expansive power since it takes longer to bring the steam down to the condensation point. The superheater upon a locomotive is a series of tubes in the smoke-box or in the forward section of the regular boiler-flues. In hauling extra-heavy traffic, two or more locomotives are hitched to one train. Since this is expensive in equipment and crew and not easy to control, two or more locomotives are now built into one machine. The locomotive built for the Virginian Railway is really three in one, for it has two cylinders under the boiler and one under the tender on each side.

279   The largest "iron horse" in the world, courtesy of the American Locomotive Co., New York

THE ELECTRIC LOCOMOTIVE

OF recent years the steam locomotive has had a competitor in the electric locomotive. As early as 1895, electric locomotives were used to pull trains of the Baltimore & Ohio through the tunnels of Baltimore. It was quickly recognized that the electric engine by eliminating gas, smoke and cinders, was indispensable for tunnel and subway service. It was next discovered that the electric engine is excellent in mountain service or wherever heavy

280   Baltimore & Ohio electric locomotive hauling the first train under electric power, 1893, courtesy of the General Electric Company, Schenectady, N. Y.

grades are encountered, since it can exert its maximum power continuously upgrade, whereas a steam locomotive loses power the longer it climbs. The electric also on downgrades by a slight change can convert its motor into a dynamo, and *make* electricity instead of *using* it; the force necessary for turning the dynamo acts as a brake on the downgrade. In winter weather upon these grades the electric locomotive performs better than the steam, for the latter in severe cold has difficulty in keeping up enough steam to pull its load, while an electric motor is little affected by temperature. The steam locomotive, like a horse, has to be fed whether it is working or not. Even in a roundhouse a locomotive burns a couple of hundred pounds of coal an hour, and, standing at stations, it consumes more than twice that amount. The electrics, on the contrary, are like automobiles; they burn nothing when standing still. Because of their cleanliness electric locomotives are favored for terminal service. If the terminal also serves a large suburban traffic, electric power has a further advantage in its divisibility. Separate motors can be put in each car and as many cars run as needed, thus varying the costs with the traffic. On the other hand, a steam engine costs about as much to operate whether it has ten cars behind it or one.

ELECTRIFICATION OF THE NEW YORK, NEW HAVEN & HARTFORD RAILROAD

FOR many reasons, however, electric locomotives have not entirely displaced steam. The cost of immediate and complete change is prohibitive; though a steam locomotive is frequently in the repair shop, its total life approximates that of a man, and such equipment is too valuable to be scrapped at once. Furthermore, the enormous cost of installing electric power comes all at once; it must be complete enough to carry the immediate peak-load and the probable peak-load of the near future. Unless all this equipment can be used constantly — as in terminals — the cost burden is excessive. Steam locomotive power can be increased gradually and can be varied with the traffic without excessive cost. The electric locomotive is not an independent unit; if serious trouble occurred at a power house *all* the electric locomotives on the section served by that house would go dead and the whole section would cease to function. But one steam locomotive might

281   From a photograph, courtesy of the New York, New Haven & Hartford Railroad

blow out a cylinder head, or cast a tire, lose a wheel or explode a boiler, while every other engine on the division would continue to operate, and the train to which the damaged engine was attached would soon proceed under another locomotive. This difficulty with electrification could be met by a super-power zoning system for the interchange of power. But the electric locomotive is not likely to displace steam as readily as the steam locomotive thrust horses off the railway lines. Since the greatest cost is that of installation, railroads usually favor government projects that furnish cheap electricity. Thus the New England railroads back the "St. Lawrence Waterway," in which the public pays for installation.

282   From a photograph, courtesy of the New York, New Haven & Hartford Railroad

THE GASOLINE–DRIVEN COACH, NEW YORK, NEW HAVEN & HARTFORD RAILROAD

THE rapid extension of automobile truck service has created a problem for branch lines of railroads where business was not heavy even when the railroad got it all. In 1924–25, the Boston & Maine petitioned the public regulatory bodies of Massachusetts, New Hampshire, Vermont, and Maine for permission to abandon more than one thousand miles of branch lines and let the motor truck provide the service. One solution is a change of power, abandoning the expensive steam locomotive and substituting electricity, either in single cars operated from a power station or a gasoline-electric car that develops its own current. Another device is a gasoline motor like that employed in a gigantic truck placed in a railway car and run on rails instead of a highway. As the second quarter of the twentieth century opens, the future of the branch line railroad in competition with the highway automobile coach and truck remains uncertain. Some of the railroads, the New York Central, for instance, and the Pennsylvania, have themselves gone over to the motor truck and motor bus for freight delivery and passenger transportation over the public highways.

THE DEVELOPMENT OF RAILS

LIKE locomotives, the rails and bridges of the new transportation were evolved through years of trial. Some of the first railways used cut stone fitted together for rails, others employed timbers for this purpose. There are logging railroads deep in the forest that even at the present time lay down logs or timber for rails. The most common of the early rails was of timber or stone with iron straps fastened to the wearing surface, mortised at the ends to form a perfect joint. Unfortunately, these ends worked loose under the thrust and pound of the wheels and the flimsy wooden cars were so often impaled on these sharp rail-ends — called "snake-heads" — that every train carried a sledge hammer to pound the ends back through the floor and

into place on the timber of the track. When the sledge hammer could not loosen the snake-head, the train was delayed until the iron could be sawed off. Passengers as well as car floors were known to be caught on the ends of "snake-heads." The evolution of the rail was an engineering feat. Its composition, its shape, and its dimensions were studied in detail and subjected to the harsh test of experience. This beam carrying enormous weights, and assaulted with fierce constant blows, must not fail; defectiveness means disaster.

283   Section of first rail in use west of the Alleghenies, from the original in the
Kentucky State Historical Society, Frankfort

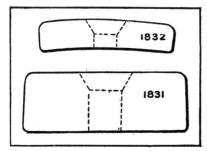

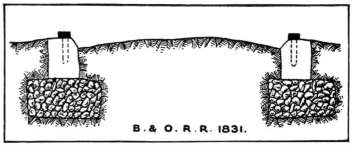

284
Strap rails used on Amboy Division, 1831–32, from G. P. Raidapaugh, *Origin and Development of the Railway Rail in England and America*, Journal of the Iron and Steel Institute, XCV, London and New York, 1917
Rails on the Baltimore & Ohio, 1831, showing substitution of long granite slabs for wooden rails, from G. P. Raidapaugh, etc.
285

THE DEVELOPMENT OF THE IRON RAIL

THE first iron rails were solid heavy bars of the same width at top and base. Next appeared a rail with a straight top and convex bottom held at the ends by iron clamps, called chairs or blocks, which in turn were fastened to stone or wooden foundations. The first bar rails were made of cast iron and did not exceed three or four feet in length. These could be made in America but were brittle and not so strong as rolled iron rails manufactured in Great Britain. No facilities for making rolled iron rails existed in the United States until 1844 when a plant was set up at Mount Savage, Maryland, and another in 1845 at Danville, Pennsylvania. The Mount Savage plant produced a rolled rail with an inverted "U" shape. These rails were spiked to wooden sleepers. The "T" rail which became the accepted standard shape was first used in 1831 on the Camden & Amboy Railroad. The model for it was whittled out of a pine stick by Robert L. Stevens, the president of the Camden & Amboy Railroad, and the son of the famous John Stevens, the steamboat pioneer. He had great difficulty in persuading British ironmasters that a rail of this shape could be rolled, but they at length succeeded in making a rail that conformed fairly well to Stevens' model. By 1840, the "T" rail became fairly common on American roads and within another decade was the accepted rail shape.

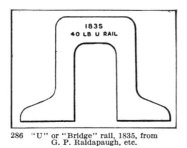

286   "U" or "Bridge" rail, 1835, from
        G. P. Raidapaugh, etc.

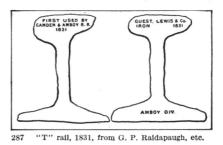

287   "T" rail, 1831, from G. P. Raidapaugh, etc.

THE BESSEMER RAIL

BY 1870, men were saying that railway development, so far as its mechanical equipment was concerned, was reaching its peak. Engines and cars could not be made bigger and heavier, because rolled iron rails could bear no greater weights. Meanwhile, Great Britain had been manufacturing steel rails cheaply by a process invented by Henry Bessemer in 1862 (see Vol. V). Some of these rails had been purchased by the Pennsylvania Railroad as early as 1863 and found superior to iron rails. The Bessemer process, after vexatious delays caused by lawsuits, was begun at Harrisburg, Pennsylvania, in 1865. Thereafter, American railroad technique forged ahead once more, for the steel rails were cheaper in the long run than iron, bore more than twice as heavy a burden, and wore four or five times as long. By the 'nineties the Bessemer rail came gradually to be replaced by "open hearth" rails, which are still in use.

288   First Bessemer steel rail rolled in America, from G. P. Raidapaugh, etc.

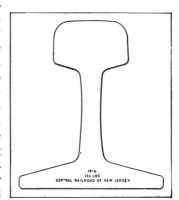

289   Modern open hearth rail, from
        G. P. Raidapaugh, etc.

290   Bridge, Conneaut River, Ohio, from an engraving in the *Cincinnati, Columbus and Cleveland Guide*, 1854

WOODEN RAILWAY BRIDGES

THE first railroad bridges were constructed of wood. Many of them collapsed of their own weight, but bridge engineers quickly learned to use truss construction that made timber bridges reasonably safe under stress and strain. But the wooden bridges were subject to fire, particularly when locomotives burned wood fuel and belched forth sparks at every exhaust; and men were placed on guard at every bridge armed with fire-fighting equipment. If it had not been for wooden bridges and trestles with their low cost, some one hundred fifty thousand miles of American railway would have been greatly delayed and perhaps never constructed. Some of the early wooden bridges were daring engineering feats; he was a bold man who risked building them — or riding over them.

291   Bridge at Elk Creek, Ohio, from an engraving in the *Cincinnati, Columbus and Cleveland Guide*, 1854

292   Viaduct of the Baltimore & Washington Railroad, from an engraving in possession of the publishers

THE PROBLEM OF THE STONE BRIDGE

FOLLOWING the lead of the highway builders some mid-century railway engineers constructed stone masonry bridges. Some of these viaducts lifting their beautiful arches high above the stream were triumphs of engineering skill and seemed destined to be enduring monuments to their builders. But the stone bridge, admirable for the highways, did not prove satisfactory for the railroad. The shock and pound of passing trains, failing to be absorbed by the rigid masonry, were returned with destructive force to the light locomotive and rails.

293   Bridge over Green River, Louisville & Nashville Railroad, from an engraving in
Harper's Weekly, Feb. 25, 1860

THE FIRST IRON BRIDGE

AT the time of the Civil War, the weights of rolling stock began to mount to such a degree that the old wooden bridges became dangerous. Fortunately, bridge engineers could turn to new materials. At first cast-iron was used, and soon rolled iron from mills at Pittsburgh and Cincinnati. To keep down costs, the iron bridges were constructed as light as possible. This led to some startling innovations in truss construction and girder manipulation. Rolled iron gave way to steel, and cantilever designs came into vogue. The suspension bridge was used where bridge-piers were impracticable. The first of the great iron bridges was that over the Green River on the Louisville & Nashville Railroad, a structure one thousand feet long and one hundred and eighteen feet high. It contained about five hundred and ten tons of iron, and cost one hundred and sixty-five thousand dollars. The bridge was begun in April, 1857, and was ready for trains on July 1, 1859. It shared with the Victoria bridge at Montreal the distinction of being the largest iron bridge in North America.

294   Courtesy of the Delaware, Lackawanna & Western Railroad

DELAWARE RIVER BRIDGE AT SLATEFORD JUNCTION, PENNSYLVANIA

THE bridge builders of a generation ago thought that the last word had been said with mammoth steel cantilever bridges. But the years have brought a material stronger and more durable than steel, concrete. When
properly made, concrete is impervious to weather and needs neither painting nor repairing. The rigidity of
concrete, greater than that of the old stone bridges, is overcome by carrying the cinder or rock-ballast of the
right of way on across the bridge. The structure easily bears this extra weight and the continuous ballast prevents a shock in passing from an elastic roadbed to a solid bridge, noticeable in steel bridges as well as stone.
Concrete bridges, too, are capable of more architectural beauty. What is said to be the longest concrete
bridge in the world at present is the Lackawanna Railroad bridge over the Delaware at Slateford Junction,
Pennsylvania.

295   Courtesy of the Pennsylvania Railroad

HELL GATE BRIDGE

THE Hell Gate Bridge at New York which connects the Pennsylvania Railroad with the New Haven and thus
joins the South with New England is a modern combination of concrete and steel. This bridge, which took
four years to build, has a one-thousand-foot steel span, the largest arch span in the world. To help pay the
twenty-seven million dollars cost of this modern engineering marvel, travelers on trains that cross this
bridge are assessed a small extra fare; in effect it is a toll bridge.

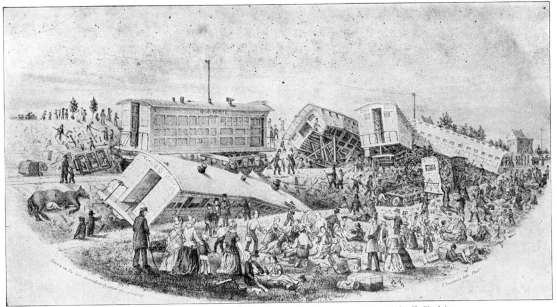

296

Accident on the Camden & Amboy Railroad, Aug. 29, 1855, from a lithograph by T. Sinclairs
in the Historical Society of Pennsylvania, Philadelphia

THE RAILROAD ACCIDENT TOLL

The construction of roadbeds and rolling stock have undergone evolution as well as the bridge. The development of the railway system in Great Britain and the United States, although starting from the same point — the triumph of Stephenson's *Rocket* — soon displayed marked disparity. In Great Britain, the railroad was laid as straight as possible, with unavoidable curves made extremely wide. Grades were kept to a minimum, even at the expense of leveling hills, extensive blasting, and the filling of valleys. The original right of way was therefore generally a permanent construction, possible in a settled country possessing ample capital. The case was far different in the United States, then a young nation with population thinly scattered over a great territory and with capital at a high premium. Construction on this side of the Atlantic had to be carried forward with speed and cheapness. Hills were not leveled if they could be got around, and gulleys were

not filled if they could be crossed by trestle or switchback. Later when earnings warranted, the right of way was straightened, curves widened, fills made and permanent construction attempted. The result of the earlier haste and cheapness of construction was a large number of accidents. During the first dozen years, accidents were few because lines were short, traffic light and the speed of trains not great. But thereafter until the Civil War the accident toll was frightful. The density and speed of traffic increased rapidly, while roadbed and rolling stock remained jerry-built. Death or injury was inflicted upon passengers, trainmen, trespassers along the right of way, and at grade crossings, terminals, yards, or stations. At length the railroads began a campaign to reduce accidents. Improved rolling stock, careful maintenance of way and installation of ingenious signal apparatus went a long way toward elimination of risks to life and limb. The maiming of trespassers has not been eradicated. The grade crossing mortality was dangerously increased with the advent of the automobile and gave rise to a campaign of caution and the realignment of highways so as to avoid crossings.

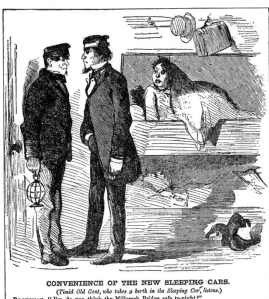

CONVENIENCE OF THE NEW SLEEPING CARS.
(Timid Old Gent, who takes a berth in the Sleeping Car, listens.)
Brakeman. "Jim, do you think the Millcreek Bridge safe to-night?"
Conductor. "If Joe cracks on the steam, I guess we'll get the Engine and Tender over all right. I'm going forward!"

297

From *Harper's Weekly*, May 28, 1859

298   From a photograph, courtesy of the Union Pacific System, Omaha, Neb.

THE LUCIN CUT–OFF ACROSS THE GREAT SALT LAKE

ALL the main lines at least of "Class One" American railroads have now been straightened, the curves have been widened and the bed well ballasted. This has not been done so much for the comfort of passengers, who incidentally profit by it, as to cut down operating expenses and to increase freight movement. In carrying out this work some remarkable "cut-offs" have been made. Among the most famous is the Lucin cut-off across the Great Salt Lake, where one may go to sea upon a train. Before this was built, Central Pacific trains made a forty-four mile circle around the Great Salt Lake, including a fifteen hundred foot climb. The development of a level right of way cost ten million dollars; all the timber for piles had to be hauled a thousand miles and all the water for the construction engines was brought from far away, since the water of Salt Lake quickly corroded a boiler tube. Yet greater efficiency in the handling of traffic made the change both inevitable and profitable.

THE LACKAWANNA LINE

THE original line of the Lackawanna in New Jersey constantly dipped into valleys, only to climb hills on the opposite side. Many of the unnecessary dips and swoops have been removed by constructing fills across the valleys, the trains running on the crest of these man-made ridges. To look straight down from the train window upon farmhouses and trees in the valley below is sometimes a breath-taking experience. The Lackawanna spent enormous sums on these causeways to facilitate its chief business, the carrying of coal. Freight trains could now be made longer and heavier and operated at a greater average speed.

299   A freight train crossing a fill, courtesy of the New York Central Railroad, New York

300   Chain coupler on the *De Witt Clinton*, courtesy of the New York Central Railroad

COUPLERS

THE three-link chains (see above) which jerked the *De Witt Clinton's* passengers out of their seats made obvious the need for a better type of coupler. The first improved device was a straight iron bar which held cars in close contact and avoided some of the snapping and bumping incident to long chains. But the iron of the period was unequal to such severe strains and a single great link, held in place with large iron pins, was finally adopted. The link coupler shortly became the standard equipment, but unfortunately did not hold cars closely together and was itself a loosely fitted device. As a result, it was extremely noisy and caused the platforms of cars to bounce out of line both vertically and horizontally. Passengers were therefore forbidden to cross the car platforms and jump the gap between the cars after the train started. Some cars showed a sign depicting a freshly made grave with an ornate monument upon which was engraved, " Here lies the man who crossed the platform when the train was moving." It seems incredible to us that railway officials, shippers and passengers so long complacently accepted the crude couplers. But the railways were chronically short of capital for improvements, shippers were interested in rates more than methods, and passengers were uncritical.

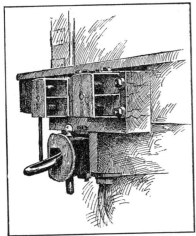

301   Link and pin coupler, from Scribner, *The American Railway*, New York, 1889

302   Automatic coupler, from Scribner, *The American Railway*, New York, 1889

ADOPTION OF THE AUTOMATIC COUPLER

THE link and pin coupler was also dangerous for the trainmen who had to stand between the cars and hold the link in order to guide it into its slot on the other car and then drop the pin in place. He was supposed to do this guiding with a stick, but he never did so for fear of the ridicule of other trainmen. So every year men were crushed between cars, often fatally. As late as 1888, in Massachusetts alone one hundred and fifty-four men were involved in coupling accidents. In the 'eighties, automatic couplers were invented, but railroads could not be induced to accept them. It was not until the 'nineties that joint action of the Master Car Builders Association and Federal legislation compelled the adoption of the automatic device.

IV—9

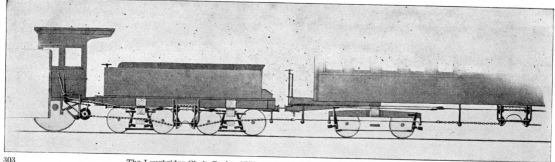

303   The Loughridge Chain Brake, 1855, courtesy of the Westinghouse Air Brake Co.

PRIMITIVE BRAKES

PRIMITIVE locomotives were for the most part fitted with brakes like those of a stagecoach: a wooden block pressed against the rims of the drive wheels by a hand lever. But at an early date the steam power that drove the engine was made to stop it, operating through a small cylinder, located between the drive wheels and so arranged that it raised a piston which in turn lifted the iron brake blocks and pressed them firmly against the wheel treads. This brake in a variety of forms was used until the air brake appeared. But it soon became evident that some method of braking the cars as well as the engine must be devised. The numberless devices fell into two classes; those whose force acted against the rim of the car wheels, and those in which it was applied to the rail, bringing the car to rest by friction. The latter type ultimately fell into great disfavor, for not only was it heavy and slow, but it broke the rails; and tended to derail the cars. The brake shoe was applied to the rim of the wheel by winding a chain on a straight bar or tube or by forcing the shoe into position by levers or screws. Many other devices involving springs, hydraulic action, compressed air, and electricity were used in an effort

304   Railway Tender Brake, 1830, courtesy of the
Westinghouse Air Brake Co.

to find a substitute for hand power, but the hand brake was well nigh universal until the air brake appeared. Even after the air brake was adopted some kind of a hand brake was also attached to the cars for use in an emergency. Certain blasts on the locomotive whistle meant "set brakes." The brakeman hurried to the brake control to apply the brakes. This irregular application of brakes made the stopping of a train a series of jolts and shudders.

305   Railway Tender Brake, 1831, courtesy of the Westinghouse
Air Brake Co.

306   Railway Carriage Brake, 1839, courtesy of the
Westinghouse Air Brake Co.

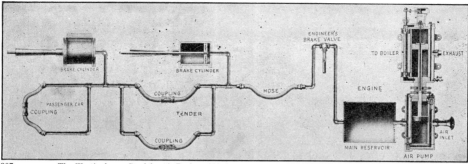

307   The Westinghouse Straight Air Brake, 1869, from a diagram, courtesy of the Westinghouse Co.

AIR BRAKES

IN 1868, George Westinghouse invented an air brake applicable to passenger cars. Crude, slow, and non-automatic, it was not much used until Westinghouse invented his triple valve. This mechanism reduced by two-thirds the time required to operate the brakes and led to the adoption of air brakes for passenger-car service. The air-braking system as devised by Westinghouse comprised an air pump run by steam, attached to the locomotive, and controlled by a governor sensitive to changes in air pressure. This filled a large air storage reservoir on the locomotive. There were smaller reservoirs under each car connected in a continuous system by pipes and flexible hose. The brake cylinder was supplied with air from the small reservoir of the car. When the brakes were off, the whole system was filled with compressed air at the same pressure. To apply the brakes, the engineer turned a valve under his hand. This released or reduced the air pressure and acted upon the triple valve which was placed in the piping system between the brake cylinder and the car reservoir. When the pressure was reduced, a small piston in the triple valve was driven to the extreme left by the pressure from the air in the car reservoir. This permitted the air from the car reservoir to flow into the cylinder and applied the brakes. To release the brakes, the engineer turned his valve back so as to permit compressed air from the storage tank to flow through the train pipes, establishing connection between the train pipe and the car reservoir and permitting the air in the brake cylinder to escape to the open air. If the air in the car-tank lost pressure from any cause, the piston in the triple valve moved so as to open a connection between the train pipe and so restore the pressure. Since the brakes operated upon release of pressure, they would be applied automatically if the train broke or air leaked out of the train pipe.

Scene.—OFFICE OF THE —— RAILROAD COMPANY.

PRESIDENT (to anxious Applicant for a situation as Brakeman). "Want a berth, eh!—(to Doorkeeper)—Mr. JONES, has there been a Brakeman killed on the road within a day or two?"
Mr. JONES. "Well, no, Sir, none this week."
PRESIDENT (to Applicant). "Ah! well, my man, call next Monday, and by that time I guess there'll be a vacancy."

[Exit Applicant, not so much elated at the prospect as he might be.

308   Cartoon illustrating dangers in the life of the brakeman, from Harper's Weekly, Nov. 1875

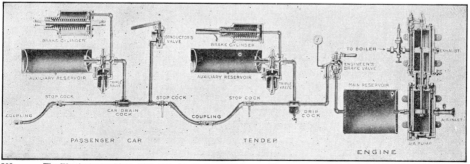

309   The Westinghouse Plain Automatic Air Brake, 1872, from a diagram, courtesy of the Westinghouse Co.

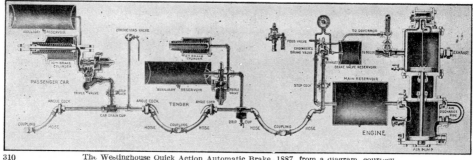

310   The Westinghouse Quick Action Automatic Brake, 1887, from a diagram, courtesy
of the Westinghouse Co.

TESTS OF AIR BRAKES, 1887

ALTHOUGH the air brake was used on passenger trains after 1868, it was not until 1888 that it was in great demand in the freight service. Trials under the auspices of the Master Car Builders Association were held in July, 1886, and May, 1887, with freight trains of fifty cars each. The first tests proved that on a fifty-car train the air brakes set eighteen seconds sooner at the head of the train than on the rear car, causing collisions within the train. The trials of 1887 were equally unsatisfactory, but immediately thereafter Westinghouse so improved his triple valve and the train pipe that he was able to apply brakes throughout a fifty-car train in two seconds. He fitted out a fifty-car train and took it on a three-thousand-mile tour, giving demonstrations several times daily. Despite the impressiveness of these tests, some railroads were reluctant to equip their freight service with air-brakes. Eventually, the public compelled all railroads by law to furnish their cars with this efficient method of stopping. The air brake since 1887 has undergone many minor improvements, so that to-day its action is practically simultaneous on a train of any length.

311   From a lithograph *Burlington Test with 50 Freight Cars*, by Bartlett & Co., courtesy of the Westinghouse Co.

"TURN–OUTS"

WHEN the first trains left stations, there was no way of telling where they were or what was happening to them, or predicting when they would arrive at the next station. Since there was no method of central control, each train was a law unto itself. As soon as traffic was dense enough it became imperative to build side-tracks or "turn-outs," at which two trains might meet at scheduled time and pass. Half way between such turn-outs were center posts. But if one train was late, train A for example, train B waited until the flagman had walked ahead to signal train A. Train B then proceeded. If train A was signaled, after the flagman had passed the next center post, it was forced to back up to the turn-out it had last passed, allowing train B to proceed. If on the other hand the flagman had not reached the center post before train A appeared, train B was forced to back up to its turn-out and wait for the other to pass. At stations a tall pole was erected with a lookout at the top. At train time, the station agent climbed the pole and scanned the horizon for a glimpse of the smoke of the approaching train. When he espied it, he descended to the platform and rang a bell to warn all that a train was about to appear.

312   Lookout Tower, from *Harper's New York and Erie Railroad Guide*, New York, 1851, in Columbia University Library

313 From an engraving by the National Bank Note Company, New York, in possession of the publishers

FLAGMEN

At particularly dangerous places, such as curves that hid the tracks ahead, at high bridges or tunnels, the early railroads stationed flagmen to signal the engineers the condition of the track before them. Flagmen were sometimes replaced by little tower houses equipped with semaphores. Eventually the telegraph, telephone, and block signals did away with the need for the kind of flagmen just mentioned, except in emergencies.

314 Emergency Flagman, from an engraving after the drawing *Danger Ahead*, by W. L. Sheppard in *Harper's Weekly*, Feb. 10, 1872

THE INTERLOCKING SWITCH SYSTEM

How complicated a terminal may be, and how dangerous, when every switch depends upon the right action of a man, may be realized by glancing about the approach to any large railway terminal. The mazes of signals and switches in such a yard are all controlled by interlocking devices and operated by central towermen. The greatest enemy of this modern system is snow and ice which clogs the switches and puts the control devices out of commission. But modern railways cannot let weather hinder them, so small electric heating appliances are now attached to the interlocking switch system. Snow and ice in such places have ceased to be a nightmare to towermen and train dispatchers.

315   Railroad Yards, South Station, Boston, showing Interlocking Switch System. © Keystone View Co.

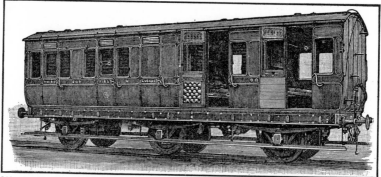

316   British Passenger Coach, from *The American Railway*, Charles Scribner's Sons, New York, 1889

BRITISH PASSENGER COACH

IN Great Britain, the first railway cars were nothing but stagecoaches with fixed axles and grooved or flanged wheels. Indeed, the modern British passenger car is a series of stagecoaches joined together on one frame, each compartment being entered from the side and forming a complete unit. The railway vocabulary of the British smacks strongly of stagecoach days. The engineer is called the "driver," the conductor is a "guard," the cars are "carriages," the roundhouse location of a locomotive is a "stall," the roundhouse engine-groomer is a "hostler" and the station ticket office is the "booking office." American railroad men talk of roundhouse "stalls" and roundhouse "hostlers," but other stagecoach nomenclature has largely disappeared.

317   Tappan Landing, eastern terminus of the Erie Railroad on the Hudson River, from an engraving by P. Ostrander after a drawing by A. C. Morton, in possession of the publishers

DIFFERENCES BETWEEN AMERICAN AND BRITISH CARS

THE original passenger cars on American railways were, like those of the British, merely modified stage-coaches. The Baltimore & Ohio, the Charleston & Hamburg, and Mohawk & Hudson all used at first passenger cars of this type. Almost immediately, however, changes in car design appeared. Logically, the first thing that was done was to mount three or more coach bodies on one frame which could easily be supported at the ends by four swivel trucks. Here the stagecoach influence was still visible.

318   The Locomotive *Planet* and Coaches, Camden & Amboy Railroad 1834, from the painting by E. L. Henry (1841–1919).
© C. Klackner, New York, 1904

THE AMERICAN PASSENGER COACH

THE American passenger coach had a nearly flat roof with no method of ventilation except the side windows. With dust, sparks and soot pouring through the windows, cleanliness among railway travelers was impossible. The seats were hard wooden benches with no upholstery or springs and with straight backs. A railway journey was not for the timid or the delicate. In winter the cars were heated with stoves at the ends. With no ventilation, the atmosphere of a crowded car became well nigh unbearable.

319 American Passenger Coach, 1835, from *Harper's Weekly*, August 25, 1888

In the railway wrecks the stoves became a deadly menace by setting fire to the flimsy wooden cars. The artificial light in the cars was furnished by candles stuck in holes, one at each end of the car. Since petroleum was not discovered until 1859, it was not until after the Civil War that centrally hung kerosene lamps were available. Despite these crudities, the demand for travel was so great and the discomforts of other modes of land transportation so much worse that passengers flocked to the railroads. The officials had calculated the probable demand from figures of travel by the older methods and were astounded by the enormous increase in traveling induced by the new means. The opening of the Charles-

320 American Passenger Coach, 1844, showing primitive platforms and windows, from *Harper's Weekly*, August 25, 1888

ton & Hamburg Railroad at once caused a fifty-fold increase in the number of travelers between the two places.

AMERICAN "FIRST CLASS"

PERHAPS it was because a brakeman walking on a board on the outside of a passenger coach was subjected to fatal hazards on the sharp curves of American railways that the partitions between the coach-like bodies gave place to a central aisle with doors at the ends. At any rate this type of car early appeared on American rail-

ways in marked contrast with British railway carriages then and now. Another explanation of the difference between American and British passenger cars may be found in social conditions. The Americans of 1830 were resolutely democratic. The prosperous merchant did not mind rubbing elbows with a farm hand. The English compartment cars with their various designations permitted a certain privacy and luxury. In America, every one had to travel first class, even though a first-class car was little better than a cattle car. It was not until the Pullman Company began to function that a real "first class" service was offered by American railroads.

321 Interior of an American Railway Car, from an engraving by E. Landells after a drawing by J. Burton in *The Illustrated London News*, April 10, 1852

322   Earliest type of passenger coach, Pennsylvania Railroad, from the model in the Carnegie Institute, Pittsburgh

IMPROVEMENTS IN CAR BUILDING

THERE was considerable variation in car design on different roads. The Pennsylvania Railroad did not make its passenger cars after the model of stagecoaches but produced a car that bore a resemblance to a modern freight caboose. When this was lengthened and equipped with two four-wheeled trucks, the normal passenger car of the 'forties was brought into existence. Like-wise some but not all of the early railroads had roof seats for passengers, sometimes protected by an awning. Occasionally, passenger cars were fitted with flags and pennants and a few had sight-seeing cupolas on the roof. By 1840, the central aisle passenger car was the accepted standard on American railroads. Until the time of the Civil War there were few improvements made in it. Owing to the insistence of passengers, springs were put under the cars, and cushions were provided for the hard wooden seats. In the 'fifties the frame of the seat was generally of iron instead of wood and the seat itself was upholstered. Springs and upholstery

helped to alleviate some of the worst bumps of railway travel. Beginning in 1836, car ventilation was improved. At first this improvement was limited to one hole cut in the center of the roof. Soon there were four holes at the four corners protected from rain by tin covers. Then someone thought of raising the whole central portion of the roof and inserting movable "deck-

323   Passenger coach, 1857, from the model in the Carnegie Institute, Pittsburgh

lights" to admit fresh air and draw off foul. It took a great many years, however, to make the deck roof a universal feature of passenger cars.

Private Carriage   Carriage for Passengers   Car with Freight
324   From an engraving by A. J. Mason after a drawing by A. J. Davis, in Edwin Williams, *The New York Annual Register*, 1832

PRIVATE CARS

ALMOST from the inauguration of American railways, passengers who wished special privacy or exclusiveness have been permitted to hire private cars. At first private cars were either a regular coach placed at the disposal of those who paid for its exclusive use, or flat cars upon which those who so desired could sit in their own horse-drawn coach. As soon as passenger cars became distinguishable from private horse-drawn vehicles, private cars were always selected from among the newest and most ornate of the railroad's passenger cars. Since George Pullman began building his "Palace Cars" in 1867, private cars have been generally of the Pullman type. At all times, travelers in private cars have paid the regular railway fare plus surcharges for the rental of the cars and the service (porter, chef, etc.) it provides.

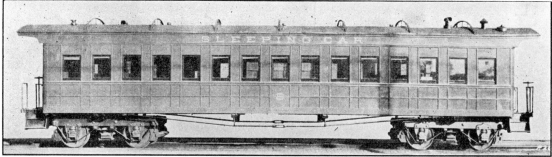

325   The first sleeping car, *ca.* 1864, from a photograph, courtesy of the Pullman Company, Chicago

EARLY SLEEPER — PULLMAN'S "PIONEER A"

WHEN night passenger travel began on the railroads in the late 'thirties, no special provisions were made for the passengers; they slept as well as they could in the regular day coaches. But since people insisted on traveling at night, and inasmuch as canal boats and steamboats made special accommodations for night travelers, the railroads too were compelled to furnish sleeping facilities. Regular coaches were fitted on one side of the aisle with sleeping bunks. These were in three tiers, the seats forming the lowest row, while shelves that stood flat against the side of the car by day were lowered to a horizontal position at night and suspended by chains or supported by posts to form the middle and upper rows. The railroads at first furnished neither mattresses nor blankets for these bunks, but soon provided the mattresses which by

326 George M. Pullman, 1831–97, courtesy of the Pullman Co., Chicago

day were piled in a heap at the end of the car and dragged down the aisle at night to be placed in the bunks. Probably the first sleeping cars of this kind appeared in the winter of 1836–37 on the Cumberland Valley Railroad of Pennsylvania between Harrisburg and Chambersburg. In 1858 George M. Pullman, making a trip from Buffalo to Chicago on the Lake Shore Railroad, was struck with the discomfort and inadequacies of night-travel accommodations. He then began experiments in connection with the Chicago & Alton Railroad to better the comfort of sleeping cars. He continued until 1864, when he constructed a sleeping car called the "Pioneer A." This car cost eighteen thousand dollars to construct at a time when other sleeping cars could be built for four thousand five hundred dollars. When finished, it was too big for the bridges and station platforms, but it happened that the "Pioneer" was needed for the transportation of the body of President Lincoln in 1865 and so the railroad was altered to fit the car. A similar thing happened when President Grant wanted to take a trip in the "Pioneer." The car was then put into regular service and proved so extraordinarily popular that a number of others like it were ordered. This began the Pullman sleeping car business and marked the end of unusually uncomfortable night travel.

327   Interior of an early Pullman car, from *Harper's Weekly*, August 25, 1888

328   329   330

Interiors of early Pullman cars, from *Harper's Weekly*, August 25, 1888

THE PULLMAN CAR

THE special car business was large enough in 1867 to warrant George M. Pullman forming the "Pullman Car Company" to manufacture the cars and operate them over the railroads of the country. The Pullman sleeper was followed by the parlor or drawing-room car, popularly called "palace cars" at the time of their introduction to the public. Next came what was known as the "hotel car," which is now most nearly approximated by the "buffet car." The original hotel cars were provided with a kitchen and pantry and small portable tables that could be placed between the seats. The first hotel car, "The President," was used on the Great Western Railway of Canada in 1867. The hotel car quickly developed into the diner. The Chicago & Alton Railroad ran the first Pullman dining car in 1868. In order to impress the public with the character of this car, it was called the "Delmonico." Although some railroads have provided all or a part of their own equipment of the Pullman type, most of the roads have found it more convenient to enter into traffic arrangements with the Pullman Company. The railroads do not themselves ordinarily operate this service because the need for special equipment varies greatly at different times. Since the cars are very expensive, the charges against them for idle time are high. The Pullman Company, by balancing the peak and slack demands of the railroads against each other, may keep its cars fully employed. When it was first organized the Pullman Company granted a through travel privilege not furnished by the railroads themselves. Although it is not so called, the Pullman operation really constitutes a "first-class" railroad service comparable to the foreign first-class designation.

THE VESTIBULE CAR

THE Pullman dining car brought an unlooked-for result. To reach the diner, passengers had to cross the open platforms between cars, prohibited as dangerous. In 1857, the Naugatuck Railroad, operating between Bridgeport and Winsted, Connecticut, had, indeed, put canvas diaphragms over the platforms, forming a covered passage between cars, but this was for purposes of ventilation and had not proved useful. George M. Pullman in 1886–87 invented the "vestibuled car": a bellows diaphragm on a steel frame ran the length of the platform, forming a narrow corridor with doors opening on to the steps. The first vestibuled train of this type was run on the Pennsylvania Railroad in 1886. The full vestibuled Pullman of to-day, made of steel, is the safest car in America. It cannot be burned, splintered or easily telescoped. The vestibule feature was slowly added to all new passenger coaches; but there are thousands of wooden coaches with exposed platforms still in use on American railroads.

331   Vestibule cars, courtesy of the **Pullman** Company, Chicago

RAILROAD TICKETS

PASSENGERS on the earliest railroads paid a cash fare; and, although nearly all railroads soon adopted tickets, passengers for a long time preferred to pay in cash. The railroads did not provide adequate facilities for the sale of their tickets nor protection against counterfeiting. The payment of cash fares on trains, however, led to thievery on the part of conductors; and as facilities for the sale of tickets were developed, passengers were compelled to buy tickets at the stations and show them before boarding a train. To discourage the cash fare the railroads exacted an extra charge — five or ten cents — for fares so paid. Sometimes this surcharge was kept by the railroad; sometimes it was given back to the passenger if he presented a proper certificate at a station. For protection against counterfeits, tickets are printed on special paper and according to special forms. In addition, each ticket carries a form number and a serial number together with a stamped device (usually containing the date of sale) on the back. Time limits, too, invalidate tickets. The first tickets were of odd sizes, some very large. Colored and glazed papers were used as well as cardboard, and in a few instances metal tokens were employed. Coupon tickets or strip tickets valid for through journeys over different lines were not often used in the earlier years of railroading because of the mutual jealousies and suspicions of railroads and the difficulties of coöperating in a division of the receipts from such tickets. Through tickets became general as consolidations of railroads

332   New England railroad tickets, from F. B. C. Bradlee, *The Boston and Maine Railroad*, Essex Institute, Salem, 1921

were effected. Modern tickets are of almost infinite variety to meet every type of travel. A passenger may travel from New York to San Diego, returning by way of Seattle and Chicago, all on one ticket.

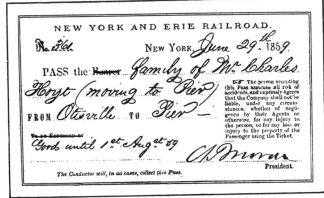

333   Pass on the New York & Erie Railroad, from E. H. Mott, *The Story of Erie*, New York, 1899

RAILROAD PASSES

RAILROAD passes have their legitimate use, but when railroads were young passes were issued in a manner that caused public scandal. In an effort to secure legislative favors, passes were issued wholesale, and, once established, the railroads could not easily stop the practice, although many of them would have liked to do so. Eventually public opinion was aroused against the pass evil, and legislation strictly limited their use. It is difficult even for railroad employees to get passes outside their regular runs.

334　　Baltimore & Ohio freight car, 1832, from a reconstruction, courtesy of
the Baltimore & Ohio Railroad

THE FIRST FREIGHT CARS

THE original freight carrier was a flat car upon which the freight was piled and held in place by ropes. Soon the sides were built up for a couple of feet to hold the goods more securely. As a protection from the weather, cloth covers were used. These cars looked much like Conestoga wagons, and they may have been suggested by that familiar overland freighter. About the time of the center-aisle passenger coach, a small crude box car was introduced, of about four or five tons capacity. Springs were early applied to freight cars — almost as soon as to passenger cars — for the damage to freight in a springless car was considerable. Other changes in passenger-car construction were likewise applied to freight cars, such as swivel trucks, coupling devices and brakes. Special freight cars came later.

335　　Clearing yards, Belt Railway Co., Chicago. © Diggins Aerial Photo Co., Chicago

FREIGHT TERMINALS

FREIGHT terminals are necessarily equipped with greater and more complicated trackage than passenger terminals. They are located with reference to the offerings of freight within the city, but they require plenty of room in which to shift and store the freight. The "yard" of a freight terminal not only contains tracks for switching in "making up" and "breaking down" trains, but tracks from which coal, grain, stone, heavy machinery, and the like may be unloaded perhaps with derricks or cranes, directly into trucks or received from them into the cars. The buildings of a freight terminal are generally in three sets, one devoted to "inbound freight" where goods consigned to local parties are received. A second set of buildings handles "outbound freight," while a third, called the "transfer house," re-assorts freight.

TRANSFER HOUSE

ALTHOUGH everyone concerned with shipping desires to load cars to capacity either with a single commodity for one consignee or at least with commodities all going to one city or town, it is not always possible to do so. "Mixed cars," having a variety of freight for several destinations, are shunted into the terminal "transfer house" where the freight is unloaded and assorted so far as possible into full carload lots. The freight terminal is the crucial factor in the railroad's freight business. Out on the line it is

336   Handling freight at the Cedar Hill, Conn., Freight Terminal, courtesy of the New York, New Haven & Hartford Railroad

fairly easy to keep trains moving, but the efficiency and dispatch with which the terminal is operated determine how much freight a railroad can handle. When terminals are clogged, the whole railroad becomes congested and in critical periods may have to declare embargoes on certain classes of freight or freight destined for certain places. The New York Central in 1924 completed the Castleton cut-off which relieved the worst congestion point on the whole system, the Albany freight terminal.

337   United States Mail Terminal, Chicago, courtesy of the Post Office Department, Washington

THE RAILWAY POST OFFICE

AT the present time, considerably more than three-fourths of the total weight of mail is carried on railroads and a goodly proportion of this in railway post offices. The railroads supply the cars and haul the mail, transfer it from station to station as necessary, load and unload it when the government itself does not furnish labor for these purposes, and carry it from the stations to the post offices except in the larger cities. In addition, the railroads must furnish adequate convenient space for mail cars at terminals and have the requisite number of cars ready in advance of the time for the scheduled departure of trains. Not even the Twentieth Century Limited can start until all the mail it is supposed to carry is aboard; and if the New York Central has not provided enough mail space for all the mail offered, the "Century" cannot leave any of the mail behind but must wait until enough mail cars are put into the train. If any single mail weighs over fifty thousand pounds, a special train made up wholly of mail cars must be dispatched. The railroads receive payment of about one hundred million dollars a year for the service. Formerly the payments were based on weight and mileage but in 1916 payment by space was adopted.

FUNCTIONS OF THE RAILWAY EXPRESS

338   Railway express office, Ellenville, N. Y., about 1890, courtesy of the
American Express Company

AMONG the most important of the early express companies were the Wells Company, organized in 1845, the American Express Company, started in 1850, and the Wells-Fargo Company of 1853. In the following year, the United States Express Company was started. By the time of the World War, these companies had been reduced to four — Adams, Wells-Fargo, American, and Southern — which did more than ninety per cent of the express business of the United States. As a war measure, these four companies were combined into the American Railway Express Company. In March, 1920, when the government turned all railway and express properties back to their owners, the American Railway Express Company elected to continue as a unit. A competitor appeared in 1921 in the Southeastern Express Company, having a monopoly of the express business on the Southern Railway system and the Mobile & Ohio Railroad (nine thousand three hundred and fifty-nine miles of track).

The railroads carry the express matter, provide cars, set aside station facilities for handling the traffic and grant free transportation to employees and supplies of the express company. The express company in turn solicits business, collects and delivers the articles shipped, and assumes full responsibility for the commodities entrusted to it, even when on railroad property. In addition, the express company cares for railroad money and packages free of charge. The express companies and the railroads were thus virtually in partnership; and before express companies were regulated by public utilities commissions and prior to the establishment of the parcel-post system they managed to pay high returns to their stockholders and at the same time pay a large revenue to the railroads. (See Chapter VII.)

PASSENGER TERMINALS

THE railway passenger terminal must be carefully planned to afford a place for the sale and purchase of tickets, a room where passengers may wait for trains, a series of platforms for access to trains, a head platform, easily reached from the waiting room and the street, connecting all the train platforms, and facilities for the expeditious handling of baggage. In addition to these fundamentals, most passenger terminals also contain a number of conveniences for travelers, such as restaurants or lunch rooms, stands for the sale of newspapers, tobacco and candy, telegraph and telephone facilities, little shops of various sorts and a taxi stand. These concessions are rented to private concerns and the income so derived helps to pay the expenses of operating the terminal. The express company and Pullman company are likewise provided with suitable quarters. The use of electrical power permits the construction of office and hotel buildings in connection with the terminal and allows tracks to be laid underground.

339   Interior of the Grand Central Terminal, New York, courtesy
of the New York Central Railroad

340   Union Railroad Station, Washington, from a photograph, courtesy of the Pennsylvania Railroad, Philadelphia

RAILWAY PASSENGER TERMINALS — EXTERIOR VIEWS

PASSENGER terminals, large and centrally located, are expensive, and it is usual for two or more railroads to join in the ownership and operation of a "union station." Sometimes the proprietor railroad leases the use of the terminal to one or more other railroads, thus reducing expenses for all. Passengers find joint terminals convenient, since changes may be made without leaving the building. The South Station in Boston holds the record for the number of people who use it yearly. This is owing to the large suburban traffic, which in New York is divided among the Grand Central and Pennsylvania Stations, the ferries, and the tubes. The first passenger terminal in America notable for its beauty was the Union Station at Washington, D. C. This was later eclipsed by the triumphs in New York, erected by the New York Central and Pennsylvania railroads. Other noteworthy American passenger terminals are the new Union Station and Northwestern station in Chicago, the Union Station at Kansas City and the Michigan Central Station at Duluth, but for the most part American passenger terminals suggest past glories and present poverty.

341 Grand Central Station, New York, from a photograph, courtesy of the New York Central Railroad

CHAPTER VI

THE RAILROAD BUILDERS

THE railroad was the first tie that bound the distant and diverse sections of the United States together. The improved highway and the canal had each made important contributions to the work of uniting the nation. In the day of its greatest popularity, the advocates of the canal dreamed of artificial waterways which, uniting with natural waterways, would cover the United States with a network of trade routes. In the Canal Era the western boundary of the nation ran along the Rockies and did not include Texas. Obviously the canal could never overcome the obstacles of those mountain barriers between the broad valley of the Mississippi and the Pacific. While statesmen still thought in terms of canals, there was little interest in Oregon or California. They were too far away ever to become a part of the nation. The advent of the first practicable railroad inaugurated a profound change in the outlook of the American people.

After the experimental decade of the 'thirties, the swiftness of railroad expansion in the United States is one of the outstanding achievements of the nineteenth century. In America the railroad, after the first years, was primarily an adjustment to distances that the European would have considered vast. While the canal was still in its heyday, a few visionaries were dreaming of iron bands that would unite the oceans. Not without significance is the fact that within less than a decade after the practicability of the railroad had been demonstrated, the United States extended its domain to the Pacific. In the 'forties railroads were rapidly extending their first tiny lines. In the 'fifties Chicago was connected with the Atlantic coast and the first great lines between the North and South were established. But, unfortunately, they came too late. In the same years that the railroad builders were advancing swiftly toward the great objective of giving the nation by means of efficient trade routes a unity that it had never known before, disruptive political forces were bringing about a civil war. Could the crisis of 1861 have been avoided, the railroad might possibly have prevented the fratricidal conflict. The railroad builders as well as the politicians determined the destiny of the nation.

Perhaps the most striking early result of the successful operation of railroads was the change in the flow of commerce in the Mississippi valley. Heretofore trade had followed the course of the rivers and the larger part of the commodities had tended to move southward toward the great port of New Orleans. The railroad replaced this north and south flow with one which ran east and west. In a sense the railroad relieved the upper Mississippi valley country of its dependence upon the markets of the South and bound this section more closely to the northeastern states. Much of this shift occurred in the fateful decade of the 'fifties when war was approaching. Had the Compromise of 1850 failed and secession occurred at that time, it is more than likely that the Union would have been permanently dissolved. It is hard to exaggerate the importance of the railroad in the development of the United States in the nineteenth century.

THE BUILDING OF THE BALTIMORE &
OHIO RAILROAD

COMMERCIAL rivalry was in part responsible for the eagerness with which Americans seized upon railroads. Baltimore, Philadelphia and Boston saw in railroads a means of regaining and retaining the commercial superiority which New York had suddenly gained when the Erie Canal made it the outlet of the Middle Western interior. In Baltimore, Philip Evan Thomas, a Quaker merchant and banker, and George Brown, likewise a banker, heard simultaneously of the new railroads then building in England. Both were struck with the idea that this successful innovation might be the salvation of Baltimore's commerce; and, after consulting together and with influential friends, they secured from the Maryland legislature a charter of incorporation for the Baltimore & Ohio Railroad. On April 24, 1827, the company was organized with Thomas as president, and on July 4 of the next year construction was begun amid popular enthusiasm. It was not, however, until twenty-five years later that the first train rolled into

342 Philip Evan Thomas, 1776–1861, from the portrait, artist unknown, courtesy of the Baltimore & Ohio Railroad, Baltimore

Wheeling, (West) Virginia. The first western terminus of the horse-railroad was Vinegar Hill, seven miles from Baltimore. Ellicott's Mills, thirteen miles from Baltimore, was the next railhead, and it was over this line that locomotives were first demonstrated (see p. 107). By 1832, the railroad had been built to the Potomac River at Point of Rocks, seventy-two miles west of Baltimore, where it was halted by an injunction of the Chesapeake & Ohio Canal Co., claiming exclusive transportation rights in the Potomac valley. By this time, however, the railroad had proved its value, for it had carried three hundred thousand passengers, and had shown that goods could be marketed, with proper freight facilities. The injunction dismissed, the railroad was carried on to Harper's Ferry by December 1, 1834. At that time the road owned eight locomotives and operated many cars with horses. At Harper's Ferry connection was made with the Winchester & Potomac Railroad which tapped the northern end of the Shenandoah valley. Eight years later, the Baltimore & Ohio reached Cumberland, one hundred and seventy-eight miles from Baltimore, eight years ahead of the canal building toward the same terminus. Between Cumberland and Wheeling the hardest engineering problems were encountered, but by means of eleven tunnels and one hundred and thirteen bridges the line reached Wheeling on January 1, 1853. The road had one hundred and thirty-nine locomotives, ninety-six passenger cars, and twenty-five hundred and sixty-seven freight cars. Since Wheeling was a dead-end stop without westward connections, the Baltimore & Ohio officials chartered and constructed the Northwestern Virginia Railroad from Grafton to Parkersburg. This road was opened on May 1, 1857. From Parkersburg a reasonable connection was made with the Marietta & Cincinnati Railroad; and from the latter city, by way of the Ohio & Mississippi Railroad, Baltimore was at last more or less closely joined by rail with St. Louis four years before the opening of the Civil War. But a traveler had to change cars three times and transfer twice to steamboats and twice to ferryboats in making the journey. Through freight service was as yet impossible.

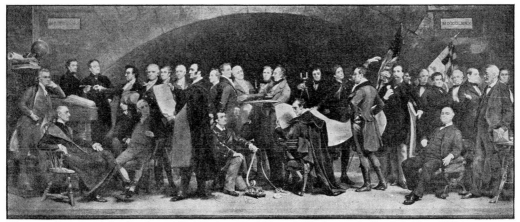

343   From the painting *Founders and First Directors of the Baltimore & Ohio Company*, by Francis B. Mayer (1891–) in the offices of the Baltimore & Ohio Railroad, Baltimore

344   An Early Transportation Advertisement, from the original in the
Philadelphia Commercial Museum

PHILADELPHIA TO PITTSBURGH

IN Pennsylvania, a state Board of Canal Commissioners embarked upon an elaborate scheme for connecting Philadelphia with Pittsburgh and the Mid-West trade. The first link in the Pennsylvania Public Works was the Philadelphia & Columbia Railway, the second a river and canal route from Columbia on the Susquehanna to Hollidaysburg on the Juniata, where progress was barred by the Alleghenies, thirty-six miles beyond which lay Johnstown with canal connections to Pittsburgh. Hollidaysburg and Johnstown were connected by means of a series of ten inclined planes, the Portage Railroad, November, 1833, surmounting the heights. Of the three hundred and ninety-five miles between Philadelphia and Pittsburgh, one hundred and eighteen were covered by railroads (Columbia and Portage) and two hundred and seventy-seven by river and canal. It took ninety-one hours to make the entire journey and the fare was fifteen dollars. The saving of time and money made the route popular for twenty years. (See No. 169.)

FIRST CHARTER OF THE PENNSYLVANIA RAILROAD

THE Pennsylvania System was in theory an improved state highway open to the use of the public upon the payment of tolls. At first traffic on the rails moved at the speed of the slowest horse-drawn cart behind which the locomotive panted impatiently. Later, horse-drawn vehicles were restricted to the night hours. But the traffic management under state control was never quite satisfactory. Passes were granted to officeholders in vast numbers. Political hangers-on were placed on the pay roll, and on election days trainloads of employees were said to ride from village to village along the line casting ballots at each stop. Meanwhile an old unused railroad charter was granted to the Pennsylvania Railroad Company by the commonwealth of Pennsylvania. Under it the company built a railroad from Harrisburg to Pittsburgh, work commencing at the eastern terminus July 7, 1847. In 1852, this new railroad joined the state's Portage Railroad for passage of the mountains, but two years later it finished a trackage of its own through the Alleghenies, avoiding the use of the inclined planes. The same railroad in 1849 had gained control of a line running from Harrisburg to Lancaster, a cut-off junction with the Philadelphia & Columbia Railroad. In 1857, the state in despair of profitable operation of its twenty million dollar enterprise sold it to the Pennsylvania Railroad for seven and a half million dollars. This railroad then had a through line from Pittsburgh to Philadelphia. Acquiring the Camden & Amboy Railroad, it gained access to New York and started on its modern career.

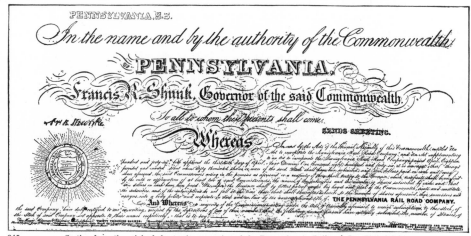

345   Section from the original charter in possession of the Pennsylvania Railroad Co., Philadelphia

NEW-YORK AND ERIE RAIL-ROAD,

RATES OF TOLL IN CENTS, PER 100 POUNDS.

BETWEEN NEW YORK AND THE STATIONS NAMED.

GREATLY REDUCED. . . . . ADOPTED NOVEMBER 1st, 1849.

NAMES OF THE SEVERAL Depots. AND FREIGHT STATIONS, ON THE RAILROAD.	RATES in Cents per 100 lbs for ARTICLES IN CLASSES No. 1.	No. 2.	No. 3.	No. 4.
Pier, - - - - -	8	6	4	3
Piermont. - -	10	8	5½	5
Blauveltville. -	11	9	6	5½
Clarkstown. -	12	9	6¾	6
Spring Valley -	13	10	7	6½
Monsey, - - -	13	10	7	6½
Suffern - - -	14	11	7½	7
Ramapo, - -	15	12	8	7½
Sloatsburgh. - -	15	12	8½	8
Monroe Works.	16	13	9¼	9
Wilkes' - - -	17	14	9½	9
Turner's - - -	18	14	10	9
Monroe. - - -	19	15	10½	9

ENUMERATION AND CLASSIFICATION OF ARTICLES.

NOTE—The character † refers to the estimated weights or some other particular relative to the Article under the head of Conditions. The * refers to the Special Rates.

CLASS No. 1.
ACIDS, in glass,
BASKETS, loose
BLINDS, loose,
BOOKS, b'xd at owners' risk of chafing.
BOOTS and Shoes,
BROOMS, brushes,
BUFFALO Robes,
CANDY, in boxes,
CARDS, for cotton or Wool.
†CARRIAGES, new
CARPETS,
CHINA ware,
CLOCKS, boxed,

CLASS No. 2.
ALE, Porter in bottles
ALCOHOL, in wood
BAGGING, cotton or tow,
BASKETS, in nests.
BATTING, cotton,
BEEF, Mutton, fresh
BERRIES. Bells,
BOILERS for engines
BRANDY, RUM, in casks,
BROOM CORN, in bales,
BURLAPS or Duck,
†BUTTER, Lard,

CLASS No. 3.
ASHES, pot & pearl
Do. dry house,
ALE, BEER, in casks
ANVILS, Axletrees, iron
BACON, HAMS, in casks
BEANS, PEAS green
*BEEF, salted in bbls
BLINDS, in shooks,
BONES, Horns Hoofs
BOXES, Barrels em'ty
CANDLES, Cheese,
†CHARCOAL, in boxes
CHAIR STUFF, Turned Stuff
COPPER Sheets or Plates

CLASS No. 4.
ASHES, leached
ANCHORS,
†APPLES, in bags, barrels or baskets
†BARK, Tanners'
BEANS, PEAS dry,
BEETS & sim'lr roots
†*BOARDS & Plank
BRAN and FEED,
†* BRICK, TILES,
BUILDING STONE
CABBAGES and similar vegetables
CIDER, VINEGAR,
*CLAY, MARL,
*COALS, mineral

Special Rates.

SOLE Leather & Dry Hides: PER SIDE	PER HIDE	CATTLE, except OXEN: PER HEAD	PER CAR LOAD	CALVES, NOT MORE THAN 3 MONTHS OLD: 1 to 44 per HEAD	45 or more per HEAD	STORE HOGS, and PIGS LIVE: 1 to 44 per HEAD	45 or more per HEAD	SHEEP: 1 to 49 per HEAD	50 or more per HEAD	LAMBS: 1 to 49 per HEAD	50 or more per HEAD	FLOUR AND MEAL: 1 to 9 bbls per bbl.	10 to 49 bbls. per bbl.	50 or more per bbl	PORK, BEEF, FISH, salted, per 100 lbs	Iron Bars, Pigs, Scraps, Blooms & Steel: per 100 lbs	per 2000 lbs	NAMES OF THE SEVERAL Depots, AND FREIGHT STATIONS ON THE RAILROAD.
...	...	42	...	9	7.2	7¼	6	6	...	4¼	...	8	6.4	6	3,2	2,4	48	- Pier - - -
...	...	56	...	12	9.6	10	8	8	6.4	6	4.8	11	8.8	8¼	4,4	4,	80	- Piermont -
...	...	63	...	13½	10.8	11¼	9	9	7.2	6¾	5.4	12	9.6	9	4,8	4,4	88	- Blauveltville
...	...	63	...	13½	10.8	11¼	9	9	7.2	6¾	5.4	13	10.4	9¾	5,2	4,8	96	- Clarkstown.
...	...	70	...	15	12.	12¼	10	10	8.	7½	6.0	14	11.2	10½	5,6	5,2	104	- Spring Valley
...	...	70	...	15	12.	12¼	10	10	8.	7½	6.	14	11.2	10½	5,6	5,2	104	- Monsey - -
...	...	77	$11	16½	13.2	13¾	11	11	8.8	8¼	6.6	15	12.	11¼	6,	5,6	112	- Suffern. - -
...	...	84	$11	18	14.4	15	12	12	9.6	9	7.2	16	12.8	12	6.4	6,	120	- Ramapo, - -
...	...	84	$11	18	14.4	15	12	12	9.6	9	7.2	17	13.6	12¾	6.8	6,4	128	- Sloatsburg -
...	...	91	$12	19½	15.6	16¼	13	13	10.4	9¾	7.8	19	15.2	14¼	7,6	7,2	144	- Monroe W'ks.
...	...	98	12½	21	16.8	17½	14	14	11,2	10½	8.4	19	15.2	14¼	7,6	7,2	144	- Wilkes' - -
...	...	98	12½	21	16.8	17½	14	14	11.2	10½	8.4	20	16.	15	8,	7,2	144	- Turner's - -
...	...	105	$13	22½	18.	18¾	15	15	12.	11¼	9.0	21	16.8	15¾	8,4	7,2	144	- Monroe. - -

346 Rates of Toll on the New York & Erie Railroad, section from a print in the New York Historical Society

THE NEW YORK & ERIE

In New York State itself, a railroad competitor of the Erie Canal was promoted as early as 1831. De Witt Clinton, the father of the canal, projected a system of turnpikes and canals for southern New York. But two of his associates, Jeremiah Pierson and Eleazer Lord, were attracted to the idea of a railroad, stimulated by the account which Pierson's son gave them of a honeymoon journey on the first passenger train of the Charleston & Hamburg Railroad. On April 24, 1832, Pierson secured a charter for the New York & Erie Railroad Company against the violent opposition of the canal interests. A year later the New York & Erie Railroad Company was organized and Eleazer Lord, Pierson's son-in-law, was elected president. But private funds were slow to support a scheme which held out to investors such a slight promise of reasonable returns. It was not until 1839, after years of discouragement and abandoned beginnings, that a serious start was made at grading, and then only for forty-six miles between Piermont, the eastern terminus on the Hudson, twenty-four miles north of New York city, and the western terminus at Goshen. Once actually started, the Erie Railroad slowly and with extreme financial pain crept westward. The Goshen line was opened for traffic in 1841, and seven years later the first train entered Binghamton. The next terminus was Elmira, and in 1849 Corning was reached. Two years later, in 1851, Lake Erie echoed to the triumphant whistle of the first Erie Railroad engine to pull a train into Dunkirk, the predetermined western terminus. Although it took twenty years to join Piermont and Dunkirk and cost six times the original estimate per mile, the Erie was the first through line railroad between the Atlantic coast and the Middle West. It was at the time of its completion the longest single railroad in the world, although Moscow and St. Petersburg in Russia were connected in the same year and shared world honors with the Erie. The Erie reached the lake before the Baltimore & Ohio entered Wheeling, before the Pennsylvania connected with the Portage Railroad at Hollidaysburg and before the New York Central united the string of individual roads from Albany to Buffalo. The Erie was, therefore, the first trunk-line railroad.

347 Jeremiah Pierson, first President of the New York & Erie Railroad, from David Cole, *History of Rockland County*, New York, 1884

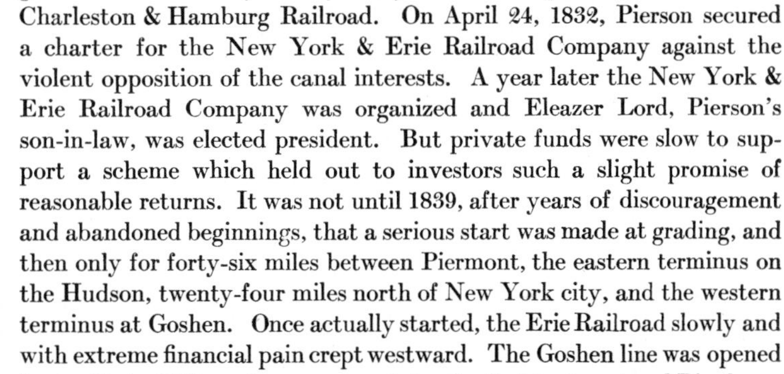

348 Early Train on the New York & Erie Railroad, from an engraving on an original bank note of the Bank of Port Jervis, N. Y., courtesy of W. L. Cuddeback, President

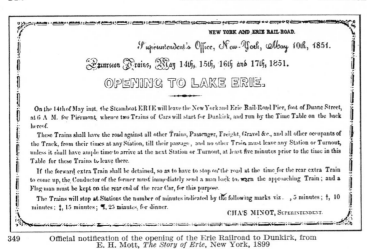

349   Official notification of the opening of the Erie Railroad to Dunkirk, from E. H. Mott, *The Story of Erie*, New York, 1899

350   Jay Gould, 1836–92, from an engraving by Williams, after a photograph, in possession of the publishers

THE ERIE'S WESTERN CONNECTIONS

ALTHOUGH the Erie was the first trunk-line railroad, it began in a swamp and ended on a sand dune. Piermont was twenty-four miles from the harbor of New York and Dunkirk was not of great commercial importance. By its charter the Erie was forbidden to make any connections which might bring it in touch with either Philadelphia or Baltimore. If the Erie produced any business at all, New York State meant to have it. A boat-line connected Piermont with New York city, which, however, soon had to meet the competition of a railroad from Suffern to Paterson, the Ramapo & Paterson Railroad, and the Paterson & Hudson Railroad, which entered Jersey City opposite New York. Erie passengers preferred these lines to the boats. The Erie to secure a terminal in New York city took them over under perpetual lease in 1851. It required many more years to make western connections equally valuable. Ohio had railroad connections that could have carried the Erie as far west as St. Louis, but to enter Ohio from Dunkirk necessitated crossing the lake front of Pennsylvania, which state was not of a mind to aid a New York railroad to make western connections. By methods of doubtful legality, a line, the Atlantic & Great Western, was eventually built across Pennsylvania, which enabled the Erie to lift its nose out of the Dunkirk sand hills and proceed westward to Cleveland which Erie trains entered in 1863. From there the way was eased to Dayton in 1864, and then Cincinnati was accessible by way of the Cincinnati, Hamilton & Dayton Railroad. A St. Louis outlet was available at Cincinnati by means of the Ohio & Mississippi Railroad. Eventually, therefore, there was a through railroad line from Jersey City to St. Louis, and the Erie terminals became the North River and the Mississippi.

351   Resolution extending the thanks of the City of New York to the builders of the New York & Erie Railroad (showing terminus at Piermont, Cascade Bridge, and Starrucca Viaduct), from E. H. Mott, *The Story of Erie*, New York, 1889

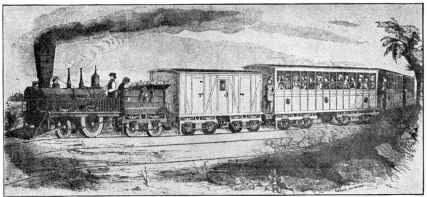

352   Afternoon Train between Springfield and Albany, from a daguerreotype, 1842, in the
American Antiquarian Society, Worcester, Mass.

RAILROAD BEGINNINGS IN MASSACHUSETTS

BOSTON's dismay at the changes wrought by the Erie Canal was as great as that of Baltimore and Philadelphia. Boston too dreamed of a canal across Massachusetts to the Hudson River, but before construction was started turned its attention to railroads that would accomplish the same object, namely divert the Erie Canal traffic from New York city to Boston. The first step in this plan was the chartering of the Boston & Worcester Railroad on June 23, 1831. Work in the construction of this road was commenced in 1832. The first nine miles to Newton were opened for regular passenger service on May 16, 1832. Service was extended first to Needham (thirteen and a half miles), then to Ashland (twenty-four miles), next to Westboro (thirty-two miles), and, finally, on July 4, 1835, to Worcester (forty-four miles). Some fifteen hundred people enjoyed the new means of travel on the opening day; and the railroad at once proved popular and profitable. The stagecoach line had taken a day between Boston and Worcester and charged two dollars; to do business in Boston therefore cost a Worcester man three days. The new railroad charged him a dollar and a half and took him to Boston and back with ample time for business in an afternoon. Before the Boston & Worcester Railroad was finished a new line, the "Western Railroad," was chartered to run from Worcester to the western boundary of Massachusetts. This road passed through Springfield, Westfield and Pittsfield, and reached the New York boundary in 1841. There another road, the Albany & West Stockbridge, carried passengers to the Hudson River. The "Western" leased the Albany & West Stockbridge in 1842. In 1870 the two Massachusetts roads were both absorbed by the Boston & Albany Railroad.

BOSTON'S DREAM OF A NORTHERN TRUNK LINE

BOSTON supplied managers and money to the transcontinental lines, but she built no trunk line of her own.

Before Vanderbilt entered the New York Central, there was talk in Massachusetts of buying it to form with the Boston & Worcester, and the Western Railroad, a through line from Boston to Buffalo. But the opportunity passed. Another project was to use the Boston & Lowell, Lowell & Nashua, and Northern Railroads as a nucleus for a system from Boston to Montreal and Boston to Ogdensburg via Rouse's Point. At Montreal and Ogdensburg, Boston boats were to traverse the Lakes picking up traffic for the railroads. Except for the boats, this system now exists, but it was completed too late effectively to compete with the Baltimore & Ohio, Pennsylvania, or **New York Central**.

353   Original Train, Boston & Lowell Railroad, 1835, from F. B. C. Bradlee,
The Boston & Lowell Railroad, Essex Institute, Salem, Mass.

REMARKS

ON THE

PRACTICABILITY AND EXPEDIENCY

OF ESTABLISHING

A RAIL ROAD

ON ONE OR MORE ROUTES

FROM BOSTON TO THE CONNECTICUT RIVER.

BY THE EDITOR OF THE BOSTON DAILY ADVERTISER.

Boston:

WILLIAM L. LEWIS, PRINTER, CONGRESS STREET.

1827.

354   Early Boston Program for Railroad to the West, from the title-page of a pamphlet in the New York Public Library

NEW ENGLAND'S HANDICAPS

BOSTON was less favorably situated than her rivals in the struggle for mid-western trade. Maryland, with (West) Virginia, Pennsylvania and New York all reach far westward. New England is a kind of island bounded by the Atlantic, the St. Lawrence, Lake Champlain, Lake George and the Hudson, and so cut off from the West. Railroads running westward through Massachusetts ended in a *cul-de-sac* in the Hudson valley. Vermont and New Hampshire's jealousy of Massachusetts checked railroad building from Boston northwestward. Moreover the early New England lines were built in territory much more thickly settled than the trunk-line projects and found their powers so taxed from the start to supply service for passengers that they could not give attention to developing local or long distance freight.

THE ORIGIN OF THE NEW YORK CENTRAL

THE Baltimore & Ohio, the Pennsylvania, the Erie and the Boston & Albany represent conscious efforts on the part of their promoters to connect the great Atlantic ports with the Middle Western farms. Before the railroads or the separate links that composed them were constructed, men had in mind the complete projects, and realized their commercial importance. That is, the whole was foreseen and planned carefully in advance before the parts were put in place. The New York Central, on the contrary, represents a system whose originally unrelated parts were constructed into a unified system by the vision of a master mind. The first of the series of little unconnected roads that followed the path laid out by nature in the Hudson and Mohawk River valleys and defined by the Erie Canal was the Mohawk & Hudson Railroad. This road, seventeen miles long, was designed as a short cut between Schenectady and Albany, saving passengers a forty mile journey by canal and river by way of Troy.

It was not expected, and the charter expressly forbade, that freight should travel over this route. Of scores of petitions for railroad charters during the next few years only six were granted. These were (1) the Schenectady & Utica (78 miles), (2) Syracuse & Utica (53 miles), (3) Auburn & Syracuse (26 miles), (4) Auburn & Rochester (78 miles), (5) Rochester & Attica (45 miles), (6) Attica & Buffalo (32) miles. These roads were finished through the 'thirties and early 'forties, so that by 1845 a passenger could travel by rail all the way from Albany to Buffalo. But the seven roads were operated independently, had varying types of equipment, honored no through tickets, made no attempt to coördinate schedules, and established no common stations at junction points, a situation which was regarded as advantageous to local business. There was no approach to a through system from Albany to Buffalo.

NEW-YORK CENTRAL RAIL ROAD.

BAGGAGE CHECKED THRU FROM NEW-YORK or BOSTON

TO ALL POINTS WEST, NORTHWEST AND SOUTHWEST.

Shortest & Most Direct Route from all Points in New England.

FIVE EXPRESS TRAINS LEAVE ALBANY DAILY,

(SUNDAYS EXCEPTED)

CONNECTING AT BUFFALO WITH THE
LAKE SHORE & BUFFALO & LAKE HURON R.R.

CONNECTING AT SUSP. BRIDGE WITH THE
GREAT WESTERN RAILWAY,

Well Ventilated SLEEPING CARS commodiously fitted up with every necessary requisite for comfort, are attached to the Night Trains, thereby affording Travelers the luxury of a Nights Sleep, without the necessity of laying over on their route

SMOKING CARS ATTACHED TO ALL PASSENGER TRAINS

An Emigrant Passenger Train Leaves Emigrant Depot Daily (Sundays Excepted), at 12 M.

FOR FURTHER PARTICULARS SEE SMALL BILLS.

E. CORNING, President.   C. VIBBARD, Gen'l Supt.   S. DRULLARD, Gen'l Freight Agent.
GEORGE BANKER, Chief Clerk.   JOHN S. DALEY, Eastern Traveling Agent.

355   Early New York Central Poster-Advertisement, from a print, *ca*. 1853, in the American Antiquarian Society, Worcester, Mass.

THE WORK OF VANDERBILT

But the seven roads were forced into union. Those that were prohibited by charter from carrying freight were at a disadvantage. Combination, in order to extend the freight privilege, to reduce terminal charges and trans-shipment costs and to establish standard-gauge track and equipment, was therefore inevitable. On May 7, 1853, the seven railroads and three other independent but connecting roads combined to form the New York Central Railroad, operating between Albany and Buffalo. By 1858, there were sixteen roads in the combination. Meanwhile another railroad, the Hudson River, had been chartered in 1846 to construct a line from Troy and Albany to New York. This road, on the east bank of the Hudson, was opened in 1851. From the outskirts of New York city to Prince Street on the Bowery, the New York & Harlem Railroad Co. had operated since 1832. Cornelius Vanderbilt first bought the New York & Harlem Railroad and then by a stock market coup in 1863 gained control of the Hudson River Railroad. He next obtained a state charter to consolidate these two roads. Two years later, Vanderbilt, at the close of river navigation, served notice on the New York Central that the Hudson River Railroad would accept no more of the Central's freight. This notice, together with Vanderbilt's "bear-short sales" of Central stock, depressed the price of Central shares which the Commodore then bought in. At the next meeting of the New York

356 Cornelius Vanderbilt, 1794–1877, from a photograph by Howell, New York

Central's directorate Vanderbilt was elected president of the road. His first move was to consolidate the New York Central with the Hudson River Railroad, which had been combined with the New York & Harlem. The outcome was a unified railroad system from New York to Buffalo.

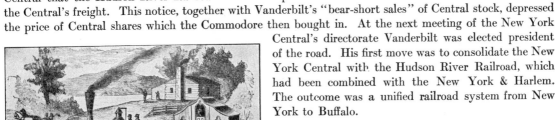

357 Early Locomotive, Erie & Kalamazoo Railroad, from E. T. Andreas, *History of Chicago*, Chicago, 1884–86

MIDDLE WESTERN RAILROAD CONSOLIDATION

A similar development of railroad systems was taking place in the Middle West. The longest of these corn-belt lines was the Illinois Central, with some seven hundred miles of track, but other noteworthy companies were the Chicago & Northwestern; Michigan Central; Lake Shore & Michigan Southern; Pittsburgh, Fort Wayne & Chicago; Chicago & Rock Island; Erie & Kalamazoo; and Hannibal & St. Joseph. Some of the Middle Western railroads had working agreements for through traffic with the Eastern trunk lines; and, with a similar situation existing in the South, the way was prepared for the next act of the railroad drama, the building of the transcontinental railroad. In the 'thirties and 'forties visionaries dreamed of a railroad from the Great Lakes to the coast of Oregon. By the 'fifties the nation had been convinced, but the question of its location became a most bitter sectional and political issue

358 Through line to the Southwest, from W. P. Smith, *The Railway Celebrations of 1857*, New York, 1858

NO. I.
SOMETHING NEW.

Every great enterprise has been ridiculed in the outset. Every thing that is worth doing has had the fate of being regarded as chimerical—only common projects meet at first with public confidence—indeed the great difficulty in the way of accomplishing these great designs that require the combination of numbers and the exertion of higher powers is not so much any inherent obstacle, as want of public faith.

Situated as the United States are, with the Atlantic upon one shore and the Pacific upon another, she might be the first maritime nation in the world, and it will be our fault if we are not.

It is in our power by the same effort to open an immense interior country to market to unite our Eastern and Western shores, firmly together, to embrace the whole of the fur trade, to pour those furs into India and in return to enrich our interior with the spices and silks and muslins and teas and coffee and sugar of that country. It is in our power to build up an immense city at the mouth of the Oregon, to make it the depot for our East India trade & perhaps for that of Europe—in fact to unite New-York and the Oregon by a rail way by which the traveller leaving the City of New-York shall at the moderate rate of ten miles an hour, place himself in a port right on the shores of the Pacific.

We are perfectly aware that many will laugh at this and display their wisdom by condemning it without examination.

The distance between New-York and the Oregon is about three thousand miles—from New York, we would pursue the most convenient rout to the vicinity of Lake Erie, thence along the south shore of this lake and of Lake Michigan, cross the Mississippi between forty one and forty two of north Latitude, cross the Missouri about th' mouth of the Platte, and then on by the most convenient rout to the Rocky Mountains, near the source of the last mentioned river—thence to the Oregon, by the valley of the south branch of that stream, called the southern branch of Lewis' river.

The Illinois, the Mississippi, and the Missouri might be crossed by Ferries, most of the other streams by bridges.

This as we have said would be about three thousand miles, and might occupy about a fortnight from New-York to the Pacific, at the moderate rate of ten miles an hour.

We hope that the United States will not object to conducting this national project—it would be no local benefit, but in its effects coextensive with the Union.—It deserves their attention in many points of view—the improvement of the interior—increasing the value of the public domain—binding the East and West together—raising the Oregon at once to importance—and making it, what it can hardly be other ways, an efficient part of the Union—the interests of commerce, agriculture and manufactures would be essentially advanced—in fact our western coast brought into life and being. Nothing could contribute more to prosperity at home and reputation abroad than a magnificent effort like this.

The expense of it would not surpass one year of war.

It might be completed within six years—and if expense were the only obstacle, three years would be sufficient.

359 Section of editorial by S. W. Dexter, advocating a transcontinental railroad, in *The Emigrant*, Feb. 6, 1832, from a copy in the library of the University of Michigan, Ann Arbor

FORECASTS OF A TRANSCONTINENTAL RAILROAD

THE first dreamer who expressed in print his idea of a Pacific railroad seems to have been Judge S. W. Dexter, publisher and one of the editors of *The Emigrant*, a weekly newspaper at Ann Arbor, Michigan Territory. An editorial of February 6, 1832, proposed a railroad from Lake Erie to Oregon. The United States Government, if disinclined to construct this line, was to encourage private capital by means of a land grant of three million acres. Similar articles appeared during the 'thirties in Massachusetts, Missouri, New York and Iowa. It was a bold project, for in 1830 there were only twenty-three miles of railway in the United States. Even in 1840, the two thousand miles of railroad then in existence were all close to the Atlantic seaports. None of the railroad companies owned and operated more than one hundred miles of track and few of them so much as thirty miles. During the 'thirties there were only two states west of the Mississippi, Louisiana (1812) and Missouri (1821). The Oregon country itself was not definitely acquired until 1846; all of the Southwest, including California, still belonged to Mexico in the 'thirties, and Texas did not become an independent republic until 1836. To extend a form of transportation, as yet scarcely tested, across a continent but little explored and largely owned by foreign powers, was not a scheme to attract hard-headed business men.

THE PIONEER WORK OF ASA WHITNEY

IN the 'forties the situation was changed. Texas was annexed in 1845; the Oregon country was acquired the next year; and Mexico ceded us the Southwest, including California, in 1848. Meanwhile the railway mileage in the East was quadrupled and the importance of the railroad better understood. During the 'forties the Pacific Railway project received its most energetic support from Asa Whitney, a New York merchant who had been impressed by a ride on the Liverpool and Manchester Railroad in 1830. Between 1842 and 1844, business took him to China where he became enthusiastic over that country's commercial possibilities. A railroad across the continent, he urged, would secure this commerce to the United States and form a link in an international commercial highway from Shanghai to Liverpool. As he himself said, "I have undertaken this mighty work because I know someone's whole life must be sacrificed to it."

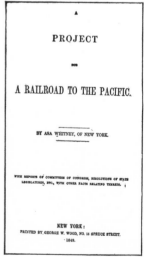

PROJECT

FOR

A RAILROAD TO THE PACIFIC.

BY ASA WHITNEY, OF NEW YORK.

WITH REPORTS OF COMMITTEES OF CONGRESS, RESOLUTIONS OF STATE LEGISLATURES, ETC., WITH OTHER FACTS RELATING THERETO.

NEW YORK:
PRINTED BY GEORGE W. WOOD, NO. 18 SPRUCE STREET.
1849.

360 Whitney's published project, from the title-page of the original pamphlet, 1849, in the New York Public Library

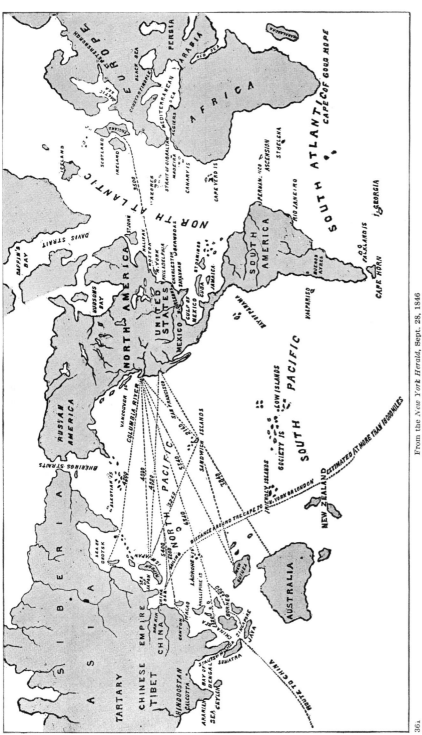

From the *New York Herald*, Sept. 28, 1846

WHITNEY'S PROPOSAL TO CONGRESS

WHITNEY's plan was to build a railroad as nearly straight as possible from the Great Lakes to the Pacific coast. He asked Congress to aid him by ceding to him a strip of land thirty miles wide on each side of the railway for which he was to pay ten cents an acre. This land he was to sell to settlers and with the money build the railroad. Settlers in their first year would be given employment on the construction and thereafter have at their door a means of transporting surplus agricultural products. If Whitney failed to complete his railroad, what was built was to become governmental property. If he did finish it, he was to operate it until the income equaled the expense; any further profits were to be turned over to the government, or used for educational or other public purposes. Whitney estimated the cost of construction at about sixty-five million dollars. Needless to say, Congress never granted Whitney's petitions. After exhausting his own considerable fortune in advocating his scheme, Whitney eked out a living by peddling milk in Washington, where he died unhonored. But the agitation started by Whitney did not pass with him. He was a lone herald of a movement that swelled yearly.

362 Thomas Hart Benton's Statue in Lafayette Park, St. Louis, by Harriet Hosmer (1830–1908), courtesy of *The St. Louis Star*, St. Louis

THOMAS HART BENTON, 1782–1858

WHITNEY's efforts were not without effect in winning men to a realization of the importance of a Pacific railroad, and these men in the 'fifties took up the agitation where Whitney left off. Whitney seems to have had no personal or selfish aims, and at the beginning of his campaign there was but one possible route, from Lake Erie or Michigan to Oregon by way of Salt Lake and South Pass. But the men of the 'fifties were each eager to advance the interests of his own locality; and since several routes were now possible, conflicting plans warred fruitlessly with one another in Congress. Perhaps the most persistent "booster" was Thomas H. Benton; in season and out he maneuvered for St. Louis. After the first transcontinental line was built, St. Louis erected a statue of Benton in one of the city parks in recognition of his indefatigable services, carrying upon it the words which he used at a Pacific Railroad meeting at St. Louis in 1849: "There is the East. There is India." A station on the railroad was named after the Missouri tribune. Yet no man did more to delay the building of the Pacific railway than Benton. He took the ground that it was better to have no railroad at all than one detrimental to St. Louis. Benton was most prominent but by no means the sole representative of the people who placed local interest above national welfare. Together they delayed for years the Pacific railroad.

SECTIONAL RIVALRY

IN Congress the South was less enthusiastic for the railroad than the North. But both North and South wished it to be built, if it was to be built, within its own territory. Within these two camps there were local interests that further subdivided the forces. On the side of the South. Charleston, South Carolina, claimed to be the logical eastern terminus of the proposed road; while the states which comprised the lower Mississippi Valley region were especially active in forwarding the claims of Memphis as the best starting point for the transcontinental enterprise. There appeared in *Niles' National Register*, March 14, 1849, the following announcement of a meeting sponsored by Memphis promoters: "A public meeting was held at Memphis on the 22d ult., to respond to the suggestions of the citizens of Arkansas and elsewhere, proposing a convention in Memphis on the 4th of July next, to devise and adopt measures for establishing a national railroad from the Mississippi to the Pacific. Resolutions were adopted approving of the proposition, and a committee of twenty-five persons was appointed to prepare a suitable address to the people of the United States on the subject." Texas in turn demanded that the road should run from California to the Gulf of Mexico or be located so that the route passed through Texas connecting the Pacific with the Atlantic. The northern group in turn was divided into a faction that favored Chicago as the eastern terminus and another demanding that the road should end in St. Louis.

C l. Benton concluded his speech as follows:.

We live in extraordinary times, and are called upon to elevate ourselves to the grandeur of the occasion. Three and a half centuries ago, the great Columbus—the man who was afterward carried home in chains from the New World which he had discovered; this great Columbus, in the year 1492, departed from Europe to arrive in the East by going to the West. It was a sublime conception. He was in the line of success, when the intervention of two continents, not dreamed of before, arrested his progress. Now, in the nineteenth century, mechanical genius enables his great design to be fulfilled. In the beginning, and in barbarous ages, the sea was a bar to the intercourse of nations. It separated nations. Mechanical genius, in inventing the ship, converted that barrier into a facility. Then land and continents became the obstruction. The two Americas intervening have prevented Europe and Asia from communicating on the straight line. For three centuries and a half this obstacle has frustrated the grand design of Columbus. Now, in our day, mechanical genius has again triumphed over the obstacles of nature, and converted into a facility that which had so long been an impassable obstacle. The steam car has worked upon the land, and among enlightened nations, and to a degree far transcending it, the miracle which the ship, in barbarous ages, worked upon the ocean. The land has now become the facility for the most distant communications, the conveyances being invented which annihilates both time and space. We hold the intervening land: we hold the obstacle which stopped Columbus: we are in the line between Europe and Asia.

We have it in our power to remove that obstacle—to convert it into a facility—and to carry him on to his land of promise and of hope, with a rapidity, a precision and a safety unknown to all ocean navigation. A king and a queen started him upon his great enterprise. It lies in the hands of a Republic to complete it. It is in our hands.—We, the people of the United States, of this first half of this nineteenth century. Let us raise ourselves up. Let us rise to the grandeur of the occasion. Let us complete the grand design of Columbus, by putting Europe and Asia into communication, and that to our advantage, through the heart of our own country. Let us give to his ships, converted into cars, a continued course, unknown to all former times. Let us make the iron road—and make it from sea to sea. States and individuals making it east of the Mississippi, the nation making it west. Let us now, in this convention, rise above everything sectional, personal, local. Let us beseech the National Legislature to build the great road upon the great national line which unites Europe and Asia—the line which will find, on our continent, the Bay of San Francisco at one end, St. Louis in the middle, the national metropolis and great commercial emporium at the other—and which shall be adorned with its crowning honor, the colossal statue of the great Columbus, whose design it accomplishes, hewn from the granite mass of a peak of the Rocky Mountains, overlooking the road—the mountain itself the pedestal, and the statue a part of the mountain—pointing with outstretched arm to the western horizon, and saying to the flying passenger, there is the East; there is India.

363 Thomas H. Benton's plea to avoid sectional bitterness by granting St. Louis' demands, from the Philadelphia *Public Ledger*, Nov. 1, 1849

THE PACIFIC RAILROAD CONVENTION IN PHILADELPHIA.—The resolve of the Railroad Convention, at St. Louis, to meet in Philadelphia in April next, will excite renewed interest in this great work among our citizens. Philadelphia interests are immediately connected with any undertaking of the kind, and through the system of internal improvements, which our State has adopted, our city may reasonably look for a large share of any benefit which may arise from connecting by railway the eastern and western borders of the continent. Years of course must elapse before any undertaking so vast can ever be accomplished, but that it will be consummated in time there is every reason to believe, especially when the active energy of our population and its rapid increase are taken into consideration. Already in the heart of the great interior basin of California a youthful State is asking for admission into the Union; east and west, in our new possessions, similar republics are rapidly growing into strength and power, and these youthful states will require, in time, the extension of the great chain of connection which is linking the Union together in bonds the most durable. However long this period may be postponed, it is not too early for our citizens to turn their attention to the fact, with the view of deriving ultimate advantage from it. The Convention, which has been discussing this important subject at St. Louis, is composed of several hundred delegates, and is probably one of the most numerous and intelligent that has ever assembled in the United States. Its presence in our city will impart additional interest to its discussions, and proper measures should be taken to make its stay among us agreeable as possible to its members.

364 Announcement of Pacific Railroad Convention at Philadelphia, from the Philadelphia *Public Ledger*, Oct. 20, 1849

PACIFIC RAILROAD ACT OF 1862

WITH the outbreak of war and the withdrawal of the southern representatives from Washington, the differences within the northern railroads were quickly composed. The conflicting claims of Chicago, St. Louis, and a group that wanted a Northern Pacific Railroad were satisfied by making the eastern terminus of the railroad a point near Fort Kearney on the one hundredth meridian, two hundred and forty-nine miles west of Omaha and Council Bluffs. From this point four branch roads were to be constructed eastward to Sioux City, Omaha, Atchison and Kansas City. As a war measure to defend and keep within the Union the Pacific coast, to control the Indians and facilitate the carrying of dispatches, troops and supplies, Congress passed the first Pacific Railroad act in June, 1862; it was signed by President Lincoln on July 1. Because of the partial failure of this act to attract private capital it was made more liberal in 1864. These two acts constitute the charter by which the first railroad was built across the plains, the Rocky Mountains and the Sierras to the Pacific Ocean. Just as the issue of the Civil War was unity between North and South, so the building of the transcontinental railroad resulted in a union of the East and West.

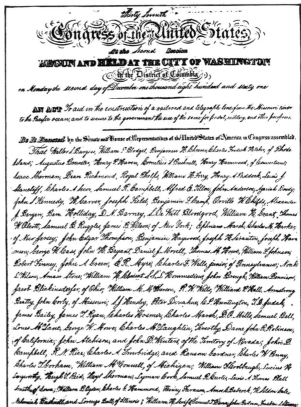

365   First page of the Pacific Railroad Act, July 1, 1862, from the original in the Department of State, Washington

THE RACE TO BUILD THE PACIFIC RAILROAD

THE actual construction of the Pacific railroad was allotted to two railroad companies: the Union Pacific was to build westward, the Central Pacific to proceed eastward. A tentative limit for each was the eastern boundary of California; later the Central Pacific was instructed to build one hundred and fifty miles beyond the state line, and finally both roads were to build until the two joined wherever the junction might be. Thus the grading and track laying of the two companies became a race, the prize being the land grants and bond subsidies to the road that actually put down the iron highway in the region of the junction together with control of the traffic originating in the valley of the Great Salt Lake. The difficulties confronting each road were about equal. The Central Pacific in its first one hundred and twenty-five miles had to climb seven thousand feet to cross the Sierras, necessitating fourteen tunnels, one of which was one thousand six hundred feet long. Every bit of material except wood and water had to be shipped by sea around South America. But this road was to be only six hundred and eighty-eight miles long as against one thousand and eighty-six for its rival. The Sierras, moreover, furnished ample supplies of timber and lumber for snow sheds, bridges, tunnel braces and ties, while cheap Chinese coolie labor was available for construction. The four principal promoters of the Central Pacific too were in much better accord with one another than the backers of the Union Pacific.

366   From the painting *An Early Railroad Train delayed by a Herd of Buffalo*, by N. H. Trotter (1827–) in the United States National Museum, Washington

367   The Summit Tunnel, Sierra Nevada, from *Frank Leslie's Illustrated Weekly*, Jan. 9, 1869

THE PROGRESS OF CONSTRUCTION

On the other hand, the Union Pacific was forced to build through a region with no white settlements except those of the Mormons and a few miners, with little water, with no timber except the inferior cottonwood and a territory infested with hostile Indians. Despite the fact that the Union Pacific was building from the East, it had no eastern railway connection until 1867 between Omaha and the terminus of eastern lines in Iowa, so that overland freighting was necessary for all railway supplies. Against these odds, the Union Pacific was for most of the way nearly level or with easy gradient; and through the Rockies a much easier pass was found than the Central Pacific had through the Sierras. The Central Pacific had nearly a year's start on the Union Pacific and had fifty-six miles laid to eleven for its rival. In 1866, however, the Union Pacific put down two hundred and forty-seven miles of track to thirty-eight for the Central Pacific. Again in the next year the eastern road finished more than two hundred miles of track while the western struggled to lay less than fifty. In the two following years, the race was more even, for the Central had surmounted its worst difficulty, the Sierras, and in the final year actually spiked over fifty miles more rails than the Union Pacific.

DIFFICULTIES OF CONSTRUCTION

Each contestant used about the same plan of construction. A hundred miles in advance went the surveyors. They were followed by the graders who in turn were a hundred miles more or less ahead of the track layers. Between the gaps of graders and track layers were other gangs of bridge builders and tunnel workers. At the end of the track was set up a temporary terminal town called at the time "Hell-on-Wheels." Cheyenne, Laramie and other towns to-day mark the temporary resting place of "Hell-on-Wheels." In the towns and various gangs there were as many as ten or fifteen thousand laborers. Discipline was military in character; indeed the Union Pacific gangs contained hundreds of Civil War veterans. At times the work itself was military, for Indian attacks compelled half the force to defend the other half at work and no man moved without a gun. Soldiers from frontier forts were called upon to protect the railroaders when the Indians became too meddlesome. With engineering, climatic and military obstacles at the scene of work, the promoters of the two roads were further harassed by financial and political perplexities at headquarters. Toward the end of the construction animosity between the two companies themselves added to the trials of both. Unconquerable determination alone overcame all difficulties.

368   From a painting *Building the Union Pacific Railroad — Attack by Indians*, in the
possession of the Union Pacific System, Omaha, Neb.

THE FINAL COMPROMISE

At all times and particularly in the two last years (1868-69), the work went forward feverishly. In 1869 the graders of the two companies met and passed each other throwing up grades roughly parallel for many miles. Not a penny was ever collected for this work. Conflicts arose between the Chinese coolies of the Central Pacific and the Irish workmen and Civil War veterans of the Union Pacific. Company officials, too, were in hot dispute as to the location of the junction. Congress in

369   Work on the last mile of the Pacific Railroad, from an engraving after a sketch by
A. R. Waud in *Harper's Weekly*, May 27, 1867

1869 attempted a settlement, but while the matter was under debate the belligerents compromised on Promontory, Utah, west of Ogden, as the official junction. Congress in April, 1869, sanctioned this compromise and the rails met at Promontory Point just a month later, May 10, 1869, with the honors in the race fairly even but slightly in favor of the Central Pacific.

370   From the painting *Driving the Last Spike*, 1881, by Thomas Hill, in the M. H. de Young
Memorial Museum, San Francisco

THE COMPLETION

The junction of the Union Pacific with the Central Pacific was marked by elaborate ceremony. The last tie to be placed was of polished California laurel and bore a silver plate reading: "The Last Tie Laid in the Completion of the Pacific Railroad May 10, 1869." To this the rails were spiked. Arizona furnished a spike of iron, silver and gold, and Nevada one of silver. Lastly, the gold spike of California, together with a silver sledge hammer, was handed to Leland Stanford, President of the Central Pacific, and to Thomas C. Durant, Vice-President of the Union Pacific.

371 Leland Stanford, 1824–93, from the portrait by S. W. Shaw in the E. B. Crocker Art Gallery, Sacramento, Cal.

THE CELEBRATION

STROKE by stroke turnabout, these two men drove the gold spike into the laurel tie. Each blow was carried by telegraph wires to the principal cities of the country. In San Francisco the strokes were repeated by peals of the bell on the City Hall, and in New York the chimes of Trinity played "Old Hundred." The final stroke was marked in San Francisco by a salute from a cannon, while in New York and in Omaha a salvo of cannon roared the news that East and West had met. In Chicago an immense civic parade celebrated the completion of the task, while the citizens of California pouring into San Francisco and Sacramento turned the day into tumult and the night into day. Appomattox had reunited the North and the South; Promontory Point had joined the East and the West; the two made a nation, one and indivisible. With the Civil War finished, though its wounds had not healed, and with iron rails spanning the continent, the country deemed that a new era of unprecedented prosperity was dawning. So the rejoicing over the event at Promontory Point was not only for what was accomplished but for what it was hoped lay in the future.

THE CRÉDIT MOBILIER

THE shouts of jubilation over the completion of the Pacific Railroad had hardly subsided when a low rumble of protest against the financial measures connected with the construction of the road began to be heard. This rumble gradually grew into an angry roar, the echoes of which have never ceased. The obvious method of paying for construction by the sale of capital stock had in the case of most of the earliest American roads proved disastrous to the stockholders. Long before the Union Pacific was chartered, it was customary to promote new railways by a small issue of stock to a few favored individuals. These insiders then formed a separate construction company which built the road, paying themselves from the proceeds of a bond issue based on the physical property of the line. Such bonds became readily salable, the insiders made a quick profit on construction, and, as stockholders, managed the railroad in their own interest after the bondholders had built the road for them. The promoters themselves put up little of their own money. This well known method was employed in financing the Union Pacific, but on so large a scale and with so many devious steps not yet wholly clear that a national scandal resulted. The Central Pacific was financed similarly by the "Contract and Finance Company."

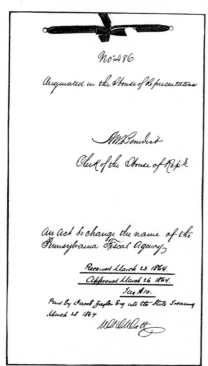

372 Title of Charter incorporating the Crédit Mobilier, March 26, 1864, from the original in the Pennsylvania House of Representatives, Harrisburg

373 Text of the Charter incorporating the Crédit Mobilier, from the original in the Pennsylvania House of Representatives, Harrisburg

DURANT *VERSUS* AMES

THE Union Pacific began its corporate existence in October, 1863, with two hundred and eighteen thousand dollars paid in for two thousand one hundred and eighty shares. Thomas C. Durant, the vice-president, was the real manager of the company. A year later Durant granted a construction contract to one H. M. Hoxie, a ferry employee at Omaha, for the building of one hundred miles of road from Omaha to the 100th meridian. Durant then formed a construction partnership among his Union Pacific friends and took over the Hoxie contract by assignment. After putting up eighty thousand dollars the members of the construction coterie became frightened at the unlimited liability and hesitated to advance further sums. Durant thereupon discovered an inactive corporation, the "Pennsylvania Fiscal Agency," with a charter that permitted almost unlimited activity but restricted the liability of stockholders to the amount of stock held. Durant bought the charter for one thousand six hundred dollars from a political "lame duck" named Duff Green, to whom it had been originally granted, changing the name to "Crédit Mobilier." To the Crédit Mobilier, the stockholders of which were Durant's

374 Thomas C. Durant, first Vice-President of the Union Pacific Railroad, from an engraved portrait in *Harper's Weekly*, Feb. 12, 1870

Union Pacific friends, the Hoxie contract was assigned, and all succeeding contracts, some by indirect methods. Within the Union Pacific and the Crédit Mobilier were two factions, one headed by Durant who saw no hope for profit in the Union Pacific itself and intended to wax fat from the Crédit Mobilier, the other led by Oakes and Oliver Ames, New England capitalists, who were willing to take profits from the Crédit Mobilier but were against impoverishing the Union Pacific to the extent that it could never be a good investment in itself. The Ames contingent became the more powerful in the affairs of both corporations. The Union Pacific paid the Crédit Mobilier for construction in government subsidy bonds, land-grant bonds, and first mortgage income bonds of the Union Pacific as well as stock in the railroad. The scandal arose over the fact that the amount paid to the Crédit Mobilier greatly exceeded the actual cost of building. The profit of the Crédit Mobilier ranged from twenty-five per cent to over two hundred per cent, depending upon how computation was made and what allowances were made for the difference between the par value and market value of the securities turned over to it. No one yet knows whether the Crédit Mobilier gained no more than a reasonable return or shamelessly robbed the Union Pacific bondholders. In the 'seventies the latter opinion was held, but the former has not been without adherents. Another ground of scandal was the charge that the Union Pacific "ring" used Crédit Mobilier stock to bribe Congressmen and other public officials in order to gain their ends. The scapegoat was Oakes Ames. He was a wealthy manufacturer with a seat in Congress. Originally invited by the President of the United States to help in the financing of the Union Pacific, Ames involved his private fortune of about one million dollars in its affairs. On account of his government position and because he was the leading director of the Union Pacific and the Crédit Mobilier, he became the target for criticism. Congress publicly censured him for the evils connected with the Crédit Mobilier and the public abuse killed him. (For a discussion of the political results of the Crédit Mobilier see Vol. IX.)

375 Oakes Ames, Vice-President of the Union Pacific Railroad, from a lithograph after a photograph, courtesy of the Union Pacific System, Omaha, Neb.

376 Collis P. Huntington, organizer of the Southern Pacific Railroad, from the portrait by S. W. Shaw in the E. B. Crocker Art Gallery, Sacramento, Cal.

OTHER TRANSCONTINENTAL RAILROADS

FIVE years before the Union Pacific met the Central Pacific at Promontory Point, a second transcontinental line, the Northern Pacific, was chartered by Congress. It was not until 1883, however, that it was able to operate trains from St. Paul to Portland. In the meantime, in 1881, the Atlantic & Pacific Railroad (now part of the Atchison, Topeka & Santa Fé) reached Deming, New Mexico, where it met the Southern Pacific projected from California eastward. The following year (1882), the Southern Pacific had extended another branch to El Paso where it met the Texas & Pacific, the two forming a passage from New Orleans to San Francisco. In 1883, the Southern Pacific gained its own entrance into New Orleans. Eventually, the Southern Pacific secured control of the Central Pacific. The Union Pacific had no Pacific terminus of its own, until in 1884 it acquired the Oregon Short Line and the Oregon Railway & Navigation Company with a terminus at Portland. In 1888, the Atchison, Topeka & Santa Fé gained entrance to Chicago and five years later secured an extension from Los Angeles to San Francisco. A rival road, the Great Northern, had been built between St. Paul and Seattle and opened for through business in 1893. Numerous other railroads were built and made units of larger systems. At the close of the century there existed two great divisions of transcontinental lines, the making of which changed in accordance with new mergers and combinations. In 1906 the Southern Transcontinental System was composed of the Colorado & Southern, the Wisconsin Central, the Atchison, Topeka & Santa Fé, the Union Pacific and the Southern Pacific. In the Northern Transcontinental group were the Great Northern, the Northern Pacific, the Illinois Central (Southern Territory), the Oregon Short Line, and the Oregon Railway & Navigation Company.

RAILROAD MERGERS

THE first great railroad consolidations which brought into existence the New York Central, the Pennsylvania and other systems were mostly end-to-end combinations of non-competing roads. New motives appeared after the Civil War; the restriction of competition, access to strategic railroad centers, such as New York, Chicago or St. Louis, and the exclusive interchange of traffic between two lines. The methods of consolidation have been as varied as the incentives. The simplest method of course was the outright purchase of one railroad by another. Nearly as simple was consolidation by means of long-term leases. Control as effective as consolidation was frequently obtained by the purchase by one road, or by a specially created holding company, of sufficient stock in another road to insure harmonious management. Finally, railroads were sometimes bound together through individuals holding a personal interest in each. This method has been so common and so effective that railroads have been grouped as belonging to the Vanderbilt, Gould, Morgan, Belmont, Harriman, Hill or Van Sweringen interests.

377 E. H. Harriman, from a photograph by Pach Bros., New York, in possession of the publishers

RAILROADS AND AMERICAN LIFE

To evaluate the importance of railroads to American life is an almost impossible task. They made feasible the settlement of regions otherwise unavailable, and have aided immensely in spreading one political power from the Atlantic to the Pacific. They have cheapened food stuffs in the cities and manufactured goods on the farms. They have made labor mobile and have created a demand for workers to exploit hitherto inaccessible resources. They have banished isolation and created mutual interdependence. They have raised rents by aiding the growth of cities and lowered rents elsewhere by penetrating formerly remote lands. Railroads bind together those living thousands of miles apart, and exert a unifying influence on our national life. Seasons and distances are annihilated to produce a nation of neighbors living in plenty and ease.

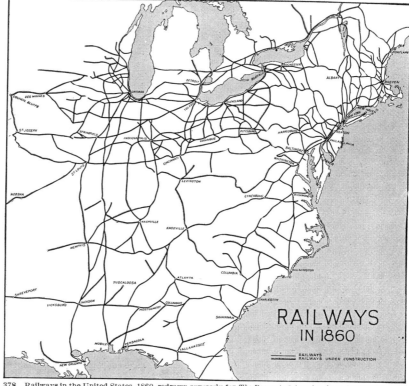

378   Railways in the United States, 1860, redrawn expressly for *The Pageant of America*, from Appleton's Railway Map of the United States and the Canadas, New York, 1860

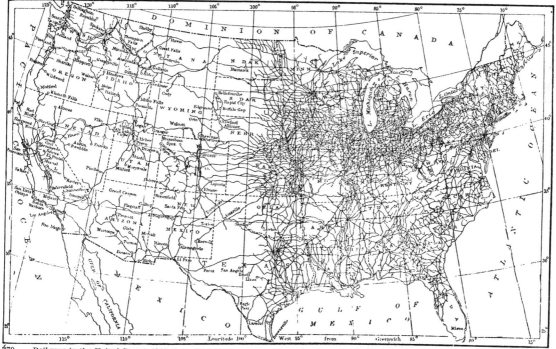

379   Railways in the United States, 1910, from *History of Domestic and Foreign Commerce in the United States*, by Emory R. Johnson, T. W. Van Metre, etc., Washington, Carnegie Institution of Washington, 1915

CHAPTER VII

THE BUSINESS OF EXPRESS

THE railroad has made the vast area of the United States an economic unit. From East and West, North and South the manufacturer may gather the raw materials for his factory and, when his product is completed, may sell it in a market as large as that in which he has bought. The service of the railroad to the American people is so fundamental to their whole life that the railroad companies have not attempted to manage all the transportation of persons or commodities that takes place on their lines. As the railroad has found that it is more efficient and hence more profitable to leave the organization of the parlor and pullman car service to another concern, so they generally have not attempted to control the business of carrying "express." Modern civilized life requires the speedy transport of vast numbers of articles whose value is high in comparison with their bulk. Companies established to perform this service are almost as old as railroads. Such concerns use every possible mode of transportation that may be necessary to deliver the package which they have accepted at its appointed destination.

The express company is an example of the transformation which industrialism has brought to American life. In the seventeenth century the individual family living usually under primitive conditions was practically sufficient unto itself. In the eighteenth century specialization began to develop as the artisan became able to support himself entirely by plying his trade, and the professional man in the person of the doctor and the lawyer became a commonplace. The second half of the nineteenth century, after the main lines of the railway net had been established, saw the simpler arrangements of the earlier times swept away. The railroad, together with a number of other factors, made possible in the United States an industrial revolution which changed fundamentally the civilization of the American people. The outstanding characteristic of the new era is specialization, division of labor. The express company which on superficial observation might seem to perform a task belonging to the work of the railroad is on the contrary the result of accurate adjustment of business organization to the needs of the day.

380 Aaron Y. Ross, 1829–1922, stage driver, employed by Wells-Fargo & Co., 1860–1916, courtesy of the American Railway Express Co., New York

381   Account sheet of the Phoenix Stagecoach Line, Washington, 1836, from the original in the New York Historical Society

THE ACCOMMODATING STAGECOACH DRIVER

STAGECOACH drivers made a comfortable income by doing errands along the route, collecting and delivering parcels, letters and messages, collecting bills, and taking care of small children on the way to visit grand-mother. When the railroads came, they hired the stage drivers, partly to silence their objections to the destruction of their old occupation, partly because their training in handling the traveling public was invaluable to the new railroad managers. The public was left without its accustomed errand runners. Conductors continued this messenger service as far as they could but the public needed, without knowing it, a new messenger service adapted to the new mode of transportation and yet flexible enough to suit all the vagaries of public demand. William F. Harnden, the original expressman, filled the need. (See No. 384.)

THE ORIGIN OF THE EXPRESS BUSINESS

WILLIAM F. HARNDEN, after five years as conductor and passenger clerk for the Boston & Worcester Railroad — he was conductor on the first passenger train run in New England — was so physically exhausted by the long hours (16 hours per day), that he gave up his job and went to New York for a visit. There he met a transplanted Bostonian named "Jim" (James W.) Hale, agent for a Providence-New York steamboat and the operator of a reading room and news service. Hale spoke to Harnden of the frequent requests made to him for someone who would do errands in Boston, and suggested that a regular service of this sort would be a good job for him. Harnden, accordingly, made a contract for express service with the superintendent of the Boston & Providence Railroad, and the manager of the *John W. Richmond*, a steamer plying between Providence and New York. Equipped with a large leather bag for packages, Harnden, in March, 1839, became the first expressman in the world, acting as his own messenger between Boston and New York.

382   Harnden's advertisement in the Boston *Annual Advertiser*, from Stimpson, *Boston Directory*, 1839

383   Harnden & Company's Boston Office, 1841, from A. L. Stimson, *History of the Express Companies*, New York, 1858

384   William F. Harnden, 1813–45, from the daguerreotype in possession of Fred Harnden, San Francisco, Cal.

HARNDEN & COMPANY

HARNDEN acted as his own messenger only for the first few months of his new business; he soon needed assistants. A clerk was established in the office on Wall Street, New York, broker's remittances and messages forming an important part of his business. Another office was maintained in Boston while Harnden's brother Adolphus acted as messenger between the two centers until he was killed in 1840 in a disaster on Long Island. In the second year of business, Harnden established an agency in Philadelphia. The steamship serv-

ice of the Cunard Company between Liverpool and Boston greatly increased the express business and its success suggested to Harnden the extension of his service overseas. In carrying out this plan, Harnden formed the partnership of Harnden & Company. The European connection led Harnden & Company away from parcel express into international banking and the forwarding of emigrants. Offices were established in the principal cities of England and France and later in Scotland, Ireland and Germany. At first, these offices handled emigrant funds between Europe and America, but soon the emigrants themselves became the chief concern. To facilitate this traffic Harnden secured special rates and privileges on the Enoch Train line between Boston and Liverpool and exclusive use of certain boat lines on the Erie Canal. Some ten thousand emigrants were billed through from their European homes to a new home in the Middle West by Harnden & Company. This was a curious business in which free human beings were the commodities of commerce.

385   Harnden Express Poster, from a contemporary lithograph in possession of the publishers

THE ADAMS EXPRESS COMPANY

Upon Harnden's death in 1845, the two parts of Harnden and Company's business, the domestic express and the European branch, were separated and sold. Eventually, the American domestic business dropped the name of Harnden and became Thompson, Livingston & Co. This firm, changing its personnel and name from time to time, enlarged its operations southward and westward until it came into competition with Adams and Company. In 1854, the latter concern absorbed all its competitors. The European branch kept the old name until 1851 when unwise investments brought it to ruin. Thus the name of Harnden disappeared from the express business, although Harnden's son (William H.) was for a short time an employee of Wells, Fargo and Company at San Francisco. William F. Harnden had died after a five year struggle against tuberculosis. For the short period Harnden was connected with

the express business he made a decent living and withstood competition. In 1866 a memorial was set up over his grave in Mount Auburn, bearing the inscription: "Erected by the Express Companies of the United States in the year A.D. 1866." Since Harnden's name is unknown to the general public there is scant recognition of the part he played in founding one of the great services the public enjoys. Fame is a fickle jade.

386   General Offices, New York, of the Adams (including the Southern, the National, and the Wells-Fargo) Express Company, from *Harper's New Monthly Magazine*, Aug. 1875

ALVIN ADAMS, 1804–77

Out of Vermont came Alvin Adams, an orphan of sixteen, to seek his fortune in Boston. For twenty years he sought it in vain as hotel clerk, family grocer, and produce merchant. In 1840, when thirty-six years old, Adams joined with one P. B. Burke to form Burke & Co. in order to enter the express business in competition with Harnden who had then been operating slightly more than a year. Few men were more unlike than Harnden and Adams. Ruggedly healthy, aggressive, alert, superlatively companionable, Adams possessed all the qualities necessary for success. But Boston looked upon Harnden as the discoverer of the express

service and gave him most of the business. Adams' partner soon became discouraged and retired; but Adams himself kept on, although up to 1842 the entire staff of Adams & Co. consisted of three men and a boy. By 1843 Harnden & Co's European ventures led them to neglect their American business. This proved to be Adams' opportunity. At first Adams & Co. confined its operations to New York, New London and Norwich, Connecticut, Worcester and Boston. In the later 'forties, the company extended southward to Philadelphia, Baltimore and Washington and in the 'fifties covered the South along the Atlantic and Gulf coasts. San Francisco was reached via Panama. The territory controlled by Adams & Co. was the most densely populated and industrially the most developed in the United States and traffic grew enormously. In the early 'fifties Adams & Co was the best intrenched express company in its territory. In July, 1854, it bought out its principal rivals and reorganized under the name "Adams Express Company," with a capital of one million two hundred thousand dollars. This was at that time divided into twelve thousand shares. From that time onward the company was a power in the land and exceedingly lucrative to its shareholders, its earnings being enormous.

387   From Ballou's *Pictorial Drawing Room Companion,* Feb. 17, 1855

388   Henry Wells, 1805–1878, from a photograph,
      courtesy of the American Railway Express Co.

THE AMERICAN EXPRESS COMPANY

FOLLOWING the success of Harnden and Adams, companies sprang up by the hundred. Many confined themselves within the limits of their own city or the collection and delivery of merchandise and other items of commerce. Other more ambitious enterprises had agents or connections in two, three or four cities or towns. Companies of still larger di-

389   William G. Fargo, 1818–81, from a photograph,
      courtesy of the American Railway Express Co.

mensions served all the principal cities and towns within a given state, along a particular trade route or within a well-defined territory. By 1860 five companies were superior to all others; they were: the Adams Express Company, the American, National, United States, and Wells-Fargo & Company. Since Adams was entrenched on the north and south routes along the Atlantic and Gulf coasts, the other companies had to seek different territory. The American Express began as a partnership between Henry Wells and George Pomeroy, operating an express service between Albany and Buffalo. With Crawford Livingston they formed five successive partnerships, the final association being called Wells & Company. For service west of Buffalo to Cincinnati, St. Louis and Chicago, Wells joined with William G. Fargo, William A. Livingston and others in various combinations, eventually becoming Livingston & Fargo. Naturally, Wells & Company and Livingston & Fargo operated together harmoniously, but a rival, Butterfield, Wasson & Company appeared in the late 'forties. Out of this rivalry a consolidation was formed in 1850, the American Express Company acting as a holding company for two new companies called Wells, Butterfield & Company and Livingston & Fargo Company.

390   Offices of Wells-Fargo Co. during the Gold Rush (reconstruction),
                    courtesy of the American Railway Express Co.

OTHER EXPRESS COMPANIES

THE Wells-Fargo Company was organized in 1852 by Henry Wells, William G. Fargo, Johnston Livingston, A. Reynolds, E. B. Morgan and others to conduct an express business in California and between that state and New York city by water. Before 1860, the company had a firm grip on the Pacific area and had bought out the principal local express companies in California. Its chief business was the carrying of gold.

THEIR FIELDS OF OPERATION

HARNDEN & COMPANY also operated a lucrative letter post. The company acted in the closest harmony with the American Express Company. The National Express Company worked the territory between the Adams and the American Express companies. This territory lay north of Albany via Troy and Burlington to Canada. The company drew upon all of northern New York and western Vermont and did a large business within Canada, particularly at Montreal. The organiza-

391   Interior of a Wells-Fargo Express Office (reconstruction), from a photograph, courtesy of the American Railway Express Co.

tion was perfected in 1855 after the usual series of partnerships and combinations. The National did not conflict with the American because it had on its directorate some of the same men. In addition, D. N. Barney, a New York banker, was president of the National and the Wells-Fargo. These three — American, Wells-Fargo, and National — were therefore more or less allied to one another. The United States Express, another company of which D. N. Barney was president, was formed in 1854. It operated primarily across southern New York along the route of the Erie Railroad and over the western connections wherever there was no conflict with the American's territory. It is apparent that even before the Civil War the largest express companies had hewn out separate fields of operation, and that four of the five were interrelated not by corporate or partnership bonds but through personal ties. One peculiarity of the express companies was that they were not corporations but joint stock associations. They had a small capital compared to the volume of business done, but a large one in view of the amount of capital actually used or required.

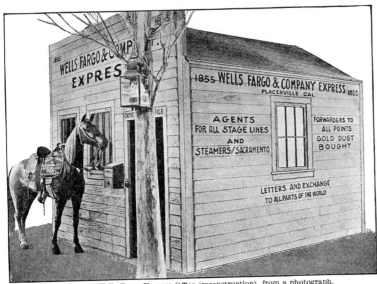

392   Exterior of a Wells-Fargo Express Office (reconstruction), from a photograph, courtesy of the American Railway Express Co.

393   Wells-Fargo Letter Box, from a photograph, courtesy of the American Railway Express Co.

394   An army express office, from *Harper's New Monthly
                   Magazine*, August 1875

THE EXPRESS BUSINESS IN
THE CIVIL WAR

In the 'fifties the Adams Express Company had built an extensive business throughout the South under the energetic direction of Henry B. Plant, who in 1854 had established himself at Augusta, Georgia. The threat of war endangered its strong position as long as it retained its northern connections and personnel. When Fort Sumter was fired upon in 1861, among those who watched the dropping shells was the northern president of the Adams Express Company. With a full realization of what that cannonade meant the president of the Adams called into consultation H. B. Plant, then superintendent of the southern express business. Hardly had the smoke cleared before a new express company was born, the Southern Express Company, with Plant as president, which took over the Adams interest below Mason and Dixon's Line. Throughout the war the express stations within the field of military operations displayed the emblems of the *Adams* or the *Southern* according to the shifts in the fortunes of battle. At the close of the war the Southern was permitted by the Adams to continue its separate existence which lasted until all the express companies were merged during the World War. Between the Southern and the Adams the closest and most harmonious business relations continued to exist.

395   Adams Express office at City Point, Va., on pay day, from an engraving
         after a sketch by J. R. Hamilton in *Harper's Weekly*, Nov. 5, 1864

A STAGE LINE TO CALIFORNIA

The discovery of gold in the Pike's Peak region of Colorado gave rise in 1858 to some of the most interesting phases of express history. From St. Joseph, Missouri, and Leavenworth, Kansas, a few miles apart on the Missouri River, there stretched for two thousand miles westward to Sacramento an unknown territory without a single permanent settlement except the recently established Mormon colony at Salt Lake City and a few garrisons of the United States army. But, where gold was, men, supplies, and news must go. A stage line was established by Russell, Majors & Waddell from St. Joseph to Denver, called the Central Overland, California & Pike's Peak Express Company. A mail route from Sacramento to Salt Lake City, operated by one Ben Holliday, and another from Salt Lake City to St. Joseph owned and run at long intervals by John Hockaday, were absorbed by the new express company, which thereupon conceived the daring idea of a regular fast mail route over the entire two thousand miles from St. Joseph to Sacramento and San Francisco. This idea developed into the "Pony Express."

396   A Central Overland, California & Pike's Peak Express Co. coach, from an
                 engraving in possession of the publishers

397   From the mural painting, 1920, *The Pony Express Rider on his first Relay after leaving St. Joseph, Mo.*,
by Edward J. Holslag, in the First National Bank, St. Joseph, Mo.

THE PONY EXPRESS

On April 3, 1860, at 4 P.M., Henry Wallace, riding at one hundred and twenty pounds, mounted a swift pony before the offices of the United States Express Company at St. Joseph and dashed across the prairie. Twenty-five miles out a fresh pony awaited him and at fifty miles, another. At seventy-five miles from St. Joseph another rider took up the race and in this manner for nine days the precious saddle bags were rushed across the plains, the Rockies and the Cascades to Sacramento, amidst the uproar of anvils, church bells and cannon. At Sacramento the swift steamer *Antelope* hurried the bags to San Francisco. The California Band and Volunteer Firemen paraded from the boat dock to the offices of the *Alta Telegraph* at one o'clock in the morning, the eleventh day from St. Joseph. Men and horses had vanquished time and distance.

THE PONY EXPRESS RUNS TWICE A WEEK

The day the Pony Express left St. Joseph another rider, Harry Roff, started eastward from Sacramento. Exactly on schedule ten days later the first Pony Express from the West arrived in St. Joseph. For two years in summer and winter, fair weather or foul, despite hostile Indians and white bandits, a regular schedule was maintained between St. Joseph and Sacramento, at first in ten days making an average speed of eight miles per hour, but soon in eight days, at an average speed of ten miles per hour. Before the Pony Express the mail schedule from New York to San Francisco via Panama was twenty-two days. The Pony Express at first ran weekly from each terminus but after June 10, 1860, it operated twice a week. The distance between relay stations was shortened from twenty-five miles to ten where the nature of the country required it, and the riders rode between three stations. When circumstances such as an Indian war prevented a rider from being relieved at the third station, he sometimes continued in the saddle for many hours. Among the famous riders were Buffalo Bill (W. F. Cody) and Jack Slade. The history of the west is full of color and picturesque features but there are few that have stirred the imagination and given the shade of romance to history to the extent furnished by the short-lived pony express. Nearly every trip of every rider had its thrills and the complete story was an epic.

398   Monument at St. Joseph, Mo., marking the spot where the first Pony Express started, April 3, 1860, from a photograph, courtesy of the American Railway Express Co.

399   From the mural painting, 1920, *Missouri River Packet Landing at St. Joseph*, by Edward J. Holslag,
                     in the First National Bank, St. Joseph, Mo.

THE PONY EXPRESS ROUTE

LETTERS and news items, wrapped in oiled silk and written on the thinnest paper, were carried by the riders
for ten dollars an ounce. The papers were placed in four locked pockets of a light leather "mochilla" or pair
of saddle bags, which were shifted from pony to pony at the relay stations. The Pony Express route was
due west from St. Joseph to Fort Kearney, thence by way of the Platte to Julesburg. From that point the
way was by Forts Laramie and Bridger to Salt Lake City. Beyond the Mormon metropolis the riders pointed
for Camp Floyd, Ruby Valley, Humboldt and Carson City. From there the trail was plainly indicated to
Placerville, Folsom, and Sacramento. In 1860 the Overland Telegraph Company began at St. Joseph and at
Sacramento to string a line across the two-thousand-mile gap. As the lines advanced the Pony Express
traveled only between the ends of the wire, and when the wires joined in 1862 the Pony Express became a
picturesque memory. As a service the Pony Express was a success but financially it ruined its promoters, the
deficit amounting to two hundred thousand dollars. The upkeep on one hundred and ninety relay stations,
four hundred station employees, eighty riders and five hundred horses in a country then without local supplies,
was too great a strain although the receipts per trip ran as high as one thousand dollars.

THE OVERLAND MAIL COMPANY

Two years before the "Pony Express" the Wells-Fargo Company had organized the Overland Mail Company,
which carried mail, express matter and passengers by stage from St. Louis through New Mexico and Arizona
to Los Angeles and San Francisco. The success of the "Pony Express" and the threat of war caused the
Wells-Fargo interests to take steps in 1861 to transfer the Overland Mail Co. to the central route of the
"Pony Express." George Chorpening was then operating a stage line from Salt Lake City to Sacramento.

The Central Overland, California
& Pike's Peak Express Company,
owned by John Hockaday, was
also in service. Ben Holliday,
protected by a Colorado charter,
ran a stage line called the Overland Mail & Express Co., from
St. Joseph to Salt Lake City. All
of these rivals were successively
bought by the Wells-Fargo Company, which from 1866 to 1869
continued to run a stage mail,
express, and passenger service
from St. Joseph to Sacramento.

400   An Overland Stage Line ticket to the West, from an engraving
                     in possession of the publishers

401   The Overland Mail starting East from San Francisco, from *Harper's Weekly*, Dec. 11, 1858

RAILROADS AND EXPRESS COMPANIES

WHEN in 1869 the Union Pacific and Central Pacific met at Promontory Point, Utah, to form a continuous transcontinental railroad, the Wells-Fargo Company sold out their transportation business and reverted to an express and banking company, contracting with the Union Pacific for carriage. The Central Pacific did not at first serve the Wells-Fargo Company but contracted with another competing express called the Pacific Express. But the Wells-Fargo bought off this rival and in 1870 became the dominant express company in all the far western territory. Later the American, the United States, and newer companies associated with the new transcontinental railroads, entered the Wells-Fargo territory; but at the time of the merger of all the express companies during the World War the Wells-Fargo operated over more than twice as many miles of line as its nearest rival, the Adams Express Company.

402   From a mural painting, 1920, *Stage Coach Held up by half breeds and Indians*, by Edward J. Holslag, in the First National Bank, St. Joseph, Mo.

HIGHWAYMEN BESIEGE THE WELLS–FARGO STAGES

IN the wild, uninhabited country through which the Wells-Fargo stages carried their valuable parcels highwaymen plied a lucrative trade. Guards on the stages were not of much value except to soothe the nerves of passengers, because the attacks were generally a surprise from ambush.

403   A stagecoach hold up (reconstruction), courtesy of the
American Railway Express Co.

MEASURES OF PROTECTION

THE losses to Wells-Fargo were so great that the company organized a special corps of detectives, some of whom were not without experience as highwaymen. The work of the detectives was so effective that attacks became infrequent and less often successful. The tales clustering around the robberies of stagecoaches are now part of the "color" of the Far West.

FUNCTIONS OF THE EXPRESS COMPANIES

ALTHOUGH the express companies are most closely allied with the railroads, they have always used other means of forwarding their business. Harnden himself made part of his journey from Boston to New York by boat, and vessels still carry express matter on the rivers, lakes and oceans. Stage, horseback and dog train are still resorted to wherever railroad service ceases. The express companies seek the best mode of getting the work done regardless of what that may be. The forwarding of valuable or perishable freight has been the mainstay of the express companies, but they have also derived considerable revenue from the execution of papers, writing money orders, making collections and doing an order and commission business. These services are not confined to the United States but are world-wide. Of late personally conducted tours have been added to the express service, a logical development from the check and money privilege long extended to travelers. The offices of the express companies never have been confined to continental America, but since the way was opened by Harnden European branches have been maintained. To-day offices of the express companies are found in every part of the world. Although there is nothing to prevent any or all of the American railroads from refusing to make a contract with the express companies and operating their own express business, the express companies even then would still be left with much business to do besides the forwarding of fast freight over railway lines.

404   Interior of the American Express offices, Paris, France, from a photograph, courtesy of the American Railway Express Co.

405   Exterior of the American Express Building, Paris, France, from a photograph, courtesy of the American Railway Express Co.

CHAPTER VIII

OCEAN AND LAKE COMMERCE IN A MECHANICAL AGE

ONE of the most striking results of the American industrial revolution in the latter half of the nineteenth century was the almost complete disappearance of the American merchant marine engaged in foreign commerce. With practically two centuries of maritime experience and achievement behind them the American people suddenly abandoned the sea. The great clipper ships which defied so successfully their British rivals passed into relative insignificance but left a glorious record. At the same time the British kept steadily on improving and developing their ships with the passing decades and maintaining their maritime world supremacy.

A number of factors combined to drive the Stars and Stripes from the sea. During the Civil War Confederate commerce raiders destroyed a large amount of shipping and by compelling an advancement of insurance rates forced hundreds of vessels into foreign registry. But this setback might easily have been overcome had the American people willed to direct their energies toward the sea. The reason why they did not was primarily because of the opportunities which were offered on land. By the middle of the nineteenth century the time had come when Americans were ready to begin the exploitation on a vast scale of the unparalleled natural wealth which lay within the national boundaries. What capital and energies they had went into the mining of coal and iron, gold, silver, and copper; into the tapping of oil pools; into the refining of these raw products hewn out of the earth; and into the manufacturing of an ever increasing variety of articles that were wanted to make life more comfortable or more convenient. Money and energy went into perfecting the railway system, into the building of urban transportation lines, into the network of wires that made communication by telegraph and later by telephone possible from one end of the United States to another. Busy with the great task of laying securely the foundations of the economic life of the new day in an undeveloped country, the American people turned for the time being from the sea. The greater part of their foreign trade was carried in vessels which they did not own.

As the Civil War brought about a sharp decline in the merchant marine of the United States so the World War played an important part in its swift revival. By 1917 the new industrial era had been firmly established. The vast equipment of transportation lines and factory buildings which were characteristics of the new era had come into being. The capital which had been "frozen" into this equipment was beginning to bring in rich returns. Americans were seeking opportunities for the further investment of this surplus. Moreover, the change in their life had brought a change in the character of their exports, and a merchant marine became desirable in order to aid American industry in securing adequate raw materials and disposing of manufactured goods in foreign markets. So an American merchant marine again appeared, which in the first half of the nineteenth century took a place second to that of Britain among the merchant marines of the world.

406   The *Great Western*, from an engraving by G. Lansing, in Ithiel Town, *Atlantic Steamships*, New York, 1838

THE *GREAT WESTERN*

THE clipper ship was America's challenge to the commercial carrier nations of the world. But even before the first clipper was designed, changes in ocean commerce had begun that eventually almost banished American ships from the deep seas — changes in materials and in motive power in which the United States had little share. The British steamer *Great Western*, plying without recoaling between trips from Bristol to New York and operated for nine seasons, may be credited with initiating in 1838 scheduled continuous passages by steam vessel across the Atlantic. The *Great Western* was a paddle wheel steamer built of wood with a gross tonnage of one thousand three hundred and twenty and a net of six hundred and seventy-nine. She was two hundred and sixteen feet long by thirty-five and four-tenths feet broad with a depth of twenty-three and two-tenths. The modern *Leviathan* could carry the *Great Western* on her deck without much difficulty. Sailing packets and clippers could and did make just as fast voyages as the early steamships. But the advantage of the sailing ship, larger cargo space enabling it to carry freight cheaper than a steamer whose hold was partially filled with machinery, could not outweigh the drawback of sail, namely its inability to keep to schedule. Calms might add days to a voyage while the sail ship rolled idly on the ocean or adverse winds might either delay the trip or blow the ship leagues off her schedule. On the contrary the steamship plodded steadily toward port regardless of calm and was only slightly affected by adverse winds. Steamers therefore were preferred to sailing vessels by passengers and merchants to whom time had value. As the world became geared to a faster pace, steamships were more and more favored.

407   The *Sirius*, early British steamship, from Ithiel Town, *Atlantic Steamships*, New York, 1838

408   Steamship *Great Britain*, from *The Illustrated London News*, July 15, 1843

THE STEAMSHIP *GREAT BRITAIN*

THE Great Britain Steamship Company, not satisfied with inaugurating regular transatlantic steamship service, built and operated in 1840 the first overseas iron steamship, the *Great Britain*, with a screw propeller. Iron had been suggested for ship construction as early as 1809 and a patent for iron boats had been taken out in 1815; but the idea was generally ridiculed. It was said of course that iron would not float and even if it did that it would soon rust and leak, besides offering an excellent security for barnacles and weeds. It was further asked how a compass could be kept accurate on an iron ship. The wiseacres were confounded by a small iron ship, the *Vulcan*, built for Clyde service in 1818, a vessel which not only floated but gave a half century of service. In 1821 a small iron steamship, the *Aaron Manby*, was constructed for shoal waters, and this was followed by several others for like purpose. These vessels demonstrating the feasibility of iron for ships, the British seafolk tried iron for longer voyages on the ocean, first to Africa and then to India. The largest of the first iron boats was the *Rainbow* of six hundred tons burden built in 1837. The *Great Britain*, designed in 1840, was to be a ship of three thousand tons five times the size of the *Rainbow* — three hundred and twenty-two feet long, fifty-one feet broad and thirty-two feet deep. Bold men indeed were they who projected such a ship at that time. But the *Great Britain* justified their daring; she floated, she withstood the buffets of the rough Atlantic, she more than earned her keep; in short in every way she was a success as a steamship. The greatest proof of her stanchness and also a demonstration of the strength of iron construction occurred in September, 1846, when the ineptitude of her captain ran her ashore on the coast of Ireland. There she lay all winter pounded by seas that would have reduced a wooden ship to splinters but so little was the *Great Britain* damaged that she was hauled off the following summer, reconditioned and operated in the Australian trade for twenty-one years. After her long years as a steamer she was converted into a sailing ship

for another decade of creditable service. Finally she ended her career — as has many a fine ship — as a coal barge in coastwise trips among the Falkland Islands. Despite the success of the *Great Britain*, iron construction made its way slowly; but in 1856 even the conservative Cunard Company adopted iron hulls and by the time of the Civil War it may be said that iron was recognized as the best ship building material of the day. Iron ships were strong, iron was adaptable to all sizes and intricacies of design and was easily procured in Great Britain. But iron ships doomed the small ship-yards.

409   Launch of the *Great Britain*, from *The Illustrated London News*, July 29, 1843

410   Sir Francis Pettit Smith, from *The Illustrated London News*, Sept. 9, 1871

THE SINGLE–SCREW PROPELLER

THE screw propeller of the *Great Britain* was not a new device; claims for the origination of the screw propulsion idea date back into the eighteenth century and even the seventeenth. It will be remembered that Stevens, the American, had built and run a small screw steamboat in 1804; but the *Clermont* had paddle wheels, and all the early steamboats on inland waters and upon the high seas had followed Fulton's example. In the reintroduction of the screw credit should go, among others, to John Ericsson and Sir Francis Pettit Smith.

411   The Propeller of the *Great Western*, from J. R. Hill, *Year Book of Facts*, London, 1843

THE ADVANTAGES OF THE SCREW PROPELLER

THE *Great Britain* in commercial service and the *Rattler*, launched in 1843 for the British Admiralty, both gave convincing evidence of the fuel economy of screw propulsion in large ocean-going ships. In rough weather the screw lay deep in the water, but paddle wheels, with the rolling of the vessel, were frequently out of water and in the air, a severe strain upon the ship. On the other hand a single screw ship was harder to steer than a paddle wheel steamer whose wheels could be made to assist in steering; and damage to the screw likely to occur in shallow water was well nigh fatal to the ship. Despite the disadvantages of the screw the economy was so great that after 1850 it displaced paddle wheels in deep water service, and the side wheel or stern wheel steamer was relegated to shallow or inland waters where it has remained to this day.

JOHN ERICSSON, 1803–1889

JOHN ERICSSON evidenced his inventive and executive ability at an early age. When he was a boy of eleven he built a miniature saw mill and only three years later he was a division boss over six hundred workers engaged in building the Gotha Canal. Ten years later he was drawing army maps and engaged in improving cannon, guns, and steam engines. In 1829 he built both a steam fire engine and a locomotive. His screw propeller for ships, consisting of several blades or segments of a screw, was patented in England in 1836 and tried on the Thames in 1838. His propeller was based on such correct principles of twist that it was an immediate success. The following year he came to the United States and supervised in 1841 the installation of a screw propeller on the warship *Princeton*, the first step toward our modern navy. At the same time he fitted propellers to steamboats for the Delaware & Raritan Canal, the Erie Canal and the James River Canal. The *Witch*, an iron steamship with a propeller, was built under his instruction. His place in American history, due to his armored steam *Monitor*, is well known. The year after his death his body was carried by an American naval ship to Sweden for final burial. Though American only by adoption, his name stands high in our annals.

412   From the portrait by Ballin, 1862, in the American Society of Mechanical Engineers, New York

413   Cunard Royal Mail screw steamship *Bothnia*, from a lithograph, courtesy of the
Cunard Steamship Co., Ltd., New York

THE STEAMSHIP *BOTHNIA*

THE general adoption of the screw after 1850 increased the use of iron hulls, since a wooden stern was not stanch enough to withstand the constant great strain of a whirling submerged propeller. Improvement in the engine speedily followed. The first engines were all "simple," that is, they used but one expansion of steam at low pressure. In the late 'fifties the British began using compound (double) expansion high pressure engines in their smaller boats. The first Cunarder with a compound engine, the *Bothnia*, built in 1874, showed a decided economy in fuel. The double expansion engine was followed by the triple and then by the multiple which produced much higher speeds and permitted a great increase in the size of ships both as to cargo capacity and passenger accommodation. Iron and wooden sailing ships could carry weights that were less than half the tonnage of the vessel itself, whereas the multiple engine steamships transported with ease weights that were sixty per cent more than the boat's own tonnage. The carrying capacity of the improved steamship, therefore, was some four times that of the wooden sailing ship.

414   Cunard Royal Mail steel screw steamship *Servia*, from a lithograph, courtesy of the
Cunard Steamship Co., Ltd., New York

THE STEAMSHIP *SERVIA*

WITH the multiple expansion engine and a correspondingly larger vessel the limit of iron ships seemed to have been reached in the late 'seventies. At this point railroad experience afforded a hint to shipbuilders. When the iron rail could no longer stand increased locomotive size and train weight, railroad men had discarded iron in favor of steel. Ship designers did likewise. Since steel is stronger than iron a ship may be made of steel with less weight of material, and hence more cheaply than one of iron. The steel ship, being lighter for its size, will float more buoyantly and can therefore carry a greater weight of cargo. A steel ship of the same weight as an iron one will be much larger. Experiments with steel ships began in Great Britain in 1875. Within five years these trials had been so successful that the Cunard Company built the *Servia* of this material. The Atlantic Ocean is a severe testing laboratory for a novel ship material, but so well did the *Servia* pass the trials that within a decade after she left the ways the British yards were constructing deep sea vessels of almost no other material than steel. In 1880 about ten per cent of the new tonnage in British yards was of steel, whereas by 1890 considerably more than ninety-five per cent was of this material alone.

415   The steamship *City of New York*, from an engraving by F. S. Cozzens in *Harper's Weekly*, March 30, 1889

TWIN-SCREW SHIPS

THE *Servia* was in her day the last word in ocean shipping, but her fame was eclipsed in 1888 when the Inman line put on the *City of New York* and the *City of Paris*. The former was the first twin-screw vessel to cross the Atlantic. The second screw did not add much to the speed, but was a great advance in assuring safe

navigation. If a single-screw ship lost or damaged its screw or the propeller blades, or had an accident to its rudder, it floated at the mercy of wind and wave. With two independent sets of machinery, however, repairs could be made in cne set with the ship under way. In spite of a damaged rudder the ship could be steered, after a fashion, by varying the speed or direction of the screws, an old trick of the paddle-wheel steamers. In case of fire at sea it has sometimes been possible in twin-screw ships to drown the flames with water pumped by one of the engines while still proceeding under its power. The twin-screw vessel could dispense with sails, together with the masts and yards carried on single-screw ships. This did away with much dead weight which made possible more cargo space and by reducing the resistance of the ship to the wind increased the speed. The twin-screw ship soon led to the adoption of multiple screws. No first class deep-sea ship, freighters excepted, has been built with a single screw since the twin

416   Twin screws on the *City of New York*, from Henry Fry, *The History of Steam Navigation*, London, 1896

screw proved its value.

THE TURBINE

WITH steel construction, multiple expansion engines and multiple screws it might appear that nothing more could be done to make ships larger, faster and safer. But the bulky multiple expansion reciprocating engines of the 'nineties were to give place to the smaller, more easily operated, turbine invented in 1883 by a Swede, De Laval, and in 1884, by Parsons, an Englishman. These improved engines were demonstrated first on the tiny *Turbina*, built in 1894 expressly for experimental purposes. Five years later a small torpedo boat destroyer (two hundred and ten feet long), the *Viper*, and then the *King Edward VII*, a Clyde River steamer, were successfully equipped with turbines. At length, in 1905, the turbine entered the Atlantic service and two years later met with extraordinary success in the *Lusitania* — of sad memory — and the *Mauretania*. For the turbine as against the reciprocating engine is claimed lower initial cost, great saving in space, freedom from noise, vibration and minor accidents, economy of steam and greater speed.

417   Steamship *King Edward VII*, early ship equipped with turbine, from a photograph. © Rischgitz, London

418   Steamship *Olympic*, first vessel employing reciprocating and turbine engines, courtesy of the White Star Line, New York

RECIPROCATING AND TURBINE ENGINES

THE year after the *Lusitania* raced across the Atlantic propelled by turbines, the *Olympic*, a huge White Star Liner, appeared with both reciprocating and turbine engines, the first using the steam under high pressure and the latter converting the low pressure steam into power. But turbines operated best at very high speed and screws at moderate speeds. To offset this difficulty, electricity generated by the turbine was carried by cable to the screws where motors "stepped" to the right speed whirled the propellers. This type of transmission saved much cumbersome, space-taking and sometimes dangerous shafting. An American coastwise ship, the *Powhatan*, renamed the *Cuba*, was the first electrically-driven ocean passenger liner. The first general cargo-carrier with a turbo-electric plant was the *Eclipse*, built for the American Shipping Board and chartered to the American Line in 1920.

THE ADOPTION OF FUEL OIL

COAL was the only fuel used on the Atlantic until, in 1902, fuel oil appeared. This fuel had been employed by steamships on the Caspian Sea as early as 1870. By saving time in refueling, conserving storage space aboard the vessel, reducing by three-fourths the stoke hold personnel, and eliminating the worst job around ship, that of firing the boilers, fuel oil became at once popular. The first oil burner was the *Arab*, crossing the Pacific in 1902. Up to the opening of the World War oil burning equipment gradually but steadily increased. During the war and after it the marine interests of the world plunged pell mell into fuel oil installations. By 1920 more than three-fourths of the ocean tonnage under the American flag was oil-burning, and a third of the British ships were similarly equipped. To-day new steamships are all oil burners and old ones are being converted at an amazing rate. Of the oil supply stations throughout the world, America controls a large part, just as Great Britain formerly monopolized the coal bunkers. The use of oil marks an important step in the development of an American merchant marine.

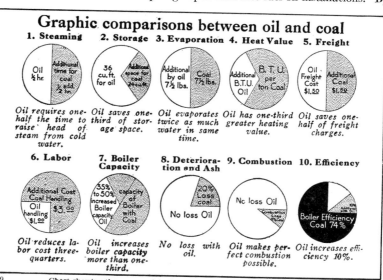

419   Chart showing the commercial advantages of fuel oil, prepared, 1919, by the Tidewater Oil Co., Bayonne, N. J., reproduced by permission

420 Launching of the *Asturias*, the largest motor ship, Belfast, 1925, from a photograph. © Wide World Photos

THE MOTOR SHIP

THE most recent development in ocean shipping is the supplanting of the steamship by the motor ship. When the steamship adopted the turbine engine alone or in combination with reciprocating engines and used oil to turn water into steam to drive those engines, the next logical step was to burn oil directly without the intervention of steam as a motive power. The internal combustion engine of the Diesel type has nearly all the advantages of a turbine plus the further saving of nearly all the space, equipment, and labor necessary to run steam boilers. The typical motor ship of 1910 was the *Vulcanus*, a six-cylinder single screw vessel of one thousand one hundred and seventy-nine tons. In 1914 the world's tonnage in ships of five-hundred gross tons and over, using oil engines, amounted only to one hundred and ninety-four thousand. By 1920 the tonnage of such ships had increased to six hundred and ninety-three thousand. In 1922 fifteen per cent of the new ship construction under way in the world was designed for motor propulsion. One of these ships was a twenty-two thousand ton vessel, six hundred feet long, to be driven by a two-cycle Diesel engine at an average speed of eighteen knots an hour, a duplicate of the largest, fastest *Empress* liner of the Canadian Pacific Railway fleet, and to be used as a passenger liner for the Union Steamship Company. In 1924 five hundred motor ships were constructed with a gross tonnage rising to one million five hundred and fifty-nine thousand. The superior advantages of the motor ship began to be even more widely acclaimed. During the year 1925 the number of ships employing the oil-engine motor rose to six hundred and eight, with a total tonnage of two million one hundred and fifty-seven thousand. We appear (1927) to be at the beginning of a new era in ocean shipping. The motor ship promises to do to the steamship what the latter did to the sailing packet.

THE CONCRETE SHIP

WOOD, iron and steel have all had their day as construction materials for ships; it remained for the urgent demands of the World War to give *concrete* (a Frenchman had patented a concrete rowboat in 1849) a chance to prove its worth for the hulls of sea-going ships. The proposal to use concrete in ship construction met as much ridicule as did the first steel ships. Much the same objections were raised against concrete. But once again the scoffers were confounded by facts, for concrete ships were a success. The United States Shipping Board in 1917 gave orders for the construction of a couple of score of concrete hulls, the largest of which was the *Faith*, launched in the spring of 1918, three hundred and twenty feet long, forty-four and a half feet wide and thirty feet deep, with a cargo capacity of five thousand tons. Her oil-burning engines gave her a speed of ten knots an hour. It is claimed for the concrete ship — as it is for the concrete building — that it is rat and vermin proof, cannot rot or rust, need not be painted, and may be built quickly with low priced labor. Although during the war the concrete ships were given the highest ratings by such agencies as Lloyd's, the contracts for them were canceled after the Armistice, and little has been heard since of concrete sea-going vessels. The present lack of interest in them does not mean necessarily that the world will never again hear of concrete ships.

421 Steamer *Faith*, concrete construction, from a photograph, courtesy of the Department of Commerce, Washington, D. C.

THE FLETTNER–ROTOR SHIP *BUCKAU*

422 © Wide World Photos

Soon after the World War it was discovered in Germany that wind would exert from four to nine times more pressure on cylindrical towers rotating at a high rate of speed than on sails having the same area. So the *Buckau* was constructed with two cylinders instead of masts, cylinders forty-two feet high and revolved by electric motors at an average speed of one hundred and twenty-five revolutions a minute. Wind power, small crew, and tiny space allotted to machinery, promised cheap operation, but the experimental voyage failed to prove convincingly the effectiveness of this new sort of navigation. In the summer of 1925 the first American rotor boat was operated off the coast of New England, built and run by two students of Massachusetts Institute of Technology. It was not identical in detail with the German ship but copied its principle of locomotion. The *Buckau* herself was advertised for sale in American newspapers in July, 1925. We cannot yet tell whether the rotor ship has a future.

THE TRAMP SHIP

Before 1812 men such as Stephen Girard of Philadelphia and Elias H. Derby of Salem not only owned and controlled ships but themselves dealt in the commodities borne by the vessels. With the increase in the safety and regularity of sea-borne traffic merchants no longer owned and operated ships, and shipmasters ceased to be concerned personally with the buying and selling of the commodities their craft transported. Merchants hired — chartered — ships as they needed them; shipping men sought contracts for carrying cargoes wherever they could find them. This was the origin of the "tramp ship," a vessel without schedule which takes any kind of cargo anywhere at any time. In the seventeenth and eighteenth centuries "tramps" carried general cargoes, but in the nineteenth they usually loaded for one voyage entirely with one bulk commodity. Despite the enormous development of "line traffic" and "liners," tramp — chartered — ships carried at least half of the total freight commerce of the world until 1914. Tramp ships have been owned by the captains who commanded them, by a small group of associates owning one or several such craft, and by large companies controlling a great number of vessels open for charter. The utmost skill and the widest, most accurate knowledge is required to operate profitably a fleet of "tramps."

423   Tramp Ship *Nokatay*, Oakland, Cal., Sept. 22, 1919, from a photograph, courtesy of the Office of Naval Records and Library, Navy Department, Washington

424   Tramp Steamer *Laurel*, Baltimore, Md., March 1919, courtesy of the Office
of Naval Records and Library, Navy Department, Washington

DECLINE OF TRAMP STEAMERS

BEFORE 1914 tramp steamships offered an effective competition to liners in the regulation of ocean freight rates. Between 1913 and 1924 the average carrying capacity of vessels increased twenty-four per cent. In the same period the normal speed of the average ship increased from twelve knots an hour to close to twenty knots an hour and the number capable of more than twenty knots also increased. In 1914 only sixty out of two thousand seven hundred and fifty-eight liners were oil burning, whereas in 1925 there were one thousand four hundred and eleven out of three thousand three hundred and seventy-four. This change increased cargo space and lessened time in port. The tramp steamship owners with less capital than liner organizations have been unable to keep pace with these modern developments. As a consequence in 1925 out of every one hundred vessels only twenty-seven were tramps while ten years earlier there were about forty-two tramps in every one hundred ocean carriers. The greater frequency of liner voyages due to their space increased their numerical and tonnage superiority to tramps.

425   Steamship *Majestic*, courtesy of the White Star Line, New York

GROWTH OF THE LINE BUSINESS

WHEREVER the commerce between two ports is sufficiently large and regular, it has paid to put into service the "liner" that specializes in scheduled passages between the two ports. The packet lines have been pictured and described earlier in this book. Steamship lines to America began with the Great Western Steamship Company and continued with the Cunard Company, the Allan line, White Star, Red Star, Inman, Hamburg-American and many others. Up to 1850 the steamship line as contrasted with the sailing packet line was an experiment but by the time of the Civil War the steamer in line service overshadowed the sailer. Since the Civil War liners have run from the Atlantic ports to all the ports of Europe and from the Pacific harbors to the Far East, Pacific Islands, Australia and the South Seas. Indeed all the principal ports of the world are connected with each other directly or indirectly with some kind of steamship line service. The line business quickly developed specialities. The most spectacular was the speed record ship designed to carry passengers, express and mail at the fastest pace and in the greatest comfort and luxury. The *Majestic* is a vessel of this sort.

TYPES OF FREIGHTERS

A SMALLER and less speedy type of liner carries passengers and a small cargo of freight that in railroad terms would be classified as "fast freight." A third type is designed primarily for freight but may carry as many as sixteen passengers. Finally there are freight liners that transport freight alone. No provision is made for passengers and of course no mail or express is shipped on freight lines. In short, the services are as varied as the needs of commerce.

426   Freight steamer *El Ocano*, Morgan Line, courtesy of the Southern
Pacific Company

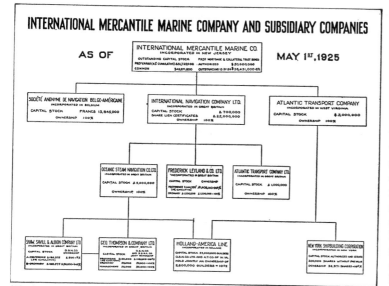

427   Organization of the International Mercantile Marine and of Subsidiary Companies, from
Report of International Mercantile Marine Company for 1924

ORGANIZATION OF THE SHIPPING BUSINESS

OCEAN traffic has followed the general drift of business organization from small independent units to large combinations, the object of which is the control of competition, the spreading of risks, and the provision of "feeder" lines for the collection and distribution of traffic. Shipping interests have further extended their control to shipbuilding corporations, coal and oil companies and financial institutions. On the other hand railroad, automobile, and a variety of other transportation companies have entered the field of the shipping business.

CONVENIENCES TO TRAVELERS

ONE of the results of this network of affiliation is that a traveler may entrust himself, say, to the Canadian Pacific Railroad and take a leisurely three-year tour of the whole world, never, ashore or afloat, stepping beyond the dominion of that railroad; or a shipper may with assurance hand over to the Hamburg-American Company at New York a package addressed to almost any port, big or little.

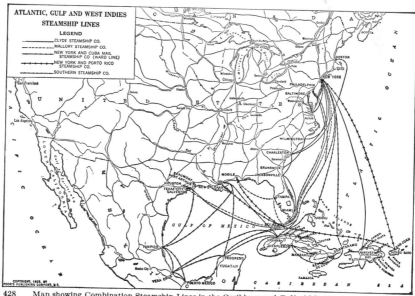

428   Map showing Combination Steamship Lines in the Caribbean and Gulf of Mexico, from *Annual
Report of the Atlantic, Gulf and West Indies Lines for 1924*

429   Steamship *Empress of France*, from a photograph, courtesy of the Canadian Pacific
Steamships, Ltd., Montreal

A SHIP OF THE CANADIAN PACIFIC RAILROAD

RAILROADS with a port terminal must make it attractive to shipping companies in order to secure a fair share of the import and export freight business. At the larger ports there is usually enough commerce to satisfy the needs or desires of the roads; elsewhere special contracts or traffic agreements are necessary, and sometimes the railroad has deemed it expedient to establish a steamship line of its own. Thus in 1871 the Pennsylvania Railroad organized the American line to operate between Philadelphia and Liverpool, following the example of the Baltimore & Ohio Railroad, which had aided, in the late 'sixties, in the establishment of the Atlantic Transport line (Johnson line) between Baltimore and Europe. On the Pacific, the Southern Pacific Railroad until recently controlled the Pacific Mail Steamship Co., while the Great Northern Railroad owned the Great Northern Steamship Co. The Northern Pacific Railroad had its own subsidiary Pacific shipping company but chartered the vessels that ran upon the line. Few ship lines owned or controlled by railroads have been profitable as shipping ventures but they have served the railroad purposes for which they were created. They have been curtailed or abandoned wherever satisfactory agreements could be reached with shipping corporations. On the Great Lakes, little of the shipping is independent; nearly all of it is tied up with land corporations. Railway ownership on the Lakes has, however, been largely eliminated by law.

GROWTH OF SPECIALIZED SHIPPING BUSINESS

IN addition to the railroad shipping lines, certain other land corporations have entered a specialized shipping business. Outstanding among these have been the United Fruit Company, the oil companies, steel corporations and sugar refineries. The United Fruit Company, in order to avoid demoralizing the American market with alternate gluts and famines, found itself forced to control the shipment of bananas from the West Indies, Central and South America. To transport so perishable a cargo, special fast ships were built and chartered under long contracts to the United Fruit Company. To keep the ships busy, the company went into the production of bananas which led them into politics in Central and South America. The "Great

White Fleet" has become one of the most important freight and passenger lines from American Atlantic ports to the islands of the Caribbean and the republics of Central and South America. The oil companies of which the Standard Oil is the greatest have controlled their own ships because their cargoes required a vessel constructed for the sole purpose of transporting these products. In 1920, the Standard Oil Company of New Jersey owned fifty-one "tankers" aggregating a deadweight tonnage of four hundred fifty-six thousand, the largest commercial fleet both in number of craft and carrying capacity listed for ocean service under the American flag. Some of the latest of these ships carry cargoes for the public as well as for the oil company.

430   Steamship *Ulua*, of "The Great White Fleet," from a photograph,
courtesy of the United Fruit Co.

PRIVATE AND SEMIPRIVATE STEAMSHIP LINES

On the Atlantic the Bethlehem Steel Corporation carries ore from Spain, Sweden and Cuba to Baltimore, Philadelphia and Boston. Some of these inbound ore-boats carry oil on the outward journey; the others travel outward in ballast. The United States Steel Products Company, a subsidiary of the United States Steel Corporation, is a marketing

431   Steamship *Cubore*, modern ore boat, Atlantic service, from a photograph, courtesy of the Bethlehem Steel Company, Bethlehem, Pa.

company abroad for the great American steel producer. As such it has a fleet of its own and charters other vessels as need arises. New links in the Steel Corporation's world-wide operations are two common carrier fleets known as the New York & South American Line and the Isthmian Line whose names are significant of their field of endeavor. The American Sugar Refining Company has laid plans for a fleet of tankers to carry molasses, but the boats also may transport a limited amount of general cargo. Henry Ford entered maritime circles with five vessels — to be expanded into a fleet, as conditions warrant — for shipping knocked-down Fords to foreign markets or to carry parts and supplies to foreign branch factories. All of these private or semiprivate steamship lines have grown out of the needs of particular American industries. Their ships are designed for highly specialized cargoes operating between points not adequately served by regular shipping companies. The private ship-line, like the private railroad freight-line, enables the owner to eliminate intermediate profits and at the same time exercise control over the handling and destination of shipments.

VALUE OF THE FOREIGN TRADE OF THE UNITED STATES

THE total foreign trade (exports and imports) of the United States has grown with our national expansion. The dollar value of our total foreign trade in 1860 was four times that in 1800. Between 1860 and 1890, we reached a total figure that was ten times that set at the beginning of the century; and by the opening of the twentieth century our trade was about fourteen times what it had been one hundred years before. The succeeding years of the new century have marked a more rapid advance, ranging from two billion dollars in 1900 to thirteen billion in 1920 and eight billion in 1924. Of course, changes in the values of money distort these statistics; but apparently our trade in 1925 was twenty-five times what it was in 1800. During the first seventy-five years of the century we bought more abroad than we sold, but since 1875 the contrary is true. The differences have been equalized by "invisible balances": interest and dividends to foreign investors in domestic enterprises, payments to foreigners for freight-carriage, insurance and other services, expenditures of tourists abroad and domestic funds sent to relatives abroad, etc. Before 1875 we paid these "invisible balances" abroad, chiefly to England; but with the turning of the tide in trade the balances flowed to us. Since 1914, the flood tide of these incoming balances has floated us to the position of the principal creditor nation in the world. We cannot continue to hold this position and at the same time export more than we import. The United States tariff policy, a relic of our debtor days, prevents an easy flow of imports. No nation yet has succeeded in maintaining an excess of exports while acting at the same time as the world's chief loan merchant.

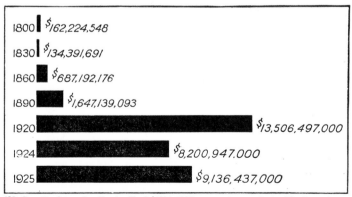

1800	$162,224,548
1830	$134,391,691
1860	$687,192,176
1890	$1,647,139,093
1920	$13,506,497,000
1924	$8,200,947,000
1925	$9,136,437,000

432 Growth of America, Foreign Trade 1800–1925, prepared expressly for *The Pageant of America*, from statistics in the *United States Statistical Abstract*

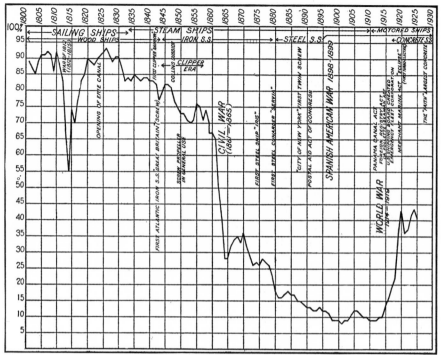

433   Chart showing amount of foreign trade carried in American bottoms, 1801–1925, prepared expressly for *The Pageant of America*, from statistics in *Statistical Abstract of the United States*

THE DECLINE OF THE MERCHANT MARINE

WITH the growth of trade the American merchant marine has steadily declined.   In 1826, ninety-three per cent of our foreign trade traveled under the Stars and Stripes.   American commerce carriers had fallen to sixty-seven per cent in 1860, and in 1901 had reached a humiliating eight per cent.   The actual tonnage of American merchant marine engaged in foreign trade increased until 1861, but thereafter steadily shrunk except for a brief period, 1898 to 1909.   The tonnage of our coastwise shipping surpassed that engaged in foreign trade in 1836 and continued to gain throughout this period so that by 1911 we had about eight times as much coastwise tonnage as that engaged in foreign trade.

ELEMENTS IN THE DECLINE OF OUR MERCHANT MARINE

OF the positive factors that hastened the decay of our deep-sea commercial fleets the first was the shift from sail to steam.   For two hundred years America had developed and brought to perfection both the sailing ship and the sailor.   But ocean steamships made our long training in sail useless.   To be sure, the steamboat was first perfected by an American, but our subsequent experience with steam-craft was confined to rivers and protected waterways.   Europeans, and particularly the British, at once ventured forth under steam on the open seas.   Secondly, the British, lacking wood, began to build their steamships after 1843 of iron.   Our first anthracite iron furnace was not started until about 1840 so that even the iron bolts of our clippers were imported from Great Britain.   From 1840 until 1900 our iron industry seldom caught up with the enormous domestic demand for iron (and later, steel) for railroad construction and the equipment for bridges, dwelling construction, machinery, tools and everything else that a rapidly growing nation demanded.   It is not difficult to see why we did not build iron steamships — calling for a special knowledge and experience — in successful competition with Great Britain.

IS HE TO BECOME ONLY A SPECTATOR?

434   From the cartoon *Is He to Become only a Spectator?* by Williams in the *Public Ledger*, Philadelphia, Nov. 8, 1908

435   Opening of the Suez Canal, from *The Illustrated London News*, Dec. 18, 1869

EFFECT OF THE CIVIL WAR ON COMMERCE

THE iron steamship had barely started effective competition with the wooden sailing ship when the storm of the Civil War broke over us. Our own brothers, the Confederates, as a justifiable war measure, started to exterminate the Union's merchant shipping. Some nineteen Confederate war cruisers — the two most famous of which were the British-built, British-coaled and largely British-manned steam cruisers the *Florida* and the *Alabama* — destroyed two hundred and fifty-seven Northern commerce carriers. Marine insurance rates on American commercial ships immediately advanced to prohibitive figures and many an American shipowner in desperation sold or transferred his vessel to foreign flags. Under the American Navigation Laws of that time no such ship could ever again sail under our colors. We came out of the Civil War with a third of our foreign trade tonnage gone. Hardly was the war ended when the Suez Canal was opened (1869). This waterway, so advantageous to the world's commerce, was a staggering blow to sailing ships, for such vessels could not use it. The cream of the Far Eastern commerce therefore went to steamships — and to Great Britain. Navigation laws were designed to protect American shipping which only laid insuperable handicaps upon it. They forbade Americans to buy foreign-built ships and put them under American registry. They refused American registry to any ship that was in any degree owned by a foreigner. They provided that American ships must be commanded wholly by American officers above the rank of watch-officers. They penalized American ships repaired abroad or foreign ships repaired in American yards. And finally, they loaded American ships with taxes, charges and duties.

HANDICAPS OF AMERICAN SHIPPING

AMERICAN shipping was further handicapped by high costs of building and operation. Wages, representing one half to two-thirds of the cost of a ship, were twenty-five to eighty per cent higher than in foreign yards. Economies effected in British yards by specializing in one type of craft were unobtainable in the miscellaneous construction undertaken by American builders. At sea, higher wages, a larger quota of officers and crews and better accommodations placed American ships at a competitive disadvantage. Governmental subsidy, either direct or in the guise of mail contracts, had lamentably failed in the case of the Collins line and the Pacific Mail Steamship Co. Since the Civil War it has been steadfastly opposed. Mail contracts, however, were entered into in 1891.

436   Senator W. P. Frye, author of the bill authorizing ship subsidy, 1910, from a photograph. © Harris and Ewing from Wide World Photos

OUR SHIPPING GREATLY INCREASED BY THE WORLD WAR

THE withdrawal of European ships for war service or the laying up of ships to escape the risk of capture or destruction — six million tons in Germany and Austria — produced a shortage in carrying capacity. At the same time the demands of the war nations upon America for

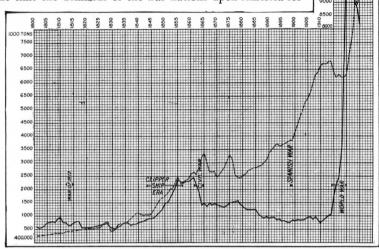

food and war materials greatly augmented our need for ships. To buy them or build them was our only recourse. As the world's greatest neutral (1914–17) and the world's greatest exporter, America offered a registry that was attractive to foreign-owned ships and to American-owned ships flying foreign flags, and many were thus transferred. In response to the challenge of the submarine, our shore line hummed with ship-building activity. Ships of wood, iron, steel and concrete began to slip off our ways, and gigantic new shipyards sprang up, the largest of which was Hog Island

437   Tonnage of the American Merchant Marine, engaged in Foreign (solid line) and Coastwise Trade (broken line) 1800–1925, prepared expressly for *The Pageant of America* from data in the *Statistical Abstract of the United States*

on the Delaware River. Ships built by new methods, ships built regardless of cost, ships by the dozens, by the score and by the hundred put to sea flying the American flag. Hog Island alone launched one hundred and twenty-two steel ships. On June 30, 1912, the gross tonnage of American steel steam or motor vessels of over one hundred tons was one and a half million; the United Kingdom had eighteen million. On June 30, 1923, the United Kingdom still had her eighteen million, but we had twelve million, four times as much as any other country except Great Britain. We are now (1927) the owners of the world's second largest merchant marine engaged in foreign trade. The United States has "come back" on the seas.

THE UNITED STATES SHIPPING BOARD

To create and control the merchant marine of the war period, the United States Congress, on September 7, 1916, brought into being the "United States Shipping Board." The following April an executive arm of this board, called the "Emergency Fleet Corporation," with a capital of fifty million dollars, was authorized by Congress. These bodies during the war built and operated ships, improved harbors, recruited shipyard workers and ship personnel, adjusted disputes with labor and shippers, and arranged coöperative working facilities with railroads, tugboats and lighterage companies, to create and maintain a merchant marine amid

438   The United States Shipping Board, 1925. © Keystone View Co.

the turmoil of war. After much discussion following the close of the war, the Merchant Marine Act of 1920, popularly known as the Jones Act, created a new Shipping Board to control the government-owned ships until they could be disposed of to private, preferably American, owners, without undue loss to the government. The Board was given wide powers over America's merchant marine, both publicly and privately owned, and was authorized to extend public aid to private individuals in the construction of ships as a loan, not a subsidy, the funds to come from the Board's ship sales and revenues from ships operated by it.

COASTWISE SHIPPING

439   Barges towed at sea, from a photograph.   © Edwin Levick

THE sad story of our mid-nineteenth-century decline does not apply to American coastwise shipping. In July, 1789, when Congress imposed a tonnage tax on coastwise shipping of six cents a ton per year, the provision was made that for foreign ships the tax should be fifty cents a ton, collected every time the foreign ship entered or left an American port. In 1808, and again in 1817, Congress declared that no ship owned wholly or in part by a subject of a foreign power should carry goods or passengers from one American port to another. For more than a century, therefore, American coastwise commerce has been free from any kind of foreign competition, except during the World War when foreign-built ships and ships of foreign registry were temporarily granted the privilege of coastwise trade. "Port to port American commerce" was extended in 1900 to include Hawaii and Porto Rico, and the Jones Act of 1920 made this rule apply to all American territories wherever situated. This means that Alaska, the Philippines, American Samoa and Guam are limited to American ships for commerce with each other and with American mainland ports. As a result of this gigantic monopoly, the gross tonnage of American shipping, even in the darkest days of the foreign-trade tonnage slump, was the second largest in the world. The ocean voyages of our coastwise ships on the Atlantic coast alone are often as long as those of British ships whose trade with Europe is classified as foreign. The distance (two thousand five hundred and ninety-seven miles) from Calais, Maine, to Point Isabel, Texas, is greater than that from Cardiff to Greece (two thousand four hundred and fifty-five miles).

THE ENLARGING OF THE SAILING VESSEL

THE marine engine has never replaced sail in coastwise tramp ships as it has in the chartered vessels that operate to foreign ports. Such traffic does not require speed so much as cheapness, and the whole of the Atlantic coast, except the tip of Florida, and the Pacific coast north of Los Angeles, enjoys steady winds. In 1860, there was twice as much sail-tonnage as steam in coastwise commerce, and even to-day (1927) there is almost half as much sail-tonnage as steam. To keep down its rates the sailing vessel has been enlarged,

440   The *George W. Wells*, from a photograph.   © N. L. Stebbins, Inc., Boston

and for ease of handling by a small crew the schooner-rig has been preferred. The two-mast schooner was generally replaced in the 'seventies by the three-mast ship. The largest of these was the *Bradford C. French*, a wooden vessel of seven hundred tons. The booms and gear of a three-mast ship were so large as to approach the limit in man power, so when still larger ships appeared using four, five and even six masts mechanical aids were installed. The two largest six-masters were the *Eleanor A. Percy* of Bath (three thousand four hundred and one tons) and the *George W. Wells* of Boston (two thousand nine hundred and seventy tons), ships which in a fair wind were as fast as the ordinary coastwise steamer and far cheaper to build and operate.

441　　The *Thomas W. Lawson*, from a photograph, courtesy of the Bethlehem Shipbuilding Corporation, Ltd., Fore River plant, Quincy, Mass.

SAILING SHIP COASTWISE CARGOES

THE largest schooner yet built was the *Thomas W. Lawson*, constructed in 1901–02 by the Fore River Ship and Engine Company (now a subsidiary of the Bethlehem Steel Corporation of Quincy, Massachusetts). This schooner had seven masts, the lower portions of which were steel, and a steel hull with a double bottom. She had a gross tonnage of five thousand two hundred and eighteen, more than seven times as great as the *Bradford C. French*. Yet the *Thomas W. Lawson* carried a crew of only sixteen men; a square rigger of her size would have needed a crew of forty men. The sails were manipulated by donkey engines. This ship, the only seven-master yet constructed, was lost (in 1907) after six years of service. Sailing-ship cargoes in coastwise commerce since the incoming of steam have always been bulky, heavy commodities. On the Atlantic southbound they have carried ice, coal, stone and lumber, while northbound they transported cotton (now carried mostly by railway), lumber, sugar and coal. On the Pacific and in intercoastal traffic they have been used mostly for lumber. Sea-going tugs trailing a string of barges can in fair weather underbid sail ships. In protected waters this type of transportation has almost eliminated sail; but on the open ocean, especially in winter, the greater safety of the ship able to navigate by itself has, despite the barge, kept the sail vessel in trade. Barges were at first the hulls of dismantled sailing ships; some of the proudest clippers ended their days in this humble rôle. But losses were great enough to bring into use barges made of steel especially constructed for sea-going service. Coal is the principal cargo transported along the coast in barges.

THE STEAMSHIP *BANGOR*

COASTWISE steamships at first supplanted the sail packets only in protected waters such as Long Island Sound and Chesapeake Bay. But by the 'fifties steamers were running regularly along the coast with all the improvements that had appeared in the transatlantic service. The year following the first voyage of a screw-propelled iron steamship across the Atlantic (1843) saw the launching of the *Bangor* at the Harlan and Hollingsworth yards on the Delaware, the first iron sea-going steamship used in coastwise trade. This boat ran for years between Boston and Bangor, Maine. The coastwise steam lines centered at New York, but each of the principal Atlantic ports had its own line. Those out of Boston mostly ran "down east" to ports in Maine and the Maritime Provinces of Canada, those out of Philadelphia and Baltimore southward. From 1850 to 1870, the coastwise steamship was the principal means of transporting passengers, mail, express and fast freight to and from points connected with the Atlantic Ocean. But the steamship was not without competition from railroads running along the coast. These rapidly encroached on the steamer's business.

442　　Steamship *Bangor*, 1844, from S. W. Stanton, *American Steam Vessels*, New York, 1895

RAILROAD CONTROL OF STEAMSHIPS

By the 'seventies the railroads had made through connections along the coast and had so improved that a journey could be made more quickly, and fully as safely, by land as by sea. Speed attracted both passengers and mail and express. Coastwise steam lines met the change by putting on slower but much larger boats for the transportation of merchandise and package cargoes, fruit and vegetables.

443   Morgan Line Freighter *El Coston*, from a photograph, courtesy of the Southern Pacific Co.

Most of the steamers retained passenger accommodations for the few to whom time was no object. But the railroads, by purchase, long-term lease, stock control, interlocking directorates, community of interest and agreements, speedily acquired control of the steamship lines. In some cases, as the "Morgan Line" (the Sunset Route), from New York to New Orleans, a part of the transcontinental route of the Southern Pacific Railway, the steamers are large, luxurious and fast.

THE BUILDING OF THE PANAMA CANAL

One of the most significant events in coastwise shipping was the construction of the Panama Canal. In 1879 the builder of the Suez Canal, Ferdinand de Lesseps, organized a French company to cut a waterway across the Isthmus of Panama. Four years later excavation was begun, but the work stopped because there was too little money and because of the disease-breeding mosquitoes. A new company made but little advance. President Cleveland in 1895 furthered the project by appointing a board to investigate and report on the feasibility of a canal across Nicaragua. In 1897, the board was succeeded by the Nicaraguan Canal Commission, and this was replaced in turn, two years later, by the Isthmian Canal Commission. By 1901, the imminence of a decision in favor of the Nicaragua route caused the dormant French Panama Company to place a reasonable price on its property and franchise which was agreed to by our government. This turned interest to Panama. A treaty with Colombia was negotiated and ratified by our Senate in 1903 but rejected by Colombia. Then a "timely" revolution separated Panama from Colombia. The new republic ratified a treaty with the United States and in 1904 work started on the Panama Canal. Dr. William C. Gorgas, an army colonel, waged war on the mosquito, the carrier of yellow fever and malaria that had defeated the French. Gorgas conquered the mosquito and made the Panama Canal Zone one of the most

444   From the mural painting *Building the Panama Canal*, by W. B. Van Ingen, in the Administration Building, Canal Zone

healthful regions in the tropics. For three years, owing to divided authority, the work dragged. In 1907 the army took over the job. Colonel George W. Goethals was made chief engineer, and the task was successfully completed in 1914. During the construction the world watched with keen interest the program of the work, and were filled with dismay when slides threatened destruction of the great undertaking. Its eventual success thrilled everyone.

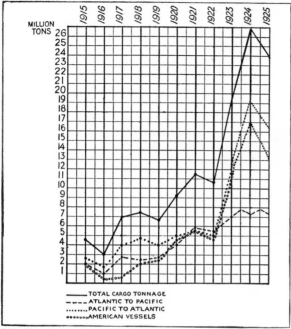

445 Chart showing Commercial Traffic through the Panama Canal, 1915–25, prepared expressly for *The Pageant of America*, from statistics in the United States Department of Commerce, *Yearbook*, 1925

TRAFFIC THROUGH THE PANAMA CANAL

THE Panama Canal established ocean traffic between the Atlantic and Pacific. Immediately after the World War steamship lines extended their routes through the canal and several new lines were opened. About half the vessels using the canal are under the American flag and most of these ships are engaged in coastwise commerce. The transcontinental railroads, although alarmed by the diversion of traffic, are forbidden by the Panama Canal Act of 1912 to operate company vessels through the canal. More tonnage passes from the Pacific to the Atlantic through the canal than vice versa. This is due to the large amounts of sugar brought by the American-Hawaiian line and the oil carried by tankers from California fields to eastern refineries. The fleet engaged in intercoastal traffic in 1923 numbered two hundred and fifty ships, totaling one million six hundred and thirty-five thousand gross tons. Some of the best privately owned ships under the American flag are in this service.

The fleet was composed of twenty-six thousand gross tons of passenger ships, eight hundred twenty-seven thousand tons of cargo vessels and seven hundred eighty-one thousand tons of tankers. Additions constantly are being made to the fleet and intercoastal service.

GREAT LAKES COMMERCE

THE Great Lakes connect the greatest raw-material producing region in the world with the world's largest manufacturing centers. Although all the lakes except Michigan border on Canada, the United States gives rise to ninety per cent of their commerce, and this must therefore be borne in American ships. The total tonnage is a little less than half that of coastwise traffic. The lake trade developed passenger-steamship service after the opening of the Erie Canal, and, as had happened several decades earlier between the ports along the Atlantic, in the case of steamboat traffic the competing railroads gained control of this business, but did not wholly suppress passenger traffic. On Lake Erie, especially, since the journey between certain towns on its shores is cheaper, more pleasant and shorter in mileage by water than by rail, large, luxurious and fast passenger steamers ply between Buffalo, Cleveland and Detroit. In 1915, the Interstate Commerce Commission ordered the Grand Trunk, Lehigh Valley, New York Central, Pennsylvania, and Rutland to discontinue their control of Lake boats.

446   The *Seeandbee*, a Great Lakes steamer, courtesy of the Cleveland & Buffalo Transit Co., Cleveland

447   Whaleback ore steamer *Henry Cort*, from a photograph, courtesy of the Oliver Iron Mining Co., Duluth, Minn.

STEAMERS UNIVERSAL ON GREAT LAKES

ON the Lakes, steam has supplanted sail. Closed to commerce from the middle or end of December to the middle or end of April, the Lakes call for speed in the open season; and several "bottle necks," at the Welland Canal, Lake St. Clair, the Detroit River and St. Mary's River (Soo Canal), as well as harbors, completely or in part artificial, place sail navigation at a competitive disadvantage. The steamships for the most part are not "tramps" but operate on "lines" belonging to the steel companies and oil corporations. Hence there is very little free competition, and there are few individually operated boats open to charter. The largest line is the Pittsburgh Steamship Company, a subsidiary of the United States Steel Corporation, with a fleet which has a tonnage about half that owned by the Hamburg-American line, the largest shipping company in the world. There are not many wooden ships left on the Lakes. The region is the heart of the iron and steel industry of the United States and oak for shipbuilding is not easily obtainable. The largest shipbuilding concern on the Lakes is the American Shipbuilding Company, with yards at Buffalo, Cleveland, Lorain, Wyandotte and Superior. But there are more than a half dozen other fair-sized companies with yards at various Lake ports. The size of the Lake ship is limited only by the size of the smallest lock through which it must pass. Bulky cargoes of low unit value encourage the building of large ships. Whaleback steamers now nearly obsolete were an early example of specialized Lake ships.

448   A Great Lakes freighter, the *Merton E. Farr*, from a photograph, courtesy of the Detroit Shipbuilding Co., Detroit, Mich.

THE STRUCTURE OF LAKE SHIPS

THE typical Lake ship is a strange sight to a salt-water mariner. Its ends are blunt, its sides are straight, and its bottom is almost flat — a glorified canal boat. The wheelhouse is away forward, and the quarters, the engine room and stacks, are aft. In between are only the thinnest of masts or none at all. Cargo-hoisting machinery is on the wharf, not on the ship. The deck is pierced from wheelhouse to quarters with full-length hatches across the ship. This weakens the structure but facilitates loading and unloading. To see one of these ships is to see them all, for they differ only in size. Sidewheel steamships are found only in the passenger service. All the freighters have screw propellers.

IV—13

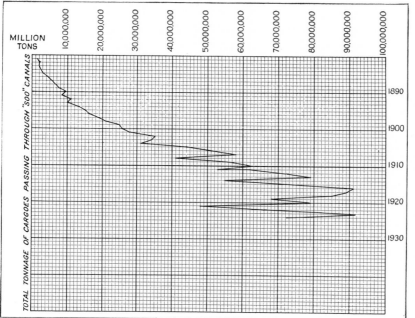

MILLION TONS

TOTAL TONNAGE OF CARGOES PASSING THROUGH "SOO" CANALS

449   Chart showing Total Tonnage passing through the Soo Canal, 1881–1925, prepared expressly for *The Pageant of America*, from statistics in the *Blue Book of American Shipping* and from *Statistical Abstract of the United S ates*

COMMERCE ON THE LAKES

About half of the Lake commerce passes over Lake Superior through the "Soo" locks, which has had traffic more than double that of the Suez in every year since 1895. But such tonnage comparison is hardly fair, since the contrast is between iron ore and silk, grain and tea, lumber or coal and porcelain. The east-bound cargoes on the Lakes are iron ores originating around Lake Superior and carried to points on Lakes Michigan or Erie for use in blast furnaces.   Grain origi-nates on Superior or at Chicago and is shipped to Buffalo, which receives about three-fourths of all the east-bound grain. The rest goes to Canada (Montreal) and a half dozen American Lake ports. At Buffalo the grain is transshipped to the railroads and the Erie Canal. When business is thriving, Buffalo receives as much as two million bushels of grain per day. Lumber is another large item in east-bound traffic. The west-bound cargoes are coal — both bituminous and anthracite — stone, oil and general merchandise. Since this traffic is lighter than the eastward trade and many ships return westward in ballast, western rates are low on any bulky commodity that can be transported in a boat designed to carry ore or grain. Iron ore east and coal west account for eighty per cent or more of the total volume of Lake commerce. The total sailing distance across the Great Lakes is one thousand two hundred miles, equal to a journey from Liverpool to Bilbao, Spain. Most of the cargo on the Lakes travels about two-thirds of this distance. But the traffic is so standardized and handled by so many labor-saving devices that the rates are the lowest ton-mile charges in the world. They are about one-fourth the rates for equal service on the American railroads. Therein lies the secret of the prosperity of Lake commerce.

450   Grain Elevators at Buffalo.   © Detroit Publishing Co.

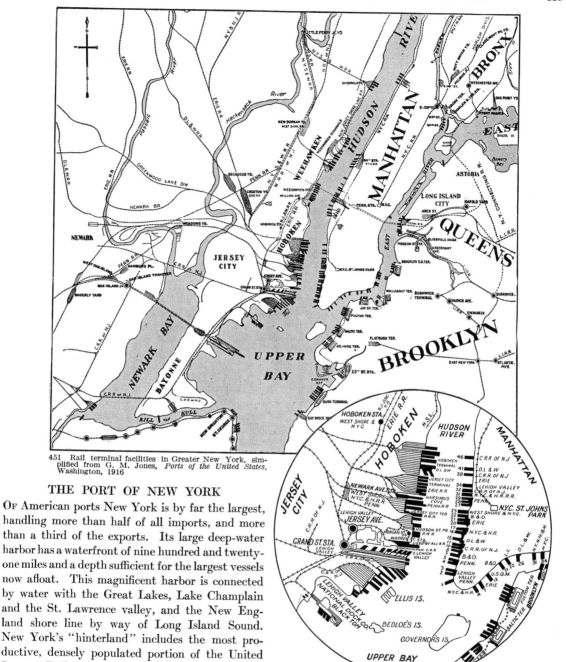

451 Rail terminal facilities in Greater New York, simplified from G. M. Jones, *Ports of the United States*, Washington, 1916

THE PORT OF NEW YORK

OF American ports New York is by far the largest, handling more than half of all imports, and more than a third of the exports. Its large deep-water harbor has a waterfront of nine hundred and twenty-one miles and a depth sufficient for the largest vessels now afloat. This magnificent harbor is connected by water with the Great Lakes, Lake Champlain and the St. Lawrence valley, and the New England shore line by way of Long Island Sound. New York's "hinterland" includes the most productive, densely populated portion of the United States. Railroads, following the waterways, have increased New York's grip on the interior, thirteen principal railroads converging upon the city. The traffic that flowed to New York involved changes of ownership and means of transport at the metropolis. These again involved financial transactions, and hence the upbuilding of financial institutions. To handle the cargoes and to staff the money centers a great population was required, which in itself became a large producing and consuming unit. The city branched into all sorts of activities and attracted to itself the offices of nearly every variety of enterprise found anywhere in the United States. The metropolis became the switchboard for the nation's mining, manufacturing, lumbering, farming, transportation and communication. Consequently, this great magnet drew to it nearly one hundred ocean lines, both freight and passenger, and was the focus for a score of river and Sound lines. Indeed, New York became the leading port of the world. Its commerce is more generally carried in liners than in charter vessels.

452　　　　The harbor of Seattle, Washington, from a photograph.　© Keystone View Co.

OTHER LARGE AMERICAN PORTS

SINCE water carriage is cheaper than land, ocean vessels seek to penetrate the interior as far as possible. Such ports as Philadelphia, Baltimore, New Orleans and Portland, Oregon, are all more than a hundred miles from the ocean. But costs can also be cut by increasing the size of the ships, and big ships fully loaded cannot enter inland ports on shallow waters. Only four American ports can receive the largest ships now afloat: New York, Seattle, Tacoma and San Francisco. Fortunately for the older inland ports, it is only the liners that have become gigantic; the world's freight "tramps" are relatively small. Yet these too have enlarged with the passing of years. Once there was hardly a bay or cove too small to serve existing ships. Gradually the smaller, shallower ones have been abandoned and shipping concentrated in places with deeper waters. What has been true of seaside harbors has been even more emphasized in river ports; long ago the smaller streams saw their last ocean-going vessel. Obviously it is not the miles of deep channel but the short stretches of sand bars or rapids that block rivers from deep sea boats; this is best illustrated by the Columbia.

453　　The Golden Gate, entrance to the harbor of San Francisco, from a photograph.　© Brown Brothers, New York

454   The Harbor of Los Angeles, courtesy of the Los Angeles Chamber of Commerce

SOME GREAT AMERICAN HARBORS

THE principal American harbors close to the ocean are Boston, New York, Newport News, Norfolk, Galveston and the three north Pacific ports, San Francisco, Tacoma and Seattle. Occasionally artificial ports have been created, such as Port Arthur, to the east of Galveston, Texas, and Houston and Texas City to the west. Los Angeles, twenty miles inland from the Pacific, consolidated with San Pedro and Wilmington under a pledge to expend in harbor improvements at San Pedro ten million dollars by 1919. A breakwater more than two miles long was built, and Los Angeles harbor now has the same minimum depth as Philadelphia and Galveston, offering security for large ships. It is one of our busiest Pacific ports.

455   Chesapeake & Ohio Railroad Pier, with coal pockets, Newport News, Va., courtesy of the Chesapeake & Ohio Railroad Company

COAL POCKETS AT NEWPORT NEWS

CERTAIN American ports such as Newport News and Norfolk specialize in the shipping of coal. Coal also in large amounts goes out of the port of New York. Boston stands first among American ports in receipts of coal, the bituminous variety coming by water from Norfolk and Baltimore and anthracite from Philadelphia and the Jersey section of New York harbor. Boston distributes the coal to New England's factories and homes. In tonnage, coal forms the chief item of traffic at our Atlantic ports, as it is of our railroads. Should all steamers burn oil instead of coal, and should the mine-mouth electric and hydroelectric plants supply all the land power, the railroads would make good the loss by the development of other traffic; but the fate of the coal barges would be doubtful.

456   Screwing cotton into the hold, Galveston, Tex., from a photograph. © Keystone View Co.

COTTON AND LUMBER

OTHER ports specialize in cotton. Galveston's export of cotton is the greatest in the world. Cotton is the mainstay of Wilmington, North Carolina, Savannah, Mobile, Houston and Texas City and is the leading but by no means the only export from New Orleans. Petroleum products outbound are the almost exclusive support of Port Arthur (Texas), while lumber and timber products play a similar rôle for Jacksonville and Pensacola. Lumber is an important item in several other ports along the South Atlantic, Gulf and Pacific coasts and the Great Lakes. Los Angeles claims to hold first place among ports in the receipts of this commodity, probably because the rapidly growing city needs the lumber to build her many bungalows. Tonawanda holds a similar position in the lumber traffic of the Great Lakes. Only New York and New Orleans are highly diversified in their traffic.

457   Loading lumber at Jacksonville, Fla., from a photograph. © Keystone View Co.

458   Traffic in the Hudson River, New York. © Keystone View Co.

THE CONTROL OF HARBORS

THE facilities which change a harbor into a port are anchorage
basins, anchorage posts, wharves, warehouses and other
storage equipment, the means for the transfer of cargo, and
railroad connections. Control of the harbor, as of all navigable waters, is vested in the Federal Government. The port
is subject to the state or city. Generally both private and
public facilities are available. In Boston, Philadelphia,
Baltimore and Norfolk, the facilities are the property of
trunk-line railroads, and in order to encourage traffic they
are offered free or for the lowest possible charge. The burden
of port terminals, however, is becoming so great that railroads
are encouraging public port terminals. At New York, the
city owns many of the piers and pier sites but has leased
them for long terms for a fixed annual rental to certain
railroads and steamship lines. The revenue to the city is
large, but the system limits competition and the rentals are
charged as a tax upon commerce. In New Orleans, all the
facilities with one exception are open to everyone, but a
charge is assessed against the ship on the basis of size. At
Galveston and San Francisco, the principal charge is against

459   Loading grain on the *Aquitania*, courtesy of the
Cunard Steamship Co., New York

the cargo based on its nature and quantity. Other ports have combinations of the systems mentioned. The
result is that for the same ship and cargo the charges in different ports may vary by as much as one hundred
per cent and may be higher than five thousand dollars.

460   Shifting freight between docks, New York.   © Keystone
View Co.

461   Interior of a freight shed, Cunard docks, New York, courtesy
of the Cunard Steamship Co., New York

462   Railroad lighters, New York Harbor, from a photograph.   © Keystone View Co.

463   Lighter, New York Harbor, from a photograph, courtesy of the
New York Lighterage Co.

"LIGHTERS"

BECAUSE of expense or crowding of the wharves, ships may load or unload at an anchorage basin by means of shallow draft harbor craft called "lighters." Among American ports New York makes the greatest use of lighters. Though some are owned and operated solely in the interest of a railroad or ship line, or leased to them, most lighters are open for hire. The price depends upon supply and demand and fluctuates considerably.

TRANSIT SHEDS

WHEN boats arrive at a pier or quay with a cargo of miscellaneous package freight, a large "transit shed" must be provided in which to spread out the cargo so that it may be sorted and classified. Under the cover of the shed there is likewise piled temporarily all the outbound freight of the ship except that which is loaded directly from lighters. If any of the cargo, in or outbound, has to be held for any length of time, it is kept in a warehouse, sometimes on the pier itself, sometimes at a considerable distance from it. The warehouse may be supplied with cold-storage chambers. General cargoes that are in standardized packages lend themselves to mechanical handling and move across the pier into the warehouse, to railroad cars or trucks as fast as the machinery can get the articles out of the boat. Bananas at New Orleans are unloaded by conveyors.

464   New Orleans wharf shed, from a photograph, courtesy of the New Orleans
Association of Commerce

465   Unloading fruit from a steamer to a refrigerator car, courtesy of the New York Lighterage Co.

PIER ARRANGEMENTS

BULK cargoes such as grain, ore, coal and petroleum are generally delivered at wharves especially designed to handle these products. They lend themselves most readily of all cargoes to standardization of loading or unloading and hence make the fullest use of machinery or gravity. The warehouse for grain is an "elevator"; for coal a "coal pocket"; for petroleum a "storage tank"; while ore is piled out of doors. Cargoes are raised from the holds of vessels at terminals either by the hoists (mast, booms, cable and donkey engine) at each end of the vessel itself, or by the hoists and cranes attached to the pier. Both sets may be employed at once. Specialized cargoes like ore and grain are moved by machines which almost invariably are on the pier. Through the transit shed, cargoes may be shifted by hand trucks, motor trucks or overhead monorails and cranes. The pier must be arranged to receive drays and motor trucks for local receipts and delivery of merchandise. A well-equipped pier also has a track for the direct loading and unloading of railway cars. These cars are shifted by the railroad in control of the pier, or there may be a belt-line railroad connecting the piers with all or most of the railroads serving the port city. Piers projecting from the shore are popular for they conserve land space and promote expeditious handling of ship and cargo. Only upon narrow waterways are piers built parallel to land. The upper decks of some commercial piers are in a few instances used for city recreation centers.

466   Raising cargo from the hold, courtesy of the Cunard Steamship Co., New York

467   Wharves, Bush Terminal, from a photograph.   © Keystone View Co.

THE BUSH TERMINAL

THE most complete, though not the largest, ocean terminal in the United States is the Bush Terminal in South Brooklyn, New York. First established in 1895, it includes more than half a dozen loft buildings for manufacturing purposes, a railroad of its own and lighterage facilities. There the incoming ocean-borne raw materials are received and manufactured by private companies in leased space, and the finished articles are distributed either to ships, railroads or local customers. The company acts as agent for the railroads connected with New York, and as local representative for selling the products of non-resident manufacturers. A larger terminal company, but one not so thoroughly integrated, is the New York Dock Company, also of South Brooklyn. It owns a water front of two and a half miles, including thirty or more piers, some one hundred and fifty warehouses, a couple of factory buildings, grain elevators of some two million bushel capacity, three railroad terminals, car floats, tugs and lighters. This company is credited with owning the largest bonded and free warehouse system in America, several units of which are equipped for cold storage. The oldest private terminal for public use in New York is the Brooklyn Eastern District Terminal established in 1876. This company operates three terminals, one in Brooklyn, another in Jersey City and a third in Long Island City. The three together with their auxiliary equipment are not so large as the Bush or New York Dock Company.

468   Airplane View of Bush Terminal, from a photograph.   © Keystone View Co.

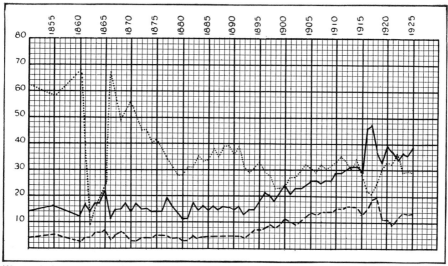

469   Graph showing exports from the United States, 1850–1925, of manufactures ready for consumption (solid line); manufactures for further use in manufacturing (broken line); and crude materials for use in manufacturing (dotted line); prepared expressly for *The Pageant of America* from statistics in the *Statistical Abstract of the United States*

OUR PRINCIPAL EXPORTS

FROM the Civil War to 1880, our exports were predominantly drawn from American farms. Manufactures ready for consumption and partly manufactured goods have grown from less than fifteen per cent of the total exports (1880) to more than half in 1925. Along with this advance has gone a decline in the relative importance of exports of crude materials for use in manufacturing. These changes in our exports have been a mirror of our domestic progress; we have passed from a pioneer agricultural society to an industrial nation. Of late we have needed at home more of our own foodstuffs and raw materials and have sold abroad more of the products of our workmanship. Canada, Argentine and Australia are taking the place we once held as exporters of food products and raw materials. The leading export, however, is still raw cotton, and a glance at the list shows that industrialization is still far from complete. The following constitute the chief exports of the United States: cotton; refined petroleum; automobiles and parts; leaf tobacco; copper and copper manufactures; lard; coal; wheat flour; wheat; fruits; lumber; cotton cloth; electric machinery; agricultural machinery; hog products. The United States is not an international merchant; that is, our exports are nearly all domestic merchandise. Our re-export of foreign goods in the same form in which they are imported has seldom amounted to more than one and a half per cent of the total exports and never to more than two and a half per cent.

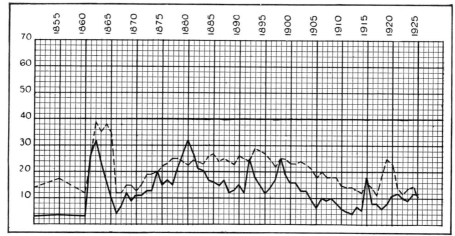

470   Graph showing exports from the United States, 1850–1925, of foodstuffs in crude condition and of food animals (solid line); and foodstuffs wholly or partly prepared (broken line); prepared expressly for *The Pageant of America* from statistics in the *Statistical Abstract of the United States*

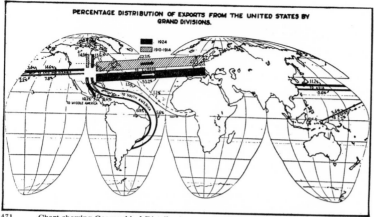

PERCENTAGE DISTRIBUTION OF EXPORTS FROM THE UNITED STATES BY
GRAND DIVISIONS.

471   Chart showing Geographical Distribution of Foreign Trade in the United States,
1910–25, from the United States Department of Commerce, *Yearbook*, 1925

OUR PRINCIPAL EXPORT CUSTOMERS

Europe has always been the best customer for our exports, buying on an average about sixty per cent of all we had to sell abroad. Despite the unsettled conditions in European nations since the World War, they have continued to purchase more than half of our exports. Europe favors our foodstuffs and raw materials, buying nearly all of these items we have for sale. Since it is this type of export which is falling off in relative importance, it seems likely that Europe's long preëminence as our best customer will suffer a diminution in the future. Countries like England and Germany have little use for our manufactures and indeed sell their own in competition with ours in the world markets; consequently, as our export of manufactures grows the purchases of western Europe should decline. Russia, being agricultural, may continue to take our manufactured articles. Next to Europe, North America absorbs our exports, generally taking about twenty-five per cent of the total, or about half as much as Europe. Canada and Cuba account for four-fifths of our sales to North America. The shift in the character of our exports ought to increase rather than diminish our trade with these neighbors, although Canada has industrial ambitions of her own. Some of the trade credited to Canada should really be attributed to Europe, for Canada re-exports much of what we sell there. Until the World War, Asia and South America each took about six per cent of our exports; but since that conflict Asia has almost doubled her percentage, while South America has stood still. If our export of manufactured articles continues to expand, it will probably be in Asia and South America that we shall make the most strenuous efforts to sell them, in competition with European manufactures which by long established trade relations have a firm foothold in these markets. Australasia and Africa, taking about five per cent of our exports, will doubtless be given more attention in the future.

OUR FOREIGN TRADE

For a long time Europe sold to us as much or nearly as much as to all the rest of the world. Great Britain and, to a less extent, Holland, Belgium, Germany and France were international merchants, combing the world for products to re-sell to us and others. Thus, prior to the World War, we purchased most of our crude rubber, wool, mahogany, diamonds and some of our silk from Europe rather than from the countries where these articles originated. Since the World War, much, but not all, of this intermediary trade with Europe has been discontinued. Europe, now supplying us with only thirty per cent of our needs, has been slightly surpassed by Asia, while North America now accounts for about a fifth of our imports. South America is able to sell us very few commodities, the total reaching about twelve per cent of all our imports. The proportion of the rest of the world (Oceania and Africa) in our imports is negligible (three to four per cent). Generally we sell more to Europe, North America and Oceania than we buy from them; with Asia and South America the relation is reversed. The value of our exports is exceeded only by that of the United Kingdom. Our total foreign trade is twice as much as that of any other country except the United Kingdom.

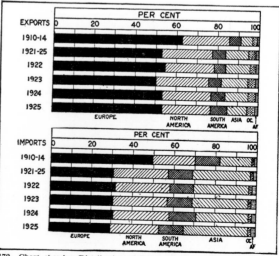

472   Chart showing Distribution of Foreign Trade of the United States, 1910–25, from the United States Department of Commerce, *Yearbook*, 1925

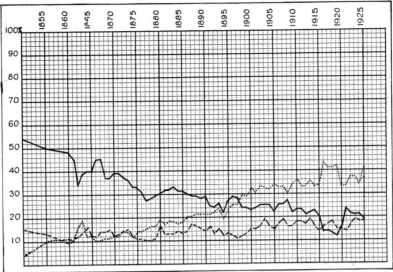

473 Graph showing imports into the United States, 1850–1925, of manufactures ready for consumption (solid line); manufactures for further use in manufacturing (broken line); crude materials for use in manufacturing (dotted line); prepared expressly for *The Pageant of America*, from statistics in the *Statistical Abstract of the United States*

FOODSTUFF IMPORTS

THE foodstuff imports of the United States have seldom amounted to as much as twenty per cent, but they have never been less than ten per cent of our total imports. The foods bought abroad have been almost entirely those of a tropical or semi-tropical origin. Sugar was for many years our leading food import, with coffee, tea, cocoa beans, vegetable oils, and fruits such as bananas, olives and figs of importance. As compared with our steady imports of foodstuffs, our foreign purchases of manufactures indicate some striking changes. For generations we were eager buyers of foreign manufactured wares, but since 1867 and quite rapidly since 1885 our purchases of such articles have fallen off. On the other hand, crude materials for use in manufacturing have mounted steadily since 1875. The following articles constitute the chief imports into the United States. Eleven of the fifteen, those indicated by (m), are crude raw materials for American factories: sugar; raw silk (m); coffee; crude rubber (m); newsprint paper (m); copper (m); cotton goods; mineral oil (m); furs (m); hides and skins (m); wool (m); jute (m); gems; wood pulp (m); tin (m).

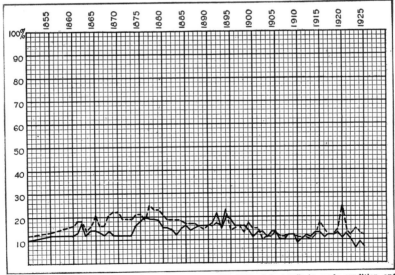

474 Graph showing imports into the United States, 1850–1925, of foodstuffs in crude condition and food animals (solid line); and foodstuffs partly or wholly prepared (broken line); prepared expressly for *The Pageant of America*, from statistics in the *Statistical Abstract of the United States*

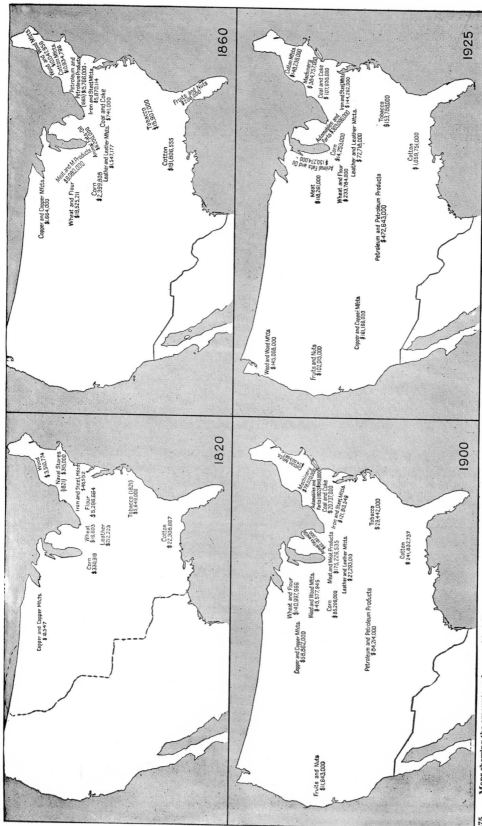

475   Maps showing the amounts and geographical distribution of the leading exports of the United States at certain periods, expressly prepared for *The Pageant of America* from statistics in the *Statistical Abstract of the United States*, 1925, and the Department of Commerce *Year Book*, 1925

THE AMERICAN EXPORTING MARKET

CROSS sections of American trade, made at specially chosen periods, pictorialize the enormous increase in the bulk of exchange in certain commodities. The names and amounts of the exported products have been placed in the geographical area where the articles were most produced at the time.

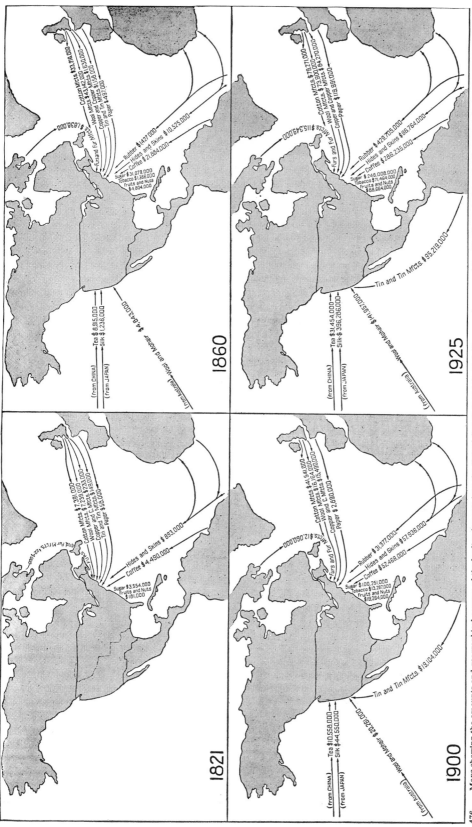

476   Maps showing the amounts and geographical sources of the leading imports into the United States at certain periods, expressly prepared for *The Pageant of America* from statistics in the *Statistical Abstract of the United States*, 1925, and the Department of Commerce *Year Book*, 1925

THE FLOW OF IMPORTS

THE first statistics available on the amounts of products imported into the United States are for 1821. At this early period of our development, to take one example, cotton manufactures and wool manufactures from Europe were by an enormous margin the leading imports. In 1860 they still led but by a much decreased percentage, and in the twentieth century, as can be traced from this pictorial tabulation, they have dropped to a relatively insignificant position.

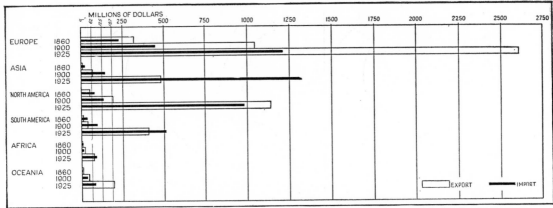

477   Chart showing the steady increase of our exports and imports, arranged by continents, expressly prepared for *The Pageant of America,*
from statistics in the *Statistical Abstract of the United States,* 1925

CONTINUOUS INCREASE

"EXPORTS to all regions of the world except Europe and the southern part of North America increased substantially during 1926. Exports to Asia increased by about one-fifth and after allowing for differences in price levels were greater than in any earlier year. Sales to Canada were also in record volume, and exports to South America, Oceania, and Africa continued to show steady expansion. Exports to Europe, on the other hand, declined considerably as a result of the decrease in the value of various agricultural commodities. There was also some decrease in our exports to Latin countries of North America. . . . Imports into the United States from every region of the world were greater in 1926 than the year before, the increase being particularly marked in the case of Asia, which furnished nearly one-third of our total imports. Increases in imports were very generally distributed among the different classes of commodities. The great prosperity of the country . . . resulted in large purchases of tropical foodstuffs and of exotic raw materials." — COMMERCE *Year Book,* 1926.

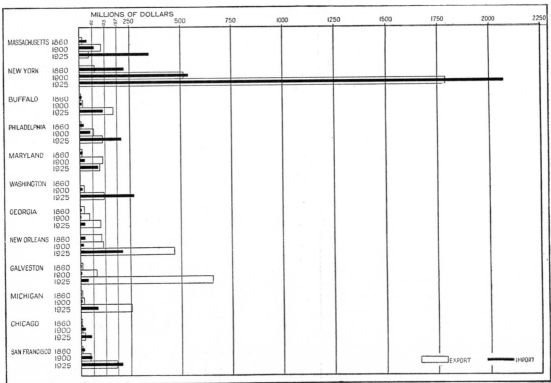

478   Chart showing the steady increase of our exports and imports, arranged by customs divisions, expressly prepared for *The Pageant of*
America, from statistics in the *Statistical Abstract of the United States,* 1925

479   Senator Tillman's Famous Allegorical Cow, from a cartoon in the *Congressional Record*, Oct. 3, 1913,
             attacking the moneyed and manufacturing interests of the East

DIVERSIFICATION AND STANDARDIZATION

THE story of the interchange of commodities within the United States has not been told with any degree of completeness. Sectional specialization in certain products made itself manifest at an early period. Great Britain recognized the clear distinction between her "fish," her "bread," and her "sugar and tobacco" colonies (see No. 18); and from this same sectional diversification, arose later the coast-wide trade between the newly formed states. Differentiation became more marked with each decade. Sections aligned themselves on great issues as their economic interests were affected. History must recognize the motives engendered by this desire to safeguard the most profitable markets and channels of distribution. The cartoon of Senator Tillman's "allegorical cow" visualizes the jealousy which persisted between the different economic sections long after the Civil War. Unfortunately the statistics necessary for a full analysis of this internal commerce are not available. For between the sections of the greatest consuming market in the world, there are no customs barriers to tabulate the amount of goods flowing backward and forward, so that the American manufacturer stands in a unique position. Protected by a high tariff wall from outside competition, he surveys the vast market — from Maine to California — confident that his product may be equally in demand throughout the country. From the same cause great mail order houses have risen, profiting by and in turn increasing the standardization of the American internal market.

480   From a cartoon representing the small retailer's fear of mail order competition, in *Cartoons*, March 1912,
             after the *Montgomery Advertiser*, Montgomery, Ala.

CHAPTER IX

RIVER AND CANAL IN THE TWENTIETH CENTURY

LIKE the merchant marine the history of the canals and rivers of the United States has been profoundly affected by the industrial development of the last half of the nineteenth century. In the days before the railroad, trade routes tended to follow the waterways because water transportation was easier and cheaper than carriage on land. For a full half-century the Mississippi and its tributaries determined the course which goods in transit should follow west of the Appalachian mountains. The Canal Era provided the nation with artificial waterways that served the regions which the navigable rivers did not reach. The perfection of the railroad changed all these commercial adjustments of the first half of the nineteenth century. The railroad, abandoning the water course, struck out in a direct line across the plains or wound its way through the passes of mountainous country. The service it offered was swift and certain. With its advent old trade routes gave place to new. In particular the canal suffered, for, as in the case of the Erie, the new mode of transportation was often found paralleling its course and furnishing a means of communication with which it could not effectively compete. As a consequence, one after another, the old canals which had been built with such high hope and which had in their day served well the regions through which they passed were abandoned. Here and there the traveler east of the Mississippi may see occasional stretches full of undergrowth with grass growing on the tow path along which the canal driver once urged his straining horses. A few canals of more than ordinary importance have been retained. Most notable among these, the historic Erie has persisted into the twentieth century. But "Clinton's big ditch" in its original form had little usefulness for the industrial population of modern times. Enlarged by the state of New York into the Barge Canal and capable of floating boats of a thousand tons the Erie Canal still plays a part in the transportation system of the United States. Rivers as trade routes have met to a slightly less extent the fate of the canals. In general river facilities cannot compete with the railroad and the motor truck. A few streams, of which the Ohio is the most conspicuous, because of their proximity to areas where bulky raw products such as coal are produced have maintained a certain importance. It may be that the time will come when transportation needs will become so great that the rivers will again be pressed into service for heavy, bulky, cheap commodities and will carry a traffic equal to that of their days of greatness. The twentieth century has seen the air ways opened. These with the railroads and the highways seem to offer the solution for the transportation of valuable, perishable articles for the generations to come. The slowness of river and canal borne freight is incompatible with an age that puts a premium on speed.

481   The Hudson River Steamer *Washington Irving*.   © Detroit Publishing Co.

OUR RIVERS IN COMMERCE

THE rivers of the United States perform two commercial services.   Their mouths are used as harbors and ports for ocean-going ships.   Then beyond tide line and deep channel the river has an inland traffic of its own employing vessels different in size and design from those engaged in sea commerce.   Few New England rivers are navigable for as much as one hundred miles.   As commercial highways, except for the logs floated down their currents, and their local passenger and excursion business, they are not important.   The Hudson is navigated for one hundred and sixty-five miles from the sea to Troy, and an extension of its traffic by means of canals and Lake Champlain carries its commercial influence into Canada, and across the state of New York to Buffalo.   The large passenger traffic is carried in luxurious steamers, which also carry some package freight. Coal, rock, sand, brick and lumber are largely transported in barges.

482   A Hudson River tow.   © Detroit Publishing Co.

483   Entrance of the Delaware Canal into the Delaware River. © Underwood & Underwood

THE DELAWARE RIVER

THE Delaware River is navigable for ocean ships below Philadelphia and for smaller boats as far as Trenton. Its passenger business, though considerable, is less than the Hudson's. However, the local freight commerce is extensive. Coal is the principal commodity, as well as iron, stone, lumber and brick. The Schuylkill lost its importance with the advent of the railway; yet some coal still loiters down its current.

484   Savannah River from City Hall, Savannah, Ga. © Detroit Publishing Co.

TRAFFIC ON SOUTH ATLANTIC RIVERS

IN general, the local freight business on the South Atlantic rivers is much smaller than that of the Hudson and Delaware. In that area coal travels by rail. Farm produce, fish and oysters are important boat cargoes. Lumber and naval stores are found on some of the rivers, particularly those in South Carolina, Georgia and northern Florida. Cotton, which was once the mainstay of southern river traffic and is still to be seen, is mostly carried by railroad. Despite their small commerce, the South Atlantic rivers are influential in keeping down railroad rates.

485 Barges on the Alabama River, from a photograph. © David Holt, Mobile, Ala.

THE ALABAMA RIVER SYSTEM

THE Alabama River system, with more than one thousand miles of connected navigable waterway, joins the cities of Montgomery, Birmingham, Tuscaloosa and Mobile. It penetrates not only one of the principal cotton-growing regions, but also one of the chief industrial centers of the South, Birmingham, the "Pittsburgh of the South." Steamers run regularly from Mobile to Montgomery on the Alabama River, and on the Tombigbee and Warrior steamboat service is maintained between Mobile and Tuscaloosa, carrying passengers, package freight and some cotton. The principal commerce, carried in barges, flatboats and rafts, comprises cotton, cottonseed, coal, iron, lumber, timber, sand and stone. Some fertilizer, grain, naval stores, provisions and general merchandise also find place in the river commerce. Above Tuscaloosa, the Black Warrior, improved by the Federal Government in 1918, reaches into the coal and iron fields. A barge line operates between Mobile, Cordova and Birmingport, transporting southward coal, rails, bar iron, steel plates, barbed wire and nails; and northward steel mill raw material, such as manganese ore and sulphur, and household supplies such as sugar, salt and canned goods. The annual tonnage is about two hundred and sixty thousand, two-thirds of which is southbound. The Alabama system and the Ohio successfully maintain river commerce despite railroad competition. It is no accident that their items of commerce are so nearly identical. Both systems serve a steel mill territory. Their mills have many freight commodities that are bulky, heavy and cheap. Consequently transportation is more economical both on the Ohio and Alabama waterways than by rail.

486 Steamer with barges, Alabama River, from a photograph. © Chamber of Commerce, Tuscaloosa, Ala.

487   Steamer *Eufaula*, plying on the Apalachicola River between Columbus, Ga., and Apalachicola, Fla.

OTHER RIVERS OF THE SOUTH

THE country bordering the Apalachicola in western Florida is almost entirely dependent upon the river for supplies and for passenger conveyance. The commerce consists of cotton, naval stores, general merchandise and forest products. In the state of Mississippi, the Pascagoula and Pearl Rivers have some local importance, but their very limited depth prevents much use for commerce. Southern Louisiana possesses, beside the mouths of the Mississippi, a maze of bayous, creeks and rivers, but the commerce on these waterways is inconsequential. The rivers of Texas flowing into the Gulf — the Trinity, Brazos, Neches and Rio Grande — have also as yet been little used for commercial purposes.

488   Transporting grain on the San Joaquin River, California, courtesy of the Stockton Chamber of
Commerce, Stockton, Cal.

TRAFFIC ON THE SAN JOAQUIN

ON the Pacific but few rivers make their way through the Coast Range out to sea. In the south, the Colorado River was navigated from 1851 until the Southern Pacific Railroad was built, and was the only route to the military reservation at Yuma. With a four-foot fall per mile the river could not compete with the railroads and later with automobiles. The great valley of California is drained by the San Joaquin and the Sacramento which flow into San Francisco Bay. Before the days of railroads these rivers with their branches had a huge passenger and freight business with fast steamboats drawing six to seven feet of water. With the coming of the railroads nearly all the passenger business and much of the freight deserted the river. The picture shows the transporting of grain on the San Joaquin.

489   On the Columbia, below the Cascades, Oregon. © Detroit Publishing Co.

THE COLUMBIA RIVER

THE Columbia is navigable for ocean ships as far as Portland, one hundred and ten miles from the sea, and for river vessels as far as the Dalles, one hundred miles above. There, the rapids are passed by a locked canal five miles long. Above the Dalles another river stretch of one hundred and twenty-four miles is available for river craft. The Willamette, which joins the Columbia at Portland, is itself navigable for one hundred and thirty miles to Corvallis, but only light draft vessels can go through the Oregon City locks in summer, due to low water. The Snake River has its confluence with the Columbia at Ainsworth and has light draft-navigation for about one hundred and fifty miles. Five other smaller rivers joining the Columbia have some navigability. Here indeed is a river system worthy of note. Yet its potentiality is far greater than its performances in commerce; few boats are ever seen above Portland. Before 1882, the Columbia was the main highway of commerce between the coast and eastern Oregon and eastern Washington. But in that year the Oregon Railroad & Navigation Co. along the river absorbed the traffic. In 1905, when the portage railroad at Celilo was built, river commerce revived. The downstream commerce on the Columbia consists of wheat, flour, miscellaneous grains, cattle and horses, wool, general merchandise, machinery and railroad supplies. The commerce of the Willamette consists of farm-stuff and forest products.

THE MISSISSIPPI RIVER

THE shallow waters, shelving banks and shifting channels of the Mississippi have kept in continuous use the sternwheel wooden vessels of early days. Nor has it been possible to increase the size of these boats. The seasonal changes in the river level render it impracticable to maintain large permanent terminals in any but the most important cities.

490   The Levee, Baton Rouge, La. © Detroit Publishing Co.

491 Mississippi towboat *Natchez* with barges. © Poland Photographers, Memphis, Tenn.

MISSISSIPPI FLEET OF BARGES IN TOW

COMMERCE on the Mississippi has declined since the Civil War. The famous steam-packet passenger boats have entirely disappeared. For freight, delays and higher insurance, amounting to as much as a third of the freight rate on river-borne goods, offset any saving as against railroad transportation. Since 1915 the river steamboat has encountered also the keenest rate cutting by small gasoline motor boats. The only through commerce of any importance on the rivers surviving competition is heavy, bulky cargo, carried on barges or flatboats pushed in flocks by a stern-wheel steamer.

492   Coal fleet, Pittsburgh, Pa.   © Detroit Publishing Co.

THE OHIO RIVER

THE Ohio River is the greatest commercial stream in the United States and its largest burden of traffic originates on its own subsidiary, the Monongahela. The leading commodity is coal, which accounts for almost exactly half of all the freight of the entire Mississippi system, and is much more than half the tonnage borne by the Ohio. In addition to coal, the Ohio River barges are filled with sand and stone, iron ore, pig iron and other iron first products. Lumber and grain too find a place of decreasing importance. Pittsburgh ranks as the foremost inland river port in the United States.

493   Along the levee, Cincinnati, Ohio. © Detroit Publishing Co.

LOWER MISSISSIPPI COMMERCE

THE commerce of the lower Mississippi (St. Louis to New Orleans) embraces the traffic that comes out of the Ohio at Cairo, and adds the coal, general merchandise or forest products that start from St. Louis. Below Memphis, cotton and cottonseed appear among the prevailing coal barges and close to New Orleans some boat loads of sugar, molasses, rice and crude petroleum may be encountered. The coal that enters New Orleans is sold there to railroads and steamships for their own use and for further transportation. The river de-

494   A Mississippi River Landing.   © Detroit Publishing Co.

liveries of coal into New Orleans are only about one-third as much as the railroads carry, and the cotton receipts by river are hardly one-tenth of the arrivals by railroad. The upper Mississippi suffers from three commercial handicaps; ice in winter; low water in summer; and insufficient draft at all times; although steamboats pass between St. Louis and St. Paul. The principal commerce on the upper Mississippi is logs and lumber. In order to encourage the waning river commerce, the Federal Government in 1918 began to operate a fleet of barges between St. Louis and New Orleans. In May, 1923, a weekly merchandise express was inaugurated between St. Louis and Memphis. Whether this attempt at the revival of the river will succeed remains to be seen.

THE DECLINE OF CANAL COMMERCE

THE record of American canal commerce since the Civil War is one of uninterrupted decline and abandonment. Of more than four thousand five hundred miles of canal nearly two thousand had been totally abandoned by 1880, and since that time about one thousand five hundred miles more have been given up. The money invested in the three thousand five hundred miles of now useless waterway was more than ninety-eight million dollars. A canal cannot live in modern times unless it is deep and wide enough to accommodate one-thousand-ton barges, propelled by their own machinery or pulled by a towboat; and three-fourths of our canal mileage, shallow, narrow and designed for animal towage, failed to meet these standards. The only state canals now (1927) in operation are in New York, Ohio, Illinois and Louisiana, and of these only the New York canals are strictly modern. One or two of the private canals are adequate for modern needs, as well as some short, deep, wide canals operated by the Federal Government and connecting important water highways. The tonnage on all state and private canals, which was sixteen millions in 1880, has fallen below three million tons. Three-fourths of the present canal traffic is local, and the principal commodities are coal, sand and stone. Forest products are also found on the barges and some iron and steel products. A small remnant of the grain trade has survived. Passenger traffic was the first to desert canals for the railroads. Perishable or valuable freight followed. Commodity after commodity abandoned the artificial waterways until only a fraction of those of great weight and low unit value were left.

495   Coal Barges on the Delaware & Raritan Canal.
© C. H. Gallagher, Trenton, N. J.

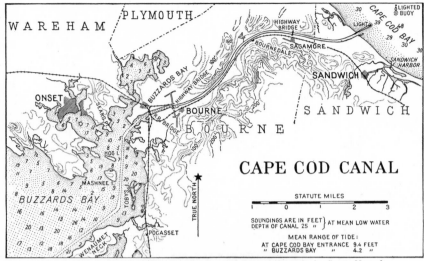

496   Map of the Cape Cod Canal, drawn expressly for *The Pageant of America* by Gregor Noetzel,
American Geographical Society, New York

TWO GREAT CANAL PROJECTS

IN recent years two ambitious canal projects, one private, the other public, have been completed, the Cape
Cod Canal and the New York State Barge Canal System. The Atlantic coast line of the United States is
nowhere more dangerous than on the ocean shore of Cape Cod. Yet a distance of three miles between the
Scusset and Manomet (Monument) Rivers and a sandy ridge thirty feet above sea level are all that have
separated the waters of Barnstable and Buzzards Bays.   As early as 1676, the idea was conceived of a canal
to avoid the dangers of the ocean passage, and in 1697 a survey was made.

THE CAPE COD CANAL

THE ground was resurveyed in 1776, and the project was broached again in 1791, in 1824 and in 1864. Protection in time of war furnished an added argument for this improvement. With the advent of steam, economy
furnished another; and the delay was due to a general inability to decide what authority should build the
canal. In 1899, Massachusetts granted a charter to the Boston, Cape Cod & New York Canal Company to
construct the waterway that had been talked about for more than two hundred years. Owing to financial
troubles, political intrigue and the opposition of competitive routes and carriers, the canal was not opened for
service until July 29, 1914. Its cost was thirteen million dollars. At high tide the Cape Cod Canal is equal in
depth to the Suez, Kiel or Manchester canals. It is short, eight miles from shore to shore and thirteen miles
from a thirty-foot depth in Buzzards Bay to an equal depth in Barnstable Bay. It is a sea-level route with no

locks or dams and with room for two
ships to pass. On Buzzards Bay the
entrance is protected by surrounding
land, but on Barnstable Bay a three-
thousand-foot breakwater gives protection. The canal has been of most
benefit to the Boston-New York
traffic, but it is used by all coastwise
carriers from Maine to Florida, and
by vessels from Nova Scotia to New
York and from the West Indies to
Boston. More than eight thousand
ships per year pass through it, carrying more than two million tons of
freight. Periodically since the canal
was opened, political efforts have
been directed to the acquirement of
this private canal by the Federal
Government.

497   Liner *Boston* passing through the Cape Cod Canal, courtesy of
Eastern Steamship Line, Inc., New York

498   Lock and Movable Dam in Mohawk River (unit of the New York Barge Canal), courtesy of the Department of the State Engineer and Surveyor, Albany, N. Y.

NEW YORK BARGE CANAL

MUCH more remarkable than the Cape Cod Canal, indeed in many respects as great an achievement as the Panama Canal, was the building by the state of New York of a barge canal system begun in 1903 and opened for traffic in 1918. The Erie Canal, which from 1825 to the close of the Civil War had made New York "the Empire State" and created at the mouth of the Hudson one of the world's greatest cities and America's chief port, had by 1900 succumbed to railroad competition. Reduced rates and lengthened locks, to accommodate larger boats, failed to secure for it its share of business. An expenditure of nine million dollars in 1895 resulted in a public scandal. Commissions appointed in 1898 and 1899 laid three plans before the public, the abandonment of the canal, a ship canal, and a one-thousand-ton barge canal. The first was unthinkable, the second expensive and of doubtful usefulness, the third a fair compromise. After much discussion, the Legislature, in March, 1903, authorized a barge canal from the Hudson to Lake Erie with branches to Lake Ontario at Oswego and to Lake Champlain at Whitehall, the funds to be derived from a bond issue of one hundred and one million dollars. The people of New York at the November polls ratified the Legislature's action. From 1904 to 1918, the new barge-canal system was in process of construction. In 1908 the original plan was extended to include two other waterways that brought Cayuga and Seneca into the state system. This same year too brought to a head a five-year campaign for the inclusion of adequate terminals principally at New York city but also at Buffalo and intermediate points. Additional appropriations were sanctioned for these objects. Still later, near the end of the construction period, provision was made for lighthouses, channel lights and other fixtures along the routes of the waterway. The total cost of the twelve-year project was one hundred and sixty-eight million dollars. This is a heavy burden even to so wealthy a state as New York.

499   Barges on the New York Barge Canal, courtesy of the State Engineer and Surveyor, Albany, N. Y.

500   Concrete lock, showing lock gates, New York Barge Canal, courtesy of the State Engineer and Surveyor, Albany, N. Y.

THE OPENING OF THE BARGE CANAL

THE new barge-canal system did more than enlarge the old Erie; much of it followed a new course. The total mileage was five hundred and twenty-five of which the part corresponding to the old Erie accounted for three hundred and thirty-nine. Of the total mileage three hundred and eighty-two was in navigable rivers and lakes; and the rest was a land-line or in locks. In the streams and lakes the channel was at least two hundred feet wide, but in rock cuts and earth bottoms the width narrowed to ninety-four or seventy-five feet. The shallowest depth was twelve feet in locks. Among the innovations were the use of concrete instead of cut stone, movable dams, lift bridges and electric power. When the barge-canal system was opened for navigation, on May 15, 1918, it was taken over by the Federal Government and remained under government control for three years. Since 1921, traffic has grown each year, until now it has recovered about half the total tonnage carried in 1880. The commodities carried over the barge system are grain, sand, stone, gravel, sulphur and lumber; also oil and automobiles. The canal boats nowadays actually make as good time as the railroads

501   New York Barge Canal Terminal, New York city, courtesy of the State Engineer and Surveyor, Albany, N. Y.

or better. Although most of the boats on the Barge Canal are engaged in local services there is a growing through fleet. In 1923, a line freight service operating from New York to Duluth via Oswego and the Welland Canal was instituted. Contrary to predictions, some Lake boats are using the Barge Canal. Yet the canal has failed to realize the hopes of its projectors and is the subject of continual criticism. Some of the strictures are unprejudiced, but others seem to bear the taint of special interest. The Barge Canal is not without enemies.

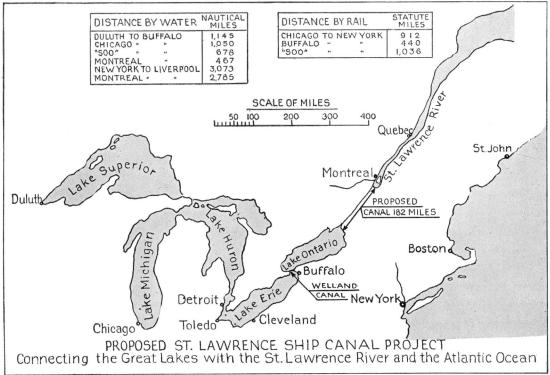

PROPOSED ST. LAWRENCE SHIP CANAL PROJECT
Connecting the Great Lakes with the St. Lawrence River and the Atlantic Ocean

502   Redrawn from a chart in A. F. Lindblad, *St. Lawrence Waterway Needed*, in *Marine Review*, August 1922

ST. LAWRENCE PROJECT

THE idea of an intra-coastal waterway from Maine to Florida and thence to the Gulf of Mexico goes back to the days of Franklin and Washington, both of whom approved it. Part of this route already exists, beginning at Portland, Maine, crossing the Gulf of Maine to Boston, proceeding across Massachusetts Bay to the Cape Cod Canal, emerging from Buzzards Bay into Block Island Sound and then into Long Island Sound. By means of the East River and Harlem River it is possible to reach the Upper Hudson and the Barge Canal System and so arrive at the Great Lakes. For passage down the coast, the plan calls for a trip from New York Bay to Raritan Bay and thence to the Delaware River by way of the Delaware and Raritan Canal. From the Delaware the route crosses to Chesapeake Bay through the Chesapeake and Delaware Canal, purchased in 1919 by the Federal Government.

Thus southward through sounds, connecting canals and dredged rivers all of which are more or less in use, a projected inland waterway is available for eighteen hundred miles along almost the entire length of the Atlantic coast. What the plan proposes is the deepening and widening and maintaining in navigable condition of the portions of this route that need these improvements. It is claimed that it would cost less to create this eighteen-hundred-mile system than it cost New York to build the five-hundred-mile Barge Canal.

A second proposal popular in the Middle West and well received in New England is the construction of a ship canal from the Great Lakes to the Atlantic Ocean by way of the St. Lawrence River. The principal natural barrier to this route is a small strip of the St. Lawrence one hundred and fifteen miles long between Preston and Montreal where three rapids interrupt through communication. It is supposed that this project would cost about twice as much as the New York Barge Canal and would pay for itself through the sale of hydroelectric power developed by dams across the St. Lawrence. The plan has been urged upon Congress and has been a matter of preliminary negotiation between the United States and Canada. Naturally, New York state and city, Buffalo and Montreal all oppose it most vigorously; while Chicago and the Corn Belt are keen to have ocean ships lying at lake ports. In June, 1927, a report on this project was published under New England auspices. The committee that prepared the report was composed of Governors and ex-Governors, influential business men and engineers. After reviewing in detail the history of the proposal the whole matter was analyzed and compared point by point with rival or antagonistic plans. The final conclusion was that the plan would be of incalculable benefit to New England, so its leaders endorsed the project.

CHAPTER X

THE LETTER POST

THE transmission of written messages has been affected profoundly by the development of industrialism. But it was not until the late nineteenth and early twentieth centuries that the full possibilities of the letter post was realized.

The mail service before the Revolution, when Benjamin Franklin was Postmaster-General for the English continental colonies, was slow, irregular and costly. For young Thomas Jefferson in Virginia to send a line to a friend in Boston cost a sum comparable to that paid to-day for a telegram, and his message required a longer time to reach its destination than a note from a twentieth-century New York business house to a branch in Shanghai. It was no accident that, when the storm of revolution approached, one of the earliest moves of the Patriot party was to establish "committees of correspondence" to quicken the interchange of information and ideas. The receipt of a letter was a rare experience in the lives of the average eighteenth-century Americans. They were, in the main, independent farmers living more or less isolated on practically self-sufficient farms. Neither their business nor their social life necessitated correspondence, except at the rarest intervals. The cost of sending a letter was, in fact, not a matter that they could ignore. Habitual correspondence was, in the eighteenth century, the privilege of the well-to-do.

A century and a half after Independence the mail has become a commonplace in the life of practically every American, bringing to his door whether it be in the city tenement or on an isolated farm letters, newspapers, magazines and advertising matter. To send a message even to a neighboring continent costs but a trifling sum. The poorest immigrant struggling to establish himself in the New World can afford a letter home, and can know that it will be delivered within a time that would have seemed incredible to the eighteenth-century American. The mail service has helped to knit the American people together and has assisted in the development of a national consciousness. The letter carrier with his leather bag signifies that in America isolation has been almost completely obliterated.

Anything that facilitates communication is a benefit to commerce. Information, advice, and exchange, all essentials of a developed commerce, are aided by an adequate organization of communication. Hence the postal service, the oldest American agency of communication, has been a vital factor in American industrial and commercial history. Messages sent by letter guide commercial agencies in adjusting the supply to the demand for goods or services. Furthermore, the means of communication may become the means of commerce. This occurs when the postal service admits to the mails such things as merchant's samples, packages of commodities, and advertising matter. It also happens when the post office itself conducts various features of the banking business such as the forwarding or safe-keeping of money or other valuables. Created to forward state papers, enlarged to accommodate private messages, the post office has been of incalculable value in the promotion of business.

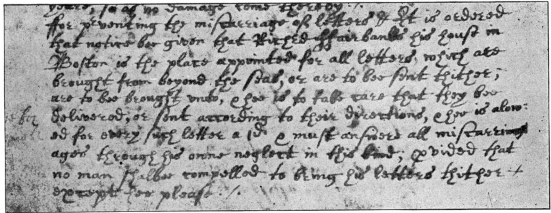

503   Massachusetts Act of 1639, making Richard Fairbanks Postmaster, from the original in the Massachusetts Archives, Boston

RICHARD FAIRBANKS APPOINTED RECEIVER OF MAIL

In America the first legislative act respecting mail was passed by the General Court of Massachusetts in 1639. It read: "It is ordered that notice be given that Richard Fairbanks his house in Boston is the place appointed for all letters, which are brought from beyond the seas or are to be sent thither, are to bee brought to him and he is to take care that they bee delivered, or sent according to directions, and hee is allowed for every such letter 1d. and must answer all miscarriages through his owne neglect in this kind; provided that no man shall be compelled to bring his letters thither except hee please." The foregoing, it is to be observed, applied solely to foreign mail, and gave Richard Fairbanks no monopoly in the handling of mail; the proviso expressly made the matter optional. A citizen of Boston could continue to hire a private messenger or he might drop his letter in the coffee-house bag if he wished or hand it directly to some ship captain, if he preferred not to patronize Richard Fairbanks.

---

52   *The Laws of Virginia.*

XC.

Publique Letters, how to be Conveyed.

WHereas the remoteneſs of divers places in the Countrey from *James*-City, and the neceſſity of communicating divers buſineſſes to the utmoſt limits of it, would, if Meſſengers were preſſed purpoſely, put the Countrey to an Annual great Expence: For prevention thereof, Be it enacted, That all Letters ſuperſcribed for the uſe of his Majeſty, or the Publique, ſhall be immediately conveyed from Plantation to Plantation, to the place and perſon they are directed to, under the penalty of Three hundred and fifty pounds of Tobacco, to each default; and if any perſon be put thereby to any extraordinary charge, the Court of each County is hereby authorized to judge thereof, and to levy payment for the ſame; the Superſcriptions being ſigned by the Governour, ſome one of the *Quorum*, or the Colonel, Lieutenant Colonel, or Major of a Regiment: And where any perſon in the Family the ſaid Letters come to, can write, ſuch perſon is required to endorſe the day and hour he received them, that the neglect or contempt of any perſon ſtopping them may be the better known, and be puniſhed accordingly.

504   Act of Virginia Assembly, 1661, regulating the conveyance of "Publique Letters,"
from *The Lawes of Virginia now in Force*, London, 1662

SOUTHERN PLANTATIONS MADE POST OFFICES

The first legislation in America that dealt with domestic mail was enacted by the Legislature of Virginia in 1661. This law provided that: "All letters superscribed for the service of His Majesty or publique shall be immediately conveyed from plantation to plantation to the place and person they are directed to, and a penalty of 350 pounds of tobacco to each defaulter." This made every plantation a post office and forced every landowner to supply a mail carrier at least as far as the next plantation.

505   Governor Francis Lovelace, 1630–1709, from
      a print in the New York Historical Society

A NEW YORK–BOSTON MAIL SERVICE

In 1673, Governor Lovelace of New York endeavored to establish a mail service between New York and Boston. The carrier was a single horseman who made the journey each way once a month. He was to carry official mail between the two colonies and was permitted to transmit private letters and packages. These were put in sealed bags and dropped at the community to which they were directed. Separate letters could be collected and delivered along the way. Although this plan was similar to one later adopted, it proved a failure. The Indians and the Dutch waylaid the messengers and completely stopped overland intercolonial communication. The attempt is interesting, however, because it was made so early, and because, as in Europe, the postal service, primarily designed for public officers and state documents, was open to the carriage of private communications.

GOVERNOR DONGAN'S PLAN

Between 1673, when Lovelace tried to establish an intercolonial postal service, and 1693, when the continuous operation of post offices began, there were several attempts by colonial legislatures to set up some means of communication within their own borders. Massachusetts, Connecticut, New York and Pennsylvania all enacted one or more postal statutes within this period. The most far-reaching plan was one put forward in 1684 by Governor Dongan of New York. He proposed a linked series of post offices extending from Nova Scotia to South Carolina, to be served by foot and horse messengers each covering a small section of the distance. This ambitious scheme dwindled in practice to an intermittent service between New York and Boston.

506   Thomas Dongan, 1634–1715, from an engraved
      portrait (not authenticated) by Charles B. Hall in posses-
      sion of the publishers

507   Andrew Hamilton, 1676–1741, first American
Postmaster, from the portrait by an unknown
artist, in the Historical Society of Pennsylvania,
Philadelphia

A MAIL SERVICE BETWEEN NEW HAMPSHIRE AND DELAWARE

In 1691 Thomas Neale a court favorite was given a monopoly over a proposed American colonial post office. Neale appointed Andrew Hamilton his resident deputy and the latter inaugurated a postal system May 1, 1693. From Portsmouth, New Hampshire, to Philadelphia and Newcastle, Delaware, Hamilton's service was supposed to be weekly, though this schedule was seldom maintained. The route was divided into sections each of which was patrolled by one rider. During the first four years of its existence this colonial post incurred expenses of three thousand eight hundred and seventeen pounds, and received returns of one thousand four hundred and fifty-seven pounds. North of New York the route was profitable, but the sections south of Philadelphia cost much more than they returned. This difference reflected the relative density of settlement and the centralization of commercial interests.

THE BRITISH POST OFFICE OPERATES A COLONIAL BRANCH

BEFORE Neale's patent expired he and his deputy, Andrew Hamilton, died. The heirs to the monopoly were an Englishman named West and Hamilton's widow, the latter being the actual manager of the system until 1706. Meanwhile, through all these years the colonial post office was in an unsatisfactory state. It suffered from the competition of ship captains and other private carriers, and it received niggardly support from the colonial governments. Everyone concerned was of the opinion that most of the difficulties arose because the post office was a private business. At length, in 1707, West and Mrs. Hamilton were induced to give up their rights for a consideration of

508 An Account of the Posts of North America, from Herman Moll, *A New and Exact Map of the Dominion of the King of Great Britain*, 1715

something between fifteen hundred and two thousand pounds. Consequently, from 1707 to the close of the Revolution, the British post office operated a colonial branch in America. John Hamilton, the son of Andrew, was the first crown Postmaster-General for America, serving from 1707 to 1730. He was followed (1730–39) by Alexander Spotswood, former Governor of Virginia, Head Lynch (1739–43), Elliot Berger (1743–53), Benjamin Franklin (1753–74) and William Hunter (jointly, 1753–61). John Foxcroft succeeded Hunter in 1761 and served until the outbreak of the Revolution. Franklin was dismissed in 1774 because of his long absences in England and the political opposition of certain interests in Massachusetts.

509 Act for establishing a Post Office in all of Her Majesty's Dominions, 1710, from *Statutes at Large*, Vol. 4. (7 Anne — 13 Geo. I)

THE FIRST COLONIAL POSTAL RATES

THE postal rates of the American colonial post office were fixed by an act of Parliament in 1711. The rates generally were fourpence for any distance up to sixty miles and sixpence for distances between sixty and one hundred miles. For longer distances the rates were higher, although not proportionally so. It costs less relatively to carry letters than it does to collect, sort and distribute them. Until after 1847, postage was payable on delivery rather than upon the posting of a letter. Since no one was sure that a letter would reach its recipient, paying postage in advance was rewarding a service that might not be rendered. In addition, there was a general distrust of postmasters; if a letter were prepaid, the postmasters might not forward or deliver it, whereas, if it were sent collect, the postmaster had an incentive to find the person for whom the letter was intended. No method of affixing stamps was invented until 1845, and even then prepayment by means of stamps was optional. If the recipient were short of funds he could get the postage "charged." Postmasters sold mail service as grocers now sell tea, on credit. Many persons were delinquent. The postmaster's job was by no means a sinecure, so it was not always easy to get capable men to assume the office. This was reflected in the service rendered.

510 Notice of Postage Money due to Andrew Hay, Perth-Amboy, from the *American Weekly Mercury*, October 23-30, 1735

511 Facsimile of *The Boston News-Letter*, April 17–24, 1724, from the original in the American Antiquarian Society, Worcester, Mass.

NEWSPAPERS IN THE MAILS

COLONIAL postal rates were based on what were called "a single letter." This was a single sheet of paper. Letters that filled two or three sheets of paper were charged double and triple the single-rate letter. None of the early postal laws established a rate for mailing newspapers. Nearly all colonial postmasters were newspaper publishers, partly because they were in an excellent position to get news, partly because news items reached them as official business free of postal charge, and partly because the post riders could be forced to deliver the postmasters' newspapers. The postmasters could and did rigidly exclude all other publishers from using the privilege of the post riders. The first newspaper published in America to be distributed by post was the *Boston News-Letter*, issued by Campbell, the postmaster of Boston. Benjamin Franklin was delighted to be appointed postmaster of Philadelphia in 1737 partly because it gave him a chance to increase the circulation of his newspaper and collect more revenue from advertising. Nevertheless, it was Franklin himself who in 1758, as Postmaster-General, admitted newspapers to the mails. From that day to this, newspapers have been a postal problem. Since their news is essentially a social service, it is desirable to give them wide circulation. Low postal rates and free carriage within certain limits bring about this end. On the other hand, the post office has always lost money on the actual carriage of the papers and indirectly has been hindered by the clogging of the mails. No real solution of the problem has ever been found.

FRANKLIN ASSUMES CHARGE OF THE POSTAL SYSTEM

THE greatest complaint against the colonial post office was the delay in the carriage of the mails. This condition was chronic until Benjamin Franklin and his associates Hunter and Foxcroft were put in charge. Franklin more than once toured all the colonies, and he or his co-partners visited every post office in the country.

Thereafter the post routes were laid out or changed so as to increase the speed, and the distance covered by each post rider was lessened. Next, the riders were required to journey by night as well as by day, and a check was placed on their time. The postmasters too were held more strictly accountable for the proper discharge of their functions. The result was a gradual increase in the speed of deliveries, so that it took six days instead of three weeks to send a letter from Boston to Philadelphia. The effect of Franklin's management was shown in the post-office finances. The first three years of his administration showed a deficit of six hundred and seventy-eight pounds. The fourth year saw the deficit reduced to two hundred and sixty-five pounds. From that time on the financial statement contained a surplus of from two hundred to four hundred pounds a year. The surplus in 1761 was almost as great as the total receipts in 1753, and reflects significantly the growth in business brought about largely by the improved management. To avoid the error of hero worship it ought to be noticed that the postal business probably would have increased, regardless of the management, due to the country's progress.

512 John Foxcroft, colonial postmaster, from the portrait by an unknown artist in the Historical Society of Pennsylvania, Philadelphia

"BOOTLEGGED" MAIL

THE colonial post office, although legally granted a monopoly, had a great deal of trouble with "bootlegged" mail. It was exceedingly difficult to get ship captains to deliver mail to the postmaster of the port rather than to private individuals. The law was made constantly more stringent and the captain was allowed a fee, generally a penny, for

513   Mail box carried before the Revolution, courtesy of the Portsmouth Athenæum, Portsmouth, N. H.

every letter he turned over to the postmaster. Yet shipmasters in colonial times were never completely attached to the official postal service. Competitive carriers on land also evaded the postal rules. The law permitted an individual to hire his own carrier for his own mail, and allowed carters and other common carriers to convey letters with merchandise whenever the letter had reference to the merchandise. These two exceptions opened the way to innumerable losses to the post office. After newspapers were admitted to the mails, they too were employed to evade postage; letters were concealed in them and codes were arranged by crossing out type or otherwise to convey messages. Sometimes several letters were written on one sheet and mailed on one postage instead of separately. Letters were concealed in merchandise, and travelers unknown to the senders of letters were prevailed upon to carry the missives along the journey as part of their luggage. After the Revolution, the constantly lowered postal rates gradually made such subterfuges uneconomical. It cost less to use the mail service than to evade it.

THE ESTABLISHING OF AN AMERICAN POST OFFICE

IMMEDIATELY preceding the outbreak of the Revolution, "mail bootlegging" became almost officially sanctioned. The colonial post office, of course, was in the hands of the British authorities. Postmasters who were loyal to the Crown did not scruple to open letters from suspected colonists. It was only a question of time before the Americans established a postal system of their own. In 1773, William Goddard, the publisher of the *Maryland Journal* at Baltimore, advocated a "Constitutional Post Office." He visited each of the northern colonies in 1774 and won almost unanimous support for the idea. After the firing of the shot "heard around the world," the various colonies quickly adopted "Constitutional Posts" of their own, which, being interconnected, formed a rival rebel system opposed to the official British colonial post office. After 1775, the latter, except for territories temporarily in the hands of the British garrisons, languished for lack of patronage and finally died. Meanwhile, the Continental Congress in 1775 gave the outlaw post office a semblance of legality by legislating for a postal system within New England. Later in the year, the Continental Congress called upon the experienced Benjamin Franklin to head a committee for the installation of a colonial postal service. In July, 1775, Franklin was elected Postmaster-General by Congress. Upon leaving for France, Franklin made way for his daughter's husband, Richard Bache, who served until 1782.

> **BALTIMORE, JULY 2.**
> The Printer of this Paper, with great Pleafure, acquaints the Public, that his Propofal for eftablifhing an AMERICAN POST-OFFICE, on conftitutional Principles, hath been warmly and generoufly patronized by the Friends of Freedom in all the great commercial Towns in the Eaftern Colonies, where ample Funds are already fecured, Poft-Mafters and Riders engaged, and, indeed, every necefary Arrangement made for the Reception of the Southern Mails, which, it is expected, will foon be extended thither—As therefore the final fuccefs of the Undertaking now depends on the Public-fpirit of the Inhabitants of Maryland and Virginia, it is not doubted, from the recent Evidence they have given of their noble Zeal in the Caufe of Liberty and their Country, but they will cheerfully join in refcuing the Channel of *public* and *private* Intelligence from the horrid Fangs of *Minifterial Dependants*; a Meafure indifpenfably necefary in the prefent alarming Crifis of American Affairs.

514   Proposal for a "Conftitutional Poft Office," in the *Maryland Journal*, July 2, 1774, courtesy of the Maryland Historical Society, Baltimore

515 From the painting *A Colonial Postman.* by Stanley M.
Arthurs, in possession of the artist

DIFFICULTIES OF THE AMERICAN POST OFFICE

DURING the Revolution, the post office had a struggle to survive. It had to shift its routes constantly not only to follow the American army but to keep out of the clutches of the British. Its principal task was maintaining constant speedy communication between Congress and the army in the field during hostilities. Members of Congress, army officers and even privates had their mail carried free. At first the public were charged the same rates that the British had established in 1765; but as the war dragged on the rates became chaotic because of the violent depreciation in Continental currency. In 1779, the rates were twenty times those of 1775. It was difficult, too, to secure postmasters and riders and to pay them after they were obtained. Changes in personnel were frequent, with a consequent loss in experience and efficiency. At the close of the war, the days of trouble for the post office were not over. The post office to be efficient had to be a Federal institution, and all Federal matters were in a deplorable condition up to the time of the adoption of the Constitution. It is easy to see, therefore, why postal legislation and management were a series of makeshifts and compromises between states' rights and Federal power. But some kind of postal service was so essential that, despite the vicissitudes of war and Confederation, an interstate system was maintained and even extended in its scope.

COACHES AS CARRIERS OF MAIL

WAR and its aftermath were not the only problems of Bache, Hazard and Osgood, the early postmasters. In America, as in Europe, the stagecoach threatened the monopoly of the post office in the carriage of mail. Coaches were faster than post riders. They could carry a greater weight, they could offer protection from the elements and they were more secure, for the coach sometimes carried an armed guard and each passenger was a potential additional guard. Finally, the revenue from passenger fares allowed the transport of light freight, packages and mail as by-product activities. Coaches first seriously encroached upon the province of the post office in the road between Boston and Portsmouth, about 1770. As these vehicles became more popular on the highways southward they grew most numerous on the very route from which the post office

derived the greater part of its revenue. Not only the coachman and guard but the passengers carried letters. So the post office began to use coaches as carriers of the mail. This was done first on the Boston-Portsmouth road; but by 1786 coaches were used on nearly all parts of the trunk line postal route from Portsmouth, New Hampshire, to Savannah, Georgia, and from New York to Albany. This first step in speeding up the mail served later as a precedent for the employment of steamboats, railroads, motor cars and airplanes. Each age has had its own definition of speed and the means of attaining it. The public always has insisted on speed in postal service.

516   Early Mail Stagecoach, from Isaac Weld, *Travels in North America*, London, 1799

THE CODIFICATION OF POSTAL LAWS

THE year 1794 may be taken as the starting point for the modern American post office. After the adoption of the Constitution in 1789, which in Article 1, section 8, gave Congress the power to establish post offices and post roads, no fundamental law regarding postal service was enacted for five years. Instead, a series of temporary acts maintained the post office as it had been inherited. But in 1794 a thorough-going revision and codification of postal laws was made by Congress. This, with modifications from time to time, had provided the basis for the operation of the postal service down to the present day. Behind our post office there are certain fundamental ideas. The United States post office shall have a complete monopoly over the collection, carriage and distribution of the mail. The office shall be operated as a social service and not as a source of government revenue or a means of taxation. (The office shall render services subordinate to, or in connection with, the carriage of mail that will fulfil the ideal of social service. The definition of mailable matter shall be extended or limited according to expressed popular demand and approval.) The office shall use the fastest means available for the transportation of mail, bearing in mind the factors of safety and security.

517 Samuel Osgood, 'First Postmaster-General, from the portrait by John Trumbull, courtesy of W. B. Osgood Field, New York

MAIL ROBBERIES

THE menace of "mail bootlegging" became insignificant soon after the United States post office was established by the Act of 1794. The increase in the number of offices — from seventy-five in 1790 to over fifty-thousand in 1927 — has tended to reduce evasion of postage by decreasing the convenience of it. More important still has been the decrease in the price for postal service. The more direct forms of robbing the post office, however, have always been a problem. Mail robberies have been both "inside jobs" and "outside"; that is, mail employees have been guilty of stealing within the organization, while bandits and desperadoes have "held up" post riders, mail stages and mail trains and have entered and sacked post offices. Up to date (1927) no one has robbed a mail airplane. Thefts within the post-office organization are extremely rare in proportion to the number of people handling mail matter. When pilfering does occur, the post office — like certain other famous organizations — always "gets its man." A highly efficient corps of mail inspectors keep "inside jobs" down to a negligible minimum. "Outside jobs" are harder to prevent, as is testified by the long list of famous mail robbers from Jesse James to Gerald Chapman. The original penalty in America for robbing the mail was death, but this was soon modified to flogging, and later to fines and imprisonment. When mail robberies in 1925–26 became more frequent and bold than usual, and with singularly large losses, United States Marines were placed on guard over post-office property and on postal cars. These marines had orders to shoot to kill. This indicates that the post office will go to great lengths to safeguard the valuables entrusted to it.

518 Attack on a Mail Coach, from a drawing by Frederic Remington, courtesy of the American Express Co., New York

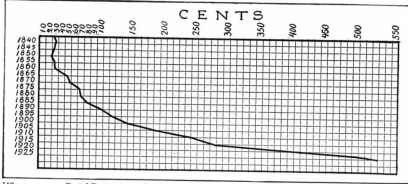

519   Postal Revenues per Capita, prepared expressly for *The Pageant of America* from data in *General Report of the Postmaster-General*, 1925

REVENUES OF THE POST OFFICE

It has not always been the theory that the post office exists to perform a social service. The Royal Mail in Britain was inaugurated partly at least as a system of espionage upon seditious or rebellious subjects. Later, both in Britain and America the mail service was a domestic commercial monopoly. This theory was succeeded by the idea that the mail service was an excellent source of governmental revenue. In America this was the prevailing theory until the Revolution; and even later the post office continued to pay into the Treasury any surplus it had. The amounts fell off rapidly until in 1828 only twenty-eight dollars was added to the funds of the government. By that time the new theory that the post office was not a means of revenue but an organization for public service was gaining recognition. Since 1799, money has been appropriated from the Treasury to support the postal service. The post office itself in the administration of Andrew Jackson was removed from the authority of the Treasury Department; and the Postmaster-General was then made a member of the President's cabinet. Political intrigue had a part in this shift, and the first Postmaster-General was subjected to virulent political attack, some of which may have been deserved, yet the change proved salutary. Since then except in time of war no American has looked upon the post office as a source of revenue. During both the Civil War and the World War postal rates were raised. In 1865, the surplus was $900,000 and in 1919 it was $73,000,000, the largest ever recorded. Since 1837, however, there has been a postal surplus only fifteen times, seven of which were between 1911 and 1919, under Postmaster Burleson. Despite the generally low rates, the postal revenue per capita advanced from twenty-six cents in 1837 to five dollars and thirty cents in 1925.

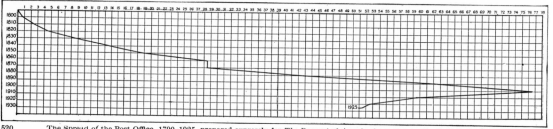

520   The Spread of the Post Office, 1790–1925, prepared expressly for *The Pageant of America* from data in the *Statistical Abstract of the United States*

THE NUMBER OF POST OFFICES

In accord with the theory that the post office is to render the greatest possible public service, regardless of revenue, it has been the practice of every Postmaster-General to extend the facilities of the service to the greatest possible number of people. At the beginning of the nineteenth century, this took the form of adding to the declared post roads and multiplying the number of local offices. Between 1790 and 1795, the number of offices increased sixfold; in each of the five-year periods following they almost doubled in number and then for a long time grew at the rate of forty to fifty per cent every five years. In 1790, in other words, there was one post office for every forty thousand people, while by 1837 there was one for about every fifteen hundred persons. In 1890 there were sixty-two thousand post offices for sixty-two million people, or one for every thousand of the population. The maximum number of offices, seventy-six thousand six hundred and eighty-eight was reached in 1900. To-day there are only a few more than fifty thousand because other means have been found of extending postal facilities than the spread of small offices. These are the city and village carrier services and the rural free delivery system. Probably all the people in the territories of the United States who are not in direct contact with some kind of postal service could be housed in one modern office building. Despite expanded facilities about fifty offices bring in nearly one half of the total postal revenue.

INSTALLATION OF THE FREE DELIVERY SYSTEM

As early as 1825, the Postmasters-General saw that the mere extension of the number of local post offices was not rendering the fullest service to the people as long as every one was forced to go or send to the post office to get or deliver mail. Consequently, in that year a carrier system was installed, a fee of two cents extra per letter being charged. In July, 1863, a free delivery and collection system was initiated, employing about four hundred and fifty carriers for some forty-nine cities of twenty thousand or more population. At first the growth of the city free delivery was based upon population; but in 1887 the population yardstick was abandoned in favor of gross revenue per office. In this way smaller communities possessing an industry or a school that yielded a large postal business might acquire a delivery and collection service. More than five hundred villages now share the delivery service once allowed only to large cities. The free delivery system was later improved by adding to the number of deliveries per day. Naturally, the volume of business determines the frequency of delivery; the commercial and trading districts of a city have the greatest number of calls per day. The largest number of deliveries in Philadelphia is seven per day; in New York it is six; in Chicago five. Many small places have only one delivery per day. The free delivery service brought the pillar-post boxes. Eventually, drop-boxes for papers and packages were also installed. Akin to these conveniences are the contract postal stations in drug stores, department stores, apartment houses and business buildings. There are more than five thousand stations of this kind, and, in addition, a thousand or more branch post offices and classified substations.

521   A Mail Carrier, from *Harper's New Monthly Magazine*, Oct. 1871

522   A Mail Carrier delivering parcel post, courtesy of the Post Office Department, Washington

523   Delivery of mail, courtesy of the Post Office Department, Washington

524   Rural carriers, French Creek, Mich., courtesy of the Post Office Department, Washington

THE RURAL FREE DELIVERY SYSTEM

As long as the post office continued to confine its offices to communities and its delivery service to villages it failed to reach the millions of people who lived on distant farms and in other isolated places. A few test

525   Rural Free Delivery, Madison, Minn., courtesy of the Post Office Department, Washington

rural routes, established in the early 'nineties, proved so successful that in 1897 the "Rural Free Delivery" service was officially inaugurated. During the first year there were only eighty-two routes; but by 1910 there were forty-one thousand in regular operation. Since then the increase has not been so rapid. Some six million families, or more than thirty million people, are now served daily by forty-four thousand rural mail carriers. The system has helped to render farm life attractive. This great public service more than justifies the excessive cost of the rural free delivery. Somewhat analogous to the rural free delivery are the "Star Routes," originally contract-carriers transporting the mail from isolated post offices to steamboat landings, railroad stations or other post offices. More recently, star route carriers have been permitted to perform the ordinary duties of rural free delivery carriers. Wherever it is possible, the star routes are converted into rural free delivery routes. The star routes are always located in sparsely settled regions difficult of access. There are more than ten thousand such routes, aggregating one hundred and fifty-nine thousand miles. In 1924, there were fifteen government operated star routes with a total mileage of seven hundred and seventy-six, and almost every one of these could provide ample material for a "thriller."

526   Rural Free Delivery Star Route from Crescent City, Cal., to Brookings, Ore., courtesy of the Post Office Department, Washington

THE POSTAL MONEY-ORDER SYSTEM

THE postal money-order service is another indication of the post-office policy. When the postal system started, people sent money through the mails. The loss was large because coins cut through the envelopes and dropped into the letter bags. Besides, this method of sending money placed an unfair temptation before the postal clerks. Almost any experienced clerk could detect the presence of coins in an envelope, and even paper money by its feel and odor revealed itself easily to clerks handling letters daily. Consequently, in order to prevent loss of currency, and to help soldiers in the field, the United States Post Office in 1864 installed a domestic money-order system in one hundred and forty-one post offices. To-day (1927) there are more than fifty thousand in the United States. At first the maximum amount on one order was thirty dollars. In 1866 this was raised to fifty dollars and in 1883 to one hundred dollars. Despite fluctuations in international exchange, the United States in 1869 made an agreement with Switzerland in regard to international money orders. Since then we have had agreements with fifty countries for the exchange of money orders. Although the amount of money orders increased from one million three hundred and sixty thousand one hundred

527 Post Office Department Money Order Application, courtesy of the Post Office Department, Washington

and twenty-two in 1865 to one billion five hundred million dollars in 1924, the rate of growth has slackened in recent years. This decrease is due probably to the greater use of checks and to the decline in immigration. The policy of the post office has been not to operate the money-order department for profit but to charge just enough to make the system self-sustaining. Consequently, the rates have been changed with great frequency.

POSTAL SAVINGS BANKS

IT took fifty years of agitation and argument to convince Congress that a postal savings bank was practicable and desirable for the United States. It was feared that this would infringe upon the domain of the banks, particularly the savings banks, and that it might injure building and loan associations. The arguments on the other side were that such a bank would encourage thrift, especially among the poor who save in tiny amounts, and that many people, particularly immigrants, who had no faith at all in the ordinary banks, would trust the government. In 1910, therefore, Congress authorized the system and it was established by the post office on January 3, 1911.

528   Immigrants at a postal savings window. © Keystone View Co., Inc.

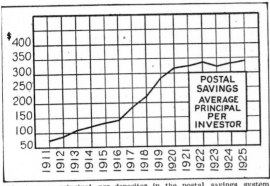

529 Average principal per depositor in the postal savings system, 1911–25, prepared expressly for *The Pageant of America*, from statistics in *The Report of the Postmaster-General*, 1925

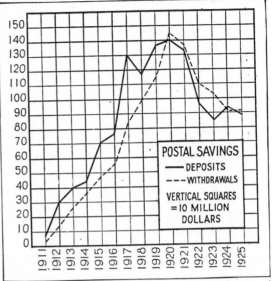

530 Postal savings deposits and withdrawals, 1911–25, prepared expressly for *The Pageant of America*, from statistics in *The Report of the Postmaster-General*, 1925

SMALL DEPOSITORS

Deposits have been accepted from one dollar to two thousand five hundred dollars (the upper limit has varied). To encourage saving the first dollar, cards with spaces for saving stamps are sold for ten cents each. The card with nine stamps, each for ten cents, is accepted as the original dollar deposit. Accounts started in one office can be transferred without loss of interest to any other office. When a person's deposits reach the maximum the deposit may be withdrawn to purchase postal bonds, and a new account may be started in the post office. The bonds pay two and one half per cent interest. Nearly half a million people per year have patronized the Postal Savings Bank. The average deposit has been slightly more than three hundred dollars. Investigations (1915) have disclosed that fifty-eight per cent of the depositors are foreign born and that this group have seventy-one per cent of the total deposits. Substantially three fourths of all deposits are hoarded savings that would never reach the ordinary investment institutions. To permit the sending of small articles of value through the mails, and to afford protection to the mail matter of the United States Treasury, a system of registered mail was instituted in 1854. Registered mail is safeguarded by a double receipt and carried in special locked strong boxes. Of course it has always been a temptation to mail robbers; but out of the ninety million registered packages that are handled in a single year the losses from theft are infinitesimal.

THE PARCEL POST

A Parcel Post System was added in 1912 to the public services of the Post Office Department. It was opened on January 1, 1913. The railway express companies had battled for years against this governmental invasion of their domain. Their opposition had been backed by timid retailers and conservatives who loathed

any plan for establishing the Government in business. In the very first year of parcel post operation, eight hundred million packages were sent through the mails despite the fact that a special stamp had to be purchased and the limits of size and weight were relatively low. Soon, however, the special stamp was abandoned, and the rates were lowered and the weight and size limits raised, and the service was opened to new commodities such as books. One immediate effect of the system was to increase postal revenue to the extent that the usual annual deficit was turned into a surplus. Lowering of rates eliminated the surplus.

531 Handling Parcel Post in a Station, from a photograph, courtesy of the Post Office Department, Washington

532   Christmas rush 'at the Washington post office, courtesy of the Post Office Department, Washington

INCREASED REVENUE FROM PARCEL POST

A SYSTEM of insurance was presently established for parcel-post merchandise, the fees being nominal; and the system was extended to permit the carriage of C.O.D. packages. The government then began to negotiate with foreign countries for the exchange of parcel-post matter. By 1920 the system had embraced all the principal countries and most of the mail-receiving communities of the world. The immediate effect of the parcel post was to increase the revenues of the Post Office Department. For the fiscal year 1913, the post office showed a surplus — not all of it derived from the parcel post — of four million dollars. This was the first time since 1883 (except for a small surplus in 1911) that any surplus at all had been recorded. Moreover, this surplus continued, reaching nine million dollars by 1917 before the war rates were applied.

533   Christmas rush at the Boston post office, courtesy of the Post Office Department, Washington

534 The Catching Post, from an engraving in
Harper's Weekly, Oct. 9, 1875

535 Catching Mail at Way Stations, from an engraving in
Harper's Weekly, Oct. 9, 1875

THE TRANSPORTATION OF MAIL

It has been the consistent policy of the American post office to use the fastest means available for the transportation of mail. From the post rider of the colonial era the carriage of mail has passed through the phases of the stagecoach and the steamboat to that of the railroad. Ever alert to new methods of transportation, the post office, as early as 1834, began to make contracts for the carriage of mails by railways. At the time objection was raised on the grounds that stagecoaches were always safer and generally quicker than railways. Indeed some rail contracts were so poorly performed that the post office returned to the use of coaches. Soon, however, the railway demonstrated its superiority and all other means of mail transportation became relatively insignificant. By 1920, about ninety per cent of all mail was carried by railroads.

536

537

Assorting the Mail, Railway Postal Service, from engravings in *Harper's Weekly*, Oct. 9, 1875

538 Railway Post-Office Car, latest type, courtesy of the Post Office Department, Washington

RAILWAY MAIL

WITH the coming of the railroad into the mail service proposals were made for sorting mail on railways cars. After seven years, in 1847, the post office sent a man to England to investigate the system there. The report was adverse. In 1862, William A. Davis, assistant postmaster at St. Joseph, Missouri, gave the

539 Distributing mail in a car, courtesy of the Post Office Department

scheme a trial between Hannibal and St. Joseph. Although the test was a success, it was not until 1879 that the railway post office was officially sanctioned. Since then it has taken on prodigious proportions. In 1926, the railway mail clerks made more than seventeen billion distributions and redistributions of mail en route, and less then one piece in a hundred was incorrectly sorted. Recently the railway mail has been speeded by the establishment of terminal railway post offices like those at the Pennsylvania and Grand Central stations in New York and the new Union station in Chicago. These terminal offices separate letters from newspapers and merchandise and make preliminary distributions of letters, sorting them for railway junctions or even by cities. At junctions where mail formerly lay idle it is now sorted in a station post office before it is put on the next connecting train. At all the larger offices labor-saving devices are installed wherever they are practicable. Letter-sorting or "facing" machines, cancelling machines, and the like are both time savers and man savers. Although the post office is often criticized, sometimes justly, for its mistakes and delays it is doubtful if any other business in the country, equally large, has a smaller percentage of error and a higher standard of efficiency. They who unduly exalt private business and condemn the government in business are often ignorant of both. Not only efficiency but heroism is a quality shown by postal employees. Those on railway cars share the dangers incident to travel and the position of the mail car near the head of the train makes it especially vulnerable.

540 Mailing Division, Chicago Terminal, courtesy of the Post Office Department

541   Pneumatic tube terminals, Chicago General Post Office, courtesy
of the Post Office Department, Washington

542   Tubes and Lamson conveyors in Pennsylvania Railroad Terminal
Post Office, New York, courtesy of the Post Office Department

MAIL CARRIED BY TUBE

A GENERATION ago, before the motor car was known, the Post Office contracted with a company that operated pneumatic tube carriers to transport mail in Boston, New York, Philadelphia, Chicago and St. Louis. This was done to avoid the delay of carting mail through congested city streets. This tube service was long the subject of controversy. It was argued that the tubes were never improved and soon became antiquated and that the mail by this method was dispatched too infrequently to meet the demands of the cities where the tubes were used. Finally, it was argued that the tube owners charged the government an exorbitant rental. Postmaster Burleson (1913–21) was an especially vigorous opponent of this means of mail transportation, and largely by his efforts the tubes were abandoned by the Post Office on June 30, 1918. However, with the incoming of a different political party in 1921, the owners of the tubes again made their voices heard in Washington; and in 1923 a limited tube service was once more installed and is now (1927) in operation in Boston, New York and Philadelphia.

THE POST OFFICE ADOPTS MOTOR VEHICLES

IN 1914, the Post Office began to operate its own motor vehicles, beginning in Washington but extending the plan to twenty-seven other cities. The practical demonstration proved a saving of time and also of expense. The scheme was amplified; the surplus war motor trucks of the War Department were turned over in part to the Post Office; so that by 1920 in one hundred and sixty-three cities the Post Office was running its own automobiles. To-day (1927) the plan is followed in about five hundred cities. In addition to various types of motor vehicles, the Post Office owns and operates an extensive fleet of motor cycles. Again, to hasten the mail the Post Office installed a boat service in New York Harbor. The vessel meets incoming ocean mail carriers down the bay, receives the foreign mail, opens it, sorts it on the way up the harbor, and delivers it ready for forwarding over the proper railway or to the New York post office. Motor boats in various parts of the country are employed by the Post Office. To electric railways and motor bus lines, the Post Office bears the same relation that it does to the steam railroads. There is also an air-mail service between Seattle, Washington, and Victoria, British Columbia, in close connection with trans-Pacific mail steamers. Between New Orleans and Pilottown, Louisiana, another air-mail service hastens the mail to and from steamers plying to Cuba, Central America and South America.

543   United States Mail motor truck, courtesy of the Post Office Department,
Washington

544 Mail Plane in Flight, courtesy of the Post Office Department, Washington

THE AIR–MAIL SERVICE

THE latest effort of the post office to speed the mails is the air-mail service. In 1911, and again in 1914 and 1915, flights were made with mail, at no cost to the post office, as exhibitions of airplanes. As a result of these trials, the post office in 1918 received an appropriation of fifty thousand dollars to experiment with air mail. The war provided the most severe tests of air machines. The War Department in the spring of 1918 furnished the post office with machines and aviators to operate an air mail between Washington and New York, and soon after May 15, 1918, regular mail flights were established between Washington and New York, relaying at Philadelphia. More than seven hundred thousand letters were sent by air during the eight months of service in 1918. The air mail started over a section of the original post route in the United States; but the post office soon decided that the first air-mail trunk line ought to connect New York and San Francisco, not Maine and Florida. Consequently, in May, 1919, Chicago and Cleveland were connected by air mail; and, in July of the same year, Cleveland and New York. More than nine million letters were sent by air mail in this second year of the service. The following year Chicago was joined with Omaha on May 15, and Omaha was coupled with San Francisco on September 8. Meanwhile, a feeder line from Chicago to St. Louis had been opened on August 16, and another in September between Chicago and St. Paul. By this time the cities were offering landing fields, buildings and cash to the post office as inducements for an air-mail service. The number of letters carried rose in 1920 to twenty-one million. By that time it was plain that air mail was destined to play an important rôle in future postal service.

545 Unloading the First Mail Plane from the West, courtesy of the
Post Office Department, Washington

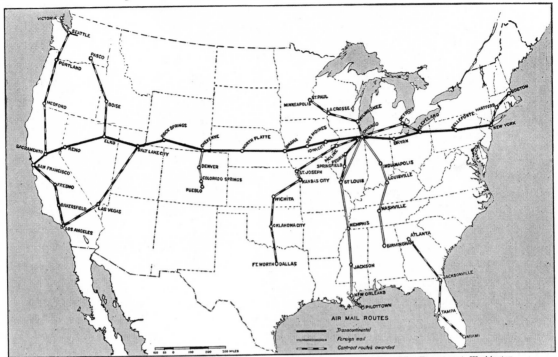

Map showing Air-Mail Routes, Transcontinental, Contract, and Foreign, courtesy of the Post Office Department, Washington

TRANSCONTINENTAL AIR–MAIL ROUTES

By 1921, the post office was definitely committed to a trunk transcontinental air-mail route and began to lop off the lesser routes. To test and advertise the trunk line, a flight from New York to San Francisco was made on Washington's Birthday. The time was thirty-three hours, twenty-one minutes. In 1926 the Eastern Division ended at Chicago (seven hundred and twenty-six miles); the Central Division at Cheyenne (nine hundred and two miles), the Mountain Division at Salt Lake City (four hundred and thirteen miles), and the Western Division at San Francisco (six hundred and twenty-four miles). The number and location of the regular landing fields and emergency fields have also been changed from time to time. Up to 1924, all the air mail was carried by daylight, but the post office had been endeavoring to institute night flying. There could be no real air mail if trains had to fill the night gaps in the service. To prepare for regular night flying the various landing fields were connected by telephone and radio for weather reporting. The fields themselves had to be lighted, and a line of ground lights twenty-five miles apart had to be established to mark the flying route. The planes, too, had to be equipped with lighted dials, two emergency flares, landing lights and flying lights. That is, flying requires navigation, and as a ship needs many types of aid in plying from port to port, so too an airplane cannot be self-sufficient.

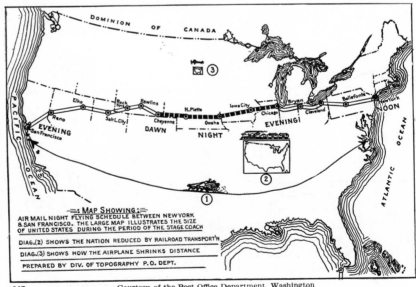

Courtesy of the Post Office Department, Washington

548   Parachute Flare, from a photograph (U. S. Army Air Service Photographic School), courtesy of the
Post Office Department, Washington

NIGHT–FLYING MAIL CARRIERS

NIGHT FLYING began in the Mountain Division on July 1, 1924, and has been continued regularly ever since that time. To fly is an achievement, to fly on a calm starlight night is a miracle, but to fly every night requires grit and nerve with a seasoning of luck. By the end of 1925, the lighted airway was two thousand and forty-one miles long, reaching from New York to Salt Lake City. The lights fall into two main groups; the routing beacons set twenty-five miles apart, and the landing-field equipment. Each night-flying plane has two parachute flares released at will by the pilot to help him locate a field in case of a forced landing. A new night-flying air-mail route was established on July 1, 1925, between New York and Chicago. The planes and pilots change at Cleveland. The income from this route in the first six months of service was about one million dollars. The greenest rookie among the air-mail pilots is paid two thousand dollars per year, plus a bonus of five, six, or seven cents for every air-mile flown, and promoted at the rate of one hundred dollars per year base salary for each five hundred miles in the air. Night-flying pilots receive a larger basic salary and a larger mileage rate for each mile flown. The average earnings for pilots during the fiscal year 1925 was six thousand seven hundred and sixty dollars, and no one begrudges them a cent of it. The cost of gasoline and oil is fifty thousand dollars more per year than the total paid to all pilots in wages. In 1925, the mileage flown was over two million miles. Air mail has passed the experimental stage.

549   Wind Indicator illumined at night, used on the
twenty-five emergency fields, Chicago to Cheyenne,
courtesy of the Post Office Department, Washington

IV—16

550   Highest Beacon Light in the World, 8600 feet above
sea level, five million candle-power light, courtesy of the
Post Office Department, Washington

551   Transferring the Mail from Plane to Truck, San Francisco, Cal., courtesy of the
                                Post Office Department, Washington

THE GROWTH OF THE
AIR–MAIL SERVICE

The post office has undertaken air-mail transportation as a demonstration school and experience laboratory. It intends eventually to withdraw from actual operation, and let contracts to private corporations, as it does with every other means of transportation. A beginning was made in 1925, when the Post Office advertised for contracts for air-mail routes to act as feeders to the trunk-line transcontinental route. This is the first step in a plan that will crisscross the nation with mail-carrying airways. The year 1925

552   Inauguration of Night Flying, July 1, 1924, Hazlehurst, N. J., courtesy of the
                                Post Office Department, Washington

probably marks the beginning of a new mail-transportation era, just as 1830 was the starting point for railway-mail service. The number of letters carried by air mail increased steadily from seven hundred thousand in 1918 to sixty million in 1924. The following year the number dropped to nine million because a new air-mail postage rate was established and only letters prepaid at the new high rate were carried by airplane. These rates were based on zones, of which there were three: New York to Chicago; Chicago to Cheyenne; and Cheyenne to San Francisco. The rate was eight cents an ounce for each zone. In 1927 the rate was changed to ten cents an ounce to any place in the United States.

553   Loading Mail Plane, Hazlehurst, N. J., courtesy of the Post Office
                                Department, Washington

THE DEAD LETTER OFFICE

THERE are many million pieces of mail that the Post Office Department cannot deliver because of defective or illegible address, insufficient or improper postage and other causes. To take care of this mail a Dead Letter Office was established in Washington in 1825. Branch offices were set up in 1917 in New York, Chicago, and San Francisco, and sub-branches at twelve division headquarters of the Railway Mail Service. Mail is not opened except as a last resort. Experts, in a surprising number of cases, are able to direct the mail to the proper person. More than three hundred thousand letters were so for-

554   One day's collection of dead letters, courtesy of the Post Office Department, Washington

warded in 1924. After letters are opened, it is often possible to send them either to the remitter or the addressee. Three million were thus treated in 1924. Of the remainder those that are plainly of no value are destroyed after opening, while the rest are filed. An astonishing number of dead letters contain valuable enclosures. Merchandise, money and other articles found loose anywhere in the mails are sent to the Dead Letter Office. A museum devoted to these articles is a fascinating exhibition. What cannot be reclaimed is held for a reasonable period and then sold. Revenue from the "dead mail" is about three hundred thousand dollars per year, which goes to the United States Treasury.

FREE MAIL

AN extremely large amount of mail is carried free by the Post Office. The greatest proportion of this is the official mail of the Washington executive departments, called "Penalty Mail" because a penalty is assessed against anyone who uses the free privilege for any personal purpose. A statement to this effect is printed on the envelope or cards in the place regularly assigned for stamps. In addition, Senators and Representatives have a large amount of correspondence, which is connected officially with their duties and which may be franked. Newspapers are transported free in the county where they are published. All other second-class matter is carried at rates less than cost. Finally, books for the blind are carried free by the Post Office, as are also the publications of agricultural colleges and experiment stations. Investigations made since 1921 indicate that some four hundred and fifty million pieces of mail are carried free. If this mail paid postage in its proper class it would yield a revenue of about thirteen million dollars. It was revealed that one of the greatest beneficiaries is the Post Office Department itself. In 1924 the World War Foreign Debt Commission enjoyed free mail to the extent of one dollar. On the other hand, the Post Office itself got five million dollars worth of its own missives transported free, the Treasury almost two million dollars worth, the Department of Agriculture about one and one half million dollars, and the War Department about one million dollars.

555   The Franking Abuse, free bags leaving the Washington Post Office, drawing by Theodore R. Davis in *Harper's Weekly*, Jan. 30, 1869

556   From a cartoon by Thomas Nast in *Harper's Weekly*, Jan. 8, 1870

557   From a cartoon *The Louisiana Lottery* in *Puck*, Sept. 3, 1879

PROTECTION OF THE MAILS

EVER since the notorious Louisiana Lottery, postal regulations have been framed to protect the American people from nefarious fraudulent schemes and to shield American homes from indecent literature. Without the privilege of using the mails, promoters or publishers of unclean matter cannot thrive. Yet this protection is afforded at the price of eternal vigilance on the part of the postmasters and postal inspectors. Upward of two thousand fraudulent schemes are suppressed every year. Not so much trouble is experienced now as formerly with indecent publications, but the picture postal cards are the source of innumerable prohibitions. Most of the cards refused are not immoral in themselves, but words, phrases, marks and the like are added by the senders that make the cards unacceptable. Censorship in the domain of morals is exceedingly difficult, for much depends on point of view or definition. Evil, like beauty, is often in the eye of the beholder.

TRANSATLANTIC MAIL

MAIL between foreign places and the United States began to assume bulky proportions with the advent of packet sailing ships, but it became of real importance only after steamship lines were established. Until after the World War, most of the money appropriated for carrying American mail overseas went to foreigners. After the World War our ocean mail contracts favored American ships, but in only two years have the payments to Americans exceeded the rewards to aliens for this type of service. The movement of mail in American ships is unbalanced, for the

558   Sea Post Office, courtesy of the Post Office Department, Washington

outbound vessels carry much more than the inbound. This is due to the fact that foreigners favor their own merchant marine. They as well as ourselves can control the mail that originates in their own country, and so dictate the carriers of outbound mail. With mail originating abroad no nation is so dictatorial. The

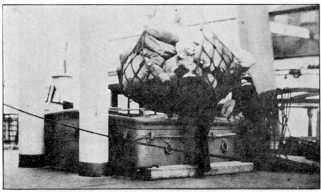

559   Unloading mail from a ship, courtesy of the Post Office Department, Washington

experience with railway post offices has been applied to ocean vessels, for many of them are now fitted with ocean post offices where postal business is transacted, and — what is still more important — where mail is sorted in transit, thus speeding delivery after the ship docks, so that foreign mail may be transferred to the next outgoing train. Indeed in many ports the mail is forwarded before the ship is wharfed into her pier, for harbor mail boats meet incoming vessels at the quarantine station and take off their mail.

CHAPTER XI

THE TELEGRAPH

THE telegraph stands with the invention of writing and printing as an epoch-making event in the history of human life. For eighteenth- and early nineteenth-century America the letter was a quite adequate supplement to the interchange of ideas by personal conversation. Life moved slowly and its paraphernalia were simple. As the century progressed, however, men, led by the scientific investigators, began to understand and to harness hitherto unused forces of nature. The power of steam and the possibilities of mechanics began to be exploited. The mysteries of electricity were studied.

The new forces that were being brought within human grasp required swift communication for their full exploitation and their adequate control. In the primitive days of railroading it was all very well for two trains, each quite unaware of the proximity of the other, to meet between stations and for one to back up to the nearest siding. But the time soon came when the speed of the locomotive and the amount of traffic made it impossible for the railroad to depend with safety upon mere visual signaling. The engineer who pulled his train out of a station must know that the track ahead was clear and he, in turn, must be directed by a dispatcher who knew at all times the location of the trains on a line perhaps a hundred or more miles in length. The telegraph made possible the almost instantaneous interchange of ideas between men separated by great distances. It made possible that modern marvel of technique and organization, the railroad system.

In the swift transport of "news" and information also, the telegraph has been basic to the development of the modern industrial and commercial era. It made possible the twentieth-century newspaper which brings each day to its subscribers an account of important happenings the world over. That moment on the western front on November 11, 1918, when along the fighting lines from Switzerland to the sea the guns suddenly lapsed into silence, should be contrasted with the useless carnage of Pakenham's defeat before New Orleans days after the War of 1812 had ended. Twentieth-century folk, living in an age of mechanical marvels, have difficulty in realizing what a fundamental change in human life occurred when it became possible for men to transmit messages from continent to continent with almost the speed of light. Wipe out at a blow the telegraph and its correlatives, the telephone and the wireless, and twentieth-century civilization would cease to be.

The telegraph was peculiarly fitted to American needs. When Morse gave this valuable instrument to us we had become a country of "magnificent distances." Our population was sprinkled over a vast area, a condition not conducive to national unity and cohesion. We were threatened either with division into local federations of states or with the stagnation of incommunicable hamlets. By making all Americans neighbors the telegraph was a mighty influence in welding these neighbors into a nation.

PRIMITIVE "TELEGRAPHS"

KING AGAMEMNON, according to legend, was the first man to transmit intelligence by a line of beacon fires by which he apprised his wife Clytemnæstra of the conquest of Troy. Messages by means of beacons are also mentioned in the Bible. In later history they are one of the most common world-wide ways of flashing news forward. Our own Indians gave signs and signals by fire at night and by a clever manipulation of columns

560   Indian Smoke Signals, from T. P. Shaffner, *The Telegraph Manual*, New York, 1859

of smoke by day. Savages in other parts of the world depended upon the beat of drums, or the clash of cymbals timed according to a code to speed information to distant places.

Civilized men too have used these barbaric methods of communication, augmenting them by the notes of trumpets and the firing of guns.

561   Indian Signaling, from *Harper's Weekly*,
March 22, 1873

562   Naval Semaphore Signaling, from a photograph,
courtesy of the Navy Department, Washington

HUMAN SEMAPHORES

A STEP above primitive beacons or tom-toms was the savage — and civilized — scheme of posting sentinels within sight of one another on prominent points of land. By the direction in which these sentinels faced or by the position of their legs or arms, a definite meaning was signaled to other watchers. A naval "rookie" sending communications with semaphore flags is a direct descendant of the barbarian human semaphore posted on a conspicuous crag.

CONTINENTAL ARMY SIGNALS

AMERICANS, during their struggle for political independence, contrived many modes of signaling. The lanterns that were hung aloft in the Old South Church, "one if by land and two if by sea," are familiar to every American. Another well-known Revolutionary War method of rapid communication was a mast on which was a crossbeam terminating in a hook. A barrel, a flag and a basket were parts of the equipment. These in many combinations communicated to watchers a variety of important messages. This really was a semaphore-telegraph, but it lacked the nicety of detail and the multitude of combinations of the instrument that appeared in Europe about 1800.

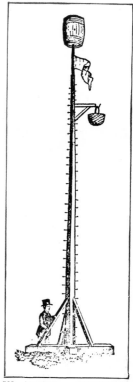

563 American Revolutionary Army Signal, from T. P. Shaffner, *The Telegraph Manual,* New York, 1859

CHAPPÉ SEMAPHORE-TELEGRAPH

A FEW years before the French Revolution, Claude Chappé, a schoolboy of d'Angers, contrived with a straight bar of wood, to which were attached two wing-pieces, a means of producing one hundred and ninety-two distinct signals. After perfecting the invention and message code,

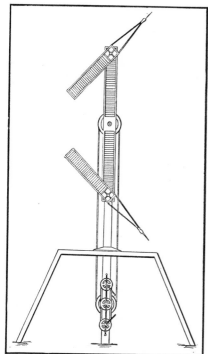

564 The Chappé Semaphore-Telegraph, from T. P. Shaffner, *The Telegraph Manual,* New York, 1859

he was granted a demonstration before a government commissioner. This officer reported favorably and Claude Chappé was appointed the first official French telegraphic engineer, with instructions to proceed with the installation of his system. The Chappé semaphore consisted of three pieces, one large piece called a regulator and two identical smaller pieces named indicators. The possible positions of the regulator were four: (1) vertical, (2) horizontal, (3) right oblique and (4) left oblique. Likewise each of the indicators was capable of seven similar positions in relation to the regulator to which they were attached. A diagram of these one hundred and ninety-two positions is shown in the cut at the foot of this page. The regulator with its two indicators was very large and was set on the highest eminence obtainable, often on a tower built for that purpose. The distances between stations varied. By experience Chappé telegraph operators found that in clear weather they could transmit about three signals per minute. This meant, for example, that a message could be sent from Toulon to Paris at the rate of about one signal every ten or twelve minutes. A chain of couriers would take at least four days. The mania for speed in communication and transportation which was so marked in the nineteenth century began in the preceding one; rapid dispatch of news was of incalculable benefit.

A=REGULATOR
B, C=INDICATOR

1. VERTICAL   2. RIGHT OBLIQUE   3. HORIZONTAL   4. LEFT OBLIQUE

565   Principle of the Chappé Telegraph, drawings prepared expressly by the author for *The Pageant of America*

566 Early English semaphore-telegraph station, from
T. P. Shaffner, *The Telegraph Manual*, New York,
1859

IMITATORS OF THE CHAPPÉ TELEGRAPH

It must not be understood that Chappé *invented* the original semaphore-telegraph. He is to be credited only with inventing the first *practical* telegraph system of this particular kind. Men in other nations modified the parts of the Chappé device or invented new methods of producing like results. Semaphore-telegraphs could not be operated in foggy weather, in heavy snowstorms or under any weather conditions that produced low visibility; and for a long time they could not be run at night. Furthermore, although they were the speediest method of their time, they were all extremely slow as compared with modern communication. In the Peninsular War, the Plymouth (England) station started a message to London reading: "Wellington defeated —" At this point fog stopped the transmission and London was in distress for twenty-four hours until the rest of the message came, reading: "— the French at Salamanca." Among the many modifications of the semaphore was one operated in England. This consisted of panels with movable slots. The relation of open or closed slots was arranged into a code which could be read at a distance. At night the position, or color of lights indicated open or closed slots and so could be used for transmitting messages. The sign language invented for the deaf or dumb is a variety of semaphore signaling, for it consists of different combinations of positions of fingers and fists each one standing for a letter.

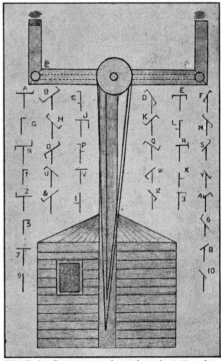

567 Early German semaphore-telegraph station, from
T. P. Shaffner, *The Telegraph Manual*, New York,
1859

568 Army heliograph signaling, from a photograph, courtesy of the
United States Signal Corps, War Department, Washington

THE HELIOGRAPH

Everyone knows that the flash of sunlight caught on any bright surface is visible at a great distance. By arranging flashes into codes, messages may be transmitted. The common heliograph is a mirror upon which codified flashes are produced by a shutter. On bright days this simple mechanism is singularly effective over surprising distances. It was long employed by armed forces, both in America and abroad.

MAGIC NEEDLES

IN the sixteenth century, and indeed until well into the eighteenth, there was a widespread faith in the tale of the "magic needles." It was said that if two pieces of steel cut from the same bar and rubbed with the same lodestone were mounted like compasses, both would turn in the same direction, whatever might be the distance between the two needles. Thus two friends could prepare two such needles and arrange letters around the circumference of their arc. It was believed that they could send messages to each other by simply turning the needle. The story of the magic needles seems to have started with Baptista Porta, who recounted it in his *Magiae Naturalis* in 1558. It was whispered about for centuries. Among those who were firmly

569 Primitive Magic Needle, from J. Leurechon, *Récréation Mathématique*, Paris, 1627

believed to possess one of these magic needles was Cardinal Richelieu. The myth of the magic needles did not die until scientists experimented in earnest with magnetism and electricity. Although the story of the "magic needles" only served to show to what lengths human credulity will go, perhaps it was not without some service for mankind. The striking similarity between the supposed action of "magic needles" and the later operation of electrical telegraphs suggests that the latter may have been prompted by the former. This is not advanced as a fact but as a possibility; as yet there is no evidence to indicate any connection between the myth and the needle telegraphs of the nineteenth century.

570 Otto von Guericke's Electrical Machine and Sulphur Globe, *ca.* 1663, from Otto von Guericke, *Experimenta Nova Magdeburgica Vacuo Spatio*, Amsterdam, 1672

EXPLORERS IN THE REALM OF ELECTRICITY

SCIENTISTS prepared the way for the electric telegraph. Among them was William Gilbert, physician to Queen Elizabeth, who first collected and published in 1600 the scattered data in reference to the form of energy he called Electricity. Otto Guericke in 1671 constructed the first frictional electricity machine, learned the property of electrical repulsion and noted the fact of electrical induction.

571 From the painting *Dr. Gilbert Explaining His Discoveries to Queen Elizabeth*, by Arthur A. Hunt

572   The Leyden Jar experiment, from Johann H. Winkler, *Von der Stätike der
          Electrischer Kraft des Wassers in Gläsernen Gefässen*, Leipsig, 1746

PIONEER SCIENTIFIC ELECTRICIANS

Von Kleist, dean of the Cathedral at Kammin in Pomerania, Musschenbrok, a professor at Leyden, and Cuneus, a burgess of Leyden, were all concerned in 1745 and 1746 in the discovery of the Leyden jar, which might be called the great-grandfather of the electric battery. The earliest experimenters in the transmission and velocity of electricity were Daniel Gralath, Joseph Franz and the Abbé Nollet. A number of other men including Benjamin Franklin were interested in electrical experiments. At first electricity was derived by friction and was volatile in quality and small in quantity. The researches of Luigi Galvani and Alexander Volta led to the furnishing and use of electrical energy that was tractable in quality and capable of quantitative production. Many workers, from Beraut in 1748 through Beccaria to Oersted, Ampère, Davy, Faraday, Henry and others, ferreted out the curious relationships of electromagnetism and magneto-electricity. All these men were scientific explorers. Generally scientists working in laboratories care little about the practical applications of their discoveries. As a rule the scientists are satisfied with learning facts; others reap where scientists sow.

THE ELECTRIC–NEEDLE TELEGRAPH

If Samuel Morse had never lived and if no one else had ever thought of the scheme he used for telegraphy, it is likely that the world would have used the electric-needle telegraph. All of the many electric-needle telegraphs depend on the fact that a magnetic needle placed within an electrical coil will be deflected to the right when a current passes through the coil in one direction, and to the left when the current is reversed. Among the first to suggest that this needle deflection could be used for telegraphy was Ampère in 1820. The most practical and one actually used for several years was the Gauss and Weber telegraph, as modified by Steinheil in 1836. Steinheil discovered that the ground is a conductor and can replace the return wire in an electric circuit. He is also credited with first organizing the system of poles and insulators for carrying telegraph wires in air.

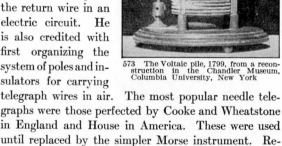

573   The Voltaic pile, 1799, from a reconstruction in the Chandler Museum, Columbia University, New York

The most popular needle telegraphs were those perfected by Cooke and Wheatstone in England and House in America. These were used until replaced by the simpler Morse instrument. Replacement was not unopposed, for both in America and England the needle telegraph had its active proponents who did not yield readily in the battle with the Morse instrument. This was particularly true in England.

574   The Gauss and Weber needle telegraph, from J. J. Fahie,
          History of Electric Telegraphy, to 1837, London, 1884

COOKE AND WHEATSTONE

ELECTRIC telegraphy was first brought from the status of
experimental theory to that of a commercial enterprise by
William Fothergell Cooke and Sir Charles Wheatstone.
Cooke was the practical inventor and Wheatstone the
scientific experimenter. In March, 1836, when Cooke was
studying anatomy at Heidelberg, he saw Professor Moncke
demonstrate an electrical telegraph. He abandoned all
other interests and devoted himself feverishly to the invention of an electrical telegraph capable of general public
use. Within three weeks he completed a device which in
its principle was the same as the needle telegraph that he
and Wheatstone afterward introduced into England. In
the latter part of 1836, Cooke tried to convince the directors
of the Liverpool & Manchester Railway that his telegraph
was what they needed in order to send signals through a
railway tunnel at Edge Hill. His attempt failed. After
this failure Cooke consulted Faraday and Roget and upon
the advice of the latter sought Wheatstone. Cooke and
Wheatstone found that they complemented each other in a
remarkable fashion. Wheatstone was reluctant to com-

575   Sir Charles Wheatstone, 1802–75, from an engraved portrait
from J. A. Fleming, *Fifty Years of Electricity*, London, 1921

mercialize his discoveries, but in May, 1837, he was persuaded by Cooke to enter a partnership of science and
business. Wheatstone was the thinker, Cooke the doer and their combination was prolific in results.

THE COOKE AND WHEATSTONE TELEGRAPH

TAKING Cooke's fundamental principle for a telegraph and adding to it all the improvements suggested and
tried both by Cooke and Wheatstone, the two men were ready for and succeeded in obtaining a patent for
their apparatus in June, 1837, the year of Morse's patent in America. Their mechanism comprised five

576   Cooke and Wheatstone's five-needle telegraph instrument, 1837,
from J. A. Fleming, *Fifty Years of Electricity*, London, 1921

electrometers mounted on one triangular bed, five
wires of primary and secondary circuits, and a
keyboard by which the sending operator directed
electrical currents over the wires so as to deflect
the proper needles in the desired way. The two
partners in 1838 and 1839 took out patents for
improvements. They also invented and introduced other forms of telegraphs; while still other
inventors produced double-needle and single-
needle instruments. Dial telegraphs and chemical
telegraphs too entered the field for popular favor.
Needle telegraphs in England, although not on the
continent, were reluctantly abandoned in favor of
the Morse telegraph. It is to be said for the needle
telegraph that it required an operator of little
skill. Against the needle telegraph were its
multiplicity of wires and parts and its purely
visual message which strained the eyes and made
two receivers necessary. The speed too was much
inferior to that of the Morse, rarely exceeding
twenty words per minute. The British railroads
which popularized the telegraph preferred the
needle machine, for many station masters could
use the needle instrument at places where traffic
did not warrant the employment of a skilled extra
man as a Morse telegrapher. In America telegraphers were hired for station masters.

577   Samuel Finley Breese Morse, 1791–1872, at the age of 24, from a self-portrait, after the reproduction in S. V. Henkels' *Catalogue*, Dec. 14, 1920

MORSE VISUALIZES THE TELEGRAPH

On October 6, 1832, the packet ship *Sully* sailed from Havre for New York. On board as passengers were William C. Rives of Virginia, American Minister to France, J. F. Fisher of Philadelphia, Dr. Charles T. Jackson of Boston and Samuel Finley Breese Morse, an American artist of considerable distinction. One night at the dinner table the conversation happened to turn on the subject of electromagnetism. Dr. Jackson described some of the recent discoveries of European scientists proving that electricity passed instantaneously through any known length of wire, and that its presence could be observed at any part of the line by breaking the circuit. Morse exclaimed, "If the presence of electricity can be made visible in any part of the circuit I see no reason why intelligence may not be transmitted instantaneously by electricity." Morse himself became obsessed with his own idea and throughout the remainder of the voyage thought about it constantly. Before the voyage was finished he was able to put into his sketchbook drawings of the apparatus by which he proposed to make electricity mankind's messenger. The basic plan for the Morse telegraph was thus conceived in mid-ocean as the result of a chance dinner-table conversation.

MORSE'S YEARS OF DOUBT

In 1832, when Morse first envisaged his telegraph, he was forty-one years old, a widower with three children to support and only his artist's brush by which to gain a living. Through all the years when he was struggling to perfect his invention he was engaged in a desperate fight to keep the wolf from his door. Years before, while a student at Yale, Morse had been interested in Professor Silliman's electrical experiments. He had the benefit of the counsel of Professor Leonard Gale and Professor Joseph Henry, the latter probably the greatest scientist in the domain of electricity in his day. After the summer of 1837, Morse had the benefit also of a young assistant, Alfred Vail. Morse's first crude instrument was made ready late in the year of 1835 or early in 1836. Its frame was an old wooden canvas stretcher such as artists use, its wheels were taken from an old wooden clock and the rest of the apparatus was equally uncouth. With it, however, Morse was able to mark down telegraphic signs and make distinguishable telegraphic sounds. In 1837, worried lest the scientists and inventors of Europe should lead him in the race for a successful instrument, he filed a petition for a patent. On January 24, 1838, Morse and his partner Vail were ready for a public demonstration. From 1838 until 1843 indifference and hostility were his only rewards. During those lean years Morse drank the bitter dregs of poverty. His precious experimenting had to be laid aside from time to time so he could earn money by his brush and by commercial photography (daguerreotypes). His daily bread and supplies for further work on the telegraph were earned by tedious labor.

578   First Electromagnetic Recording Telegraph Instrument, made and used by Morse, 1837, courtesy of the Department of American History, United States National Museum, Washington

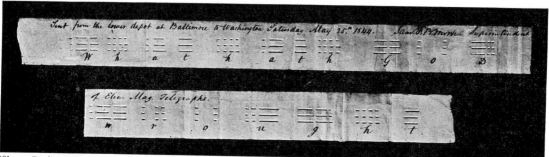

THE FIRST MORSE LINE AUTHORIZED BY CONGRESS

THE five years of effort were a blessing in disguise to Morse, for they enabled him to make many minor and a few major improvements in his invention. In 1842, Morse was able at last to get a bill presented in Congress appropriating thirty thousand dollars for an experimental telegraphic line. Then began weeks and months of agony as he watched the fate of his bill. Finally, after an uproarious debate in which several Representatives gave full play to their ideas of humor, Morse's bill passed the House. Then began another period of torment for Morse while the bill was in the Senate. The very last day of the session, March 3, rolled around with a great press of unfinished business before the Senate. All through the hours of daylight Morse sat there, and then far into the night, until at last he retired to his hotel, a temporarily crushed man. Next morning the daughter of his old friend and classmate, the Honorable H. L. Ellsworth, Commissioner of Patents, came to tell him that the bill had passed. He promised Miss Ellsworth that the first dispatch should be hers.

579 The "Old Factory" at Morristown, N. J., where Morse and Vail constructed the apparatus for exhibition before Congress, from the *Century Magazine*, April 1888

580 Original Instrument used on Baltimore-Washington line, from the original in possession of the College of Engineering, Cornell University, Ithaca, N. Y.

BUILDING THE FIRST AMERICAN TELEGRAPH LINE

As soon as the "telegraph bill" of 1843 was law, Morse decided to establish the experimental line between Washington and Baltimore and selected as assistants Professor Gale and Alfred Vail. To these was added Professor James C. Fisher, who was later replaced by a young engineer, Ezra Cornell. As building progressed, wires were strung on poles. When they reached the junction of the Annapolis, Washington and Baltimore roads, a distance of twenty-two miles, an unofficial service began. Messengers from the Whig convention then sitting in Baltimore hurried to the terminus of the telegraph line which kept Washington informed of the convention's progress. At last the line was completed. On May 24, Vail sat at the key in Baltimore and Morse in Washington. Anne Ellsworth had the honor of sending the first official message, "What hath God wrought." Morse calmly clicked off these singularly appropriate words. Vail received the message in Baltimore without an error, and flashed it back to Morse. The electric telegraph was an accomplished fact.

581 Duplicate of the First Telegraph Message sent from Baltimore to Washington, May 24, 1844, repeated by Vail to Morse May 25, facsimile from original bearing Morse's signature, in the United States National Museum, Washington

582   Type of Finger Key first used in transmitting the Morse alphabet, 1843–44, believed to be one of the original instruments, from a photograph, courtesy of the Department of American History, United States National Museum, Washington

583   Morse Telegraph Key, first used about 1845, from a photograph, courtesy of the Department of American History, United States National Museum, Washington

THE MORSE TELEGRAPH

MORSE first tried to work out a code that could be interpreted through an electromagnetic machine. He hit upon the *dot* and *dash* and later the *space*, all of which could be expressed by the length of time the circuit was closed or open. Next he planned to give every word in the dictionary a number, and then assign a dot-dash-space equivalent to each numeral from 0 to 9. Morse carried this intention far enough to start the compilation of a telegraphic dictionary. A system so complicated had little practical application. The success that finally rewarded Morse was largely due to what he threw away. The telegraphic dictionary was first abandoned in favor of a dot-dash-space signification for each letter in the alphabet and each of the numerals. By consulting a printing office, Morse learned which letters were used most and to them he gave the simplest dot-dash equivalent. Thus *A* was ·—, *E* became ·, *N* was —·, *O* was ··, and so on. These could be produced by merely pressing a key to close, hold or keep open the circuit. The elaborate recording mechanism was cast aside in the 'fifties when it was demonstrated that the operators could read the message by the sound of the electromagnet. Eventually, then, the Morse machine consisted of a sending key, a transmitting wire and a receiving electromagnet. To this was added a simple device for intensifying the action: hence the sound of the receiver, and line mechanisms for amplifying or "boosting" the current.

SAMUEL FINLEY BREESE MORSE, 1791–1872

AFTER the success of the telegraph was assured by the trial of 1843, Morse abandoned painting and spent the rest of his life — he lived to be eighty-one years of age — in perfecting, expanding and defending his invention. In 1872, shortly after receiving a tremendous ovation in New York, he passed away peacefully at his home. His life is divided into two almost exactly equal parts, the first spent as a painter, the second as an inventor and promoter. His achievements include a score of first-rate portraits, his telegraph, the dot-dash-space alphabet, a French railway telegraph, the laying of the first submarine cable (New York Bay, 1842) and the discovery (with Dr. Fisher) of the principle of duplex telegraphy. He is credited also with being the first experimenter with wireless telegraphy and the first to experiment in America with Daguerreotype. Just as the Morse telegraph dislodged all competitors in America, so too it displaced its rivals in Europe. Long before he died Morse could claim that the whole world had adopted his invention to the exclusion of all others. To this day no one has succeeded in bringing forth a superior instrument. In 1858, ten European governments came together in a representative convention to decide on some kind of suitable reward for Morse. They agreed to pay him four hundred thousand francs payable in four yearly installments. In addition, nine European governments or monarchs granted various kinds of decorations or honors to Morse. Great Britain, Switzerland and Saxony, although they all eventually used the Morse instrument exclusively, never in any official manner indicated any indebtedness to him or appreciation of his genius. But decorations and honors meant little; the universal adoption of the Morse instrument is his best testimonial.

584   From a photograph by Sarony, New York

585   Early Telegraph Office, from T. P. Shaffner, *The Telegraph Manual*, New York, 1859

THE EXTENSION OF THE TELEGRAPH

IN 1843, Morse sought to sell his patent to the government. The price he asked, one hundred thousand dollars, seems ridiculously small in retrospect but it was balked at in 1844; so Morse and his associates began to lease the right to the use of his instruments to private companies. Then began a wild scramble. Scores of little companies sprang up everywhere in America. Offices were opened for the public, clerks and bookkeepers trained, and special courses begun for the new operators. The success of Morse's invention called forth several other forms of telegraph. Companies backed these inventions and entered the fray against the lines using the Morse patents. The most pretentious of these competitors was Royal E.

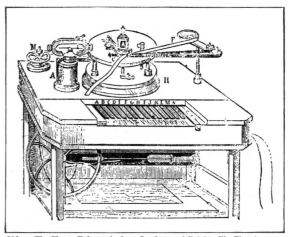

586   The House Telegraph, from Lardner and Bright, *The Electric Telegraph Popularized*, London, 1859

House, who obtained a patent for a telegraph in 1848, dated from 1846. In 1849, a House line was built between Philadelphia and New York and soon many lines were competing with the Morse system in various parts of the United States. There was a relatively short although excessively bitter contest. The last House line to operate was one from Boston to Montreal. The multitude of little licensed companies using the Morse system discovered that short local lines did not pay. Slowly but surely a monopoly was established in the telegraph industry. Men learned that competition is not invariably the life of trade; there are businesses, of which telegraphic communication is one, which are natural monopolies.

587   Early School of Telegraph Operators, from T. P. Shaffner, *The Telegraph Manual*, New York, 1859

588 From a photograph, *ca.* 1860, by Brady, in the United States Signal Corps, War Department, Washington

AMOS KENDALL, 1789–1869

BORN in Dunstable, Massachusetts, August 16, 1789, Amos Kendall worked on his father's acres until he was sixteen years of age. He entered Dartmouth in 1807, graduating in 1811 at the head of his class. Young Kendall in 1814 decided to go West. In Lexington, Kentucky, he was for more than a year tutor to the children of Henry Clay. He then moved to Georgetown, Kentucky, was appointed postmaster there, and later drifted into newspaper work at Frankfort, Kentucky. This carried him into the vigorous life of the day and place. General Jackson, on becoming President, appointed Kendall Fourth Auditor of the Treasury Department, an office he held for five years (1829–34). He was then placed in charge of the Post Office by Jackson; and when that position was made a Cabinet office, Kendall was the first Postmaster-General. Sometime after 1840, Kendall met S. F. B. Morse. The two men impressed each other favorably; and Morse, Gale and Vail placed their telegraph affairs in Kendall's hands. For the rest of his life Kendall was engaged in the telegraph business. Morse's suits, contracts and interests in mergers were all attended to by Kendall. In the process, Morse, Gale and Vail profited and Kendall himself built up a substantial fortune.

589 Making a Cable, from T. P. Shaffner, *The Telegraph Manual,* New York, 1851

590 Submerging the cable in a river crossing, from T. P. Shaffner, *The Telegraph Manual,* New York, 1851

TELEGRAPHY UNDER WATER

THE question soon arose: "How are we to get the wires across rivers?" The immediate answer was to erect poles of great height on each bank and droop the wires over the waterway. But these poles were wrecked by gales. Moreover, poles of sufficient height were difficult to procure and costly to set in place. The engineers consequently were forced to experiment with methods of running wires under water along the beds of rivers. Morse himself had foreseen this difficulty and had been the first man to make trials of immersing electric telegraph conductors. In 1842, an experiment in New York harbor failed because the cable was hauled up and cut by a passing vessel. In December of the same year, Morse again made the attempt at submarine telegraphy, this time passing his cable under the waters of a canal at Washington, D. C. The endeavor was entirely successful; but we know now that his cable, insulated as it was, could not have endured in practical everyday use. At the time when Morse in America and Cooke and Wheatstone in England were perfecting their telegraphs, a surgeon at Singapore, Dr. Montgomery, sent to England a strange substance — the juice (percha) taken from the isonandra gutta tree. This juice had the property of hardening in air but softening in boiling water and thus was easily manipulated into any desired shape. Electricians found it an almost perfect non-conductor and impervious to water. Moreover, the supply seemed unlimited. Its use led to the submarine telegraphic cable.

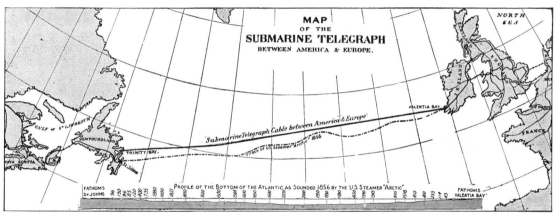

591   Map of the Submarine Telegraph between America and Europe, from Charles F. Briggs and Augustus Maverick, *The Story of the Telegraph and a History of the Great Atlantic Cable*, New York, 1858

THE FIRST OCEAN CABLES

On August 27, 1850, the cable laid between France and England was connected and messages were sent through it. But the action of the grinding waves soon wore it through. The following year a second cable was laid down between Dover and Calais. Communication was established through on October 17, 1851, and from that date has never been interrupted by reason of faulty cables. The success of the second Dover-Calais cable was followed by the laying of a dozen others joining various parts of Europe. It was the Canadian islands off the mouth of the St. Lawrence that first on this continent proposed to use ocean cables. The pioneer cable actually laid in American ocean waters ran from New Brunswick to Prince Edward Island twelve miles across the Straits of Northumberland. The full plan was much more ambitious. The engineer, Frederick N. Gisborne, had hoped to establish telegraphic communication between St. Johns, Newfoundland, and the American telegraph land lines terminating in Maine. From St. Johns he proposed to establish a line of steamers to Galway, Ireland. This plan would shorten by four or five days communication between Europe and New York. Financial reverses prevented him from carrying out his idea. Early in 1854 he proceeded to New York, from which journey came marvelous consequences.

THE FIRST TRANSATLANTIC CABLE COMPANY

The capitalist sought by Frederick N. Gisborne in New York was Matthew D. Field, who presented the idea to his brothers, Cyrus W. and David Dudley Field. Cyrus Field was fired by an inspiration. "Why not lay a cable across the Atlantic itself!" He wrote to Morse and to Lieutenant Matthew F. Maury of the United States Navy, who had just completed an extended investigation of depths of the Atlantic between Newfound-

592   From the painting *Projectors of the Atlantic Cable*, by Daniel Huntington (1816–1906) in the Chamber of Commerce of the State of New York, New York

land and Ireland. Both Morse and Maury replied favorably concerning the idea. Cyrus Field turned with enthusiasm to the project for an Atlantic cable. The first step was to buy in March, 1854, the property rights and charter of the Electric Telegraph Company, Gisborne's Canadian concern. At six o'clock, Monday morning, May 8, 1854, the New York, Newfoundland and London Telegraph Co., was organized at the home of David Dudley Field and Peter Cooper was chosen as president. For the next two years this company was busy completing its arrangements and equipment on the American end of the proposed communication system. The negotiations, the superintendence of the work, the correspondence and a goodly share of the financial expense fell upon the shoulders of Cyrus W. Field.

593   Cyrus W. Field, 1819–92, from a photograph
made during Field's visit to London, 1856

THE ATLANTIC TELEGRAPH COMPANY

In 1856, with the American terminus ready, Cyrus Field sailed to England. There he interested Brett, who had laid the Dover-Calais cable, Edward O. W. Whitehouse, a famous electrician, and Charles T. Bright, one of two brothers who were deeply interested in the British Magnetic Telegraph Company. On September 29, 1856, these three men, together with Cyrus Field, formed the Atlantic Telegraph Company. Application was made to the British Government for aid in ships and money both of which were almost immediately promised. The public applications for stock exceeded the capital by thirty thousand dollars, the capital being three hundred and fifty thousand dollars represented by three hundred and fifty shares of one thousand dollars each. Returning to the United States, Field applied to our own government for favors similar to those obtained from the British. Against violent opposition the aid was authorized. With the finances cared for, the company proceeded to the ordering of the cable. After careful deliberation the order was divided between three British companies, the contracts being signed on December 6, 1856. They completed their task on July 6, 1857.

LAYING THE FIRST (1857) ATLANTIC CABLE

The *Niagara*, the ship assigned by the United States, left New York on April 22 and arrived in the Thames, May 14. On June 5, she left for Portsmouth for fitting and for Birkenhead to take aboard the cable. The British battleship *Agamemnon* loaded at Greenwich. It took three weeks to stow the cables on the ships, which then proceeded to Queenstown, Ireland. As the two ships lay at Queenstown, the ends of the cable were joined and they tested perfectly through

594   The *Niagara* under full steam, from *Harper's Weekly*, May 2, 1857

two thousand five hundred miles of length. The test made, the cable was severed again and the ships departed for Valentia Bay, the chosen terminus in Ireland for the European end of the cable. There were nine ships all told in the cable-laying expedition, but the two named alone carried the precious freight. On

595   The laying of the cable in mid-ocean, from *Harper's Weekly*, May 2, 1857

August 5, 1857, the shore end of the cable was carried by small boats from the *Niagara* to the telegraph station. The next day the troubles began. Almost at the start difficulties in paying out the cable were encountered. For six days the *Niagara* slowly forged through the sea, the cable slipping over her stern into the ocean. On August 11, in a heavy swell, the paying-out machinery went wrong. The cable broke; three hundred and thirty-four miles of lost hopes lay on the bottom of the ocean.

596   The *Agamemnon* laying the 1858 Cable, lithograph after a painting by R. Dudley in W. H. Russell,
The Atlantic Telegraph, London, 1866

THE SECOND (1858) ATLANTIC CABLE

THE directors of the Atlantic Telegraph Company were in no wise despondent. By June 1, 1858, all was in readiness for the second contest with fate. It was decided to have the two ships assigned the previous year meet in midocean, splice the ends of the new cable, and then proceed: the *Agamemnon* toward Ireland, the *Niagara* toward Newfoundland. On June 26 the cable was spliced. Almost immediately it fouled and broke. A second splice was made and the ships steamed away from each other. But they had gone hardly forty miles when the cable broke again. A third splice was completed and once more the vessels started. On the afternoon of the next day the cable snapped a third time. Two hundred and ninety miles of cable were lost and the boats returned to harbor. With repairs, reinforcements and new appliances, the vessels were ordered to meet once more in the middle of the Atlantic on July 28, 1858. The next day the cable was once again spliced. On the seventh day the *Agamemnon* appeared in Dowlas Bay, Valentia, her task finished. At 1:45 A.M. of the eighth day, the *Niagara* anchored in Trinity Bay, Newfoundland. The big job was done!

597   Reels of gutta-percha-covered wire loaded into tanks at Greenwich, from W. H. Russell,
The Atlantic Telegraph, London, 1866

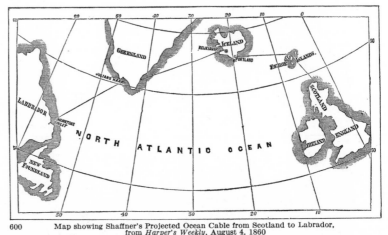

599 Celebration of the completion of the Atlantic Cable, Union Square, New York, from *Harper's Weekly*, Sept. 11, 1858

INTERNATIONAL CELEBRATION

BEFORE the two shore ends of the cables were laid, landed and fixed at the stations, dispatches were wired to the press over the land lines, announcing the success of the ocean portion of the job. Scores of messages of congratulation poured into the terminal offices. On August 16, the cable was officially opened for business. The first message came from the directors in England and read, "Europe and America are united by telegraphic communication. 'Glory to God in the highest, on earth peace, goodwill to men!'" Next a message of congratulation and felicitation came from the British Queen and was answered by the American President. But international jubilation over the success of the cable soon came to an end. The cable signals began to grow feeble; by September 3 they became unintelligible, and in October they ceased altogether. The world was apprised of this on September 7, and the heroes of a few weeks were reviled as arch-villains.

600 Map showing Shaffner's Projected Ocean Cable from Scotland to Labrador, from *Harper's Weekly*, August 4, 1860

TALIAFERRO P. SHAFFNER, 1818–81

TALIAFERRO P. SHAFFNER, a pioneer in electrical communication, after the telegraph became practicable was engaged in the task of building pole lines in the frontier areas of the Middle West. One problem he encountered was that of carrying his lines across streams. This led him to experiment with cables, a preparation for his later ocean cable projects.

OTHER CABLE PROJECTS, 1858-66

THE ultimate failure of the Atlantic cable of 1858 revived the old doubts about the limits of transmission of electricity. Based on the fears that no cable two thousand miles long would ever be able to carry electric impulses the whole distance with the regularity required for a commercial enterprise, three rival projects were put forward between 1858 and 1866 all of which advanced as their greatest claim to attention the necessity of shorter cable lengths. The first was a line running along the European and African coast across to South America and northward to the United States. The longest single stretch of cable on this route would be about one thousand miles.

601   Shaffner's expedition arriving at Kaksimiut, Greenland, from *Harper's Weekly*, Aug. 4, 1860

A second plan, calling for a maximum cable span of one thousand four hundred miles, was to proceed to America by way of the Azores. Finally, an extreme northern route was mapped and actually prospected.

602   *The Great Eastern* in the Medway receiving the Atlantic telegraph cable, from *Harper's Weekly*, March 11, 1865

This line was to start in Norway and Scotland, cross to the Faro Isles, Iceland, Greenland and Labrador and thence southward to Canada and the United States. For this plan it was claimed that the longest span of cable did not exceed six hundred miles. The principal backer of this route was Taliaferro P. Shaffner. During all the efforts to lay an Atlantic cable he was securing rights and winning support for his northern project. However, before he could obtain sufficient financial backing, the Atlantic cable of 1866 was laid down successfully and the Shaffner project was killed.

THE ATLANTIC CABLE OF 1865

THE promoters of the Atlantic Telegraph Company were indomitable. They called to their aid the best electricians, telegraphers and scientists of the world. The specific trouble with the cable of 1858 was decided to be a flaw in the cable two hundred and seventy miles from Valentia. Several attempts were made to pick up the Valentia end of the cable to repair the fault. These were unavailing. It was all the company could do to keep alive from year to year and finance investigations and experiments with cables. Meanwhile some thirty-seven ocean cables were laid down between 1858 and 1866, including one from Malta to Alexandria, a distance of one thousand five hundred and thirty-five miles, and one from Fao in the Persian Gulf to Karachi, a distance of one thousand four hundred and fifty miles. At length the financial problem of the Atlantic company was settled and the more difficult riddles of technical issues were solved. Once again Field and his associates defied Neptune to do his worst. Man set out to conquer Nature: brains, technical skill and audacity were set against unreasoning forces.

603   Coiling the Atlantic cable on board *The Great Eastern*, from *Harper's Weekly*, March 11, 1865

604   From the painting, 1866, *The Great Eastern's Arrival at Heart's Content, Newfoundland, July 27, 1866,*
by R. Dudley in the United States National Museum, Washington

SUCCESS!

IN July, 1865, the great task was once more begun. After smaller boats had laid the shore end of the cable in Foilhomurrum Bay, Valentia, this end was spliced to the cable in the three great tanks aboard the *Great Eastern* and at 7:15 P.M., July 23, the vessel pointed her bow for Newfoundland while her stern was tied to Ireland. On August 2, the cable was lost. Three separate but vain attempts were made to recover it. The efforts were not abandoned until every bit of grappling material aboard had been forfeited. Once again a useless cable, one thousand one hundred and eighty-six miles long, lay on the bottom of the ocean. The expedition of 1865 proved to Cyrus Field and his associates that while their cable was serviceable, their tackle was inadequate. Granted the right equipment, they felt certain a cable could be laid across the Atlantic. July 13, 1866, saw the *Great Eastern* once more thirty miles off Valentia splicing her cargo of cable to a shore end, and at 3:30 P.M. the Atlantic cable began to slip over her stern. On July 18, the cable became entangled but the tangle was cleared. On July 27, 1866, the *Great Eastern* steamed into Heart's Content Bay, Newfoundland, and landed the cable in perfect order.

605   From the painting, 1866, *Landing the shore end of the Cable, Valentia, Ireland, July 7, 1866,* by
R. Dudley in the United States National Museum, Washington

606   From the painting, 1866, *Receiving Messages, Sept. 2, 1866, from the Recovered 1865 Cable,* by
R. Dudley in the United States National Museum, Washington

COMPLETION OF SECOND CABLE

SERVICE began immediately. The *Great Eastern* and her convoy ship then started off to find the lost cable of 1865, pull it up two miles from the bottom of the ocean, join it to a new cable, and complete the laying that had been so disastrously interrupted the year before. In September they found the cable. A message was flashed to Valentia and answered. The cable was unbroken. Then the new cable in the vessel was spliced to the old cable and the *Great Eastern* slowly paid it out to Newfoundland, the second cable to arrive there in the same year.

CYRUS WEST FIELD, 1819–92

CYRUS WEST FIELD came of a distinguished family. His father, David Dudley Field, Sr., was a noted Congregational clergyman in Connecticut and Massachusetts and an author of histories and biographies. An elder son of the same name, brother of Cyrus, was an eminent jurist. A younger brother, Henry M., succeeded the father as a minister and author, while still another brother held a seat in the United States Supreme Court.

Of this family of ministers, authors, and jurists, Cyrus W. Field was the exception in that he sought fame and fortune not in the professions but in business. In this he was as successful as his father and brothers were in their chosen vocations. His grit was amply proven in his unconquerable determination, despite heaped-up tribulations, to span the Atlantic with a telegraphic cable. After his eventual success in this herculean effort, he was influential in laying cables in other parts of the world. A derided dreamer, he became an honored hero. In the half dozen or more cables that were proposed following the success of the Atlantic Cable Field was called upon for expert aid. His advice was eagerly sought and followed for he was the foremost authority on submarine telegraphy.

FOR BETTER OR WORSE.

607   The Achievement of Cyrus Field, from a cartoon *For Better or Worse,* in *Punch,*
August 11, 1866

CHAPTER XII

THE TELEPHONE

A CHARACTERISTIC of the modern industrialism has been that, once messages were electrically transmitted, the effort to improve and to increase the scope of such communication has been unremitting. The basic invention of the telegraph had its limitations, although, for certain kinds of service, it will doubtless never be surpassed. To send the human voice across space and to make possible a conversation between individuals widely separated was the next step. A generation, however, passed between Morse's first experimental telegraph line and the accomplishment of this feat. The stringing of Morse's wires was taking place at the same time that the Democratic National Convention at Baltimore passed by the veteran politician, Martin Van Buren, to nominate James K. Polk for the Presidency. Two years later the new device was called upon to play a part in the war between the United States and Mexico. By the outbreak of the Civil War the telegraph had become an indispensable part of the equipment of American civilization. But Lee had surrendered and the defeated South had nearly passed through the dark days of reconstruction when the first official exhibition of the telephone was made.

In 1876 the people of the United States celebrated the hundredth anniversary of their national independence. There was cause for rejoicing, for the nation had grown and prospered and the danger of its dissolution had been averted. There was exhibited that year at the Centennial Exhibition at Philadelphia an instrument which, though little heeded at the time, was to affect the habits of the American people to a remarkable degree. It would transmit speech over a wire for a considerable distance — considerable for that time. Sir William Thomson, the great English scientist, would have amazed most of the visitors if they had heard him say it was the most marvelous thing he had seen in America. With the passing of another generation the new device had firmly established its place in American life. By 1900 the United States had become the greatest industrial nation in the world; a quarter of a century later its surpassing economic power was clear to all men. During this first quarter of the twentieth century America exploited the telephone as no other nation has done. The invention entered into the very warp and woof of commercial and social intercourse. It played a great part in that speeding up of life which is one of the most striking characteristics of modern America. By so doing it has hastened the development of other devices still further to increase the speed of human life. One pauses, at times, to wonder where the process will end.

608   Vibrating Reed of Alexander Graham Bell's
harmonic telegraph, courtesy of the American
Telephone and Telegraph Company, New York

THE WORK OF ONE MAN

THE telephone in its earliest practicable form was the work of one man, Alexander Graham Bell, born at Edinburgh, Scotland. No one else was able to invent an improved instrument until after Bell had already brought his to a practical state. It is true that others before him had been experimenting with "musical telegraphs" of one type and another but no musical telegraph ever succeeded in producing speech. A number of rivals contested in the courts the priority of Bell's invention. Bell won every suit. Bell's father invented a system of characters which he called visible speech, by means of which the action of the vocal organs in uttering all possible sounds was indicated. As a boy Bell had become an expert in this visible speech and later adapted it with extraordinary success for use in teaching the deaf to talk. This was of great help to him in the invention of the telephone. With this exact knowledge of the functioning of the voice in speech he combined adequate information about electricity and the zeal of a born inventor. In the history of invention it has been rare for one man to tower above all rivals.

609   Alexander G. Bell, 1847–1922, from a photograph taken in 1879, courtesy of the New York Telephone Company

BELL THE PROFESSOR

IN 1870 Bell's father moved from London to Brantford, Ontario. The next year, it was arranged for Bell to come to Boston to teach in a public school for the deaf. He also took private pupils, among them a boy, whose father, Thomas Sanders, became interested in Bell's ideas. He supplied Bell with money for his experiments, for getting his patents, and later for starting a company. Bell met a lawyer, Gardiner G. Hubbard, who also became interested in his ideas. In these years Bell was working along three lines to invent a phonautograph, to invent a multiple telegraph, and to invent a speaking telegraph or telephone. Sanders and Hubbard considered the multiple telegraph the most important, as they saw a ready market for

it, but Bell himself was much more interested in the telephone, a fact which might have caused his backers to desert if they had known it. He said, "If I can get a mechanism which will make a current of electricity vary in its intensity as the air varies in its density when a sound is passing through it, I can telegraph any sound, even the sound of speech."

610   Thomas Sanders, 1839–1911, in 1878, courtesy of the American Telephone and Telegraph Company, New York

611   Gardiner G. Hubbard, 1822–97, courtesy of the American Telephone and Telegraph Company, New York

612   Courtesy of the American Telephone and Telegraph Company,
New York

BELL THE INVENTOR

ON June 2, 1875, Bell was working with his assistant, Watson, on his multiple telegraph apparatus, constructed on the principle of sympathetic vibration. They were tuning the transmitting and receiving instruments. A contact point had been screwed down so far that when Watson plucked the reed, the electric current was not interrupted, as it is in telegraphy. Consequently Bell heard not only the pitch of the reed sounding but also the overtones. He at once applied what he learned from this incident to his telephone experiments. He had discovered the principle of the undulatory electric current. Nearly a year before, he had thought out the theory for making a telephone instrument. Now he was able to make an instrument embodying the theory. He gave Watson directions for making a telephone and, when tested the next day, it proved successful, though it did not transmit strongly or clearly. After further work during the summer to improve the transmission he wrote out the specifications for his patent. On March 7, 1876, the United States Patent Office issued a patent to him, No. 174,465. Meanwhile he continued his efforts to improve the transmission. His labors were rewarded when on March 10, 1876, the first complete sentence was transmitted by telephone not only intelligibly but clearly. It was, "Mr. Watson, come here; I want you."

THE TELEPHONE AT THE CENTENNIAL

THE year the telephone was patented was the year of the Centennial in Philadelphia. Gardiner G. Hubbard, later Bell's father-in-law, was one of the commissioners representing Massachusetts. He got for Bell's invention a place among the educational exhibits from Massachusetts. The instruments, however, did not attract attention until Sunday, June 25, 1876.

613   The garret at No. 109 Court Street, Boston, where Bell invented the telephone, courtesy of the American Telephone and Telegraph Company, New York

614   From a drawing *Exhibiting the Telephone at the Centennial*, courtesy of the American Telephone and Telegraph Company, New York

615 Bell's Iron Box Receiver, exhibited at
the Centennial, courtesy of the American
Telephone and Telegraph Company, New
York

616 Bell's Single File Magneto Telephone Transmitter, exhibited at the Centennial Exposition, courtesy of the American Telephone and Telegraph Company, New York

RECOGNITION

On that day the Recognition Committee of Judges, including Sir William Thomson, later Lord Kelvin, of England, and the American scientist, Joseph Henry, examined the electrical exhibits in order to determine their awards. They might have passed the telephone without special attention to it if their notice had not been attracted to Bell himself by the Emperor of Brazil, who, as guest of honor, was accompanying them, and who was familiar with Bell's work with the deaf. Their amazement at the actual working of the telephone knew no bounds.

ADVERTISING THE TELEPHONE

Though it had the approval of scientists, the telephone aroused no desire among business men to pay for having one. Following lectures Bell delivered before scientific societies, there came a demand for public lectures with demonstrations of the use of the instrument. At one of these, at Salem, Massachusetts, February 12, 1877, the telephone was used for the first time to send a dispatch to a newspaper. The effect of such demonstrations was to arouse the public interest. The first person actually to sign a contract for a telephone was a man named Emery who in May, 1877, leased for twenty dollars two telephones for use in Charlestown, Massachusetts. In the same month E. T. Holmes, who was operating a burglar-alarm business in Boston, borrowed a dozen telephones, which he put in six of his clients' offices and connected with his burglar-alarm wires. Holmes then arranged a switch at his own office. For several weeks this demonstration exchange was run as a telephone business by day and a burglar-alarm system by night. This "sales promotion" for his new product showed that Bell's advertising was practical.

617   T. A. Watson explaining Bell's work to Boston newspaper men, from
Frank Leslie's Illustrated Newspaper, March 31, 1877

618   First long-distance use of the telephone, Salem to Boston, from
The Scientific American, March 31, 1877

619   Applications of Bell's new telephone, from *The Scientific American*, October 6, 1877

THE FIRST TELEPHONE INSTALLATIONS

THE first telephone line built exclusively for that instrument connected the workshop of Charles Williams, in Boston, with Williams' home in Somerville. It was completed April 4, 1877. There was also a line running from Bell's laboratory at No. 5 Exeter Place to the shop at No. 109 Court Street, but this was not a commercial line. The first line built for a client, finished in May, 1877, ran from the Cambridge Board of Waterworks to the control gates at Fresh Pond. Within a month there were two hundred and thirty telephones in regular use. In 1927 there were more than sixteen million telephones in the Bell system of the United States.

THE FIRST TELEPHONE EXCHANGES

THE first fully equipped telephone exchange constructed for commercial service was opened January 28, 1878, at New Haven, Connecticut. The American District Telegraph Service, the Law Telegraph Service and the Gold and Stock Telegraph had been supplying a special telegraph and messenger service to certain clients furnished through central offices and regulated by certain devices for notification or telegraphic communication. At first telephones were added as supplementary service, but later they became in many cases substitutes for the telegraph and the messenger.

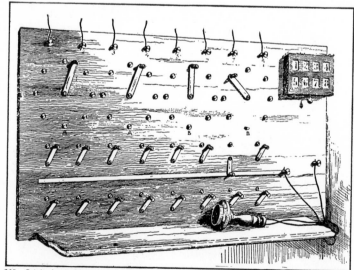

620   Original switchboard used in Commercial Exchange, New Haven, Conn., Jan. 1878, from a photograph of reconstructive sketch, courtesy of the American Telephone and Telegraph Company, New York

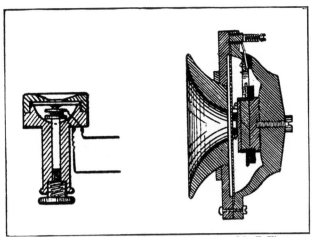

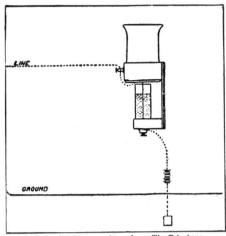

621   Edison's carbon transmitter (Clarke's illustration), from John E. Kings-
        bury, *The Telephone and Telephone Exchanges*, London, 1915

622   Gray's liquid transmitter, from *The Telephone
            and Telephone Exchanges*, London, 1915

WAR WITH THE WESTERN UNION

IN 1877 Bell, Sanders and Hubbard offered to sell the telephone to the Western Union Telegraph Company for one hundred thousand dollars. This was refused. So the Bell group organized and went into the business of renting telephones and initiating service through agents and licensed companies. Several special service companies like the American District Telegraph Company were subsidiaries of the Western Union. Soon the telephone company began to cut into their business, people preferring to talk rather than send a message. This growing loss of business aroused the Western Union. As it was too late to buy the telephone, the company, deciding to crowd the telephone company out of the field by competition, and engaging Elisha Gray, Amos E. Dolbear and Thomas A. Edison as their inventors, went into the business. The first Bell telephone used the same instrument as transmitter and as receiver. Edison invented a transmitter that was better than the Bell instrument. This was the great practical advantage the Western Union had in getting business. But the telephone company claimed that Bell had invented and patented not merely an instrument but the whole art of transmitting speech electrically. So the telephone company sued the Western Union group for infringement of patent. Finally the Western Union counsel was convinced that Bell's patents were valid and the only thing to do was settle. On November 10, 1879, an agreement was signed, whereby the Western Union acknowledged Bell to be the original inventor of the telephone, admitted the validity of his patents, and bound itself and its subsidiaries to retire from the telephone business. The telephone company agreed to buy the Western Union's telephone apparatus at cost and stay out of the telegraph business. The defeat of the Western Union did not end the telephone's legal troubles. The company was engaged in constant litigation until 1896, three years longer than the life of the patents themselves. Most of the cases were suits for infringement against companies organized to sell as much stock as they could before they were sued, and the case got through the courts. There were six hundred cases in all before the courts, including many appeals to the United States Supreme Court. Bell and the telephone company won every case.

623   From a cartoon *The Telephone Rivals were Fighting for a Shadow, and the Substance was lost*, by Thomas Nast,
                    in *Harper's Weekly*, March 13, 1886

624   Courtesy of the American Telephone and Telegraph Company, New York

THE ORGANIZATION OF THE TELEPHONE BUSINESS

In July, 1877, the owners of the telephone organized a trusteeship with Gardiner G. Hubbard as trustee and Thomas Sanders as treasurer. In January, 1878, a corporation was formed to manage the business in New England separately. In June a similar corporation was formed for the rest of the country. In February, 1879, these two companies were reunited under the name of the National Bell Telephone Company with a capitalization of eight hundred and fifty thousand dollars. The management was taken over by William H. Forbes as president and Theodore N. Vail, general manager. Local organization was effected by the telephone company granting agencies and licenses to satisfactory applicants. When a telephone business was incorporated the parent company took payment in stock of the local company. It never granted to anyone, however, the right to build lines connecting the local companies. These local companies gradually merged into the present associated companies. In 1880 the American Bell Telephone Company with seventy-one million three hundred and fifty thousand dollars capital succeeded the National Company. In 1885 the American Telephone and Telegraph Company was chartered in New York to build lines connecting the local companies. In 1900 it took over from the American Bell Company the functions of the parent company. It now stands at the head of all American corporations. At the end of 1926 its capital stock was $1,064,327,800, held by 399,121 shareholders, of whom approximately 60,000 were telephone employees. The 1926 net income was $116,990,401.

"INDEPENDENT" COMPANIES

From the first there has always been more than one telephone company in the field in the United States. During the life of the Bell patents all the competing companies were violating Bell's rights in his patents. But when the patents expired, a whole swarm of legally constituted rivals to the Bell System came into existence. After a generation of experience with independent companies the public has at last learned that the telephone is a natural monopoly. Duplication of systems does not reduce rates or improve service. The small independent companies do not render extensive trunk-line, long-distance service, nor can they indulge in expensive research, seeking improvement in equipment.

625   James M. Thomas, an organizer and chairman of the National Independent Telephone Association, courtesy of the Independent Telephone Association, Chicago

626   F. B. MacKinnon, president of the United States Independent Telephone Association, courtesy of the Independent Telephone Association, Chicago

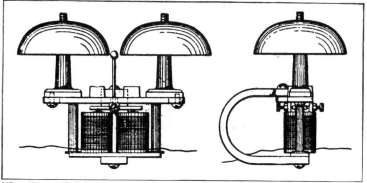

627 Watson's Polarized Ringer, from John E. Kingsbury, *The Telephone and Telephone Exchanges*, London, 1915

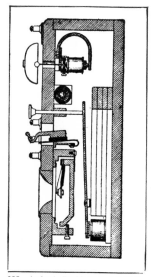

628 Anders' Pushbutton Magneto, from John E. Kingsbury, *The Telephone and Telephone Exchanges*, London, 1915

TELEPHONE SIGNALS

BELL's original telephones comprised a conducting wire and two receivers. Bell's first circular assumed that the telephone itself would give its own call, for he said: "Any person within ordinary hearing distance can hear the voice calling through the telephone." In December, 1877, Thomas A. Watson invented and applied for a patent on an induction coil with vibrator which signaled the station by producing a buzzing sound in the receiver. Other inventors tried to apply to the telephone something akin to the whistle familiar in speaking tubes. At the time of the introduction of the telephone the magneto call bell was well developed in the United States. Watson, Anders, the staff of the Western Electric Company and others now turned their attention to producing suitable telephone-call bells. Watson's centrally pivoted polarized armature bell became a standard feature of all call bells later devised. After the first few years the progress with signal devices was connected with improvements in the transmitter and central-office switchboard.

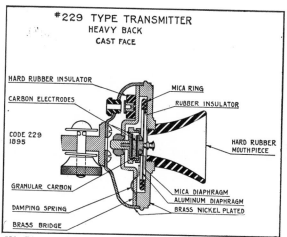

629 Wooden Hand Telephone Receiver, used commercially, 1877, courtesy of the American Telephone and Telegraph Company, New York

630 Earliest Form of the Blake Transmitter, courtesy of the American Telephone and Telegraph Company, New York

631 Diagram of the White Solid Back Transmitter, courtesy of the American Telephone and Telegraph Company, New York

THE TELEPHONE TRANSMITTER

BELL's first transmitter was like his receiver, a magneto instrument. Later he invented a liquid transmitter operated by battery current. Edison's first important contribution had been a battery transmitter, neater, more compact, and more efficient than Bell's, permitting speech over longer mileage of wire. Handicapped by the superiority that Edison had given to the Western Union, the Bell interests worked on the improvement of its own transmitter. Several men contributed to the desired result, Emile Berliner, David E. Hughes, and a Bostonian, Francis Blake. The Blake transmitter was superior to all others, including Edison's. The Bell companies now owned the best transmitter, the best receiver and the protection of the Bell patents. The Blake transmitter was improved by incorporating a discovery of an English clergyman, Henry Hunnings.

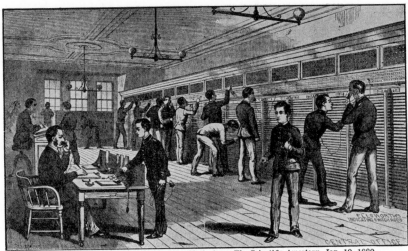

632 Merchants' Telephone Exchange, New York, from *The Scientific American*, Jan. 10, 1880

THE FIRST SWITCHBOARDS

The telephone switchboard, the core of the telephone system, has grown out of the demands of the telephone business. The story of the switchboard is too mechanical and too complicated to describe; indeed there are few men in the telephone business itself who are really masters of the detail of a switchboard. E. T. Gilliland, Charles Scribner and J. J. Carty are the principal magicians who have produced this modern wizardry, by means of which any two of sixteen million telephones may be connected with each other.

CENTRAL BATTERIES

In the early days the battery for operating the transmitter was located at the telephone station. In 1893 a method was developed for utilizing one large battery at the central office which resulted in better and quicker service. This resulted in several seconds being clipped from the time required for each call. This saving on one call was unimportant, but when calls were multiplied by the thousands the total savings by cutting the time per call became a matter of vital consideration.

633 Pyramid telephone switchboard, installed at Richmond, Va., 1882, courtesy of the American Telephone and Telegraph Company, New York

MODERN OPERATORS

Although we cannot comprehend the switchboard, we may appreciate its operator. Boys, the first switchboard employees, were found to be too careless; so girls took over the central office. The central girls are a highly selected corps of workers.

634 Local switchboard, 1927, in New York, courtesy of the American Telephone and Telegraph Company, New York

THE DIAL SYSTEM

THE development of a machine to take the place of the telephone operator has long been a challenge to inventive genius. Among the early inventors of automatic exchange systems were N. B. and T. A. Connolly, T. J. McTighe and A. B. Strowger. The use of automatic systems was at first almost entirely confined to the "Independents." As a rule these systems operated in the smaller communities where there were few central offices and little or no connection with outside communities or exchanges of different types. However, in 1915, the Bell System designed the panel type dial system which is adapted for use in the larger cities and provides interconnection with different types of exchanges. Later the

635   Machine-Switching Apparatus, Automatic System, courtesy of the American Telephone and Telegraph Company, New York

equipment based on A. B. Strowger's patents was adapted for use in the smaller communities. Since 1915 the Bell System has made considerable improvement in these systems and they are being installed extensively throughout the country. In New York city twenty-nine dial exchanges of the panel type were in operation in 1927, but for long-distance calls operators are still essential.

TELEPHONE WIRES AND CABLES

IRON wire, the only material available in 1876, was not an ideal conductor for the human voice. Copper wire was known to possess the required electrical properties, but when made into wire it had only about half the tensile strength of iron. In 1877, T. B. Doolittle, a pioneer in the telephone industry, made a series of tests in the shops of the Ansonia Brass and Copper Company which resulted in a method for producing hard-drawn copper wire which is as strong as iron wire. Copper wire is used to-day for practically all open-wire telephone lines. The multiplicity of wires, especially in cities, created a new problem. After a great deal of work, a method of combining wires for an aerial cable was discovered, and later a method of laying cable or wires underground. In the country, the open lines were retained, for the most part.

636   Network of Telephone and Telegraph wires on Broadway at John Street, from *Harper's Weekly*, July 27, 1889

637   Cables and Loading Pots, courtesy of the American Telephone and Telegraph Company, New York

638   Broadway at John Street after wires were removed, from Moses King, *King's Handbook of New York*, 1893

639   J. J. Carty, 1861–, courtesy of the American Telephone and Telegraph Company, New York

METALLIC CURCUIT

"ANOTHER important subject which profoundly affected the development of the telephone art was the discovery by J. J. Carty in 1883 of the balanced metallic circuit. By abandoning the ground return in favor of a second wire closely paralleling the first, troubles from overhearing telephone conversations on adjacent lines and disturbing noises from nearby electric wires were greatly reduced. The success of the metallic circuit depended upon the interchange in position of the wires of the circuit at certain definite intervals, each point at which the interchange occurred being called a transposition. A proper coordination between the location of transposition points in circuits on the same pole was found to be essential to successful working. The extension of this principle to cable construction . . ., laid the foundation for the great advances that have taken place in this branch of the art." — NELSON'S ENCYCLOPEDIA.

The discovery referred to in the above quotation was first applied practically in the experimental line from New York to Boston.

640   Michael Pupin, 1858–. © Underwood
& Underwood, New York

LOADING

SHORTLY before the year 1900, Pupin, a professor at Columbia University, and G. A. Campbell of the Bell research staff, independently discovered a means for making the wires better conductors of electricity. Applications were filed with the Patent Office, which declared that Pupin's invention was about two weeks earlier than Campbell's. The American Telephone and Telegraph Company purchased Pupin's patent, and after further technical work developed and manufactured loading coils that would work successfully. The first commercial application was completed and put into service May 18, 1900, on a cable between Jamaica Plain and West Newton, Massachusetts. The first application to open-wire lines was completed July 2, 1900, by the American Telephone and Telegraph Company on a twelve-gauge circuit between New York and Pittsburgh. The first large installation of loading on underground cables was put into service August 13, 1902, on a cable between the Cortlandt office, New York, and Newark, New Jersey. Loading is a practical method of increasing the efficiency of telephone circuits by equipping them at periodic intervals with inductance coils of special design.

641   Inter-City Aerial Cable, showing Loading Pots, courtesy of the
American Telephone and Telegraph Company, New York

642   Building the Transcontinental Telephone, 1914, courtesy of the American Teletelephone and Telegraph Company, New York

LONG–DISTANCE TELEPHONY

In the organization of the telephone industry, subsidiary companies might develop the business within geographic areas, but the parent company reserved for itself the construction and operation of lines connecting the geographic areas. The landmarks in telephone history may be listed as follows:

643   Bell opening the Chicago-New York Long Distance Line, 1892, courtesy of the New York Telephone Company, New York

TERMINI	DISTANCE: MILES	DATE
Boston to Cambridge	2	1876
Boston to Providence	45	1882
Boston to New York	235	1884
New York to Chicago	900	1892
New York to Denver	2100	1911
New York to Salt Lake City	2600	1913
New York to San Francisco	3400	1915
Jekyl Island, Ga., to San Francisco	4300	1915
New York to London (wireless)	3515	1927

This record may be translated into terms of telephone equipment. The Boston-Providence venture succeeded because of improved transmitters and line. The first Boston-New York line was a direct consequence of the introduction of the metallic circuit and hard-drawn copper wires. Loaded phantom circuits together with improved repeaters, provided the way for long-distance underground cable lines and transcontinental wireways.

The final transcontinental circuit was opened with a ceremony that befitted such a remarkable achievement. On January 25, 1915, Thomas Watson sat in San Francisco, Bell in New York, President Wilson in Washington and Vail at Jekyl Island, Georgia. They all exchanged messages, Watson and Vail being 4300 miles apart. At present the loading has been removed from the transcontinental circuits and additional repeaters installed.

644   Official Opening of the Transcontinental Line of the Bell System, Jan. 25, 1915, courtesy of the New York Telephone Company, New York

The Telephone.

THE proprietors of the Telephone, the invention of Alexander Graham Bell, for which patents have been issued by the United States and Great Britain, are now prepared to furnish Telephones for the transmission of articulate speech through instruments not more than twenty miles apart. Conversation can be easily carried on after slight practice and with the occasional repetition of a word or sentence. On first listening to the Telephone, though the sound is perfectly audible, the articulation seems to be indistinct, but after a few trials the ear becomes accustomed to the peculiar sound and finds little difficulty in understanding the words.

The Telephone should be set in a quiet place, where there is no noise which would interrupt ordinary conversation.

The advantages of the Telephone over the Telegraph for local business are

1st. That no skilled operator is required, but direct communication may be had by speech without the intervention of a third person.

2d. That the communication is much more rapid, the average number of words transmitted a minute by Morse Sounder being from fifteen to twenty, by Telephone from one to two hundred.

3d. That no expense is required either for its operation, maintenance, or repair. It needs no battery, and has no complicated machinery. It is unsurpassed for economy and simplicity.

The Terms for leasing two Telephones for social purposes connecting a dwelling-house with any other building will be $20 a year, for business purposes $40 a year, payable semiannually in advance, with the cost of expressage from Boston, New York, Cincinnati, Chicago, St. Louis, or San Francisco. The instruments will be kept in good working order by the lessors, free of expense, except from injuries resulting from great carelessness.

Several Telephones can be placed on the same line at an additional rental of $10 for each instrument; but the use of more than two on the same line where privacy is required is not advised. Any person within ordinary hearing distance can hear the voice calling through the Telephone. If a louder call is required one can be furnished for $5.

Telegraph lines will be constructed by the proprietors if desired. The price will vary from $100 to $150 a mile; any good mechanic can construct a line; No. 9 wire costs 8½ cents a pound, 320 pounds to the mile; 34 insulators at 25 cents each; the price of poles and setting varies in every locality; stringing wire $5 per mile; sundries $10 per mile.

Parties leasing the Telephones incur no expense beyond the annual rental and the repair of the line wire. On the following pages are extracts from the Press and other sources relating to the Telephone.

GARDINER G. HUBBARD.

CAMBRIDGE, Mass., May, 1877.

For further information and orders address

THOS. A. WATSON, 109 Court St., Boston

645   Advertising Circular, Announcing Telephone Rates, 1877, courtesy of the American Telephone and Telegraph Company, New York

TELEPHONE RATES

THE present-day method of providing telephone service, whereby telephones are rented to subscribers, not sold, has been in effect since telephones were first furnished to the public in 1877. At that date, telephone service consisted only of communication between fixed points, the subscriber being furnished with two telephones at twenty dollars a year for social purposes, and forty dollars a year for business purposes. In 1878, the first exchanges were established, rates being generally quoted on a "flat" or "unlimited use" basis. Message rates were introduced shortly thereafter in certain exchanges and now are quoted generally in the larger cities for business service, and in a few large metropolitan areas for residence service. Rates fixed by the companies are subject to regulation by public utility commissions in practically all states.

THE TELEPHONE ABROAD

THE United States has more than three-fifths of the world's telephones. Germany ranks next in total number of telephones but in point of development, that is, telephones per hundred inhabitants, the United States is more than three times better equipped. Canada ranks second in telephone development, followed by the Scandinavian countries, and then by New Zealand. Russia has but one telephone per hundred inhabitants. In foreign countries most telephones are located in the larger cities. In the United States, however, there has been such a wide distribution of the telephone that communities of less than fifty thousand people are on the average better equipped with telephones than inhabitants of most large foreign cities. There are more telephones in New York city than in the whole of Great Britain and northern Ireland.

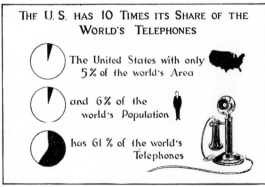

646   Statistical graph, courtesy of the American Telephone and Telegraph Company, New York

647   From a map, *More Telephones in One City in United States than in Three Continents*, courtesy of the American Telephone and Telegraph Company, New York

648   From the drawing *Weavers of Speech*, courtesy of the American Telephone and Telegraph Company, New York

COMMERCIAL ASPECTS OF THE TELEPHONE

IN the year 1926, there were over twenty-three billion telephone conversations in the United States. Of the strictly business conversations the principal commercial aspect was the saving of time. In one day a business man may get in personal touch with scores of scattered people. In this respect the telephone is preferable to the telegraph. Perhaps it is not much of an exaggeration to say that the development of the modern commercial city would be impossible without the telephone. Railroads telephone much of their business messages within and outside of their organization. Newspapers depend on the telephone; telephonic connections are made at hourly intervals throughout the day between news agencies in the principal cities with daily newspapers in the smaller towns. In this way each news item is received simultaneously at thirty or forty newspaper offices. Captains of ships telephone their instructions to sub-officers scattered throughout the immense hulls of modern liners. Mine operators above ground telephone orders to mine foremen stationed far below. Central offices of great business organizations keep in constant touch with scattered factories by means of the telephone; and farmers keep in contact with the market. Not infrequently a firm with headquarters in one city and with a factory or branch office in another city perhaps a thousand miles away will lease a toll line for one hour regularly each day and eliminate delay by transacting their business by telephone. Several firms have gone so far as to eliminate the necessity of branch offices in a distant city by leasing a toll line for the full business day. A Boston bank, for instance, has a through trunk line terminating in a New York telephone number. For a New York business man to talk with the Boston bank he has merely to call the New York telephone number. This instrument is inextricably woven into modern American business and commerce.

649   The Merger of East and West, courtesy of the American Telephone and
Telegraph Company, New York

CHAPTER XIII

VOICES ACROSS SPACE

FROM the very inception of telegraphic transmission men dreamed of sending messages without wires. Alfred Vail and Rogers made experiments none of which had practical results. If two coils of uninsulated wire are in proximity but not connected, any electric current in one coil sets up similar electric currents in the other coil. Electricians call this "induction." It occurred to several inventive men that it was possible to use induction currents to transmit telegraphic codes without wires. One attempt to employ the idea was to telegraph from moving railway trains. Along the railway track a wire conductor was erected and within a moving car another circuit was set up. The electric impulse within the car was induced across the space to the wire alongside the track. The scheme succeeded in a measure but was never adopted to any considerable degree. Quite analagous were experiments between a mainland and nearby islands. A circuit was constructed on the shore of the mainland, and another parallel to it was strung on an island. Pulsations in the mainland circuit were induced across the intervening space and repeated in the island circuits. This made it possible to telegraph to the island without cables or wires connecting the island to the mainland. These kinds of wireless, however, were rigidly restricted in their application because of the feebleness of the ordinary electric currents used in telegraphy. Wireless communication is the product of the twentieth century. In less than twenty-five years it has been brought into direct contact with the lives of a great majority of the American people. The acceptance of the telegraph and telephone was slow in comparison with the swiftness with which Americans made the radio their own.

650 The Genius of Electricity, from the statue by Evelyn B. Longman, courtesy of the American Telephone and Telegraph Company, New York

651 Joseph Henry, 1797–1879, from the portrait by Henry Ulke, in the United States National Museum, Washington

652 James C. Maxwell, 1831–79, courtesy of the Bell Telephone Laboratories, New York

653 Dr. Edouard Branly, courtesy of Charles Scribner's Sons, New York

654 Heinrich Hertz, 1857–94, from William Stanley's Collection of Autographed Photographs of Noted Scientists, in the Stanley Library, General Electric Co., Pittsfield, Mass.

655 Sir Oliver Lodge, 1851–, from a photograph in William Stanley's Collection of Autographed Photographs of Noted Scientists, in the Stanley Library, General Electric Co., Pittsfield, Mass.

THE SCIENTIFIC FORBEARS OF RADIO

THE modern systems of wireless transmission go back to many scientific experimenters working in quiet laboratories. Professor James C. Maxwell at the University of Edinburgh, in 1864–65, announced the theory based on mathematical data that light is produced by electromagnetic undulations oscillating at the rate of four hundred million million times per second. Men knew that there are sound vibrations both so slow and so fast that the human ear cannot detect them. After Clark, men reasoned by analogy that there are probably light vibrations both too sluggish and too swift for the human eye to see. Joseph Henry had shown at Princeton in 1842 that electrical motions are under certain conditions oscillatory, and in 1853 William Thomson (later Lord Kelvin) had formulated mathematically the conditions for oscillatory electrical motions. Professor Heinrich Hertz in 1887 produced oscillatory electrical currents that vibrated at a speed between the highest audible sound-waves and the slowest visible light-waves. He demonstrated that they traveled through the air from the circuit where they were produced to another circuit nearby, actuating it into exactly equivalent vibrations. Hertz reasoned that this second circuit is to electrical waves what the ear is to sound-waves or the eye to light-waves and called it a "detector." A disciple of Hertz was Professor Righi of the University of Bologna, in whose laboratory was a young Italian named Guglielmo Marconi. Dr. Edouard Branly discovered that whereas iron filings in a tube generally set up considerable resistance to the passage of an electric current, when the electricity is oscillatory the filings lose their resistance and become excellent conductors. In 1894, Sir Oliver Lodge showed that this behavior of iron filings could be made to serve the purpose of telegraphy. In 1895, Marconi used the filings coherer for a detector in his wireless telegraph.

656   Marconi with his apparatus, taken on the occasion of receiving the first transatlantic Wireless
        signals in Newfoundland, 1901, courtesy of Marconi's Wireless Telegraph Co., Ltd., London

MARCONI'S FIRST EXPERIMENTS

By patient trial Marconi produced oscillatory electrical motions of much greater strength than those of Hertz and Righi. He also found by trial that the best way to get these oscillatory electrical motions into the air was by an upright wire connected with the ground. The higher the wire, the better the results. With an ordinary Morse key he could vary the sending of the oscillations as in the regular Morse code. Trial also convinced Marconi that the best receiver of the oscillatory electrical motions was a second upright wire extended high in the air and connected with the ground. Suitable connections with this wire led the oscillations to a filings coherer. When an oscillatory current arrived at the coherer, the filings became good electrical conductors. As soon as the oscillations stopped, the coherer was tapped automatically so as to cause the filings to fall apart and become once again highly resistant to electrical currents. The intermittency of low and high resistance allowed translation into the Morse code. The intermittent action of the coherer resulted in changes of sound in attached head phones. Other connections led to properly adjusted mechanisms that printed the intermittent pulsations as dots, dashes and space. At first Marconi was able to send and receive only two miles, but later he extended this to four and eight miles, and by 1895 he was getting distance enough to seek patent rights. The first British patent was secured in June, 1896.

EXTENSION OF THE MARCONI SYSTEM

In 1899 messages were sent from near Boulogne to South Foreland across the English Channel, a distance of over thirty miles. This success prompted Marconi to come to America to arrange for an experiment. A station was set up at Signal Hill, Newfoundland, and another at Poldhu Station, England. In 1901, faint but perceptible interchanges between these two offices aroused the Anglo-American Cable Company who, having monopoly privileges in transoceanic communication, ordered Marconi out of Newfoundland. Accordingly, he went to Table Head, Glace Bay, Cape Breton Island. On December 21, 1902, the first official transatlantic wireless telegram was sent from Table Head to England. The following year (1903) President Roosevelt and King Edward exchanged wireless greetings and good wishes. Five years later regular commercial wireless transoceanic service was started between Nova Scotia and Ireland.

657   Original Marconi Wireless Apparatus, courtesy of the Radio Corporation of America, New York City

WIRELESS AT SEA

AT about the same time (1907) the Italian and then the British navy adopted wireless. Soon wireless equipment was a matter of course on all important vessels. There is now constant communication between ships at sea and the shore or between two ships. The security the wireless has brought to sea travel is a byword. This is illustrated by the rescue of the *Antione* by the *Roosevelt* in 1926. Its commercial value is equally important; ships at sea may be directed from

658 Early Marconi apparatus on board an Atlantic liner, courtesy of Marconi's Wireless Telegraph Co., Ltd., London

the shore to change courses because of alterations in markets or other exigencies unknown when the ship left port. Some marvelous surgical operations have been conducted at sea, every move being dictated by wireless directions from a doctor on shore or on another ship.

659 Guglielmo Marconi, courtesy of Marconi's Wireless Telegraph Co., Ltd., London

660 The Marconi one-and-a-half kilowatt quenched spark installation, as supplied to most modern ships, courtesy of Marconi's Wireless Telegraph Co., Ltd., London

GUGLIELMO MARCONI, 1875

GUGLIELMO MARCONI, the inventor of wireless telegraphy, was born near Bologna, Italy, September 23, 1875. His close personal contact with Professor Righi of the University of Bologna was the determinant influence in his life. Since Marconi is still a man of middle years, his story is the tale of the wireless to which he has devoted his constant attention. The wireless apparatus of 1927 bears scarcely any resemblance to that of 1896 except in the underlying principles. To be sure, Marconi is not solely responsible for the later inventions that have advanced wireless telegraphy. He is certain, however, of his niche in the hall of fame. The universities and governments of the world have vied with each other in the bestowal of degrees, medals and titles upon Marconi; nor has there been any lack of financial tribute to his genius.

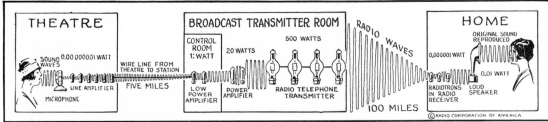

PRINCIPLES OF RADIO TELEPHONY

WHEN one person speaks to another and is heard there are three elements in the process, the motor vocal cords, air-wave transmission, and the ear-receiver. The vocal organs in the speaker's throat set in motion varying waves in the air. These spread in all directions and finally strike upon a membrane in the hearer's ear which vibrates in exact accordance with the form of the waves. The membrane communicates with certain bones and these with nerves. Finally, the hearer gets the sensation of sound. Each sound has its own peculiar form of wave, so that the number is exceedingly great and the variety of form very complex. Vibrations as slow as twenty per second are inaudible, as are also vibrations that exceed ten thousand per second. In order that speech may be transmitted by electricity over wires by the ordinary telephone it is necessary to change the air-waves of sound issuing from a speaker's throat into exactly equivalent undulatory electric currents. This was done in the telephone transmitter. The receiver of the ordinary telephone is an electromagnet acting upon a diaphragm. When undulatory currents reach the electromagnet they cause it to act upon the diaphragm in such a manner as to produce the same kind of vibrations as those that start the undulations in the transmitter diaphragm. The receiver's diaphragm vibrations therefore are heard as sounds by the human ear. In the radio telephone there are transmitters (microphones) and receivers (head phones or loud speakers) that are first cousins to those employed in the ordinary telephone. Radio vibrations of very high frequencies (vibrations per second) take the place of the wires that are used for the common telephones. It is impossible to vary radio

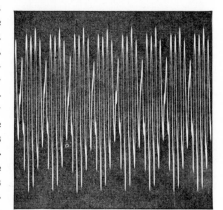

662   From a photographic record of the electric oscillations produced by broadcasting the "a" sound in "far," courtesy of D. Van Nostrand Company, New York

frequencies directly by the human voice as the weak current in a telephone transmitter is varied, because the human ear could not hear these high frequency vibrations when they were caught by the diaphragm of the receiver. Yet radio of any practical distance is impossible without employing high frequency vibrations. Therefore the radio telephone engineers had to invent a method by which the ordinary telephone transmitter and its undulatory current could control equally varying high-frequency radio oscillations. Then at the receiving end, the engineers had to transform the high frequency waves that reached the station into low frequency vibrations that would actuate a telephone receiver so that a human ear could recognize the sounds.

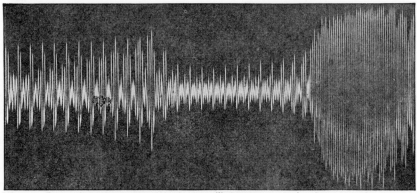

663   From a photographic record of the electric oscillations produced by broadcasting sounds in the word "Hello," courtesy of D. Van Nostrand Company, New York

APPLICATION OF THE PRINCIPLES OF RADIO TELEPHONY

To transmit sounds by wireless in a practical commercial enterprise two different sets of apparatus are required. At a transmission station some means of providing smooth, high-frequency, oscillatory electrical waves must be installed. It is necessary also to construct apparatus that will modulate the high-frequency waves in exact accordance with the waves of sound impacting upon the microphone. These waves must then be flung off into the air, taking the place of the wires of the regular telephone. The receiving station has antennæ to pick up the electromagnetic waves passing through the air. They are then guided to an instrument called a "tuner," which eliminates all the

664   Radio Telephone and Telegraph Transmitter, courtesy of the Radio Corporation of America, New York

waves except the one carrying the desired sounds. (Of course the tuner can be varied.) From the tuner the selected wave is passed into the "detector" or "rectifier." Without the detector, the diaphragm would stand still, and no sound would be produced. Furthermore, the detector changes the high frequency of the incoming waves to a frequency that the human ear can hear; this reduction does not alter the pulsations of the waves, for it only produces in miniature what the high-frequency waves have carried in magnitude. Finally, the waves from the detector actuate the telephone diaphragm of the head phones or loud speaker and so reproduce the sounds that started the operation in the microphone of the transmitting station.

665   E. F. W. Alexanderson, courtesy of the Radio Corporaton of America, New York

OSCILLATION GENERATORS FOR TRANSMISSION

THE production of radio waves has been accomplished by several different means. Hertz used a "spark" of such low frequency that it had a transmission distance of only ten to twelve feet. Marconi also employed spark-generators at audible frequency, although very much higher than that of Hertz. Improvements in wireless transmission at first took the form of raising the frequency of the spark until it was inaudible. The spark of inaudible frequency is still the most common for medium and short-distance radio telegraphy. Closely associated are the arc systems. The one most generally employed was introduced by Valdemar Poulsen and is given his name. About 1906, Professor R. A. Fessenden, together with E. F. W. Alexanderson, designed and had manufactured by the General Electric Company a dynamo capable of

generating a sustained alternating current of some eighty thousand cycles frequency. This machine was of the same general nature as dynamos used for electric lighting. The systems that depend upon dynamos are called "alternators" and have proved to be admirably fitted for radio telephony. Such basic improvements were necessary before radio could become of material benefit or enjoyment to the general public.

666   Alexanderson's Alternator, courtesy of the Radio Corporation of America, New York

THE LATEST TRANSMITTER

DE FOREST, Armstrong and others invented the three-electrode vacuum tube which is to radio what the five senses are to man. The tube may be used for transmission or reception, for amplification or modulation, and furthermore is relatively inexpensive and dependable. It bids fair to displace all other systems. A fuller description of it may be found on page 280.

MODULATOR SYSTEMS IN TRANSMISSION

IN radio transmission the modulator performs the function of the transmitter in the ordinary telephone. Modulator systems fall into two general categories. In the first there is a direct transfer of the principle of the wired telephone transmitter to the radio. The microphone is connected with the antennæ circuit in such a way that the changes in resistance set up in the microphone by sounds that strike it will cause corresponding increases and decreases in the value of the current thrown off the antennæ. By the second method microphone resistance changes affect the output of the oscillation generator while the antennæ circuit remains constant. This method has more general support. For the second method there are two devices, one the

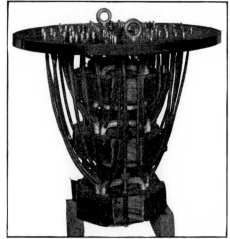

668   Magnetic Modulator, courtesy of the Radio Corporation of America, New York

667   Transmitting Vacuum Tube, courtesy of the Radio Corporation of America, New York

magnetic modulator, the other used in connection with tube-transmitters in which either the plate-voltage or the grid-voltage is varied to influence the output of the tube oscillations.
The magnetic modulator was first proposed by Alexanderson to use in connection with his dynamo alternators and has since always accompanied the installation of alternators. Where vacuum tubes with three electrodes are the source of the outgoing waves they are modulated by varying either the plate-voltage or the grid-voltage.

THE "TUNER" IN RECEPTION

THE antennæ or loop of a radio receiver is actuated by electromagnetic waves in the air. If all of these were admitted to the reproducing instruments, the wildest jumble of sounds would result or else no sound at all. So "tuners" are part of every receiving outfit. These tuners select a particular wave-length and allow it to pass through the rest of the receiving apparatus but exclude all or nearly all other waves. The electrician would say that a tuner varies the "inductance" or "capacitance" of a circuit, or does both. What happens is that an electrical wall is built up over which some few currents or one current can jump, but behind which all other currents are barred from further progress. The tuner changes the antennæ or loop from

instruments capable of vibrating in response to all the electromagnetic waves in the neighborhood to instruments that respond to one wave (or to a limited few such waves). If we held down all but one of the keys of a piano, we could sing all notes without causing a piano-string to vibrate except the one whose key we had left alone. This note would fail to vibrate until we sang its tone. A tuner acts as a damper to all the waves but one.

669   Early Radio Receiving Set, showing dials for "tuning," courtesy of the Radio Corporation of America, New York

THE "DETECTOR" IN RECEPTION

THE "detector," reducing to audible frequency the high-frequency waves that are picked up by the antennæ or aerial, is usually either a "crystal" or a "vacuum tube." The mineral crystal serves to "rectify" the high-frequency alternating currents received by the antennae so that they all flow in one direction and a condenser brings the frequencies down to audible limits. The vacuum tube-detector is now almost universally used. In connection with tube-detectors other tubes may be used as amplifiers, either before or after the current goes through the detector or both.

670   Early receiving set, showing crystal detector, courtesy of the Radio Corporation of America, New York

THE VACUUM TUBE

THE principle of vacuum tube may be said to have been discovered by Edison. He noticed that, with a metal plate sealed inside the lamp bulb between the two sides of the filament, a current would flow when the outside terminal of the plate was connected with the positive terminal of the filament but none when the connection was made to the negative terminal. The discovery remained dormant for twenty years until Fleming adopted it to his uses. Knowing that positive and negative impulses rush up and down the antennæ he built a receiving circuit wherein the positive impulses caused the current to flow in the tube while the negative impulses left it unaffected.

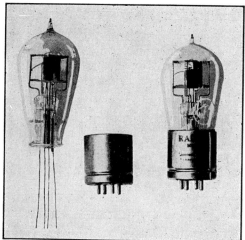

671   Receiving vacuum tubes showing tungsten filaments, courtesy of the Radio Corporation of America, New York

THE TUNGSTEN FILAMENT

EACH atom has a nucleus or positively charged portion around which cluster negatively charged electrons. When the tungsten filament is heated to incandescence certain negatively charged electrons escape from the atoms. If a positively charged plate is near by, the electrons flee to this plate and so set up the current observed by Edison. If the plate is negatively charged, then, since two electric charges of the same kind repel rather than attract, the electrons escaping are driven back to their parent atoms, and no current results. No electrons could leave the plate because it was cold. In this series of actions an experimenter in radio, Professor John A. Fleming, English scientist, saw an identity to the rectifying action of a crystal detector; so he introduced the two-electrode vacuum tube to radio users, calling it the "Fleming Valve." Although this was an improvement it was far short of perfection, so it was left to other men to bring the vacuum tube to a higher state of usefulness.

672   Back of a modern receiving set, showing tube-detectors and amplifiers, courtesy of the Radio Corporation of America, New York

673   John Ambrose Fleming. © Swaine, London

THE FLEMING VALVE (Two-Electrode Tube)

THE Fleming Valve comprised an incandescent lamp filament and a plate fixed inside a glass bulb which was exhausted of air and sealed in the usual manner. The incandescent filament shot off negatively charged electrons, leaving the filament a positively charged body. The discharged electrons were attracted to the plate when the latter was charged positively. When the plate was charged negatively, no flow of electrons occurred and hence no current was set up. It is evident then that if the plate and the filament wave applied between them an alternating voltage—half positive and half negative—only half of this voltage would constitute a current, all of it flowing in one direction. It is also apparent that the action of the tube is similar to that of a crystal detector, and so the tube can take the place of a crystal detector in a radio set. Thus in 1904 the Fleming "oscillation valve," as it has ever since been known, came into radio communication. Remarkable as was this first of modern radio vacuum tubes, still more so was the improvement made by Lee DeForest, the American Engineer.

THE DE FOREST TUBE (Three-Electrode)

EXPERIENCE with the Fleming Valve proved that the current evolved by the electrons did not equal the theoretical electrons given off by the filament. Dr. Lee De Forest, in investigating this problem, discovered that if a third electrode in the form of a wire grid were added to a Fleming Valve the theoretical limit of all the electrons sent off by the filament were utilized and what is called "a saturation current" was produced. Moreover, by suitable arrangement of the grid and by changing properly the wire connections at the externals of the electrodes with other external apparatus, the tube could be made to function as an amplifier, an amplifying rectifier, an oscillator, or a modulator. The original De Forest tubes, extremely erratic in their behavior, have been perfected by the research staffs of the General Electric Company and the Western Electric Company. De Forest's name and apparatus are familiar to all those interested in radio because of the many private sets he sold, and the radio patents he secured, his name being attached to over one hundred and twenty United States and foreign patents in radio, telegraphy and telephony.

674   Lee De Forest, 1873–, courtesy of the De Forest Laboratories, New York

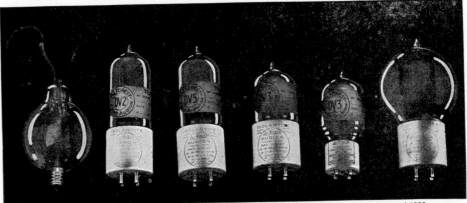

675   Audion tube, invented by Lee De Forest in 1906, and the latest highly specialized radio audions of 1926, courtesy of the DeForest Laboratories, New York

676 Interior of Broadcasting Studio of Station WJZ, courtesy of the Radio Corporation of America, New York, Department of Broadcasting

BROADCASTING

BROADCASTING, or the transmitting of radio, is expensive and has not yet (1926) been put on a commercial basis. Broadcasting began in November, 1920, when the Westinghouse Company transmitted the election returns and then began to send out daily concerts and other entertainment from Pittsburgh. This station was followed by another operated by the same company at Newark, New Jersey (WJZ), while still other stations were inaugurated at Schenectady, Springfield, Chicago, Detroit and on the Pacific coast. Their number by 1926 created a serious problem in allotting wave-lengths and averting a threatened congestion in the air. To take advantage of the public service rendered by the broadcasting stations, the American public bought or made for themselves radio receiving sets at a furious rate between 1920 and 1926. The figures of growth are startling. According to Secretary Hoover, there were scarcely fifty thousand transmitting and receiving radio sets in the United States in 1922, but by the end of 1925 an estimate placed the number of receiving sets alone in use at over five million. The number of companies manufacturing receiving sets in the same period advanced from a bare half dozen to about six hundred. Reception is more accurate in winter than in summer, at night than in the daytime. It is worst at dawn and at sunset. Transmitting stations further north get better results than those to the south. The distance obtainable varies enormously and in the most erratic manner. These are among the many things that await explanation.

677 View of Control Room of Station WJZ, New Jersey, courtesy of the Radio Corporation of America, New York, Department of Broadcasting

678 From an original line-cut reproduction made from a photograph of President Coolidge, transmitted to the New York laboratory from the station at Marion, Mass., courtesy of the Radio Corporation of America, New York

SOME COMMERCIAL ASPECTS OF RADIO

BESIDES the usefulness of radio to ships at sea, broadcasted weather reports, storm warnings, time signals, and market reports all have their commercial value. Catching the criminal and saving the lost are among the services of radio. It is now easy to connect the wire service of telephone and telegraph with the wireless, effecting a saving of time in the transmission of news and business messages. Wonderfully promising work has been done in transmitting by wired-wireless pictures and photographs of prominent people and news events. An international, transoceanic wired-wireless telephone demonstration between New York and London was held on March 7, 1926, the fiftieth anniversary of Bell's telephone patent. The American Telephone and Telegraph Co., the Radio Corporation of America and the British General Post Office joined forces in this demonstration. Scores of leisurely conversations were held between 8 A.M. and 12 M. (1-5 London), the speakers sitting in New York and London. The hearing in New York was equal to the local service, while the Londoners admitted it was better than they were accustomed to get in London. This was the most successful but not the first transatlantic telephone conversation. In 1915, the American Telephone and Telegraph Co. transmitted a speech from Arlington, Virginia, to the Eiffel Tower in France but only occasional words got through. The first newspaper dispatch by international transoceanic wired radio was sent during the 1926 experiment. Commercial transatlantic (New York–London) radio telephone service began early in 1927. Indirectly, the progress of radio is having commercial effects. The phonograph business, after being nearly wiped out, used radio equipment and discoveries to improve its own product.

679   General Operating Room at Broad Street, New York, where radiograms are sent and received from all over the world, from a photograph, courtesy of the Radio Corporation of America, New York

CHAPTER XIV

AMERICAN MONEY

TRANSPORTATION–HIGHWAYS — canals, steamboats, railroads — have been as vital to the development of the commercial life of the American as of any other people. Communication — mail, telegraph, telephone — has also played its indispensable part. But commercial interchange cannot rest on these alone. Money or a medium of exchange is likewise necessary. Almost from his earliest appearance on earth man has exchanged what he had for what he had not and coveted. For many ages the exchange was of goods for goods, or barter. However disguised by the intervention of money and credit instruments, this direct exchange of goods for goods underlies all trade.

America has seen in its history the swift development from primitive barter to trade in its most complex modern forms. Captain John Smith traded with his Indian neighbors after the methods of primitive peoples. For corn and pelts he gave the redskin articles which caught the Indian fancy. Until nearly the end of the nineteenth century the frontier persisted in American history and, so long as it lasted, barter continued to be one of its characteristics. In the seventeenth and early eighteenth centuries all the English colonies in North America were frontier communities which, as they grew more populous, developed a life more independent of the mother country. This growing complexity of colonial life made barter an unsatisfactory solution of the problem of colonial trade. But, because it was a frontier community, colonial America, like all frontiers, had difficulty in retaining an amount of English currency in circulation sufficient for the needs of its people. As a consequence greatly varying media of exchange were used by the colonial people as temporary expedients.

By the time of the American Revolution the colonies were large enough and sufficiently developed in an economic sense to be said to have definitely passed the frontier stage. One of the early national tasks was to establish a monetary system and the present decimal system was inaugurated.

The average twentieth-century American thinks little of the form or character of the currency he uses. This has not been true of his forefathers in several decades of the nineteenth century. A monetary system, in order to meet the need for which it is created, must be carefully adjusted to the economic life of the people. It required more than a century of experience before Americans developed their money to a point of maximum efficiency in its service of the commercial needs of the nation, and this end was not achieved until some of the fiercest and most dramatic political battles in our national history had been fought.

680 Scales and weights used for weighing colonial money, *ca.* 1740, in the collections of the American Antiquarian Society, Worcester. Mass.

681   From the painting *The Fur-Trading Period* by Douglas Volk, in the County Court House, Des Moines, Iowa

BARTER IN AMERICA

NEARLY all the earliest trade between the American colonists and the Indians was by barter. The Indians had no use for the gold and silver money of the whites, nor had the whites at first for the Indians' shell or bead money. As the Indian trade developed barter became less common, but as long as the trade lasted some of it was conducted by barter. Even among themselves the colonists at first, with little European money and no coinage of their own, traded largely by barter. This practice too never entirely disappeared in colonial times. To-day the farmer's wife may swap eggs for groceries at the crossroad store, a transaction akin to barter. Since the calculation of value, however, is in terms of money, it is not true barter although no money passes.

682   From the drawing *Rival Companies Soliciting Trade* by W. A. Rogers, in *Harper's Magazine*, 1879

July 14th. 1703.
Prices of Goods

Supplyed to the

Eastern Indians,

By the several Truckmasters ; and of the Peltry received by the Truckmasters of the said *Indians*.

ONe yard Broad Cloth, *three* Beaver skins, *in season*.
One yard & half Gingerline, *one* Beaver skin, *in season*
One yard Red or Blew Kersey, *two* Beaver skins, *in season*.
One yard good Duffels, *one* Beaver skin, *in season*.
One yard & half broad fine Cotton, *one* Beaver skin, *in season*
Two yards of Cotton, *one* Beaver skin, *in season*.
One yard & half of half thicks, *one* Beaver skin, *in season*.
Five Pecks Indian Corn, *one* Beaver skin, *in season*.
Five Pecks Indian Meal, *one* Beaver skin, *in season*.
Four Pecks Pease, *one* Beaver skin, *in season*.
Two Pints of Powder, *one* Beaver skin, *in season*.
One Pint of Shot, *one* Beaver skin, *in season*.
Six Fathom of Tobacco, *one* Beaver skin, *in season*.
Forty Biskets, *one* Beaver skin, *in season*.
Ten Pound of Pork, *one* Beaver skin, *in season*.
Six Knives, *one* Beaver skin, *in season*.
Twenty Scaines Thread, *one* Beaver skin, *in season*.
One Hat, *two* Beaver skins, *in season*.
One Hat with Hatband, *three* Beaver skins, *in season*.
Two Pound of large Kettles, *one* Beaver skin, *in season*.
One Pound & half of small Kettles, *one* Beaver skin, *in season*
One Shirt, *one* Beaver skin, *in season*.
One Shirt with Ruffels, *two* Beaver skins, *in season*.
Two Small Axes, *one* Beaver skin, *in season*.
Two Small Hoes, *one* Beaver skin, *in season*.
Three Dozen middling Hooks, *one* Beaver skin, *in season*.
One Sword Blade, *one & half* Beaver skin, *in season*.

What shall be accounted in Value equal
One Beaver in season : *Viz.*

ONe Otter skin in season, is one Beaver
One Bear skin in season, is one Beaver,
Two Half skins in season, is one Beaver.
Four Pappcote skins in season, is one Beaver.
Two Foxes in season, is one Beaver.
Two Woodchocks in season, is one Beaver.
Four Martins in season, is one Beaver.
Eight Mincks in season, is one Beaver.
Five Pounds of Feathers, is one Beaver.
Four Raccoones in season, is one Beaver.
Four Seil skins large, is one Beaver.
One Moose Hide, is two Beavers.
One Pound of Castorum, is one Beaver.

683   Value of Articles of Commerce expressed in beaver skins, 1703, from a broadside in the New York Public Library

Know All Men By These Prints that Daniel
Boone hath Deposited Six vi beaver Skins
in my keep in good order and of the worth
of vi shillings each skin and i Have took
from them vi shillings for the keep of them
and when they Be sold i will pay the balance
of xxx shillings for the whole lot to any
person who presents this certificate
an delivers it up to Me at My keep Louisville
falls of ohio May 20 1784   John Sanders

684   Receipt for beaver skins, with value of circulating money, from an original in the collection of the late
Col. Durrett, Louisville, Ky.

BEAVER SKINS AS MONEY

ONE of the few natural resources of early New England and New York that found a ready and constant market in Europe was furs, principally beaver. Possessing a fairly constant value in the export trade, beaver pelts served as a medium of exchange and measure of value, that is, as money, in colonial transactions.

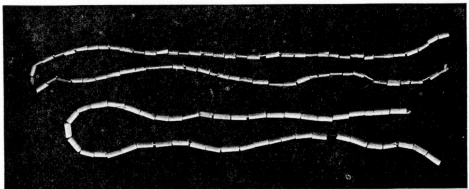

685   Strings of purple and white wampum, in the collections of the American Numismatic Society, New York

WAMPUM AS MONEY

LONG before any English boat had touched the shores of New England, Indians had fashioned beads from the inner portions of quohaug and periwinkle shells which they called "wampumeage." Wampum was used not only for money but for ornament. Belts of it were part of the sign-language of the Indians and entered into negotiations of war and peace as well as those of love. The beads were either black (blue or purple) or white; the former being scarce had double the value of the latter. The unit was a chain consisting of three hundred and sixty white beads reckoned by the settlers as worth sixty pence. This value fluctuated greatly, and in the final years of the seventeenth century it rapidly declined. In New England, wampum not only passed as money but was for a time officially legal tender receivable for taxes. Records show that it was used to pay tuition at Harvard in the seventeenth century. It entered into the trading relations of the Dutch at New York even before the New Englanders took it up and occasionally it was used as money as far south as Virginia. It did not entirely disappear until well into the eighteenth century. The gradual abandonment of wampum in colonial currency was due to the decline of the fur trade with which wampum was most intimately connected. Then too the whites, especially the Dutch, "manufactured" wampum in such quantities as to depress its value. English, Dutch, and Spanish coins superseded wampum.

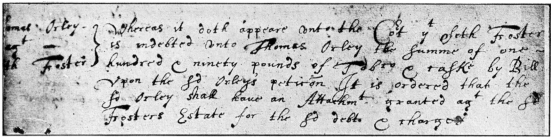

686   Record of Northumberland County, Va., March 23, 1656, showing the use of tobacco as money, from the original court
                         order in the Archives Department, Virginia State Library, Richmond

THOMAS OXLEY *vs.* SETH FOSTER: Whereas it doth appear unto the court that Seth Foster is indebted unto Thomas Oxley the sum
of one hundred and ninety pounds of tobacco & casks by bill, upon the said Oxley's petition, it is ordered that the said
Oxley shall have an attachment granted against the said Foster's Estate for the said debt and charges.

OTHER SUBSTITUTES FOR MONEY

TOBACCO was the local currency in Virginia and Maryland. The first law passed by the General Assembly of Virginia was an act setting the price of tobacco. From 1642 to 1656, Virginia forbade the making of contracts payable in money, and for about two hundred years nearly all payments, including the salaries of

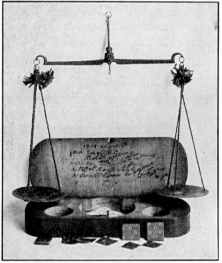

687   Balance for weighing money, Boston, 1722, from
the original in the Massachusetts Historical Society,
Boston

officials and ministers, were made in tobacco currency. In 1727, tobacco-warehouse receipts were legalized as currency in Virginia. Each receipt represented an amount of tobacco of specified grade deposited. In 1734, special casks of tobacco were inspected, sealed and branded, and receipts issued against them which were called "crop-notes." When the inspector had a good reputation, crop-notes had a higher money value than ordinary warehouse receipts. What was true of tobacco in Virginia and Maryland was also true of rice in South Carolina. In 1719, rice was there made receivable for taxes. In anticipation of the collection of this rice upon which a price per pound was set, the legislature issued slips of paper called "rice orders" which were used as money, like the Virginia warehouse receipts. Corn — a name for all grain including peas — bullets, powder, fish, sweet potatoes, deerskins, raccoon skins, hogs, sheep, turkeys, pups, and pieces of soap have been used as money in different American communities at various times.

COLONIAL COINS

A COIN is a piece of money metal of a convenient shape bearing official marks to guarantee its genuineness. Since under English law the issuing of coins was a prerogative of the Crown, the colonies in America, without coins of their own, were forced to depend upon trade to supply them with "hard money."

C A P. XXX.

An Act for afcertaining the Rates of foreign Coins in Her Majefty's Plantations in *America.*

    ' **W**HEREAS for remedying the Inconveniencies which had arifen from the different Rates at which
    ' the fame Species of foreign Silver Coins did pafs in Her Majefty's feveral Colonies and Plantations
    ' in *America,* Her Moft Excellent Majefty has thought fit by Her Royal Proclamation, bearing Date the
    ' eighteenth Day of *June* One thoufand feven hundred and four, and in the third Year of Her Reign, to fettle
    ' and afcertain the Currency of foreign Coins in Her faid Colonies and Plantations, in the Manner and Words
    ' following :'

Proclamation for   ' **W**E having had under our Confideration the different Rates at which the fame. Species of foreign
afcertaining the   ' Coins do pafs in our feveral Colonies and Plantations in *America,* and the Inconveniences thereof,
Currency of fo-   ' by the indirect Practice of drawing the Money from one Plantation to another, to the great Preju-
reign Coins in   ' dice of the Trade of our Subjects ; and being fenfible that the fame cannot be otherwife remedied, than by
America.   ' reducing of all foreign Coins to the fame current Rate within all our Dominions in *America* ; and the prin-
    ' cipal Officers of our Mint having laid before us a Table of the Value of the feveral foreign Coins which
    ' ufually pafs in Payments in our faid Plantations, according to their Weight, and the Affays made of them in
    ' our Mint, thereby fhewing the juft Proportion which each Coin ought to have to the other, which is as
    ' followeth, *viz.* Sevil Pieces of eight, old Plate, feventeen Penny-weight twelve Grains, four Shillings and
    ' Six pence ; *Sevil* Pieces of eight, new Plate, fourteen Penny-weight, three Shillings feven Pence one
    ' Farthing ; *Mexico* Pieces of eight, feventeen Penny-weight twelve Grains, four Shillings and Six pence ;
        ' Pillar

688   An Act for Ascertaining Rates of Foreign Coins in Her Majesty's Plantations in America, 1707,
                           from Statutes at Large, Vol. III (12 Chas. 2–6 Anne)

689   Spanish milled eight *real* pieces, 1766 and 1804 (obverse and reverse), in the collection of the American Numismatic Society, New York

690   Dutch *rigsdaler*, 1648 (obverse and reverse), called "Lion" or "Dog" dollars by colonists, in the collection of the American Numismatic Society, New York

691   Spanish-American doubloon (obverse and reverse), struck at Lima, Peru, 1740, in the collection of the American Numismatic Society, New York

692   Queen Anne shilling, 1709 (obverse and reverse), in the collection of the American Numismatic Society, New York

USE OF FOREIGN COINS

As a consequence the coins of all trading nations passed in the American colonies. Though the favorite coins were British and all accounts were kept in pounds, shillings and pence, the balance of trade continuously drained the American supply of British metallic money. From Spain, but more largely from Spanish possessions in America, with both of which the American colonists had a continuously favorable balance of trade, came "pieces of eight" — eight "reals" — worth about six shillings, or one dollar and twenty-five cents. In addition to the Spanish there were also quantities of Dutch coins, particularly the *ducatoun*, equal to three guilders or one dollar and twenty cents, and the rix-dollar (*rigsdaler*), a silver coin from Ceylon and Cape Colony minted in Britain and worth from thirty-six to eighty cents. There were minor coins of copper, brass or tin. Coins of full weight and not badly worn, clipped, or sweated were generally sent abroad in payment for debts, so that light-weight depreciated coins and counterfeits predominated in colonial circulation.

THE FIRST NATIVE COIN

NEW ENGLAND, the leading commercial colony, suffered most from the state of the currency. From 1652 to 1686, Massachusetts operated a mint which issued two coins, a twelve-shilling piece and a six-shilling. These were roughly rounded by clipping and bore upon one plain surface merely the letters N.E., and on the other the Roman numerals XII or VI.

693   Massachusetts twelve-shilling piece (obverse and reverse), in the collection of the American Numismatic Society, New York

694   Oak and Pine Tree shillings, 1652 (obverse and reverse), in the collection of the American Numismatic Society, New York

THE MASSACHUSETTS MINT

PROVING too plain even for the Puritans, these coins were succeeded by others which bore on one side a double ring enclosing a tree with the inscription "Massachusetts" round it, and on the reverse "New England," with the year "1652" and the Roman numeral XII, VI or III. Although minted until 1686, they all bore the date "1652," except a two-shilling piece which was first issued in 1662 and thereafter bore that date. The "tree" on the earlier coins bore little resemblance to any known species, but a later die produced a tree that looked something like a willow. The most famous was a series bearing a symbol of a pine tree or an oak tree, and hence dubbed "pine tree shillings" or "oak tree shillings." In spite of the efforts of Massachusetts to keep them at home, these coins were soon current in most of the colonies and wherever New England traded. When Charles II recovered the throne in 1660, he vigorously protested this invasion of the royal prerogative, but it was not until 1686 that the mint was closed and the colony resorted to paper money.

MARYLAND'S "LORD BALTIMORE" CURRENCY

AT the instigation of Lord Baltimore, coins were struck in England for a shilling, a sixpence and a groat. In regard to these the Maryland Assembly in 1662 ordered that "every householder and freeman take up ten shillings per poll of the newly issued coins for every taxable person under their charge and custody, and pay for all the same in good casked tobacco at two-pence per pound." Since the coins were worth in silver only about seventy-five per cent of their stamped value and the

695   Lord Baltimore six pence (obverse and reverse), in the collection of the American Numismatic Society, New York

tobacco given in exchange for them was rated at the current price, there was room for a profit to Lord Baltimore. About two thousand five hundred pounds of these coins may have been forced upon the colonists, but they soon disappeared, though a few remained in circulation for about ten years. Lord Baltimore himself was arrested at the instigation of the masters of the British mint for violating the king's prerogative.

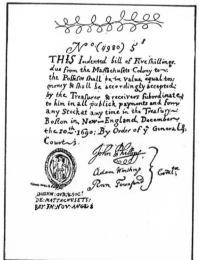

696   First Paper Money in the Colonies, Massachusetts, 1690, in the collection of the American Antiquarian Society, Worcester, Mass.

A DANGEROUS EXPEDIENT

IN 1690, with an empty treasury and the mint closed by royal order, Massachusetts was confronted with the problem of paying immediately the wages of soldiers returning from an unsuccessful expedition against Canada. In this emergency the government of the colony was forced to issue paper promises to pay when the taxes were collected. The total issue was forty thousand pounds, the bills being receivable for taxes and exchangeable for any commodities in the treasury such as European coin, wampum, beaver skins, corn and the like, but were not legal tender — that is, the soldiers could not force them upon any creditor in payment of a debt. Nor did the notes bear interest. Consequently, the soldiers who passed these notes had to accept a discount of forty per cent of their face value. In 1692, the legislature brought the notes to par by making them legal tender and receivable for taxes at five per cent premium over silver. The notes were to be retired and paid in silver when the taxes were collected. This experiment was one of the most disastrous successes in colonial financial history. Until the Revolution all colonies issued paper money.

697 Shilling bill, New Jersey, 1756, in the collection of the
American Numismatic Society, New York

698 Five pound bill, New York, 1758, in the collection of the
American Numismatic Society, New York

699 One and one third dollar bill, Maryland, 1775, in the collection of the American
Numismatic Society, New York

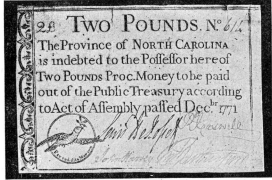

700 Two pound bill, North Carolina 1771, in the collection of the
American Numismatic Society, New York

701 Five shilling bill, Georgia, 1762, in the collection of the
American Numismatic Society, New York

COLONIAL PAPER CURRENCY

THE first Massachusetts bills were redeemable in silver and so were worth their face value. Massachusetts herself in later issues and all the other colonies overlooked the redemption feature. In many cases the promise to redeem was made when the issue was put forth but the promise was forgotten or ignored. Hence the bills rested solely upon the general credit of the issuing colonies. If the notes had been small in number regardless of the fact that they were irredeemable they might have remained at or near their face value. But they were issued in successive floods, therefore each issue depreciated rapidly until it finally failed to pass at all. Then or prior to it a new issue would be made with the same result. At first the notes were put out to pay war debts, then to defray governmental operating expenses and finally to accommodate private individuals. Maryland once issued some as a gift to her taxpayers. The colonial notes were counterfeited wholesale and had the effect of legalized robbery and constituted a debtor's paradise. The efforts of England to suppress the note evil in the colonies created strife between the colonial legislatures and the royal Governors and was one of the underlying causes of the ill-feeling that brought about the Revolution. Later similar evils were to produce political upheaval in the United States.

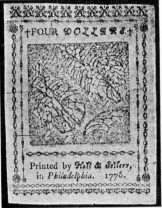

702 Fifty dollar bill (reverse), South Carolina, 1778, in the collection of the American Numismatic Society

703 Fifty dollar bill (obverse), South Carolina, 1778, in the collection of the American Numismatic Society, New York

706 Fifty dollar Congressional bill, Philadelphia, 1778, in the collection of the American Numismatic Society

704 Thirty shilling bill, New Jersey, 1778, in the collection of the American Numismatic Society

705 Four dollar Congressional bill, Philadelphia, 1776, in the collection of the American Numismatic Society

"NOT WORTH A CONTINENTAL"

707 Six dollar Congressional bill, Philadelphia, 1776, in the collection of the American Numismatic Society

THE Continental Congress, which convened on May 10, 1775, was denied the power of levying taxes, yet was made responsible for the financial obligations of the war. Following the example of the colonies, the Continental Congress began within six weeks of its inception to pay its war debts in paper bills of its own printing. Congress urged that the states redeem these bills by taxation according to population, but the states, continuing to issue bills of their own, gave the scantiest heed to the desires of Congress. Before the end of 1775, six million dollars of bills had been put in circulation, and by the close of 1779 no less then two hundred and forty-one million five hundred thousand dollars had been issued. The states in the same time had put out an almost equal amount. The paper bills amounted to a tax on the creditor class to pay the expenses of the war, and debtors, relieved of their obligations, indulged in extravagant luxuries. The phrase "not worth a Continental" became fixed in our language. Most of the two hundred millions of bills were repudiated, although seven million were redeemed in 1790 by a bond issue, one hundred dollars in bills bringing one dollar in specie. The only hard money in the states during the early days of the Revolution came from the British army in payment for supplies and quarters, and from the individual expenditures of the British soldiers. Toward the end of the conflict, French money from similar sources flowed into circulation, and French loans bolstered the flabby Congressional treasury in the latter months of the war. But coin from these two European sources falling into American hands was generally hoarded and the almost worthless Continental bills were used for daily expenditures. Germany's experience with fiat money after 1917 resembled our own between 1775 and 1790.

708   Vermont one cent piece, 1787 (obverse and reverse), in the collection of the American Numismatic Society, New York

709   New Jersey one cent piece, 1786 (obverse and reverse), in the
collection of the American Numismatic Society, New York

STATE COINAGE UNDER THE CONFEDERATION

UNDER the Articles of Confederation adopted in 1778, the states retained the power to coin money coördinately with the Confederation, but the power to regulate its value was given to Congress. Vermont, in 1785, empowered Reuben Harmon, Jr., to establish a mint and to strike copper coins. Harmon operated the mint until 1791, when Vermont was admitted to the new Union. Connecticut, too, having a supply of native copper, established a mint in 1785 and continued until 1789 to issue coins which were frequently counterfeited. Massachusetts (1786–1788), New Jersey (1786–1788) and New York (1787) also authorized the minting of copper cents. Foreign silver coins supplied the needs for larger denominations.

710   Massachusetts one cent piece, 1788 (obverse and reverse), in the
collection of the American Numismatic Society, New York

711   Connecticut one cent piece, 1787 (obverse and reverse), in the
collection of the American Numismatic Society, New York

FIRST FEDERAL COINS

THE Confederation itself began to issue copper coins in 1787 called "Fugios" or "Franklin Pennies," the former because the device on the cent was a dial with the hours expressed on the face with "Fugio" on the left and the date; on the right, a meridian sun above the dial and below it the legend "Mind your Business." The reverse bore thirteen linked circles forming a larger circle in the center of which was "United States" and around it Franklin's sentiment, "We Are One." This was the first Federal coin. Silver coins were not struck until after the Constitution was adopted. The Confederation Congress declared the money unit to be one dollar, the Spanish milled silver dollar being the most widely used coin in America at the time. One such dollar was the equivalent of two hundred of the smallest copper coins in use. At Jefferson's instigation, fractions and multiples of the dollar were placed at decimal ratio. In August, 1786, the Congress of the Confederation fixed the silver content of a dollar at 375.64 grains of pure silver. It authorized half-cents and cents of copper, dimes or tenths of a dollar, double dimes (twenty cents), half dollars and dollars of silver. Gold five-dollar and ten-dollar pieces were also provided for, the gold to be coined at 24.6268 grains pure metal to the dollar. But the mint established in October of that year produced only the cents. Before the dollars could be minted, the Confederation had given way to the Constitutional Republic.

712   "Nova Constellatio" penny; 1783 (obverse and reverse), in the
collection of the American Numismatic Society, New York

713   "Franklin" or "Fugio" penny, 1787 (obverse and reverse), in the
collection of the American Numismatic Society, New York

714   From the painting *Inspecting the First Coins* by John Ward Dunsmore, in Independence Hall, Philadelphia

THE UNITED STATES COINAGE

THE Constitution that defined the powers of the new government which succeeded the Confederation provided among other things that no state should issue bills of credit or coin money and that Congress alone had the power to coin money, regulate its value and the value of foreign coin. Acting under this grant, Congress, in September, 1789, created a Treasury Department. Alexander Hamilton, chosen for its executive head, turned his attention immediately to the establishment of a comprehensive Federal monetary system. After an exceedingly careful survey, he recommended to Congress (January 21, 1791): 1. That the dollar be the money unit; 2. That the silver dollar contain 371.25 grains of pure silver; 3. That the gold dollar contain 24.75 grains of pure gold; 4. That the decimal system be adopted; 5. That coins contain eleven-twelfths pure metal, the alloy for gold to be silver and copper; for silver the alloy to be copper; 6. That coinage be free to all who brought bullion to the mint; 7. That foreign coins be permitted to circulate for a limited time. Congress had this report before it for more than a year when, in April, 1792, it passed an act establishing a coinage system. In March, 1791, it had provided for a mint. The laws as finally enacted were in substantial accord with Hamilton's recommendations but have been modified constantly ever since. Half dimes, the first coins, were struck in October, 1792. Foreign coins were accepted frequently as legal tender until 1857.

715   The first Mint, Philadelphia, 1792, from a photograph. © International News Reel Corporation, New York

716 First type of gold half eagle, 1795 (obverse and reverse), in the collection of the American Numismatic Society, New York

717 Gold half eagle, 1818 (obverse and reverse), in the collection of the American Numismatic Society, New York

BIMETALLISM

718 Silver dollar, 1795 (obverse), in the collection of the American Numismatic Society, New York

THE double standard of coinage was adopted because of the scarcity of the metals and the popularity of silver coins. But the ratio between silver and gold, fixed by Congress at fifteen to one, was disturbed by the production of silver to such an extent that gold dollars by 1818 had entirely disappeared, through hoarding. Silver dollars, commercially more valuable than the legalized Spanish milled dollars, were also hoarded. In 1834, when the

719 Silver dollar, 1795 (reverse), in the collection of the American Numismatic Society, New York

commercial ratio was 15.6 to 1, Congress made the coinage ratio 16 to 1. Silver, thus undervalued at the mint, took flight.

720 Private credit coins issued during the Civil War, in the collection of the American Numismatic Society, New York

TOKEN MONEY

THE law of 1834 so reduced small silver coins in circulation that in 1853 Congress adopted the principle of "token money," by which the actual silver content of a dollar's worth of subsidiary coins was seven per cent less than the content of the silver dollar itself. Private individuals were denied the privilege of taking bullion to the mint and getting fractional silver coins having a greater value than bullion value. The token silver coins were made legal tender up to five dollars by the law of 1853, and to ten dollars in 1879. In suitable amounts small silver coins are always redeemable at par in standard dollars. Since 1853 we have maintained an adequate fractional silver currency. Many persons in defiance of the law issued coins for small denominations on their own credit and for their own account.

721 Silver half dollar, 1853, Token Money (obverse and reverse), in the collection of the American Numismatic Society, New York

722   Boston "shinplaster" of the Civil War, in the collection
      of the Massachusetts Historical Society, Boston

723   Boston "shinplaster" of the Civil War, in the collection of the
      Massachusetts Historical Society, Boston

GREENBACKS AND "SHINPLASTERS"

AT the beginning of the Civil War, owing to the government's laxity in laying taxes to provide Federal income, Congress, although it had grave doubts of the constitutionality of the act, passed a law in February, 1862, authorizing the Secretary of the Treasury to issue one hundred and fifty million dollars of bills of credit in denominations of not less than five dollars. A second issue for a like amount was authorized in June, 1862, and a third for one hundred million dollars in January, 1863. These notes, called United States notes, or, popularly, "greenbacks," were legal tender except for the payment of duties on imports and interest on public debt. They were payable to bearer without interest. Congress at first took steps to redeem these notes and to limit their amount, but such precautions were soon abandoned. Excessive amounts of paper notes of doubtful security caused gold to be quoted at a premium. The greenbacks, in 1864, were worth only thirty-five cents on the dollar; it took about three one dollar notes to buy what could formerly have been bought with one gold dollar. Subsidiary silver coin took flight when the greenbacks had depreciated seven per cent and people used postage stamps for small change, until Congress in 1862 issued fractional currency in paper, derisively termed "shinplasters." The maximum amount of "shinplasters" in circulation at one time was twenty-seven million dollars.

"GREENBACKISM"

THE original intentions of Congress to retire and cancel the greenbacks at the earliest possible moment were thwarted by political pressure from people who desired the inflation of the currency. In the 'sixties and 'seventies, the Middle West and mountain regions, as well as the non-commercial sections of the East, were in a situation akin to that of the colonists of America in the eighteenth century. As the West bought more from the East than it sold there, its coin flowed eastward just as colonial coins were always draining toward Europe. The dearth of coin in the West made the people there long for measures that would furnish quantities of money. They were deluded into believing that paper money issued by their government, even though irredeemable, would cure all their financial ills. That the irredeemable paper money depreciated and so raised prices they saw was beneficial to them. The debtors of the 'sixties and 'seventies, like the debtors of 1750–1800, welcomed the indirect repudiation of debts that depreciating currency offered. The first step toward easy money was taken in March, 1863, when Congress decreed that the greenbacks were not to be converted into bonds at par. Then in 1868 Congress repealed the Contraction Act of 1865 after forty-four million dollars of greenbacks had been retired and canceled.

724   From the cartoon *The Grangers' Dream of Cheap Money* by Dalrymple, in *Puck*, July 8, 1891

FEDERAL PAPER MONEY AT PAR

INSTEAD, in 1870–71, some six millions of the retired green-backs were reissued. These were soon again retired, but in 1873 a total of twenty-six millions of retired greenbacks were again reissued. In 1874, Congress tried to pass the Infla-tion Bill, which would have set a maximum limit of four hundred millions to greenbacks, although only three hun-dred and eighty-two millions were then outstanding. When Grant vetoed this act, Congress made three hundred and eighty-two millions the maximum of greenbacks. In 1877, only one vote in the Senate saved the Specie Re-sumption Act of 1875 (providing for specie resumption on January 1, 1879) from repeal, and the following year Congress enacted a law which forbade any attempt to redeem and cancel the greenbacks then outstanding. Those that thereafter were presented to the Treasury for re-demption were to be reissued. The amount of them then was $346,681,016, and that same amount of Civil War

BROTHER JONATHAN (loq.) "Ah, Specie! Glad to see you, Specie! Been looking for you for some time. Your substitute, Greenback, was very well in his day.; but, fact is, I wanted some Change!"

725   From a cartoon in *Harper's Weekly*, April 9, 1870

indebtedness is still a part of our currency. Since January 1, 1879, greenbacks have passed at face value. This is due to the fact that the Specie Resumption Act of 1875 declared that on and after January 1, 1879, any person who presented a greenback at the Treasury could if he wished secure for it standard money. That this might always be possible, Congress in 1882 au-thorized the Secretary of the Treasury to keep available a sum of one hundred million dollars, to redeem, in case of emergency, any greenbacks or other legal tender notes presented to him. The Gold Standard Act of 1900 pro-vided that the gold reserve be increased to one hundred and fifty millions. If at any time the reserve fund should fall below one hundred millions, the Treasury was em-powered to issue bonds to buy gold with which to restore the fund. With these reserves behind them, our legal tender notes are always convertible at will and hence are as good as gold and pass at their face value.

726   The Republican Caucus Committee, which formulated the Resumption Act in December 1874, from E. B. Andrews, *History of the Last Quarter Century*, New York, 1896, courtesy of Charles Scribner's Sons

THE GOLD EXCHANGE

To set the price of gold in paper money, New York brokers in 1862 established the Gold Exchange, and later the Gold Exchange Bank. Though necessary to the commercial world, this method of settling the price of gold in paper money was capable of manipulation. The gold market was cornered by Jay Gould and a group of politicians, producing the panic of September 24, 1869, known as "Black Friday." With the passage of the Specie Resumption Act in 1875, the days of the Gold Exchange were numbered. In December, 1878, when it was apparent that specie payments would be resumed on January 1, 1879, the premium on gold sank to zero. So quietly, on December 17, 1878, the Gold Exchange ceased.

727   The Scene in the New York Gold Room on Black Friday, September 24, 1869, from E. B. Andrews, *History of the Last Quarter Century*, New York, 1896, courtesy of Charles Scribner's Sons

RAGS FOR OUR WORKING-MEN—SPECIE FOR THE FOREIGNERS.

COLUMBIA. "Dear me, I do think it very wrong that the good nice Trade Dollar (worth one hundred cents) should be sent out of the country for the benefit of the 'heathen Chinee.' For if these gentlemen are permitted to have their own way, it will take a basketful of their Greenbacks (worth ——?) to buy a dinner for my children."

728   Cartoon protesting against trade dollars, by C. S. Reinhart, in *Harper's Weekly*, April 25, 1874

THE SILVER QUESTION

THE silver dollar, as defined by the law of 1834, at no time worth less than one dollar and three cents and sometimes as much as one dollar and seven cents, continued in use in foreign trade with the Far East where they passed by weight. Congress in 1873 omitted the silver dollar but included the overweight trade dollar of four hundred and twenty grains. By this law, the gold dollar of 25.8 grains standard gold became the unit of value and opened the way for further trouble, for although the silver dollar was still a standard unit so that all outstanding silver dollars had all their old rights and privileges, practically we had adopted the single gold dollar standard.

The eastern commercial and banking groups rejoiced in the gold standard because it continued this ratio in the same category with the principal commercial nations of the world. The enhancement of gold value with concurrent shrinkage in prices enabled us to export our products advantageously to foreign markets. On the other hand the farmers saw the prices of their products decline. Since they were in debt, declining prices were catastrophic. Moreover the *amount* of money in circulation was seemingly too small for current transactions. The silver miners were dismayed at the rapid drops in the price of silver and the curtailment of the silver market. Hence the Middle West farmers and Rocky Mountain miners joined forces against eastern merchants and capitalists and Pacific Coast gold producers.

The "Silver Question" that divided the country from about 1875 to 1900 grew out of the great increase in the world's production of silver: for example, our own mines output increased to two million in 1861, twelve million in 1868, twenty-eight million in 1872, forty million in 1875. The output of gold was relatively less each year until 1891, when a rapid advance began. Contemporaneously, the principal nations of the world and many of the secondary ones adopted the single gold standard for their currencies. The increase in the supply of silver when demand for it was falling, and the decrease in the amount of gold when the demand for it was advancing, increased the value of gold where it was the standard, and consequently depressed prices. In America this situation was beneficial to the commercial and banking interests and apparently detrimental to the farming and silver-mining communities.

729   Trade dollar (obverse and reverse), in the collection of the American Numismatic Society, New York

"THE DOLLAR OF OUR DADDIES"

THE farmers and miners thought that the cure for their troubles lay in the restoration of the silver dollar — "the dollar of our daddies." Their representatives urged Congressional action and succeeded in 1878 in passing the Bland-Allison Act which restored to circulation the silver dollar of 1837 as full legal tender except where contracts otherwise specifically provided. Furthermore, the law required the Treasury to buy not less than two nor more than four million dollars of silver per

730 Silver dollar, 1840 (obverse and reverse), in the collection of the American Numismatic Society, New York

month to be coined into silver dollars. At this time the market price of the silver in the silver dollar ($412\frac{1}{2}$ grain) was ninety-three cents. Since this law did not bring relief either to the farmers or the silver miners, Congress in 1890 passed the Sherman Silver Purchase Law, instructing the Treasury to buy four million five

731 Silver dollar, 1890 (obverse and reverse), in the collection of the American Numismatic Society, New York

hundred thousand ounces of silver per month, to be paid in Treasury notes redeemable either in gold or silver at the Treasury's discretion. The effect of this law was to reduce the Treasury gold supply by one hundred and thirty-seven million and to add to the silver supply by one hundred and forty-seven million. The threatened exhaustion of gold reserve and the substitution of depreciated silver, together with other drains on the Treasury, produced a severe depression. Congress in 1893, under Cleveland as President, therefore repealed the Sherman Law of 1890.

THE GOLD STANDARD

THE cry for the free coinage of silver and the inflation of the currency, which had been raised by the People's party, later the Populist party, was taken up by the Democratic party in the 1896 campaign, under the leadership of William Jennings Bryan of Nebraska. Mr. Bryan, being thoroughly imbued with the silver program, swung the Democratic party into line for silver. His "Cross of Gold" speech at the convention is one of the most famous in our annals, gaining him the nomination. His Republican opponent, William McKinley, won by a narrow margin of the popular vote. Since the election was so close, McKinley and the Republicans feared to take a positive stand on the silver issue. It was not until the Spanish-American War of 1898 united the country in support of the administration and forecast its success at the next election that Congress, stimulated by the executive, passed in 1900 the Gold Standard Act. This law declared that the gold dollar of 25.8 grains was the single standard of American money. It created a reserve fund of one hundred and fifty million dollars in gold to redeem the Treasury notes of 1890, and provided that notes of denominations larger than ten dollars be gold notes while the notes smaller than ten dollars were to be silver certificates. Silver bullion in the Treasury was to be used to the extent of one hundred million dollars for subordinate silver money, halves, quarters and dimes. The silver dollar in circulation was to be full legal

tender and the executive was charged with the duty of coöperating in any international effort to restore silver as a standard money. In the campaign of 1900, Bryan again opposed McKinley on the free-silver issue, but McKinley was returned to office by such an increased majority that it was generally felt the nation had endorsed the gold standard policy. This policy has been maintained, even in the trying period of the World War, when the United States was the sole nation to maintain the gold standard within its own limits without a break.

732 Gold double eagle, 1915 (obverse and reverse), in the collection of the American Numismatic Society, New York

CHAPTER XV

BANKING

HAND in hand with the growth of industry and commerce in the United States has gone the development of banking. Without such fiscal institutions, in fact, the expansion of the other two to their present proportions would have been quite impossible. A bank performs functions that are vital to the complete organization of the economic life of a community or a people. It takes existing tangible values, like the goods of a manufacturing concern which have been sold and converts them, through credit, into a form which can be used at once. It does the same thing for prospective values such as the future earnings of a farmer. It creates credit upon which the development of both industry and commerce depends. It makes possible the mobilization of funds. It devises instruments, like checks and drafts, which greatly facilitate exchanges. It performs these services through the carrying out of four basic functions.

The bank receives into its vaults for safe keeping the money of individuals or organizations. Sometimes, if these deposits are in savings banks, they cannot be withdrawn without a certain warning. Ordinarily, however, the bank stands ready to return his money to the depositor upon demand. With the money at its disposal the bank makes loans on credit and discounts the paper of business men. The bank, therefore, is a community reservoir of capital whence the individual may derive funds providing he can offer adequate guarantees they will be returned. Many banks, moreover, issue bank notes, their own promises to pay certain sums on demand to whomsoever presents the notes at their counters. Finally the bank invests its own funds in bonds and, at times, acts as an agency through which securities may be purchased or sold. A century and a half of development in the United States have been required to bring the banks to their present multiplicity of functions in the economic life of the people. During this time Americans have learned many costly lessons.

With the exception of the first and the second Bank of the United States practically all American banks have been private institutions. In the early days the man or group of men who would establish a bank found but few laws or regulations to restrict their independence. The result was the appearance of many unsound institutions which too frequently collapsed in the face of adversity. The surrounding of banks by adequate legal restrictions has been a long and painful process. Nor has it been the only serious problem to be solved. One of the most serious defects of the past was the almost complete lack of coöperation between banks in times of crisis. When such a system or lack of system as we had was tested out, it was found that most banks made every possible effort to strengthen their own reserves even at the expense of other banks. Taking the country as a whole the panic periods demonstrated a serious weakness. With the introduction of the federal reserve system a large measure of coöperation has been achieved.

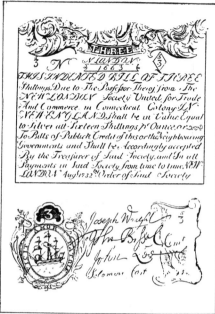

733 Three Shilling Bill, issued by the New London Society United for Trade and Commerce, from *Public Records of the Colony of Connecticut*, Hartford, 1873, after original then in possession of the J. H. Trumbull family

734 Paper Bills Issued by the Bank of North America, 1789, from L. Lewis, *A History of the Bank of North America*, Philadelphia, 1882

COLONIAL FINANCING

IN colonial America several companies or partnerships were formed to supply notes as a medium of exchange. These "banks" used mortgages on real estate as security for their notes. The first "bank" of this kind was "the Fund at Boston in New England," established in 1681. In 1714 another such enterprise was undertaken in Boston, and in 1732 in New London, the "New London Society United for Trade and Commerce" petitioned for a "bank" charter which was refused. The promoters began business, however, without a charter and issued a considerable number of notes which attained a respectable circulation in Connecticut. Groups in Rhode Island (1731), New Hampshire (1735), and Massachusetts (1740) inaugurated similar "banks" but they all fell before the ban of official disapproval. Robert Morris in 1781 at Philadelphia gave America its first real bank, the Bank of North America. After the Revolution the bank financed the revival of Philadelphia commerce, making large profits thereby. Since the original charter secured from the Confederation was of doubtful legality, the bank secured a second charter from Pennsylvania, which was later withdrawn because of popular opposition. Threatened, however, with the loss of the bank to Wilmington, the legislature of Pennsylvania in 1787 granted a new charter to the bank. After the

735 Thomas Willing, 1731–1821, president of the Bank of North America, 1782–91, from L. Lewis, *A History of the Bank of North America*, Philadelphia, 1882

Revolution social unrest, growing out of widespread private debt with its train of poverty and imprisonment, found expression in the growth of a paper money party. Seven states issued paper currency while in the remainder demonstrations in favor of paper became frequent. Rhode Island went so far as to make the refusal of its paper medium a penal offense. The famous test case of Trevett against the Newport butcher, Weeden, resulted in a decision declaring the act unconstitutional, but popular sentiment was demonstrated in the failure of four of the judges rendering the decision to be returned at the next election.

" The 25th Ultimo, an important Cause (the first that ever occurred in this State) on a Complaint against a Butcher, for refusing the new Paper Medium, came on before the Superior Court, then sitting at Newport.——General Varnum and Mr. Marchant (Attornies for the Defendant) spoke long and very ably against the Paper-Money Acts, adducing a Variety of the best Authorities to prove them unconstitutional, and repugnant to every Idea of natural Right in Property honestly acquired.——Mr. Goodwin (Attorney for the Plaintiff) spoke as well on the Subject as could be expected.——Four of the Judges appeared decidedly against the Acts, and two of them spoke to the Subject.——The Chief Justice did not publicly declare his Sentiments, as the Cause was decided without his Voting. A large Concourse of People attended the Trial, and when the Decision of the Court was publicly announced, it was received with an almost universal Plaudit.——The Plea was to the Cognizance of the Court.——Two Points were insisted upon, and unanimously agreed to by the Court.——First, The Act of Assembly erected Trials before Special Courts, uncontroulable by the Supreme Judicial Power of the State.——Particularly in this, that the Judges of the Supreme Court were made Judges, in concurrent Jurisdiction with the Courts of Common Pleas; and therefore, whenever applied to by legal Process, to commend or prohibit the Special Courts, in any of their Excesses, their Judgment, as Supreme, would be biassed by a former Decision upon the same Question.——Second, The Act denies the Trial by Jury.——The Trial by Jury is a Matter of constitutional Right; and therefore above the Reach of the Legislature, who are formed upon the Constitution."

736 Account of the Newport Butcher's Case, in *United States Chronicle: Political, Commercial, and Moral*, Providence, R. I., Oct. 5, 1786

737   The Girard National Bank, from J. G. Leach, *The History of the Girard
       National Bank of Philadelphia, 1832-1902*, Philadelphia, 1902

738   Original home of the Massachusetts
       National Bank, 1784, from a print in pos-
       session of the publishers

THE FIRST BANK OF THE UNITED STATES

As a result of these chaotic finances, Federalists like Hamilton realized the necessity of a banking system which should assign to the central government a directing and coördinating rôle. Massachusetts in 1784 had granted a charter to the "Bank of Massachusetts," while Vermont and New York had soon afterward taken similar steps. But these isolated state banks had failed to afford in time of distress any general relief. They were totally incapable of directing the budget of an increasingly complex Federal Government such as Hamilton visualized. In spite of strenuous Jeffersonian opposition, the advocates of a central banking system succeeded in 1791 in obtaining a charter for a National Bank. The bank had an authorized capital of ten million, of which the United States subscribed one fifth, the other eight million being taken by the public within two hours after the books were opened. The principal seat of the bank was in Philadelphia, but branches were established in Boston, New York, Baltimore, Norfolk, Charleston, Savannah, Washington and New Orleans. One of its purposes was to perform for the government the services which a bank offers to an individual — to act as a depository for public funds and to make short-term loans to the Treasury in the event of temporary need. In the next two decades the number of banks increased steadily. State governments took measures to establish new banks or to improve their old ones. Private commercial enterprises such as the Delaware & Hudson Canal Company began to establish credit houses, which were soon incorporated as banks.

739   Bank of the Delaware & Hudson Com-
       pany, 13 Wall Street, from an engraving
       by H. Fossette, courtesy of the Delaware
       & Hudson Railroad Company

Mr. POULSON,

By inserting the annexed list of Banking Institutions in the United States, in your paper, you will confer an obligation on
                              A SUBSCRIBER.

Philadelphia, Feb. 12th. 1806.

Number of Banks in the United States.

MAINE.
Portland 2.—Wiscasset 1.—Hallowell 1. } 4

NEW HAMPSHIRE.
Portsmouth 2.—Exeter 1. } 3

PENNSYLVANIA.
Philadelphia 4.—Lancaster 1.—Pittsburg 1. } 6

MASSACHUSETTS.
Boston 5.—Salem 2.—Newburyport 1.—New Bedford 1.—Plymouth 1.—Nantucket 1.—Marblehead 1.—Gloucester 1.—Beverly 1.—Worcester 1.—Northampton 1. } 16

RHODE ISLAND.
Providence 2.—Newport 3.—Bristol 1.—Warren 1.—Westerly 1. } 8

CONNECTICUT.
New Haven 1.—Hartford 1.—Norwich 1.—Middleton 1.—New London 1. } 5

NEW YORK.
City of New York 4.—Albany 1.—Hudson 1. } 6

NEW JERSEY.
Newark 1—Trenton 1.—Jersey 1. } 3

DELAWARE.
Wilmington 1. 1

MARYLAND.
Baltimore 3. 3

DISTRICT OF COLUMBIA.
Washington 1.—Georgetown 1.—Alexandria 2. } 4

VIRGINIA.
Richmond 1.—Norfolk 2.—Fredericksburg 1. } 4

NORTH CAROLINA.
Newbern 1. 1

SOUTH CAROLINA.
Charleston 3. 3

GEORGIA.
Savannah 1. 1

Total number of Banks in the United States. 68

740   Distribution of Banks, 1806, from a newspaper clipping in the New York Historical Society

SECOND BANK OF THE UNITED STATES

IN 1811 the renewal of the charter granted to the Bank of the United States became a political issue. The Federalist party had lost power. The Republicans denounced the Bank bitterly, and by a close vote in Congress, the charter was lost. Stephen Girard bought its assets and under a state charter continued it as Girard's Bank.

The War of 1812 left our national finances in a deplorable condition. President Madison urged a second United States Bank, and on April 10, 1816, such a bank was authorized. Its early operations were marked by irregularities. The prudence of Langdon Cheves, who became president of the institution in 1819, made enemies of many men who had been more easily accommodated under the first president, as well as of private and state banks the notes of which were refused. The greatest foe of the Bank was to be the democracy of the newer section of the country who suffered in the depression of 1819, and when this democracy elected Andrew Jackson to the Presidency the Bank was doomed.

During the years immediately following the War of 1812 there had sprung up, especially throughout the rapidly growing West, an enormous number of new banks, largely of an unstable if not fraudulent character. The consequent high overissue of notes stimulated a feverish speculation in western lands and internal improvements, in farms, crops, merchandise, and goods for a foreign export the demand for which was vastly overestimated. A crisis was inevitable. As bank after bank suspended payment throughout 1818, they became so unpopular that by 1819 candidates for Congress and the state legislature were pledging themselves to oppose the establishment of any bank whatsoever during their terms of office. The attempt of the Second Bank of the United States to establish a specie basis for its notes only served further to arouse the suspicions of those suffering from the panic. By 1832 the renewal of the Bank charter had become the political issue of the day, and Jackson's reëlection by implication closed its career as a national bank.

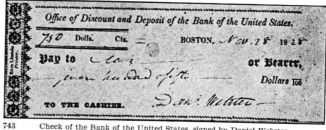

743   Check of the Bank of the United States, signed by Daniel Webster, from F. A. Cleveland, *First Lessons in Finance*

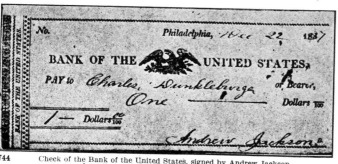

744   Check of the Bank of the United States, signed by Andrew Jackson, from F. A. Cleveland, *First Lessons in Finance*

EARLY BANKING REFORMS

THE first attempt to restrict the issue of state and private banknotes and thus remedy the demoralizing fluctuations which constituted one of the worst features of our early banks, was made by the Suffolk Bank of Boston. It offered to redeem at par all notes received from banks throughout the country, provided that the issuing banks had deposited with the Suffolk a permanent redemption fund. Accepting banks discovered their credit so boosted that their notes passed at par in all

745   Joshua Forman, from Elias W. Leavenworth,
      Leavenworth Genealogy, Syracuse, N. Y., 1873

parts of the United States. Nearly all the solvent banks of New England joined the system. The state legislature strengthened the system in 1845 by prohibiting banks from paying over their counters any banknotes but their own. This forced the country banks to send notes, received elsewhere in trade, to the

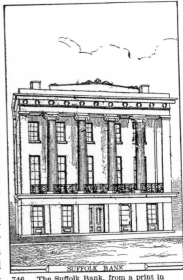

746   The Suffolk Bank, from a print in
         possession of the publishers

Suffolk for redemption. New York State enacted in 1829 a scheme of bank insurance which Joshua Forman had proposed. The act provided that every bank chartered after 1829 should pay a certain per cent into a central bank fund, from which, in case of failure, it was privileged to draw an amount sufficient to meet its outstanding liabilities. Although this system gave New York a stability hitherto found only in Massachusetts, an antimonopoly party, the Loco Focos, still attacked the remaining evil of legislative jurisdiction over the granting of bank charters. In 1838 they put through the state legislature an act whereby any bank could open, provided it had turned over to the state comptroller a certain definite amount of collateral security, in the form of bonds, stocks, or mortgages on productive real estate.

747   From a cartoon *The Times*, used in the Loco-Foco Campaign of 1837, showing the evil effects
           of the existing banking system, in the New York Historical Society

748   Run on the Bank, from J. S. Gibbons, *The Banks of New York*, New York, 1858

THE BANKING SYSTEM STILL UNSOUND

IN 1833 the government deposits were removed from the United States Bank by heavy drafts upon it, which were deposited in state banks in New York, Philadelphia and Baltimore, and cashed within a short period. The Girard Bank had originally been selected as a place of deposit for public funds, but by the close of the year twenty-three banks in all had been chosen for this purpose. Although these "pet" banks were carefully selected and their finances thoroughly investigated, charges of political favoritism were nevertheless made. By an act of Congress passed in 1836, at least one bank in each state and territory, wherever possible, was to be designated by the Secretary of the Treasury as a depository for public funds. Each bank chosen was required to redeem its notes and bills in specie on demand, and it was not to hold government deposits to an amount greater than three fourths of its capital stock. Despite the crisis following the removal of deposits in 1833, the year 1836 found the country in the midst of its greatest boom. Expansion and inflation marked every department of commercial life. Railroads and other internal improvements had been built to meet the demands for transportation. The sale of western lands had increased four hundred per cent between 1834 and 1836, much of it speculative. Banking capital boasted a one hundred per cent increase between 1830 and 1838. In 1829 three hundred and thirty state banks were in existence; in 1836, there were

six hundred and seventy-seven. In the midst of all this the specie circular of 1836, requiring that all government land should be paid for in specie, came as a blow to speculators and honest purchasers alike. The year 1837 saw a precipitation of panic conditions which were in part a phase of international depression. The failure of the wheat crop, simultaneous with the collapse of New Orleans cotton houses, brought about a final crisis, and on May 10, specie payments began to be suspended in New York banks.

BROTHER JONATHAN'S APPEAL.

749   From a cartoon in the New York Historical Society

750   Wall Street in 1850, from a print. © D. Appleton & Co., New York

THE INDEPENDENT TREASURY SYSTEM (OR SUB–TREASURY)

As early as 1834 a proposal had been introduced into Congress for the creation of an Independent Treasury System. In the absence of the National Bank, protection from other sources had been necessary against the alarming danger of loss to the government by the failure of banks and by speculation in money derived from government deposits. In 1837, more sustained attempts had been made to push the bill through Congress, but its Democratic sponsors had been defeated by the opposition of Henry Clay and Daniel Webster, campaigning for the reëstablishment of a powerful National Bank. After three years of party controversy, President Van Buren finally succeeded on July 4, 1840, in securing a Congressional majority for the Independent Treasury Act, which provided that the government's money should be received and kept in the central treasury and in its own vaults at New York, Philadelphia, Boston, Charleston, St. Louis and New Orleans — with the added provision that all receipts and disbursements should be in gold and silver. On August 13, 1841, the Whigs, who had succeeded to power with the program of overturning all that Van Buren had accomplished, repealed the former act, and, during the remaining years of Tyler's administration, wrangled ineffectively over a proper substitute. With the return of the Democrats under Polk, the independent treasury was reëstablished on August 6, 1846. The new act was patterned on that of July 4, 1840. There

were the same centers of deposit, the same general system of financial control. Treasury notes, however, were now acceptable along with specie, and government funds were not to be lent or deposited in banks. As the system began once more to function, a more settled state of finances resulted, in spite of the noisy opposition of various state banks. During the period of financial stress caused by the Mexican War, the new system was of great assistance. It never ceased, however, to be a disturbing factor in the money market. Two defects were that (1) money collected in taxes was hoarded in the Treasury and Sub-treasuries, and (2) when deposited in selected banks upon sudden withdrawal might start a money stringency.

751 Stock Exchange in 1850, from a print. © D. Appleton & Co., New York

No. 14.   New-York Clearing House,

March 23rd 1887

Debit   NATIONAL BANK, Amt. rec'd $ _957,853 13_

Credit   "   "   brought $ _5,001,319 27_

$_____ Debit balance due Clearing House

Cr. bal. due   NATIONAL BANK, $ _1,043,466 14_

Ths. Rogers   Settling Clerk

752   Clearing House Certificate, from *Harper's Weekly*, Aug. 27, 1887

CLEARING HOUSES

WITH the increasingly pronounced accentuation of New York city as the financial capital of the United States, the necessity there for a more mobile supply of credit and capital became pressing. Even during the prosperous decade of the 'forties, and in the years immediately following the discovery of gold in California, financial transactions in New York were effected slowly, because of hours of wasted activity in sending from one bank to its creditor the proper amount of money. There was danger that in a period of deflation credit might be destroyed. To facilitate mobility a large Clearing House was opened on Wall Street, October 11, 1853. Viewed with the perspective of the intervening years of banking history, this date must emerge in its true significance. Healthier banking conditions resulted immediately. Bankers were forced to be less reckless, when daily settlements and reports revealed their true condition. All of the leading New York banks became members; definite rules and regulations of procedure were drawn up; and instead of being forced to send out messengers with packages of actual money for the various other banks, each member had only to send an accredited representative to the central meeting place, where clearing house credit certificates were sufficient to balance accounts. One of the most serious defects of the banking system had been removed. Boston introduced the clearing-house system in 1856, and Philadelphia followed two years later.

753   Interior of the New York Clearing House, from *Harper's Weekly*, Aug. 27, 1887

PANIC OF 1857

IN 1857 there were one thousand four hundred and sixteen banks in the country. Seventeen years of unprecedented railroad building and commercial expansion along all lines had produced inflation with attendant high prices. The unfavorable balance of trade, caused by the movement of California gold to Europe, seemed incapable of remedy. In 1854 there had been scattered bank failures, but no city had been forced to suspend specie payment. By 1857, however, a sharp reaction was inevitable and the failure of the Ohio Life & Trust Company, the tower of western monetary strength, precipitated a crisis in which provincial banks, lacking the means for concerted action, struggled for cash. In one day four and a half millions of specie were withdrawn. In New York suspension of specie payment lasted for sixty days.

NEW YORK to PHILADELPHIA BANK. "Going to suspend yourself, eh? Is that your Brotherly Love?"

754   From a cartoon in *Harper's Weekly*, Oct. 17, 1857

755   Curbstone Brokers in New York, from *The Illustrated London News*, July 2, 1864

NATIONAL BANKS

ALTHOUGH urged by the Secretary of the Treasury, Salmon P. Chase, and by Lincoln, Congress twice in 1862 and 1863 refused to sanction a National Bank system. The opposition consisted for the most part of state bank champions. John Sherman, the sponsor of the new bill, finally succeeded on February 25, 1863, in making it law. One purpose of this act was to secure a market for the government bonds floated to finance the war. In this, it was a grievous disappointment, for less than four per cent of the borrowed money was furnished by these banks. Another purpose was the establishment of banks which could issue notes secured by government bonds. The laws regulating the national banks have been changed but they have all been concerned with the same banking matters, the specification of the amount and location of national bank reserves, and the minimum capital for the inauguration of national banks in communities of different sizes. It has also regulated the character and amount of loans or discounts and erected safeguards around the issue of bank notes by these institutions. Finally the laws have provided for reports and inspection. The name "national" gave an added strength to reputation and credit. Then, too, national banks could be designated as depositories of public money. The number of national banks has generally been smaller than the number of state banks but the capital, surplus, deposits, cash and loans of national banks for a long time exceeded those of private and state banks. One of the greatest commercial blessings afforded by national banks was the furnishing of a currency identical in style and of uniform value throughout the nation.

756   National City Bank of New York, largest national bank in the United States, courtesy of the National City Bank, New York

757   Dartmouth National Bank, Hanover, a small country national bank, courtesy of the Dartmouth National Bank, Hanover, N. H.

758   Office of Jay Cooke and Company, from
        Harper's Weekly, Oct. 11, 1873

759   Run on the Union Trust Co., New York,
        from *Harper's Weekly* Oct. 11, 1873

PANICS OF 1873 AND 1893

WITHOUT the National Bank system the war's drain on national finances might have proved fatal, and the unprecedented commercial expansion, which followed the conclusion of peace, curtailed. Yet with all the benefits which ensued, there was a serious weakness in the form of organization. A monopoly of banker's deposits was concentrated in the hands of fifteen of the national banks, centered for the most part in New York city, and holding from seventy to ninety per cent of the country banks' deposits. The nation as a whole was still dangerously immobile. In the summer months of 1873 there appeared symptoms of a sharp reaction from the inflation of the frenzied railroad building in the West. In September New York banks began to fail. The final blow came on the eighteenth with the closure of Jay Cooke & Company, and Fisk & Hatch. Clearing House loan certificates failed to relieve the inelasticity of credit. On the 20th the Stock Exchange closed. In this panic and later ones, the bank notes themselves were never distrusted, as in 1837 and 1857. The depositors, in demanding their money, were as willing to accept notes as specie. In 1873 suspension of payment was never complete. Twenty years later, at the end of a similar cycle of headlong railroad building followed by depression here and in Europe, there was complete suspension over the country. Legal tender notes sent in to the Treasury for redemption had increased from six million dollars in 1890 to one hundred and two million in 1893. Uneasiness increased as Treasury holdings dropped below one hundred million. Starting with the failure of the Philadelphia & Reading railroad, the panic spread to the Erie, the Northern Pacific, the Union Pacific and the Santa Fé. One hundred and fifty-eight national, one hundred and seventy-two state, and one hundred and seventy-seven private banks failed in the first nine months of 1893.

760   Scene on the New York Stock Exchange, from *Frank Leslie's Illustrated
        Newspaper*, May 18, 1893

DISAPPOINTED DEPOSITORS BESIEGING KNICKERBOCKER TRUST CO.'S BUILDING AFTER BANK HAD CLOSED ITS DOORS.

KNICKERBOCKER TRUST REPORTED AS READY TO ASK FOR A RECEIVER

President Higgins Appeals in Vain to Heads of Other Trust Companies. Att'y-General Jackson in Town to Consult with Bank Superintendent.

CORTELYOU ISSUES A REASSURING STATEMENT

761   From *The New York American*, Oct. 23, 1907

PANIC OF 1907

THE financial uncertainty from which the country suffered during the decade of the 'nineties was attributable in the main to the unsettled status of the currency question. The legal tender notes sent to the Treasury for redemption increased from six million in 1890 to one hundred and two million in 1893. Just prior to the panic, the Treasury reserve dropped considerably below the customary minimum of a hundred million. The resulting uneasiness in the public mind was one of the factors contributing to the crisis, while it was the repeal of the Sherman Silver Bill that finally restored a moderate stability. The attention of statesmen and of the public was diverted from the equally serious economic problem of the most efficacious reorganization of the banking system. The first years of the new century witnessed an over-expansion of credit throughout the entire world, with an enormous development in our domestic and foreign trade, with huge harvests, and with a market expanded by the million new immigrants arriving each year. By 1906, the cash reserve of the National Banks had dropped to the low figure of thirteen per cent. State banks with precariously low reserves had increased threefold in the preceding decade, and there were over five times as many trust companies, with even lower reserves. As increasing tension began to be manifested in the year following the wild speculation of August, 1906, the New York banks found themselves in the position of central banks, with insufficient reserves. Call loans, "notoriously unliquid during a crisis," aggravated the situation. On October 23, 1907, the crisis which had been precipitated by the questionable speculation of Charles W. Morse and F. A. Heinz, reached its climax with the failure of the Knickerbocker Trust Company. The attempts of the Federal Government to come to the aid of the National Banks, as it had done in the past, proved inadequate. J. P. Morgan's private capital and private prestige were alone able to prevent chaos.

GOV'T AND PRIVATE CAPITAL RELIEVE WALL STREET STRAIN.

TRUST CO. OF AMERICA MEETS PAYMENTS PROMPTLY—WESTINGHOUSE TROUBLE A CENTRE OF DISTURBANCE.

Call Money Rates Soar to 96 Per Cent. and Stocks Reach New Low Records—Westinghouse Trouble Caused by Shortage of Funds—Trust Co. of America's Prompt Payments a Bright Feature—Knickerbocker Fails to Open Its Doors.

762   From *The Wall Street Journal*, October 24, 1907

Even more impressive than the immense throng which filled Wall and Broad streets was the spectacle of the Secretary of the Treasury—a man of few words, but large executive ability—sitting calmly all day in the office of Assistant Treasurer Fish, at the Sub-Treasury, assuring all his callers of his determination to do everything which his powers as Secretary permitted him to do for the protection of the financial situation.

He was impressive because he represented the great authority and strength of the United States Government. His presence there during the scenes of excitement which were enacted outside recalled the memorable words of James A. Garfield, uttered from the Custom House steps on the day following the assassination of President Lincoln:

"God reigns and the Government at Washington still lives."

Scarcely less impressive than this was the spectacle of J. Pierpont Morgan in his office directly opposite from the Sub-Treasury representing the power of private capital directed for the relief of the financial situation. Mr. Morgan represented confidence. It is significant how in this time of strain Wall Street has turned to Mr. Morgan as to the only individual in private life who seemed to have the prestige and the ability to lead it out of danger, and in this connection it is noteworthy that Mr. Morgan has come out of the stress and storm of the past two years without any cloud upon his fame as a financial leader.

Impressive also was the spectacle of the Clearing House committee representing the associated banks of New York putting behind every weak institution the aggregated power of all the banks. This represented the great principle of cooperation in banking and never before has the Clearing House given a more remarkable example of its power to cope with a crisis than it has at this time. It is noteworthy that it is doing this without resorting to the expedient of Clearing House certificates, a method which would involve the stigma of practical suspicion of specie payments.

763   From *The Wall Street Journal*, October 24, 1907

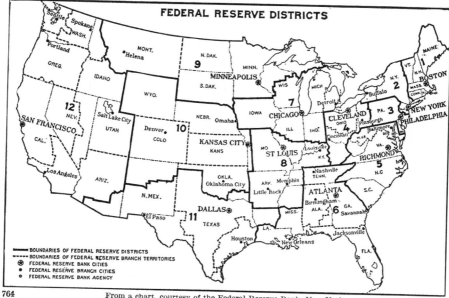

FEDERAL RESERVE DISTRICTS

764

BOUNDARIES OF FEDERAL RESERVE DISTRICTS
BOUNDARIES OF FEDERAL RESERVE BRANCH TERRITORIES
⊛ FEDERAL RESERVE BANK CITIES
• FEDERAL RESERVE BRANCH CITIES
○ FEDERAL RESERVE BANK AGENCY

From a chart, courtesy of the Federal Reserve Bank, New York

NATIONAL MONETARY COMMISSION

OUR national bank system was discovered at last to have several grave defects. There was no real central-ization, the reserve requirements were unsatisfactory, there was slight elasticity, the exchange and transfer systems were cumbersome, and the relationship with the Federal Treasury was defective. Nothing was done, until the panic of 1907 aroused the country to the weaknesses of our currency and banking system. Tacked to the Aldrich-Vreeland Emergency Currency Act of 1908 was a provision authorizing the appointment of a National Monetary Commission to study the banking system and to draft remedial legislation. In 1910 this commission suggested a plan for reform. It formed the basis for the law of 1913 that inaugurated the Federal Reserve system. The Federal Reserve Act (passed December, 1913) resulted in the opening of twelve Federal Reserve banks (November, 1914), each organized in an assigned district with the local national banks as compulsory, and with such state banks and trust companies as might care to join (subject to rules of the system) as voluntary stockholders. In form, the reserve banks are corporations organized much like other banks but differing in important details. Each has a board of nine directors of which six are chosen

by the stockholding banks, three representing the banks themselves and three the business in-terests of the district, while three are named by the Federal Reserve Board at Washington to represent the public. The latter board consists of six members named by the President and con-firmed by the Senate while the Secretary of the Treasury and the Comptroller of the Cur-rency are ex-officio mem-bers. Before July 1, 1922, there had been only five appointive members.

765

Federal Reserve Board, 1923. © Harris & Ewing, Washington

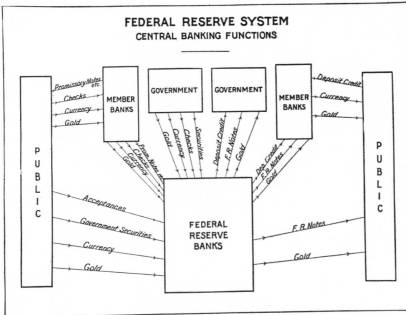

FEDERAL RESERVE SYSTEM
CENTRAL BANKING FUNCTIONS

766   From a chart, courtesy of the Federal Reserve Bank, New York

FUNCTIONS OF THE FEDERAL RESERVE BANKS

THE reserve banks exercise functions quite different from those of the ordinary bank. Their business relations are chiefly with the stock-holding banks and with the Treasury; but they may buy paper of specified kinds in the open market. Their chief duties are to hold the reserves of members (which must be deposited with them), and to control the issue of currency — the so-called "reserve notes." In order to promote the use of the check and deposit system, and to avoid the growth of excessive collection charges, the reserve banks act as clearing houses for their members, and operate a gold settlement fund for the purpose of national clearing. In order to control the growth and contraction of credit, the reserve banks, subject to the approval of the Reserve Board, name rates of rediscount and fix buying rates for open market paper; and, by the proper use of these rates, act upon prices and control the movement of gold out of, and into, the country. The combined capital of the twelve Federal Reserve banks on May 25, 1927, was $129,030,000,000 and the surplus $228,775,000,000. On December 31, 1926, there were seven thousand nine hundred and six national banks and one thousand three hundred and fifty-four state banking institutions members of the system.

767   Board of Governors of the Federal Reserve System, composed of the Chief Executives or Operating Officers of the District Banks. © Harris & Ewing, Washington

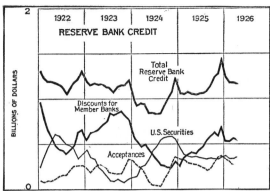

768   One of three shifts of clerks, which together work twenty-four
hours a day in the Federal Reserve Bank, New York, from a photograph, courtesy of the Federal Reserve Bank, New York

769   From a chart, courtesy of the Federal Reserve Bank,
New York

WORK OF THE RESERVE SYSTEM

THE reserve system, however, is not merely significant because it is a great system of central banking which now controls more than one third of the available reserve gold of the world. Its importance is far broader than any of a purely financial sort. Although, when it came into being, its authors had no conception of the use to which it would immediately be put as the result of war, its earliest service on a large scale was in placing more than twenty-five billion dollars of Liberty bonds and certificates and in carrying on the entire financing of the World War from the time the United States entered the struggle. Superseding the United States subtreasury system, it vastly economized gold and entirely obviated the necessity of movements of specie from one part of the country to another. Its clearing system, the greatest in history, has eliminated intersectional transfers of currency, and greatly reduced the enormous outstanding indebtedness or "float" in the form of unpaid checks which constituted so serious a menace to banking safety in former times. Its note currency, flexible and amply secured, is used the world over, as was the case with sterling before the war. The law allows the Federal Reserve banks to purchase and sell certain classes of paper in the open market. The open market consists of banking concerns and individual traders who stand ready, for a consideration, to buy or sell two-name commercial paper, bankers and trade acceptances, municipal warrants, and Treasury certificates and other forms of standard obligations. Rates at which the various types of paper can be bought and sold are regularly quoted. Federal Reserve banks are required by law to hold forty per cent gold against notes in actual circulation, and thirty-five per cent in gold or lawful money against net demand deposits. In spite of the numerous stringencies and serious embarrassments which have beset the business and financial community of the country and of other nations during the disturbances consequent to the war and its after effects, the foundations of the American business structure have remained secure, without the slightest suggestion of banking or financial panic even during the most hazardous periods in world affairs. Commercial credit has been strengthened and commercial paper standardized. The actual saving in collection charges and interest resulting from the working of the system is by many estimated at more than one hundred million dollars cash per annum, and its indirect benefits are undoubtedly many times that sum.

770   The Federal Reserve Bank Building, New York,
from a photograph, courtesy of the Federal Reserve
Bank, New York

CHAPTER XVI

A NATION ON WHEELS

LAND transportation for thousands of years showed scarcely any advance. Tut-ankh-Amen and Thomas Jefferson each traveled to a state ceremony astride the same kind of steed. In America, however, the nineteenth century opened amidst considerable popular enthusiasm for highway improvement. The turnpike era was in full swing and the stagecoach was passing through the heyday of its development. Turnpikes continued to be built well into the middle years of the nineteenth century but the turnpike era had long since passed. First the canal and then the railroad absorbed popular attention. The turnpike which made but a beginning of the solution of the problems of surface, grades, and bridges was considered ample for American needs.

The last decade of the century saw a revival of interest in roads. The "safety bicycle" with low wheels (when compared with the earlier high-wheeled type) and pneumatic tires became a popular craze giving a vast number of urban people a quite unwonted interest in the character and condition of public highways. The League of American Wheelmen pressed for better roads, or, if they could not be obtained, for cycle paths along the roadsides. The vogue of the bicycle, however, was short. Before 1900 the automobile had become a mechanical fact and only awaited its commercial development.

Within the first quarter of the twentieth century the new invention was to transform the countryside and to influence fundamentally American life. No other American industry, with the possible exception of the "movies" and the radio, has had such an instantaneous success as that of the automobile. The whole population of the United States in 1925 could have been put into automobiles at the same time, for there was one motor car for every five and eight-tenths persons.

In thirty years the automobile has changed nearly every aspect of our national life. It has brought traffic congestion to cities and has made the country more accessible. Schools and churches have been modified. Farm life has been revolutionized. Mining and lumbering have been quickened. Manufacturing has been fundamentally over-hauled to meet the demands for mass production, standardized units, and interchangeable parts. The automobile is the most taxed commodity in the nation and yields to governments a greater revenue than any other single thing. Electric and steam railways have been both harmed and aided by the new transportation on the highways. Automobiles enter largely into our exports, while our imports are swelled by the imports they require.

As a result of the automobile the nation is crossed and recrossed by an ever increasing mileage of broad highways with hard surfaces, easy grades, wide curves and durable bridges. Along these rush countless motor cars until at times the congestion on the country highway almost equals that of the city street. There is hardly a department of life, either for the individual or for the state, that has not been influenced for good or ill by this machine which prior to the opening of the twentieth century was practically unknown.

ANCESTORS OF THE AUTO

CAREFUL research has found what is believed to be the earliest record of a self-operating wagon in an illustrated Italian manuscript on the *Art of War*, written about 1430. This paper, preserved in the Uffizi Museum of Florence, contains a drawing of a wagon propelled by sails. The records of the city of Memming for 1447 tell of a mysterious covered wagon that moved under its own power. The first illustrated book printed in Italy in 1460,

771   Drawing of self-propelled vehicle by Sir Isaac Newton, reproduced in the *Scientific American*, Jan. 6, 1917

written on the subject of military art by Roberto Balturio, presents a picture of a cart actuated by paddle wheels beating against the air. In 1479, the city of Antwerp paid twelve pounds in silver to one Gilles de Dorn for a wagon that ran itself by means of concealed machinery. Sailing wagons come into the records again about 1600 when Maurice Prince of Orange is said to have constructed one. The next authentic drawing of a self-propelled vehicle is found in the papers of Sir Isaac Newton. His conception was a steam boiler mounted on wheels that moved forward by the kick of the escaping steam against the air. It is unlikely that it would have run if he had built it.

772   The Cugnot steam wagon for ordinary roads, 1771, original in the Conservatoire National des Arts et Métiers, Paris

THE FIRST "AUTOMOBILES"

IN the Conservatoire des Arts et Métiers in Paris, one may still see the first automobile that actually generated its own power and was really run. It was designed and built in 1771 by a French military engineer named Nicholas Joseph Cugnot, and was intended for a gun carriage which was propelled by a self-contained steam engine. Apparently it was never put to any practical use. Shortly after Cugnot, an Englishman, W. Symington, built and ran a steam coach (1784), and the American, Oliver Evans, in the same year and again in 1804 put steam wagons on the highway. From the opening of the nineteenth century until the 'thirties about a dozen Englishmen planned, built and operated a number of steam road wagons. Two parallel developments were going on in England, one the steam road coaches, the other railways for horse-drawn vehicles. When Stephenson put these ideas together and introduced the steam locomotive on a railroad he sounded the knell of the steam highway coaches. In 1831, Parliament carefully investigated both rail and road steam-vehicles to decide which to foster by public moneys, reported in favor of the railroad and banned steam omnibuses from public roads.

773   Sir Goldsworthy Gurney's steam carriage of 1827, courtesy of the Deutsches Museum, Munich

774   A Serpollet three-wheel carriage, 1889, courtesy of the Deutsches Museum, Munich

INVENTIONS IN STEAM, GAS, AND ELECTRIC CARS

L. SERPOLLET, a French engineer, invented the "flash boiler" wherein water was instantaneously changed to steam and by which the amount of the steam could be regulated, both by the flow of the water and by variation in the heat intensity of the fire. He also substituted petroleum products — kerosene and gasoline — for fuels in the place of wood and coal and thus eliminated dirt, smoke, ashes and difficulties of fire control. The combination of these two new features — boiler and fuel — enabled Serpollet to produce a small compact light mechanism that could be attached to existing carriages and buggies. Lenoir's gas engine, exhibited in Paris in 1878, stimulated two Germans, Gottlieb Daimler and Karl Benz, to improve the gas engine itself and to introduce better ignition and carburetion. In the field of electricity advances were being made with storage batteries. By the end of the 'eighties improvements in batteries had reached a stage that made vehicle propulsion by stored electricity feasible.

EARLY AMERICAN STEAM AUTOMOBILES

THE American reflection of the British efforts to produce a steam highway vehicle is represented by a half dozen men. The first American after Oliver Evans was Thomas Blanchard, who invented a steam car in 1825. Fifteen years later, J. K. Fisher built several steam vehicles for highway work in New York. Richard Dudgeon, as a result of a bet in 1855, built a steam road wagon in 1857. Other Americans interested in steam cars were James A. and Henry A. House of Bridgeport, Connecticut (1866), members of the Wheeler & Wilson Sewing Machine Co., and S. H. Roper of Roxbury, Massachusetts (1870). In the 'nineties, Ransom E. Olds of Oldsmobile and Reo fame and Henry Ford both were making trials with steam machines. The most notable American steam automobile was that invented by Freeland and Francis Stanley in 1897. Their cars established several speed records.

775 Stanley steam automobile, 1906 model, from a photograph in the collection of N. Lazarnick, New York

THE HORSELESS CARRIAGE

In the experimental period there was a kind of international specialization in motors. The French seized the German gas machine and made it their own. For a decade or more they led the world in the design, production and operation of gasoline cars. The steam car was in keeping with the British tradition, and British inventors and manufacturers put steam automobiles upon the British market. Americans paid most attention to storage-

776   Early Daimler Automobile, 1886, from a photograph, courtesy of the Deutsches Museum, Munich

battery vehicles. The first of these cars were extremely heavy for their time, weighing upward of two thousand pounds, and requiring large tires, an expense not then requisite for the light-weight gas or steam cars. All through the 'nineties and for some years into the new century the electric automobile was the favorite in America. It had the least vibration, had no noise or odors, was free from fire hazard, could be easily started, could be driven by anyone, and demanded no repairs except for tires, for there was little about it to get out of order. Finally, it suggested dignity and affluence.

777   Circus Poster, advertising the Duryea "Motor Wagon, or Motorcycle," from a photograph in the collection of N. Lazarnick, New York

THE DURYEA BROTHERS' AUTOMOBILE

In America the gasoline automobile was the last to enter the field but the first to dominate it. Among the earliest makers of gas automobiles were the Duryea brothers of Springfield, Massachusetts (1893). The first great achievement of the Duryea car was the winning of the Chicago *Times-Herald* race on Thanksgiving Day, 1895. The car that won this event was the fifth made by the Duryeas.

778   The original Oldsmobile, 1896, in the United States National
      Museum, Washington.   © Photoworld Service, New York

779   Henry Ford, 1863–, in his first model car, 1893, from a
      photograph in the collection of N. Lazarnick, New York

780   Alexander Winton, 1860–, at the wheel of the first ex-
      perimental Winton model, 1898, from a photograph in the col-
      lection of N. Lazarnick, New York

781   Elwood Haynes, 1851–1925, in his first car, 1893, from a photograph
      in the collection of N. Lazarnick, New York

AMERICAN GAS AUTOMOBILES

At the same time Elwood Haynes of Kokomo, Indiana (1893), Alexander Winton of Cleveland (1896) and Ransom E. Olds of Lansing, Michigan (1896) and other men including Henry Ford, were experimenting with gas cars. Ransom E. Olds did most to start the United States upon its career as the world's greatest producer and user of gasoline automobiles. By 1900 he was ready to launch a real campaign of production and sales. Having established the Olds Motor Works at Detroit, he designed a light one-cylinder curved dash runabout which could be sold for six hundred and fifty dollars. His production schedule was four hundred and thirty-three cars for 1901, twenty-five hundred for 1902, and four thousand for 1903. To appreciate the daring of this scheme one must know that the number of foreign and domestic cars owned in the United States was only nine hundred in 1896, twenty-one hundred in 1897, forty-six hundred in 1898 and eight thousand six hundred and twenty-four in 1899. The Oldsmobile was an instantaneous success.

782 Ransom E. Olds, from a photograph. © Underwood and Underwood, New York city

783 First Oldsmobile driven from San Francisco to New York, from a photograph in the collection of N. Lazarnick, New York

RANSOM E. OLDS

RANSOM E. OLDS taught the automobile industry that an enormous demand existed for a moderately priced car, that low prices could be secured by low-production costs per unit which in turn could be brought about by mass production, and that mass production could be financed by the sales provision that cars be paid for in cash upon delivery. His factory became a training school for a dozen or more young men, every one of whom became a noted figure in the industry in later years. Yet Olds retired from his own company because of a dispute with his directors. If Olds had had his way he might have contested the supremacy later attained by Henry Ford. The Oldsmobile was merged with the Buick to form the nucleus of the General Motors Co. Olds was persuaded to head a new company which has ever since manufactured the Reo car.

THE SELDEN PATENT

ANOTHER influence in the American gas-automobile industry was the Selden patent. On May 8, 1879, George B. Selden applied for a patent on a self-propelling vehicle operated by a gasoline engine. On November 15, 1895, he was granted patent number 549,160, which covered the gas automobile completely. No other person could manufacture gasoline cars during the life of the patent (until November 15, 1912) without a license at first from Selden but later from a group to whom he had sold his patent. Most of the earliest gas-automobile makers, including Selden himself, took licenses under the Selden patent and agreed to pay royalties. However, a few bold spirits headed by Henry Ford defied the patent holders. Of course, the patent holders sued the independents. In 1909, the United States District Court decided the patent was valid. All the independents except Ford were scared into the Association of Licensed Auto-Manufacturers. Ford finally carried the case to the United States Circuit Court of Appeals which in 1911 held that the Selden patent was valid but that Ford had not violated it because the Selden engine was of the Brayton type whereas Ford's was of the Otto type. The cases cost more than half a million dollars but Ford claimed that the advertising more than repaid him. When the National Automobile Chamber of Commerce was organized among the manufacturers who had been in the Association of Licensed Automobile Manufactures, Ford refused to join.

784 George B. Selden in his first automobile, 1877, from a photograph in the collection of N. Lazarnick, New York

785   Charles C. Hanch, from a photograph in the
        collection of N. Lazarnick, New York

"COÖPERATIVE COMPETITION"

THE Selden patent suits forced all the gas-automobile makers to act together in one or the other of two associations. This long coöperation paved the way for the pooling of patents and the voluntary standardization of parts. The moving spirit of this system was Charles C. Hanch of the Nordyke & Marmon Co. By 1915 the National Automobile Chamber of Commerce was created. This body cross-licensed all its members for the use of any patent gained by any one of them. The scheme covered patents on all minor improvements and numbered more than seven hundred patents. The agreement extended from 1915 to 1925 when it was renewed. In like manner, through the Society of Automobile Engineers, some two hundred or more materials and motor parts used in assembling automobiles have been standardized. This permits mass production and of course cheapens the unit cost and price. It also guarantees that cars can be finished on schedule.

"Coöperative competition" and wide acquaintance among the leading automobile manufacturers goes far in explaining why America makes the best automobiles at the least cost.

786   Early one-cylinder Cadillac, 1908, from a photograph in the
        collection of N. Lazarnick, New York

787   The first Packard, 1898, from a photograph in the collection
        of N. Lazarnick, New York

THE SURVIVAL OF THE FITTEST

THE success of the Oldsmobile between 1901 and 1904 and the equally astounding sales of the Cadillac, which was produced immediately after the first marketing of Oldsmobiles, attracted many men into the new business. Competition was exceedingly keen. Constant improvement was the only guarantee of staying in the race. Between 1902 and 1907 no less than two hundred and eighty-seven firms withdrew from automobile manufacture or failed, and three hundred and twenty-two new automobile companies were started in the same period. The panic of 1907 hit the industry hard, and during part of 1910 companies dropped out of the business at the rate of one a week.

788   The first Buick, 1904, from a photograph in the collection of
        N. Lazarnick, New York

This industry like most others has shown a tendency to reduce the number of individual units by coalescing through merger, holding companies, or amalgamation. Probably the maximum number of separate enterprises has already been reached and passed. In 1925 the automobile industry took first rank among the country's manufactures, producing eighty-seven and five tenths per cent of the total of the world.

789   The first automobile show, Madison Square Garden, New York, 1900, from a photograph in the collection of N. Lazarnick, New York

THE AUTOMOBILE SHOWS

At the World's Fair in Chicago in 1893, one solitary American automobile was exhibited, apparently a revamped wagon operated by electric storage batteries. Duryea in 1896 exhibited cars with the Barnum and Bailey Circus, and Olds in 1898 placed his car on view at county fairs. At the last bicycle "Show" in New York in the spring of 1900, a few automobiles were also to be seen on the floor; in the fall of that same year the automobile industry held its first annual show at Madison Square Garden. The floor space had a curiously empty appearance. The Silver Jubilee show of 1925 devoted more space to accessories than the original show did to cars. Yet the first show was extremely popular. Since 1900, the show has been an annual midwinter event not only for New York but also for many other cities and it has paid. In the beginning the annual models for exhibit at the show were a necessary accompaniment of a new and rapidly changing business. Of late years it is doubtful if encouragement of annual models has been of public advantage. It promotes sales for the manufacturer, but buyers find their property depreciating at an undue rate not because the car is worn out but because its style is obsolete. Some companies have taken a definite stand against yearly models in order to safeguard their customers.

790   Silver Jubilee automobile show, New York, 1925, from a photograph in the collection of N. Lazarnick, New York

791   The Locomobile, first American car to win a Vanderbilt Cup Race, from a photograph in the collection
of N. Lazarnick, New York

792   Race on Ormond Beach, Florida, from a photograph in the
collection of N. Lazarnick, New York

793   Race on the Indianapolis Speedway, from a photograph in
the collection of N. Lazarnick, New York

794   Contestants in a Glidden tour, from a photograph in the collection of
N. Lazarnick, New York

RACES AND CONTESTS

Soon after 1900 there was an automobile contest of some kind every week somewhere in the world. Among the many events those that attracted the most attention were the Bennett and Vanderbilt Cup Races, the Daytona and Indianapolis Races and the Glidden Tours. French drivers and cars won the Vanderbilt Cup in 1904, 1905 and 1906, but in 1908 the American Locomobile took first honors. Since that first triumph American cars have seldom taken the dust of one of foreign make, but the various American manufacturers continued to vie with each other until there was little point in further tests. The various early competitions were of great value both as advertisements and as laboratories, and were one more reason for the rapid development of the automobile industry.

795 Oldsmobile, 1904, from a photograph in the collection of N. Lazarnick, New York

796 Reo with rear door entrance, 1904, from a photograph in the collection of N. Lazarnick, New York

797 First American limousine, from a photograph in the collection of N. Lazarnick, New York

798 Mercer "toy-tonneau," from a photograph in the collection of N. Lazarnick, New York

799 Sport model roadster, 1907, from a photograph in the collection of N. Lazarnick, New York

DESIGN

THE name "horseless carriage" tells the design of the first automobiles. Early in the new century the motor car began to take the form that distinguished it as a new vehicle. That is, it had a metal frame wider at the rear than in front and the engine was put forward of the front seat in an accessible position. At first radiators were put either ahead of the engine or behind it, but experience soon taught that the forward location was best. The French gave the official name "automobile" and soon the world adopted that term. The next improvement in design was the addition of panel doors which produced the name tonneau for the rear compartment. The cars began to give up the height borrowed from the early horse carriages. There has been continuous progression in getting the body down near the ground and yet above road inequalities. Paneling led to stream line design and this was followed by the vogue for closed cars. Mechanical design as contrasted with body design is too complicated and detailed to recount. The invention of tungsten filaments gave electric lighting to automobiles in place of kerosene or canned acetylene, and this electric system on the car brought about electric self-starters. In like manner, tires, springs, rims, mufflers, wheels and steering mechanisms have been subjected to invention, rigid testing, adaptation, or discard. The modern car bears no closer resemblance to the automobile of 1900 than the latest locomotive does to the *Rocket*.

TOWNS UNDER 1,000 (INCLUDING RURAL)

28.5%		
11.3%	TOWNS OF 1,000 — 2,500
7.0%	" " 2,000 — 5,000
8.3%	" " 5,000 — 10,000
8.9%	" " 10,000 — 25,000
6.5%	" " 25,000 — 50,000
6.0%	" " 50,000 — 100,000
11.1%	" " 100,000 — 500,000
12.4%	" " 500,000 AND OVER

800 Distribution of automobile ownership in the United States, prepared expressly for *The Pageant of America* from statistics in the National Automobile Chamber of Commerce, *Facts and Figures in the Automobile Industry*, New York, 1926

WHO OWNS AUTOMOBILES

WHO owns automobiles? It might be answered, "everybody." But it is possible to select certain outstanding classes of owners. In 1901 the four cities, New York, Chicago, Philadelphia and Boston claimed eighteen per cent of all cars registered, distributed as follows:

CITY	ELECTRIC	STEAM	GAS	TOTAL
New York	500	800	250	1550
Chicago	200	150	100	450
Philadelphia	50	160	130	340
Boston	90	220	50	360
Total	840	1330	530	2700

Since the gas cars of that day were cheaper than the steam or electrics, it would appear that automobiles were actually what they were credited with being, "the toys of the rich." In 1910, the gas car far outranked both steam and electrics together and had a much wider distribution. After the World War the automobile was no longer the pride of the rich but had become also the tool of the farmer. In 1925 farmers were acknowledged the best buyers of automobiles, when forty per cent of all cars were in districts having less than two thousand five hundred population. Cities with populations greater than one hundred thousand had but twenty-three and five tenths per cent of the total motor-vehicle registration. That the auto is not now the toy of the rich is shown by the fact that the 1925 registrations were about four times the number making income tax returns. More automobiles are manufactured in the state of Michigan than in any other state in the union. Detroit is the leading automobile manufacturing city, Cleveland next, Indianapolis and Buffalo having about equal claims to third place. From the point of view of manufacturing this regional concentration is a good thing, for the area selected is the greatest producer of steel and coal in the country and is also a great lumber market. The automobile-accessory industry clusters in the same neighborhood because cars are made there. From the marketing point of view the area is ideal because the center of population for the whole United States has been for twenty years in the environs of Bloomington, Indiana. The localization fosters a large skilled or trained labor supply. It gives a chance for considerable division of manufacture. Similar localization is a feature of many other manufacturing industries.

THE FIRST COMMERCIAL AUTOMOBILES

To the buyers of the earliest automobiles of the passenger type, cost and performance were minor considerations. Quite the contrary was the situation in regard to motor trucks for business purposes. Economy and efficiency in transportation have been always the main desiderata, and the early automobiles were neither economical nor efficient. The only motive business men had in the purchase of motor trucks prior to 1904 was advertising. An exception to the scant heed paid by business men to the early automobile was the cab enterprise of cities. The first large buyers of electric vehicles in New York city, for example, were men who operated the cars as taxicabs. They were immediately and immensely popular. By 1900 electric taxicabs were no novelty. After 1901–02 the gas car supplanted the electric and taxicabs rapidly became ubiquitous. Within twenty years there were one hundred thousand taxicabs in the United States and the time-honored "cabby," "hansom," and "hack" had vanished from the streets. American taxicabs carry approximately three and a half million people per day.

801   First electric cabs in New York, 1897, from a photograph in the collection of N. Lazarnick, New York

802   Truck and trailer on a mountain road, courtesy of the   803   Trucks hauling electric light poles, courtesy of the General
General Motors Truck Company, New York   Motors Truck Company, New York

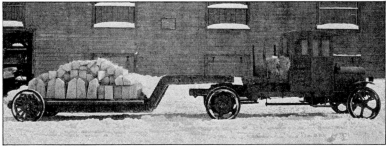

804   A truck with trailer used for carrying marble, courtesy of the General Motors Truck
Company, New York

805   Transporting automobiles by truck, courtesy of the General   806   Automobile moving van, courtesy of the General Motors
Motors Truck Company, New York   Truck Company, New York

THE FIELD OF THE TRUCK

In 1904 both the makers of automobiles and commercial houses awoke to the possibilities of cars for business uses. The number of such cars was greatly increased and the fitness of the car for special commercial services rapidly improved. In 1904 there were four hundred and eleven trucks manufactured. By 1910 some ten thousand had been produced. Five years later, seventy-five thousand was the yearly output and by 1925 almost a half million were being built per year. A motor truck is a rival of horse-drawn vehicles on the one hand and of steam railroads and electric freight railways on the other. Experience is demonstrating that the motor truck has a special field of operation. As compared with horses the motor truck is more economical on long hauls, continuous non-stop journeys, or work that involves the movement of exceedingly great weights. In this connection by long hauls are meant distances over twenty-five miles but under one hundred miles. The story is just the opposite when the motor truck is compared with the steam or electric railways. "Through" freight is more economically moved by rail than by truck, while local truck carrying may be cheaper than rail transport. The truck is then both a competitor of rails for short-haul goods and a feeder to the railways for long-haul traffic. The railways are now convinced of its coöperative features.

807 Dirt truck ascending a ramp, courtesy of the General Motors Truck Company, New York

808 Tank truck, courtesy of the General Motors Truck Company, New York

809 Use of trucks in the logging industry, courtesy of the General Motors Truck Company, New York

810 Armored Car, courtesy of the General Motors Truck Company, New York

811 Milk truck with glass-lined tank, courtesy of the General Motors Truck Company, New York

DESIGN OF COMMERCIAL AUTOMOBILES

THE typical commercial automobile differs from the passenger "pleasure" car in having a larger, more powerful but slower moving engine and a body design that puts most of the load weight over the rear wheels. The mechanical details of the truck have been subjected to the same painstaking study and experiment as those of the pleasure car. The body design of the truck, however, has not been changed as radically as that of the passenger car. Trucks of 1900 could still pass through our city streets without causing undue notice or comment. Yet special bodies for particular work have been introduced from time to time. Electric storage-battery cars for city trucking have retained favor. In 1925 there were twenty-five electric trucks in New York city that had been in service over twenty-two years. Trucks may be classified according to their load capacity or by the body design intended for special work. As to load capacity, trucks are made in various sizes from three-quarter ton to over five tons. In body design there are four classes, (1) stationary, (2) dump, (3) demountable, and (4) special. Each of these has its subclasses. Special bodies are legion, ranging from the automobile hearse to the automobile fire engine or traveling refrigerator.

812 Moving transformers by truck, courtesy of the General Motors Truck Company, New York

813 Motor-driven crane mounted on a truck chassis, courtesy of the General Motors Truck Company, New York

814   "Sight seeing wagons," predecessors of the modern motor bus, from a photograph in the collection of N. Lazarnick, New York

THE MOTOR BUS

THE motor bus is an outgrowth both of the passenger pleasure car and the motor truck but has become a separate branch of the automobile business. Bus transportation calls for a special kind of vehicle. The motor bus began about 1910 as the "jitney," an ordinary pleasure car put to the task of carrying paying passengers over a regular route upon an established schedule. It arose in opposition to street railways and surburban or interurban electric or steam lines. Overnight the country swarmed with jitneys. Generally speaking, the jitney era was short-lived. This was due partly to the hostile regulation of the jitney and partly to the appearance of the first public auto buses, which carried more passengers than jitneys could and transported people in greater comfort. The first buses were not distinguished either for beauty or comfort. The best of the modern ones are unsurpassed in public passenger transportation for speed and convenience.

815   Modern "pullman" type motor bus, from a photograph in the collection of N. Lazarnick, New York

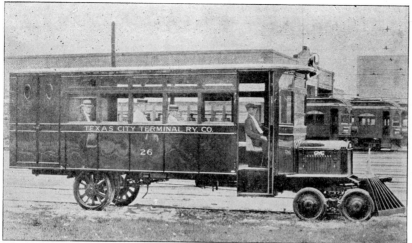

816   Motor Bus used on Railway Tracks, Texas City, Texas, courtesy of the General Motors Truck
Company, New York

THE FIELD OF THE MOTOR BUS

A FEW years ago almost everyone, including electric-traction magnates and steam-railway officials, thought that the motor bus was a dire threat to the continued existence of rail transportation of local passenger traffic. Cities such as Akron, Bridgeport, Des Moines and Toledo, which had banished the electric street railway were, however, forced to bring about their restoration, in some cases as publicly owned utilities. The place of the bus is on routes that require frequent adjustment, on streets and highways where there is no rail transportation, between points inadequately served by railway lines and in territories yielding traffic too light to support rail facilities. Automobiles, including auto buses, are fair-weather machines. In bad weather the public still needs rail transportation. Since the bus can operate where rail lines cannot, buses may be used as feeders or adjuncts for railways. The electric and steam lines have finally awakened to this fact and are becoming themselves owners and operators of bus lines. Furthermore, in regions of light traffic the railways are substituting various kinds of self-propelled bus-like cars in place of steam trains or electric cars.

817   Fordson tractor pulling a scraper, courtesy of the Ford Dealers' News, New York

THE TRACTOR

A TRACTOR is a movable power plant. It may be employed to push or pull loads, or to drag many kinds of machinery after itself. On the other hand, it can be blocked in a stationary position and its power used to saw wood, cut ensilage, pump water, or do almost any other job imposed upon a stationary engine. Equipped with wheels a tractor can go wherever a wagon can be operated. Fitted with a continuous tread it can traverse almost any kind of ground. Beyond all other markets the farm is the best customer for tractors. But the tractor is equally valuable to men engaged in forest enterprises or mining operations. Public highway departments find it valuable for road making, repairing and snow removal, while country clubs roll greens and tennis courts or cut grass with tractors. To perform all these tasks tractors are manufactured in various sizes and designed to add or subtract different kinds of auxiliary equipment. Although tractors are manufactured by thousands, most of their history is yet to be made. The automobile, truck and tractor together caused a decrease of five million horses in the United States in the ten years before 1926.

818   Road conditions encountered on the early Glidden tours, from a photograph in the collection of N. Lazarnick,
New York

HIGHWAYS

At the beginning of the nineteenth century, when the stagecoach was the last word in highway transportation, the nation burned with zeal for the improvement of roads. This promising development slowed down after 1830 when railroads filled the public mind. For the next half century roads that were not streets received scarcely any attention. Bicyclists did much to reawaken public interest in better roads but their best efforts were puny compared to the revolution produced by the automobile. When the automobile first appeared the Federal Government had long since ceased to construct highways. There were almost three million miles of highway; but only a few hundred miles were surfaced, and those nearly all within the borders of larger communities. Under these circumstances a writer of 1901 may be excused for having said that this nation would never have many automobiles because we had no roads fit for them to run on. How could a man of 1901 foresee that within a quarter of a century the people of the United States would spend on highways half a billion dollars *a year*, all derived from the automobile itself?

819   Fording a stream, from a photograph in the collection of N. Lazarnick, New York

820 A gravel road in Texas, courtesy of the Department of Agriculture, Bureau of Public Roads, Washington

821 A bituminous concrete road in Rhode Island, courtesy of the Department of Agriculture, Bureau of Public Roads, Washington

822 A concrete road in Pennsylvania, courtesy of the Department of Agriculture, Bureau of Public Roads, Washington

823 Graded dirt road, North Dakota, courtesy of the Department of Agriculture, Bureau of Public Roads, Washington

TYPES OF HIGHWAYS

THERE are in general seven types of roads in the United States: dirt, gravel, macadam, telford, concrete, asphalt and paved, divided in about the following percentages: gravel, fifty-one; macadam, twenty-three; sand-clay, sixteen; concrete, four; brick, nine tenths; miscellaneous, five and one tenth. The surfaced mileage is distributed throughout the country as follows, the percentage being the relation the surfaced mileage bears to total road mileage in the region indicated: New England, twenty-one; Middle Atlantic, twenty-one; East-North Central, thirty; West-North Central, four; South Atlantic, seventeen; East-South Central, five; West-South Central, six; Mountain, five; Pacific, twenty-one; United States, fourteen. In 1904 only seven per cent of our highway mileage was surfaced at all. There has been a constant improvement in surfacing. The type of construction depends upon the traffic and the amount of money available.

824 Snow scraper mounted on a truck, courtesy of the Department of Agriculture, Bureau of Public Roads, Washington

825 Motor-driven plow for clearing roads of deep snow, courtesy of the Department of Agriculture, Bureau of Public Roads, Washington

826 Patrolman repairing a gravel road in Maryland, courtesy of the Department of Agriculture, Bureau of Public Roads, Washington

827 Building a concrete road in Pennsylvania, courtesy of the Department of Agriculture, Bureau of Public Roads, Washington

828 Applying surface treatment to a macadam road, courtesy of the Department of Agriculture, Bureau of Public Roads, Washington

STATE HIGHWAYS

IN the 'nineties legislatures were forced to wrestle with the problem of highway improvement. The impossibility of raising the standard of all the road mileage forced the selection of certain roads for state aid — an excellent opportunity for political log-rolling. The main roads connecting the most important communities and county seats, together with those highways that linked one state to another, were designated "State Highways." Thereafter these listed roads were constructed, maintained, improved and realigned under the authority of the State Highway Department. Such routes were often called "Trunk Roads." Of course, the original selection of roads has not been kept intact. Subordinate roads were left to the counties and municipalities. Many of these entered upon a plan of road improvement; much of it upon a hit-or-miss basis.

829 Highway traffic officer, courtesy of the Department of Agri-
      culture, Bureau of Public Roads, Washington

830 Traffic regulation on a modern highway, courtesy of the Depart-
      ment of Agriculture, Bureau of Public Roads, Washington

HIGHWAY DEPARTMENT ACTIVITIES

THE work of highway improvement includes the selection of new locations and the establishment of new minimum grades. Fences and culverts have to be constructed and obstructions to clear views on curves removed. Bridges have to be widened and new ones put in their places. On the highway, traffic lines must be drawn and kept fresh. Poles along the right of way have to be whitewashed for safety's sake. Warning signs at curves, dangerous grades, crossroads, blind roads and railway crossings have to be put in place and route numbers have to be painted at frequent intervals. Some departments mark historical sights, erect signs and beautify the right of way. Work on the highways is always going on. And the automobile not only is the cause of it all but pays most of the bill.

831 A bituminous road in Connecticut, courtesy of the Department of Agriculture, Bureau of Public Roads, Washington

FEDERAL AID HIGHWAYS

ON July 11, 1916, a Good Roads Bill passed Congress and became law. This law carried an appropriation for the first year of its operation of eighty-five million dollars. The money was apportioned to the states on the basis of area, population and post-road mileage and was to be expended in the succeeding five years on the condition that at least one half the cost of road improvement should be contributed by the several states. In 1919, Congress increased the Federal appropriation by two hundred million dollars and added ninety million dollars for forest roads. Two years later President Harding signed an act that provided for a system of interstate highways. The mileage in this enterprise is about two hundred thousand. When existing highway programs of the State and Federal Governments are completed, the mileage of improved roads in the United States will be greater than the combined mileage of all the improved roads in the rest of the world.

CHAPTER XVII

AVIATION

TO fly! This dream of man is evidenced everywhere by legends of men who have actually flown or at least tried to fly. These stories are woven into the traditions of all kinds of men scattered about the world.

One of the oldest tales of India records such deeds. Similar stories are hinted at on Egyptian monuments. The Greek story of Daedalus and his son Icarus is known to every school child. The Incas of Peru had an almost identical fable. In the ancient chronicles of Britain it is said that Bladud, the ninth king, essayed to be a flier. In Finnish legend Ilmarinen and in Scandinavian legend Wieland both attempted flight. The magic broomstick of the witch and the wondrous carpet of the Arabian wizard are part of the common folklore concerning the conquest of space.

After the age of fable there are more or less authentic records of men who tried to float on the air or built models of birds or merely wrote out their theories. Among these are Oliver, the monk of Malmesbury, Roger Bacon, Leonardo da Vinci, the artist, Giovanni Baptisti Danti, Francesco Lana, Robert Hooke, Besnier and Emanuel Swedenborg. It remained for the twentieth century to see the realization of the dream. Not until a vast amount of scientific knowledge had been amassed and many natural forces tamed to the uses of man was flying possible.

Once flight had actually been achieved aviation developed with tremendous rapidity. The World War served as a great stimulus. So great has been the progress since the termination of that conflict that in the opening years of the second quarter of the twentieth century it is still impossible to forecast the final results of the conquest of the air. To achieve the progress that has been made many able and courageous men have given their lives. These heroes of peace deserve commemoration beside those of war for the supreme sacrifice in the interests of the common welfare.

832   The Langley Medal, awarded by the Smithsonian Institution only to Wilbur and Orville Wright, Glenn H. Curtiss, Gustave Eiffel, and Charles A. Lindbergh

833   From the engraving *The Ascent of the Aerial Balloon*
(Montgolfier), in the *Boston Magazine*, Vol. X

THE MONGOLFIER BALLOONS

EXPERIMENTAL aviation has taken three forms: a mechanical imitation of the flight of birds, "lighter-than-air" balloons and "heavier-than-air" planes and machines. The balloon first enabled men to soar among the clouds, but the "heavier-than-air" machines have been most popular, while bird imitators have so far always failed.

The first men to send balloons aloft were Frenchmen, Joseph and Stephen Mongolfier. A French monk Galien in 1757 set forth the theory that the air above the earth was lighter than that on the surface, so that if a suitable vessel were filled with this rare air it would float in the lower air. The Mongolfiers, impressed by the work of Galien, first tried steam and smoke and then hit upon hot air supplied by a fire of wool and wet straw. Their first balloon, made of paper, took fire, but a second and a third larger paper balloon rose to a height of about one thousand feet.

The next Mongolfier balloon, made of linen lined with paper, was destroyed by rain and wind before it had a chance to rise. The brothers used waterproof linen for their following experiment, a spherical balloon with a capacity of fifty-two thousand cubic feet. The passengers were a rooster, a sheep and a duck. On September 19, 1783, this trio made an eight-minute flight from the courtyard of Versailles. Of the three the rooster was the only one injured during the strange experience and he was trampled by the excited sheep. The king of France gave Joseph a pension of two hundred dollars a year and Stephen a medal; both brothers were appointed to the Legion of Honor.

France has honored many an air pioneer since, including Charles A. Lindbergh in 1927. In the fall of 1783, the Mongolfiers constructed a balloon of one hundred thousand cubic feet capacity, provided a place for passengers and added a fire-pan to keep hot air in the balloon during flight. Holding the balloon captive and allowing it to ascend only eighty feet, they raised one passenger on October 15, 1783. On November 21, the balloon rose free and carried Pilatro de Rozier and the Marquis d'Arlandes.

834   The Test of the Montgolfier Balloon, Versailles, 1783, from an engraving by N. de Launay in Faujas de Saint-Fond, *Description des Expériences de la Machine de Mm. de Montgolfier*, Paris, 1783

835   First Voyage of the Montgolfier Balloon over Paris, 1783, from an engraving by N. de Launay in Faujas de Saint-Fond, *Description des Expériences de la Machine de Mm. de Montgolfier*, Paris, 1783

836   From the painting, artist unknown, *Lunardi's Second Balloon Flight at St. George's Field, London*, Sept. 15, 1785, in the London Museum, London

THE FIRST BALLOONISTS

MEANWHILE, a fellow-countryman, M. Charles, was making use of Cavendish's discovery of hydrogen to fill balloons. His first hydrogen balloon went up on August 29, 1783. A second improved balloon was constructed by Charles, who, with a certain M. Robert, on December 1, 1783, took a journey of three and three fourths hours, the record for that day. These flights proved that ballooning was possible. Vincent Lunardi, on September 15, 1785, made the first balloon ascension in England. The English Channel was crossed by balloon on January 7, 1785, by Blanchard and an American doctor named Jeffries. They just cleared the coast and landed near Calais where a marble shaft was later erected to commemorate their feat. In America, two Philadelphians constructed a machine made up of forty-seven small hydrogen-filled balloons. After test flights with the machine held captive, they induced a carpenter, James Wilcox, on December 28, 1783, to take the first free balloon flight in this country. Wilcox had to cut slits in eleven balloons in order to return to earth and then came down so fast that he was badly jarred.

THE USEFULNESS OF FREE OR CAPTIVE BALLOONS

DURING the nineteenth century, balloons became common in Europe and America. Scientists used both free and captive balloons to study air currents and other phenomena of the upper atmosphere. Balloons were employed in the Napoleonic wars and to a small extent during our Civil War. In the Franco-Prussian War they became a recognized part of army and navy equipment. This caused captive kite balloons, used for observation, to be changed in shape from the spherical to the "sausage" form. During the World War hardly a mile of front was without one or more of these balloons.

837   A Modern United States Captive Observation Balloon, Macon, Ga., courtesy of the United States Army Air Service, Washington

838   Cartoon by George Cruikshank satirizing the Balloon Craze, from
        the *Comic Almanack*, London, 1845–49

MAKING BALLOONS DIRIGIBLE

OTHER experimenters sought some means of bringing balloons under control, that is, making them dirigible. Meusnier, a French army officer, found that an elliptical shape was superior to the spherical, and suggested a boat-shaped car, horizontal fins, and three propellers worked by a crew of eighty men. Except for his power plant, all of Meusnier's plans have been realized, but Meusnier himself never built a dirigible. Contemporaries of Meusnier tried to convert free balloons into dirigibles, some with oars, others with sails, and a few with paddle wheels run by hand. Rudders — vertical fins — were also tested. In 1852, the first dirigible was produced. Henri Giffard who had made a fortune by inventing a steam injector, constructed a light steam engine weighing one hundred pounds but producing five horse power. With this attached to a cigar-shaped balloon (eighty-eight thousand cubic feet capacity), Giffard, on December 24, 1852, succeeded in driving his craft at a speed of about four to six miles per hour. This was the first dirigible balloon. Three years later, Giffard built a second dirigible larger in capacity and shaped more like a pencil than a cigar. This airship was destroyed in its first landing. Later, Giffard designed a large dirigible but became blind before he got far with his plans and soon afterward (1882) died. Between Giffard's first dirigible of 1852 and those of Santos-Dumont and Count Zeppelin a half century intervened. In this period half

a dozen men, among them Charles H. Dupuy de Lome and Paul Haenlein, endeavored to perfect a dirigible, but none of them perfected a practicable machine.

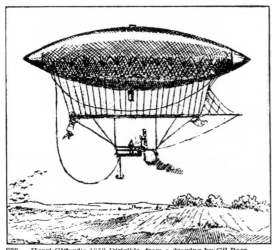

839   Henri Giffard's 1852 Dirigible, from a drawing by Gil Baer
          in Espitallier, *Aérostiers et Aviateurs*, Paris, 1913

840   The 1901 Santos-Dumont dirigible, from an engraving in
          Santos-Dumont, *My Airships*, London, 1904

DEVELOPMENT OF THE DIRIGIBLE

EXPERIMENTS with electric storage batteries as a source of power for dirigibles were made by the Frenchmen Albert and Gaston Tissandier between 1881 and 1885. Another electrically driven ship was constructed by Charles and Paul Renard, La Haye and Krebs. This airship made seven flights of which five were successful. In Germany too the dirigible was being studied by Baumgarten, Woelfert and Schwartz. The real pioneer in successful dirigible flight was Santos-Dumont, Brazilian by birth but French by choice. Between 1898 and 1904 he built no less than fourteen dirigibles, using gas engines for motive power. He was so successful that the French Government bought one of his ships for the army. The crude gas engines of that time prevented Santos-Dumont from reaching perfection in dirigible flight. About 1904, he turned his attention to "heavier-than-air" flying machines (airplanes) and became one of the most famous of the early pilots.

THE ZEPPELIN RIGID DIRIGIBLE

UP to 1900, of all the dirigibles built only one, and that one ill-fated, had been of the rigid type. Dirigibles may be of three different sorts: the non-rigid, which is merely a gas bag; the semi-rigid, reinforced by a wire net and metal attachments;

841   Alberto Santos-Dumont, from an engraving in Santos Dumont, *My Airships*, Paris

the rigid, with a frame of wood or metal inside the gas bag to stiffen and reinforce it. For this latter ship the world is indebted to the German, Count Ferdinand von Zeppelin. Zeppelin began his experiments about 1895. His first giant rigid dirigible was launched in 1900. Its trial trip over Lake Constance was attended with a series of mishaps. The Count launched a second ship in 1905 over the Bodensee. This and a subsequent trial were unsatisfactory. A third ship was constructed with which a number of successful air voyages were made. The German people then formed the Zeppelin Society by which through popular subscriptions the Count was furnished with funds for his experiments. By the opening of the World War, the Zeppelin was a reasonably safe airship with a remarkably long cruising radius. The Germans counted on it as a valuable military weapon; but, although it took part in several air raids, its vulnerability, visibility and great first cost rendered it less useful than the smaller, cheaper, swifter airplanes. The average life of the sixty-five war Zeppelins was only eighty days. Of the nine Zeppelins delivered to the Allies immediately after the war eight were wrecked in a few months.

842   Flight of the first Zeppelin, July 2, 1900, courtesy of the Maybach-Zeppelin Company, New York

843   The dirigible *Roma*, courtesy of the United States Army Air Service, Washington

844   The first trial of the dirigible *ZR2* at Cardington, England, courtesy of the United States Navy Department,
Washington

845   The dirigible *Los Angeles ZR3*) at Lakehurst, New Jersey, courtesy of the United States Navy Department, Washington

POST-WAR DIRIGIBLES

THE United States has bought since the war three rigid dirigibles of the Zeppelin type and has built one, the *ZR1*, christened the *Shenandoah*. In 1921, we purchased the *Roma* from Italy. Over Hampton Roads in 1922 the rudder of the *Roma* collapsed and the ship was completely wrecked, killing thirty-four officers and men. We next bought from the British the ship called the *R38* and renamed it the *ZR2*. During the summer it made several trial flights. In the final test flight, August 25, 1921, near Hull, England, the ship suddenly buckled and crashed to the ground, killing twenty-seven British officers and men and sixteen American officers and men who were aboard. Under the treaty of Versailles, the Germans were to supply us with one Zeppelin, which was completed in 1922, but wrecked in Germany. A second, the *ZR3*, was finished in October, 1924, and thoroughly and successfully tested in Germany. It was tested again in this country and christened the *Los Angeles*. In the spring of 1926, it was the only rigid dirigible we possessed. Under the Versailles treaty it is limited to commercial uses.

846   The *Shenandoah* moored to the mast of the airship tender *Patoka*, courtesy of the United States Navy Department, Washington

847   The wreck of the *Shenandoah*, courtesy of the United States Navy
Department, Washington

THE *SHENANDOAH*

WITH German plans and aid we built for ourselves at Lakehurst, New Jersey, another airship of the rigid Zeppelin type, the *ZR1*. This ship was finished in October, 1923, and christened the *Shenandoah*. A month later it was moored to a mast, the first time American airmen had accomplished this feat. During January, the ship broke from its moorings, tearing off its nose, and for eight hours battled with a fierce gale, but at last it was brought back to its station without a casualty. In October, 1924, the *Shenandoah* flew to the Pacific coast and returned without a mishap. During the following summer, 1925, she made a short cruise to Bar Harbor, Maine, carrying three state Governors to a conference. On September 3, she started on a western cruise. The next morning the world was shocked to learn that in a fierce storm in Ohio the *Shenandoah* had broken in the center and had crashed to the ground killing Commander Lansdowne and thirteen other men aboard the ship. Then arose furious controversies over the governmental air policy, the relative advantages of helium and hydrogen for airships and the comparison of airships with airplanes. The record of rigid airships was black indeed. This story of rigid airships, however, is no worse than that of early days of the ocean steamship. The fatalities have been lessons in construction and design. The long cruising range of the airship, together with its great weight-carrying capacity and its great speed, will retain it in service.

848   Twisted framework of the wrecked *Shenandoah*, courtesy of the United States Navy
Department, Washington

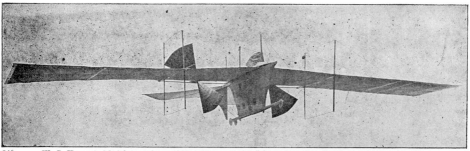

849   W. S. Henson's Model Aeroplane, 1842, courtesy of the Science Museum, South Kensington, London

850   Replica of the Original Model of John Stringfellow's Glider, 1848, courtesy of the Science Museum,
South Kensington, London

HARBINGERS OF THE AIRPLANE

To produce the "heavier-than-air" flying machine — the airplane — required the knowledge of the supporting power of thin rigid surfaces opposed to the air, an understanding of the methods of producing equilibrium in the varying currents of air, and a method of rising from the ground and producing motion through the air above the ground. To learn these things by the slow method of trial and error took a hundred years after the first balloon ascension and the work of some two score men during the nineteenth century. The absorption of the French in balloons prevented them from taking any great early interest in these matters, so the pioneers of mechanical flight were mainly British, German and American.

The first outstanding pathfinder was Sir George Cayley, who died in 1857, leaving a book, *Aerial Navigation*, which is still consulted by fliers. The scientific heirs of Cayley in Great Britain were W. S. Henson and John Stringfellow. Henson was actually granted a patent in 1842 for a plane equipped with a steam engine. Stringfellow made many experiments with gliders and engine-driven planes.

In Germany the most important forefather of the airplane was Otto Lilienthal, who, using gravity as his motive power, and flying with concave, batlike wings (sometimes with superposed surfaces), made over two thousand glides before his fatal accident in 1896. It was the report of Lilienthal's death that caused the Wright brothers to turn to flying. An Englishman, Percy Sinclair Pilcher, between 1895 and 1899, made repeated flights of short duration with gliders. His work also was known to the Wrights. A Frenchman, Clement Ader, constructed a power-driven machine in 1880 and tried a second machine before witnesses on October 14, 1897. Ader claimed that this machine really attained flight for nearly one thousand feet, but the military report said that the mechanism merely made a few ineffectual hops. Certainly Ader's machine, unlike the Wrights', led to no development of flight, except that the name of his machine, the "Avion," became the common French word for "airship."

RAPID TRANSIT OF THE FUTURE.

851   From a cartoon in *Texas Siftings*, March 10, 1888

852 Octave Chanute, from a photograph, courtesy of the United States National Museum, Washington

853 Model of Chanute's Multiplane Glider, from a photograph, courtesy of the United States National Museum, Washington

THE AMERICAN HERALDS OF FLIGHT

OCTAVE CHANUTE, 1832–1910, in the United States constructed his first man-size glider of the Lilienthal type the year before Lilienthal's death. He then began a careful study of gliders of his own devising. In 1896 and 1897, on the shores of Lake Michigan, Chanute made about a thousand test flights as a result of which he selected a biplane as the safest and possessed of the greatest inherent equilibrium. Chanute, however, did not feel that his machine had reached a point of stability to warrant trials with power-driven flight.

854 Langley's 1896 Aërodrome, from a photograph, courtesy of the United States National Museum, Washington

855 Samuel P. Langley, from a photograph, courtesy of the United States National Museum, Washington

THE ILL-FATED LANGLEY

PRIOR to 1891, a second and greater American, Samuel Pierpont Langley, 1834–1906, had arrived at theoretical proof that flight with heavier-than-air machines was possible. After 1891 he tested the theory by a series of over thirty model airplanes (which he called "aërodromes"). Next he had to devise a power plant. Since gas engines were at that time impracticable, he turned to a small, light-weight yet powerful steam engine. On November 28, 1896, his model power-driven plane actually flew about three quarters of a mile.

Two years later, President McKinley asked Langley to build a man-size plane for demonstration to the War Department. The engine, designed and built by Charles M. Manly, was the first five cylinder radial gas engine constructed. By 1903 the airplane was ready for demonstration before the War Department. The first test, October 7, 1903, failed because of an accident in launching. The second trial, December 8, again resulted in a catastrophe. Nine days later the Wright brothers achieved their epoch-making flight. To show how close was the margin by which Langley lost, it may be remarked that on May 28, 1914, Glenn H. Curtiss actually flew with the original Langley machine. There is some doubt, however, whether this flight in every particular used Langley mechanisms.

856   Wright Brothers gliding at Kitty
Hawk, N. C., courtesy of the United
States Army Air Service, Washington

857 Orville Wright, 858 Wilbur Wright,
1 8 7 1 –, f r o m a   1867–1912, from
photograph, cour-   a photograph,
tesy of the United   courtesy of the
States National   United States
Museum, Wash-   National Mu-
ington   seum, Washing-
                     ton

859   Wright Brothers' 1903 Machine, courtesy of the United States National Museum, Washington

THE WRIGHT BROTHERS

In 1896, upon learning of the death of Lilienthal, Orville and Wilbur Wright became interested in aeronautics. They read everything they could find on the subject and then constructed a wind-tunnel for laboratory experiment with different kinds of curved planes, making several thousand records. With this data they began to construct man-size gliders and in 1900 took them to sand hills south of Kitty Hawk, North Carolina. The result of the trials there was checked by study and practice with models during the winter. The next two years were spent in the same way. The summer tests of 1903 convinced the brothers that the time was ripe to apply power to their plane. They had to design and build their own gas engine and the propellers as well. On December 17, 1903, four flights were made before five spectators. The fourth, made against a twenty-mile-an-hour wind, lasted fifty-nine seconds, covering a distance of eight hundred and fifty-two feet. Said Wilbur Wright: "These flights were the first in the history of the world in which a machine carrying a man had raised itself into the air by its own power in free flight, had sailed forward on a level course without reduction of speed and had finally landed without being wrecked." By 1906 the Wrights were able to contract with the United States Government for a machine capable of carrying two men together with fuel supplies for a flight of one hundred and twenty-five miles at forty miles per hour. The brothers then sold to French, German and Italian companies the rights to manufacture Wright machines in Europe.

860 Glenn H. Curtiss, 1878–, in his Hydroplane, from a photograph, courtesy of the United States National Museum.
Washington

861 Curtiss Hydroplane alighting on Water, 1910, from a photograph, courtesy
of the United States Air Service, Washington

THE CURTISS HYDROPLANE

An American, Glenn H. Curtiss, may be credited with inventing the hydroplane (1911). He had been a
bicycle racer and had established a world's record for a motor-cycle race. In aviation he won a reputation
both as a racer and a designer. In 1910,
in order to follow the Hudson from Albany
to New York, Curtiss fitted his plane with
pontoons so that he could avoid catastrophe
if forced to descend to the river. A little
later he designed an airplane that could
rest on the water, rise from it and descend
to it again. He made a successful hydroplane in 1911.

862 Curtiss School Hydroplane, 1912–16, from a photograph, courtesy of the
United States National Museum, Washington

EUROPE PERFECTS THE AIRPLANE

For a decade or more, Americans did little
further for the development of planes or the
art of flying. Meanwhile, Europeans did a great deal. Aviation meets, races, long-distance contests and the
like kept the machine before the European public and stimulated European inventors. In experimentation
the French led. Out of conflicting types there evolved gradually something approaching standardization.
The "tractor" propeller in front of the car replaced single or multiple screws behind the wings. Stream line
design was adopted. The biplane succeeded better than multiplanes or monoplanes. The shape and angle of
wings also approached uniformity. Great diversity, however, remained in the engine types. Before the
World War the military value of the airplane had been recognized in Europe. The war itself compressed
the normal progress of a generation into five years. It developed special machines for special work, it produced the giant airplane, it greatly increased speed and height records as well as load-carrying capacity and
it introduced the metal plane. In all this America's share was limited to training hundreds of pilots, the

construction of some twenty
thousand planes on European
designs, and the design and
production of the famous Liberty engine. However, during
the war period, America established the world's first great
airplane commercial service,
namely the Air Mail. And the
flight records since the war
have been full of achievements
credited to Americans.

863   American Ship *DH4* used against the Germans for observation and day bombing, from a
photograph, courtesy of the United States Army Air Service, Washington

864 Lt. Commander Read from a photograph,   · 865   The seaplane *NC4*, from a photograph, courtesy of the United States
     courtesy of the United States Navy Depart-   Navy Department, Washington
     ment, Washington.

AIRPLANE DISTANCE FLIGHTS

DISTANCE flights with airplanes began in 1909, when, on July 25, Louis Bleriot, one of the most famous of French aviators, flew across the English Channel in seventy-seven minutes. In 1911, there were several long-distance races, as, for example, from Paris to Madrid, from Paris to Rome, and from Boston to Washington. In 1911 the first airplane crossed the American continent from New York to Pasadena, piloted by C. P. Rogers. The first flights over the Atlantic Ocean were made in 1919. In May of that year, the United States Navy seaplane *NC4* commanded by Lieutenant-Commander Read, U.S.N. made the first crossing but not in a single flight. On June 14, 1919, Captain John Alcock, D.S.C. (an Englishman), and Lieutenant Arthur Whitten-Brown (an American) in a Vickers Vimy bomber made the first non-stop airplane flight across the Atlantic. The time was sixteen hours, twelve minutes. On April 19 of the same year, Captain E. F. White made the first non-stop New York to Chicago flight.

THE FIRST NON–STOP TRANSCONTINENTAL FLIGHT

A NON-STOP flight from New York to Chicago was hailed as an achievement as late as 1920. Barely three years later pilots were preparing to fly across the continent without a single landing. On the morning of May 31, 1923, pilots Kelly and Macready soared aloft from Roosevelt Field, Long Island. They soon passed Pittsburgh, Dayton, St. Louis and Atchison. At an altitude of two thousand feet the pilots could hardly see Santa Rosa or Wickenburg, but shortly thereafter San Diego came in sight. On the landing field a great crowd saw the plane take the long glide to the ground. Before the machine had stopped rolling, Kelly jumped from the plane into the arms of the jubilant throng. Macready, too, was seized by the crowd and carried in exultation to his flying mate. The continent was conquered; two thousand seven hundred miles of distance had been covered in twenty-seven hours and fifty minutes without a single pause. Men who once had required six months to cross the United States lived to see this marvel of transportation.

866 Lieutenants Macready and Kelly before their Airplane, 1923 Transconti-
     nental Flight, from a photograph, courtesy of the Chief of Air Service, Wash-
     ington

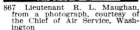

LIEUTENANT MAUGHAN'S DAWN–TO–DUSK FLIGHT

THREE times in 1923, Lieutenant R. L. Maughan tried to beat the record of Kelly and Macready by flying from the Atlantic to the Pacific between dawn and dusk, and three times he failed. But on June 23, 1924, leaving the Atlantic at 3 A.M., Maughan alighted in San Francisco at 12:48 A.M., twenty-one hours, forty-eight and a half minutes from coast to coast. He had stopped for a total time of three hours, twenty-eight minutes at five mid-continent fields for fuel and adjustments.

AROUND THE WORLD BY AIRPLANE

AVIATORS of Argentine, Britain, Italy and the United States tried in 1924 to repeat in the air Magellan's exploit by water. The Americans alone succeeded. Four American planes left Santa Monica on March 18, 1924. For seven months the world shivered at their mishaps and were apprehensive of failure. Early in April, Major Martin, the commander of the expedition, was forced down in Alaska. For nearly a month he disappeared from sight. When he was found he explained that his plane had crashed into a mountain.

870   Putting the *New Orleans* on the Beach, Reykjavik, Iceland, from a photograph, courtesy
of the United States Navy Department, Washington

THE WORLD FLIERS RETURN

MEANWHILE, the three remaining planes with their pilots, Lieutenants Lowell H. Smith, Eric H. Nelson, and Leigh Wade, had flown from Alaska to Japan. Week by week their progress was noted by the world while they crossed Asia and Europe. Lieutenant Wade met with misfortune in the Faroe Islands. For days the other two men were held up by ice, fog and storms in Iceland and Greenland; in September they landed again on the American continent, where Lieutenant Wade rejoined them and they flew across the United States to their starting point on the Pacific coast. One of the planes, the *Chicago*, was deposited in the Smithsonian Institution. The pilots were awarded the D.S.C., the first awards for a peace-time deed.

871   Commander John Rodgers, 1881-1926,
from a photograph, courtesy of the United
States Navy Department, Washington

872   The seaplane *PN9 Number 1*, from a photograph, courtesy of the United States
Navy Department, Washington

THE ILL–FATED *PN9 NUMBER 1*

EARLY in the spring of 1925, the U. S. navy launched the first of a new type (*PN9*s) of hydroplane, the largest of all metal-hull seaplanes ever built for the navy. In the fall of that year it was determined to send three of these planes in a test flight from San Francisco to Honolulu. The only one that finally got off (September 1) was the *PN9 Number 1*, commanded by J. Rodgers. For eight days nothing was heard of it. On the ninth day, when all hope had been abandoned for the fliers, the plane and its people were seen approaching Kauai, one of the Hawaiian islands. An insufficiency of gasoline had forced the plane to land on the sea, and in landing its radio transmission was destroyed. Floating without power, without means of signaling, without sufficient food or water, the men put their frail craft into the proper drift, aided by a little sail rigged out of wing fabric, and slowly navigated toward their destination.

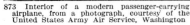

873 Interior of a modern passenger-carrying airplane, from a photograph, courtesy of the United States Army Air Service, Washington

874 Lawson "Air Liner" at Bolling Field, near Washington, from a photograph, courtesy of the United States Army Air Service, Washington

POST–WAR COMMERCIAL AIRPLANE SERVICE

In Europe after the World War experience in aviation was turned to account commercially by the establishment of regular passenger airplane service. Air lines connected England and France, and London and Amsterdam. Paris, Berlin and Vienna soon became centers for radiating passenger air lines and in 1923 a time table and schedule was published for European air lines.

The first important passenger air lines in the United States were installed by the Aeromarine Airways and were coastwise hydroplanes connecting the North and South Atlantic ports, and mainland points with outlying islands. Planes were employed as forest-fire patrols, in spreading smudges to kill forest-insect pests and in seeding inaccessible areas. In the South the attempt was made to destroy the boll weevil by airplane gas screens. Planes were found useful in mapping various parts of the United States. Seaplanes have been used to scout fish schools for the fishermen and to drive off the larger preying fish from schools of fish that are sought for the market. By 1925 the usefulness of airplanes for fast freight and express was admitted by the inauguration of several regular air lines. The Fords started a daily service between Detroit and Chicago, and there were other lines running from Cleveland, Dayton and Cincinnati. The Standard Oil Company of Indiana adopted air planes for its intercompany mail and express in ten Middle Western states. The airplane in commerce was a fixture by 1925. In that year the first dining car was installed in the London-Paris air liners, a hobo rode on the wing of a plane from Las Vegas to Los Angeles, a thief stole a plane at Sioux City, a Lascar diamond merchant was murdered on a plane while riding to Budapest, and a New York department store carried airplanes in stock for sale.

875   Ford all-metal passenger airplane, from a photograph, courtesy of John Wanamaker, New York

876   Charles A. Lindbergh and the *Spirit of St. Louis*, from a photograph.
© Wide World Photos, New York

BRIDGING THE ATLANTIC

ORGANIZED plans for crossing the Atlantic by a heavier-than-air machine were formulated as early as 1913. Their execution was interrupted by the outbreak of war. The specifications for a monoplane, submitted by Charles A. Lindbergh to the Ryan Air-Lines in 1927, embodied the technical improvements of the intervening thirteen years. On May 20–21, Lindbergh in the *Spirit of St. Louis* made a record flight from New York to Paris. The perfection of mechanical construction, which he had personally supervised, carried him without a mishap; and, with a modesty that captivated the world, he insisted that his personal rôle as navigator and pilot was in comparison a subordinate one.

877   Clarence D. Chamberlin and the *Columbia*, June 4–5, 1927, New York to Kottbus, Germany.
© Wide World Photos, New York

878   The crew of the *America*, Bert Acosta, Richard E. Byrd, George D. Noville, and Bernt Balchen, June 29—July 1, 1927, New York to Ver-sur-Mer, France. © Wide World Photos, New York

879   Lieutenant Albert F. Hegenberger. © Wide
World Photos, New York

880   Lieutenant Lester J. Maitland. © Wide World
Photos, New York

TO HAWAII

Lester J. Maitland, one of the ablest pilots in the Army Air Service, was chosen to pilot the *Bird of Paradise* from San Francisco to the Hawaiian Islands. Albert F. Hegenberger was selected as his navigator. On June 29, 1927, having completed a record non-stop sea flight of two thousand four hundred and seven miles, they made a perfect landing on the Island of Maui. Naval Commander Richard E. Byrd, navigating a similar three-motored Fokker plane, along the Atlantic trail which Lindbergh had blazed and which Clarence Chamberlin and his passenger, Charles Levine, had followed, radioed a message of congratulations to be relayed to the Hawaiian fliers.

881   The Trans-Oceanic Fliers, at a celebration in Boston (left to right, Balchen, Acosta, Noville, Byrd, Chamberlin, Lindbergh, Hegenberger, Maitland, from a photograph). © Wide World Photos, New York

THE AFTERMATH

The world waited anxiously for news of the safe arrival of Byrd and his associates. Byrd's subsequent account of the difficulties surmounted and of the contributions of their voyage to aviation, seemed the prologue to a great scene of commercial expansion in the air. The eight successful ocean fliers were regarded as an apostolic nucleus. From their achievement, however, has risen (October 1927) neither constructive confidence nor faith. They have inspired in the minds of emulators a vast overconfidence. Amateurs, eager for prizes and glory, have fancied themselves worthy successors of professionally disciplined mechanicians and scientists. Tragedy succeeds tragedy, as it has in the past, when the exploiter follows frantically in the steps of the scientific pioneer. Adjustment, however, is inevitable, and commerce ultimately the gainer.

NOTES ON THE PICTURES

2. An inspirational painting by a pupil of Jean Laurens Gérôme, overdrawn for pictorial effect. It depicts the scene on the last morning of Columbus' voyage when land is in sight. Some fifty or more canvases by Ferris are in Independence Hall, Philadelphia.

4. The painting by Millais deals with a tradition, long held by English navigators, that the Pacific could more conveniently be reached by the northwest than by the route found by Magellan.

12. Jasper Danckaerts was a Dutch draftsman who in 1679 made a number of views of New York which are among the rarities of that day. See Vol. I.

13. Jomard's work reproduces many early maps in European collections.

15. A modern illustrator's conception.

16. Original print was owned by Josiah Quincy of Boston from which this is a copy dedicated to the "Generous Founder" Peter Faneuil, whose brick building, given to the city of Boston and now used as a market, was inserted in the plate.

20. Henry Popple, died 1743, published in 1732 his "Map of the British Empire in America and the French and Spanish settlements adjacent thereto." Popple's large manuscript draft (dated 1727) is preserved in the British Museum. The French and the Spanish disputed the accuracy of this Popple map.

21. This is redrawn from the *View of Ft. George with the City of New York from S. W.*, engraved on copper by J. Carwithan, date depicted 1731–36. It differs only in a few minor details. The scene is extended a little farther to the left of Trinity Church, affording a view of Mesier's windmill.

29. Morland, 1763–1804, was a successful English painter of animals and rustic scenes. The African slave trade with the American colonies and the West Indies excited his interest at an early date.

41. Painted at Naples, 1809, and unsigned.

49. Painting the work of a Chinese.

52. Engraving by a Hawaiian.

68. Barber made illustrations of New England scenes in the 'thirties and 'forties for engravers on wood, usually based upon his personal study. See Vols. I, III and XI.

69. Wall, a popular painter of the early nineteenth century, was born at New Bedford and studied under Thomas Sully.

119. Samuel A. Mitchell, 1792–1868, made many early maps of the United States.

120. Melish, a Scotsman who traveled extensively in this country, publishing his comments and making many maps.

121. William Strickland was also an architect (see Vol. XIII) and interested himself as well in canals and railroads.

125. Reconstruction based on description. Henry an American *genre* painter who attained great popularity. See 318; also Vol. III.

128. W. H. Bartlett, an Englishman, made many drawings "on the spot" of American buildings and places, which were afterward engraved for books and prints. See 129, 133, 172.

130. Hall, an Englishman, traveled extensively in the United States in the eighteen thirties, sketching on the way. See 132, 166, 180; also Vol. III.

131. Welby an early English traveler who drew from personal observation.

140. For other pictures by Arthurs, see 145, 149, 264, 515; also Vols. I, III, VIII and XI.

167. See 125.

174. Drawn from observation by one who made the Mississippi voyage, lithographs made in Germany.

175, 177, 178. Reconstructions by a descendant of an early fur trader.

182. See 174.

183. Artist worked principally in the West, painting border scenes and history, without special accomplishments but successful in portraying primitive life.

194, 195. In these pictures the artists both depict the *Clermont* with sails fore and aft in addition to steam, while Fulton himself (letter to Barlow) claims no power was used except steam.

204. For Karl Bodmer's work, see Vol. I.

210, 211, 212. See 174.

262. See 125.

273. Jervis McEntee, 1828–91, a successful painter of landscape.

397. Holslag a Chicago mural painter chiefly for banks and industrial institutions in the West. See also 399, 402.

444. Artist made sketches "on the spot" for this painting and others in the Administration Building, Panama. He is also represented in Vol. XII.

513. This box made of tin was carried by John Noble on horseback between Portsmouth and

Boston. Noble was post-rider until 1783. The box is nine inches long.

516. Sketch by an early English traveler (see 131), valuable as an eighteenth-century view of a stagecoach, drawn from observation.

517. For an account of Trumbull and others of his paintings, see Vol. VIII.

518. Remington, after studying at the Yale Art School about 1880, went West and illustrated army life on the plains and Indian scenes, especially for *Harper's Weekly* and other publications. A collection of his pictures is preserved at Ogdensburg, New York. See also Vol. I.

581. Original message is preserved in the Connecticut Historical Society, Hartford, Connecticut.

685. The article by W. M. Beauchamp, printed in the *Bulletin* of the New York State Museum, No. 41, Vol. 8, 1901, gives an account of wampum as money and shell articles as used by the Iroquois for ornament. It has many illustrations.

592. Left to right, seated: Peter Cooper, M. O. Roberts, Moses Taylor. Standing figures, David Dudley Field, Chandler White, S. F. B. Morse, Daniel Huntington, Cyrus W. Field and W. J. Hunt.

605. In landing the shore end of the cable at Valentia, Ireland, July 7, 1866, forty boats belonging to fishermen and to H.M.S. *Raccoon*, as the painting shows, were used as a long pontoon bridge from the cable ship's tender to the shore.

606. Cyrus Field said the incident here depicted was the most exciting moment in the history of cable-laying.

INDEX

Titles of books under authors are in italics; titles of illustrations under producer are in quotation marks.